¶ LETTERS OF ST. IGNATIUS

OF LOYOLA

Selected and Translated by William J. Young, s.j.

LOYOLA UNIVERSITY PRESS

Chicago, Illinois

© 1959
LOYOLA UNIVERSITY PRESS

Printed in the United States of America

Library of Congress Catalog Card Number: 59-13459

P-ALM-R-O-E

Imprimi potest

WILLIAM J. SCHMIDT, S.J.
Provincial of the Chicago Province
October 10, 1958

Nihil obstat

AUSTIN G. SCHMIDT, S.J.
Censor Deputatus
April 30, 1959

Imprimatur

ALBERT GREGORY MEYER
Archbishop of Chicago
May 1, 1959

PREFACE

In making this selection of the letters of St. Ignatius I have availed myself of selections already published in Spanish by Fathers Macia, Casanovas, and Iparraguirre, in French by Fathers Dudon and Bouix, and in German by Fathers Karrer and Rahner. But the translation itself has been done from the collection of his letters in twelve volumes which constitute the first series of *Monumenta Ignatiana* in the *Monumenta Historica Societatis Iesu*. Other than a slim volume containing twenty-four letters, selected and edited by the Reverend A. Goodier, S.J., translated by D. F. O'Leary, and published by the Manresa Press in 1914, I know of no formal attempt to give the letters of St. Ignatius any currency in English. Here and there in biographies of the saint letters are quoted in translation, but the letters as letters do not seem to have engaged attention. This collection, therefore, of two hundred and twenty-eight letters will offer the reader a fresh revelation of St. Ignatius. It will be a portrait drawn by the saint himself. There has been no dearth of biographies of St. Ignatius, but each biographer is bound to use his own colors however close he keeps to the authentic outlines of his subject. It can hardly be otherwise even with a *selection* from the letters. But as this collection comprises all the letters that are contained in the above-mentioned selections of three Spaniards, two Frenchmen, two Germans, and an Englishman, it ought to be able to maintain some claim to being objective.

And there is need of some portrait of the kind of St. Ignatius, for perhaps no saint has suffered more from the hands of his biographers, friends and foes alike. Even his friends have not succeeded perfectly in making a satisfactory synthesis of those apparently contradictory qualities which are to be found in nearly every man of genius, and which even in St. Ignatius his sons have sometimes found so baffling. Singleness of aim and firmness of purpose can so easily be misapprehended as a heartless idealism, while tender affection and patient watchfulness will be misconstrued as weakness or partiality. Even in his lifetime Ignatius was criticized for placing too much reliance on human prudence, and that by some of his own sons, when he was merely looking for that combination of time, place, and person from which he would be able most likely to extract a greater glory for God. Thus one side of his character can easily be exploited at the expense of another, and the result will be distortion. It is hoped that the whole man—the contemplative in action, as he was called by one who knew him best—will stand revealed here in his letters. In Father de Guibert's fine phrase his was a mysticism of service, and no one can read his letters without being struck by the complete absence of that mystical language which only a few years later St. Teresa and St. John of the Cross were to make so familiar. His sights were focused on the praise and reverence of His Divine Majesty, and this he beheld with a clearness and sought with a consistency that was almost fierce and certainly unrelenting. He was indeed a mystic of the first order, one who had sounded every depth of the dark night and scaled every height of that transfiguring mountain, a contemplative who could "find God at will" but who would not permit even his enjoyment of God to encroach upon his duty of praise and service. He was first and foremost a servant, with his eyes ever fixed on his Master's interests, a liegeman sworn to safeguard the full measure of His Majesty's praise and glory.

The letters will give some idea of his varied interests. They show us how he found God in everything. They are all spiritual, whether they offer plans to Charles V for sweeping the Barbary pirates from the Mediterranean or urge John III to suppress the evil of dueling or counsel the duke of Gandia on frequent Communion. He could point a reproof without attaching a barb to it. He could threaten the rebellious—who wouldn't?—give heart to the timid, shame the selfish, and arouse the slothful with words of fire. He could pour the balm of God's love into the hearts of the bereaved and lonely. He was all sympathy with those who suffered, whether it was from sickness or poverty or persecution or slavery. But never once does he fail to point out that these are trials sent or permitted by God and that their purpose is to purify and to make more fruitful, in the case of his sons who are thus afflicted, their labors for the greater praise and service of God.

Commentators lose no opportunity to call attention to certain crudities of style in the writing of St. Ignatius. They are thinking, for the most part, I believe, of the *Spiritual Exercises*. But the same can be said, with some reservations, of his correspondence. In his *Life of St. Peter Canisius* Father Brodrick speaks of the "nodosities" of expression that are there to plague the translator, and the translator of Father Espinosa's fine work on the "Letter on Obedience" bemoans the "leisured sinuosities of sixteenth century Spanish." There are both nodosities and sinuosities in the letters of St. Ignatius, but it is not because he took little care in their composition. He himself confesses the pains he took with his letters. But he was no literary man, and one will search the letters in vain for the charm that has distinguished letter writers who were certainly more readable, and just as certainly not so profitable, as St. Ignatius. In this translation there has been no attempt to add luster to the plainness of the original, which at times can be worse than dull, or to streamline the rather courtly march of his periods. Other than breaking up some of these endless processions of gerundial platoons, no liberties have been taken with the text. It was thought preferable to preserve as much of the flavor of the original as was compatible with English idiom. It is hoped that allowing St. Ignatius at last to speak for himself will correct many a false impression and that, where he has been misunderstood, he will begin to be known and where feared, to be loved. The letters are set out in chronological order and bear the numeration of the *Monumenta*.

In signing his letters Ignatius at first wrote *Iñigo*, changing later to *Ignacio*, but just when the change was made and why is not clear. His first letters are signed with the humble formula, *De bondad pobre, Iñigo*, "poor in goodness." *Ignacio* appears for the first time in 1537 in a letter addressed to Peter Contarini, which was both written and signed in Latin. From then on for a few years both forms were used, *Iñigo* being used for letters written in Spanish and *Ignacio* for those in Latin or Italian. After 1542 *Iñigo* disappears, except for the precious letter written August 10, 1546 for the benefit of Father Barbaran. With this sole exception St. Ignatius always signed his name *Ignacio* in the numerous letters he wrote or had written during the fourteen remaining years of his life. This is the view of Father Astrain, but the editors of the *Monumenta* think that copyists and editors took the liberty of changing the form of the name to suit themselves, frequently writing, for example, *Iñigo* and *Ignatio*, while Ignatius was accustomed to write *Inigo*.

The translator wishes to acknowledge his indebtedness to the editors of the *Monumenta Historica Societatis Iesu* and the other translators and editors mentioned in this preface, especially Fathers Dudon, Macia, Casanovas, and Iparraguirre. He has drawn freely from them, as from the *Monumenta*, for illustrative information which has been incorporated in the introductions and notes to the letters. He is especially glad to express his thanks to the Reverend Aloysius C. Kemper, S.J. Father Kemper's learning is surpassed only by his charity. His long and intimate acquaintance with Spanish and his painstaking revision of the typescript will be a guarantee that the thought of St. Ignatius is faithfully rendered, but he should in no wise be held responsible for the dullness or awkwardness of the rendition. That responsibility is solely the translator's.

W. J. Y.

CONTENTS

PART I: 1524-1537

page		
	3	To Agnes Pascual
	4	To Agnes Pascual
	5	To Martin Garcia de Onaz
	9	To Isabel Roser
	12	To Agnes Pascual
	13	To James Cazador
	18	To Sister Teresa Rejadell
	24	To Sister Teresa Rejadell
	25	To The Confessor of the Queen of France
	27	To Manuel Miona
	28	To John Peter Caraffa
	31	To Peter Contarini

PART II: 1538-1540

35   To James de Gouvea
36   To Peter Contarini
38   To The Lords of Loyola
39   To Bertram Loyola
42   To Bertram Loyola
42   To The Townspeople of Azpeitia

PART III: 1540-1548

49   To Bertram Loyola
50   To Magdalene Loyola
51   To Fathers Salmeron and Broet
52   To Isabel Roser
53   To Bertram Loyola
55   To Father Simon Rodrigues
58   To Francis Borgia, Duke of Gandia

page		
	59	To Father Simon Rodrigues
	60	To John Baptist Viola
	61	To Simon Rodrigues
	62	To Peter Faber
	64	To John III, King of Portugal
	67	To Father James Lainez
	68	To Asconius Colonna
	69	To Margaret of Austria
	71	To Sister Teresa Rejadell
	72	To Father Nicholas Bobadilla
	77	To James Crescenzi
	78	To A Man Who Was Tempted
	79	To John III, King of Portugal
	81	To Cardinal Marcellus Cervini
	83	To Francis Borgia, Duke of Gandia
	86	To Father Le Jay
	87	To Doctor Peter Ortiz
	89	To Father Peter De Soto
	90	To Andrew Lippomani
	91	To Francis Borgia, Duke of Gandia
	93	To The Fathers at the Council of Trent
	96	To Peter Canisius
	98	To The Fathers and Brothers at Coimbra
	99	To Doimo Nascio
	100	To Michael de Torres
	102	To Isabel Roser
	103	To Father Michael de Torres
	106	To Francis Borgia, Duke of Gandia
	108	To Father Michael de Torres
	111	To Ferdinand, King of the Romans
	113	To Father John Polanco
	115	To Father Michael de Torres
	120	To The Fathers and Scholastics at Coimbra
	130	To Father Simon Rodrigues
	131	To Manuel Santos
	132	To Father James Lainez
	137	To Francis Borgia, Duke of Gandia
	140	To The College of Gandia
	146	To The Members of the Society in Padua
	150	To Father Anthony Araoz

page	
153	To Teresa Rejadell
154	To Father Daniel Paeybroeck
157	To Father Stephen Baroello
159	To The Community at Coimbra
162	To Father Nicholas Bobadilla
164	To Father Andrew Oviedo
172	To Father Anthony Araoz
173	To Señor Talpino
175	To Prince Philip of Spain

PART IV: 1548-1553

179	To Francis Borgia, Duke of Gandia
182	To John of Avila
184	To Prince Philip of Spain
186	To Matthew Sebastian de Morrano
187	To Jeronyma Oluja and Teresa Rejadell
188	To Andrew Lippomani
190	To Father John Alvarez
194	To Francis Borgia, Duke of Gandia
195	To Francis Borgia, Duke of Gandia
212	To The Fathers Sent to Germany
214	To Don John de Vega
215	To Doña Isabel de Vega
217	To Don John de Vega
218	To Charles Borgia
219	To John Bernal Diaz de Luco
221	To The Army in Africa
222	To Isabel de Vega
223	To The Cardinal of Lorraine
225	To The Jesuits in Rome
225	To John de Vega
226	To Charles Borgia
227	To John de Vega
228	To Isabel de Vega
229	To The Members of the Society
231	To Isabel de Vega
232	To Ferdinand, King of the Romans
233	To Father Urban Fernandes

page	
237	To Father Anthony Brandao
243	To Father Anthony Araoz
244	To Father John Pelletier
249	To Father Claude Le Jay
252	To Father Elpidius Ugoletti
254	To Father Simon Rodrigues
254	To Father Manuel Godinho
255	To Father Francis Xavier
256	To Prince Philip of Spain
257	To Father Francis Borgia
259	To Father Claude Le Jay
260	To Father Jerome Nadal
261	To Father Jerome Nadal
265	To John Stephen Manrique de Lara
267	To Those Sent to the Missions
269	To Father James Lainez
272	To Ignatius, from Lainez
274	To Joan of Aragon
278	To Father James Miron
279	To Father James Miron
281	To Members of the Society in Europe
282	To Father James Miron

PART V: 1553-1556

287	To The Members of the Society in Portugal
296	To Thomas of Villanova
296	To Simon Rodrigues
298	To Father Francis Xavier
300	To Father Simon Rodrigues
300	To The Whole Society
302	To Father James Miron
302	To Father James Miron
304	To Reginald Pole, Cardinal of England
305	To The Count of Ribagorza
306	To The Countess of Ribagorza
307	To Father Francis Borgia
308	To Nicholas Peter Cesari
309	To John Louis Gonzalez de Villasimplez

page	
310	To Margaret of Austria
311	To Father Nicholas Gaudano
313	To Hector Pignatelli
314	To Louis, Prince of Portugal
315	To Father Gaspar Berse
316	To Father Philip Leerno
317	To Theotonius Braganza
318	To Magdalene Angelica Domenech
319	To Father Jerome Domenech
321	To Mary Frassona del Gesso
322	To Doimo Nascio
323	To Father James Lainez
324	To Father Gaspar Berse
326	To The College of Coimbra
327	To Emperor Charles V
328	To Father John Baptist Viola
330	To Mary Frassona del Gesso
331	To Anthony Enriquez
334	To Father James Miron
335	To King John III
336	To Father Francis de Attino
337	To The Marquise de Priego
339	To Henry de la Cueva
341	To Father Bartholomew Hernandez
342	To Father John Nunez Barreto
343	To Ferdinand Vasconcelhos
344	To Father Peter Canisius
347	To The Widow of John Boquet
349	To Father Francis Borgia
350	To Michael de Nobrega
352	To Father John Francis Araldo
353	To Father Philip Leerno
354	To John de Mendoza
355	To Hercules Purino
356	To Father Christopher de Mendoza
358	To Asconius Colonna
359	To Violante Casali Gozzadina
360	To Father Anthony Araoz
361	To Cardinal Reginald Pole
363	To Bartholomew Romano

page	
364	To Father John of Avila
365	To Father Ponce Cogordan
367	To Claude, Emperor of Abyssinia
373	To Father Melchior Nunez Barreto
374	To Father Melchior Carneiro
375	To Gaspar de Borgia
376	To Father Robert Clayssone
377	To Gerard Hammontanus
379	To John Perez de Calatayud
380	To Father Simon Rodrigues
381	To Father John Nunez Barreto
390	On The Method of Dealing with Superiors
393	To Father Manuel Lopez
395	To Father Albert Ferrarese
396	To Francis Jimenez de Miranda
399	To Peter Camps
400	To Doña Joan de Valencia
401	To Father Francis Borgia
402	To Father Simon Rodrigues
403	To Isabel de Vega
404	To Jerome Vines
405	To Jerome Vines
406	To Henry de la Cueva
408	To Father Francis Borgia
409	To John Perez
411	To Jerome Vines
412	To The Rectors of the Society
413	To Jerome Vines
414	To John de Mendoza
415	To Alexis Fontana
416	To Alphonse Ramirez de Vergara
417	To Alexis Fontana
418	To Father Anthony Soldevila
419	To Octavius Cesari
420	To Father Adrian Adrienssens
422	To Eleanor Mascarenhas
423	To John Baptist
424	To Emerius
425	To Charles Cardinal of Lorraine
427	To John de Vega

page 429	To Father John Baptist de Fermo
430	To Father Marin Valentine
431	To Brother Joseph
432	To Father Alphonse Roman
432	To Louis de Calatayud
433	To Father Fulvius Androzzi
435	To Stephen Casanova
436	To Peter, a Priest of Bologna
437	To N. N.
439	To The Community at Alcala
441	To The Members of the Society in Portugal
443	Index

PART I

1524-1537

¶ TO AGNES PASCUAL
1, 71-73, Letter 1

This letter is addressed "To my sister Pascual in Christ our Lord." Agnes Pujol was a native of Manresa. As the widow of Peter Sagrista, she married Peter Pascual on February 26, 1512. Pascual was a weaver of Barcelona, but lived at Manresa in the Parish of St. Mary. He died and was buried at Manresa. His house in Barcelona became the home of St. Ignatius from 1523 to 1525, while he was studying grammar under Jerome Ardevoll.

Agnes wished to make living comfortable for Ignatius during his stay in her home. He preferred, however, to continue his penances. Each day he begged for his food and at night he slept on bare planks rather than the mattress she offered to him. Agnes took charge of the money and food which he collected each day. At mealtime he distributed it to the poor who gathered outside the Pascual home.

In this letter Ignatius encourages Agnes in the practice of virtue in spite of the difficulties which distract her. He bids her to take careful thought of the needs of both her body and soul. He also suggests that she consult Callistus on matters of conscience.

Barcelona, December 6, 1524

JHUS

I thought I should write you because of the great desire I know you have of serving our Lord. I have reason to think that just now you are quite fatigued, not only because of the absence of that blessed soul whom God has taken to Himself,[1] but also because of the hostility and opposition you meet with in God's service there, let alone the ceaseless temptations of the enemy of our human nature. But for the love of God our Lord be careful always to go forward, and avoid all occasions. If you do, temptation will have no power against you. In fact, you should always act thus, preferring God's praise to everything else. So far is our Lord from bidding you do anything that is fatiguing or dangerous to health that He would rather have you rejoice in Him and allow the body all that is needful. Let all your words, thoughts, and actions be in Him, and direct to this end whatever care you have to give your person, preferring the observance of God's commandments to every other good. It is this He wishes of us and this He bids us. And whoever gives thought to this will discover that there is more trouble and pain in this life . . .[2]

---
[1] Nothing further is known of this lady.
[2] The text here is faulty and lacks four or five words.

A pilgrim by the name of Callistus[3] is now in Barcelona, and I should very much like to see you consult with him. It is more than likely that you will discover in him more than appears on the surface.

For the love of our Lord let us make every effort in Him,[4] seeing that we are so much in His debt. We will sooner become weary of receiving His gifts than He of giving.

May it please our Lady to intercede with her Son for us poor sinners and obtain this grace for us, that with the cooperation of our own toil and effort she may change our weak and sorry spirits and make them strong and joyful to praise God.

¶ TO AGNES PASCUAL
I, 74-75, Letter 2

Ignatius always thought of Agnes as his mother and treated her with the greatest regard. In this letter he informs her of his safe arrival in Paris. He also includes some good advice for John, her young son, who became Ignatius' close friend during his stay in Barcelona. Ignatius spent the following seven years studying in Paris.

Paris, March 3, 1528

JHUS

May the true peace of Christ our Lord visit and protect our souls.

The thought of the deep affection which you have always had for me in God our Lord and which you have always proved by deeds prompts me to write you this letter to let you know something of my journey after leaving you. The weather was favorable, and by the grace and goodness of God our Lord I arrived here in the city of Paris in perfect health on the second of February. I will study here until our Lord ordains otherwise.

I should like very much to hear from you, and to know whether Fonseca answered the letter you wrote and what he said, or whether you spoke with him.

---

[3] Callistus de Sa was probably a native of Segovia who joined Ignatius at Barcelona, but just when we do not know. All that we know of him is what we find in the confidences shared with Gonzales de la Camara (*Scripta de S. Ignatio*, I, 84), where we are told that, shortly after their experience at Salamanca, he left Ignatius and went to Portugal and thence to the Indies, at two different times. He finally established himself at Salamanca, where he attracted considerable attention by his wealth, especially among those who had known him as a poor student in his youth. See Dudon, *Loyola*, Chapters 7 and 8.

[4] That is, following His example and in union with Him.

Remember me sincerely to John,[1] and tell him to be obedient to his parents always and to keep the feast days, because if he does he will live long in this life and also in heaven above.

Remember me to your neighbor. Tell her that the jewels have arrived. May her devout affection for me never fail. May the Lord of the world repay her and ever remain by His goodness in our souls, so that His will may be always fulfilled in us.

¶ TO MARTIN GARCIA DE ONAZ
I, 77-83, Letter 3

Ignatius expresses his approval of his brother Martin's plan of sending his nephew to Paris for study. He then goes on to explain why he did not write at first but does so now. He speaks of Christian charity and the order to be followed in charity, and encourages Martin to merit the goods of eternity by a proper use of those of time.

Paris, June 1532

IHS

May the grace and love of Christ our Lord be ever with us.

Your letter brought me great satisfaction in the service and love of the Divine Majesty because of the news it gives me of your daughter and the plans you have for your son. May the Divine Majesty be pleased with all our intentions and order them to His praise and service, and allow you to persevere, and prosper them when you so direct them. If you have no better plan, I do not think that you will make any mistake in having him take theology rather than canon law, for theology is a field in which he will find it easier to amass the riches which do not fail and which will give you added comfort in your old age. Nor do I think that you will find anywhere in Europe greater advantages than here at Paris. I should judge that, if you allow him fifty ducats a year, he will be able to meet all expenses, tutor's fees, and other charges. He will be in a foreign land, with different ways and a colder climate, and you would not want him to suffer any need that might interfere with his studies, so it seems to me. Even from the point of view of expense I am sure that he will find it cheaper, as he will be able to accomplish here in four years what it would

---

[1] An account of the familiar friendship existing between Ignatius and John, the young son of Agnes, is given in Dudon, *Loyola*, pp. 100 ff. John later gave excellent testimony in the processes for St. Ignatius' canonization.

take him six to do elsewhere—even more, I think I can say without straying from the truth. If you agree with me and send him here, it would be good to see that he arrives a week before the Feast of St. Remy, the first of October next, as the courses in philosophy begin then. If he is well founded in grammar, he could begin his philosophy by that date. Should he come a little late, he will have to wait a whole year until the Feast of St. Remy, when the course will begin over again.

I will do all I can to give him a start in his studies, and see that he applies himself and keeps away from bad company. You write: "If you decide that he is to live where you are, please let me know about what it will cost a year. If you can be of any help to me in this matter of expense, I will see that you are repaid when opportunity offers." I believe that I understand the literal meaning of your words, if there has been no slip of the pen. You mean that you will appreciate it if your son studies here and that I should do all I can to relieve you of all expense. I do not know what makes you say that or what you mean by it. If it serves any purpose, make your meaning clear. As far as justice and reason are concerned, I do not think that God will permit me to be wanting, since all I seek is His most holy service, your comfort in Him, and your son's progress, in the event you make up your mind to send him here.

You say that you are delighted to see that I have taken to writing again after so long a period of neglect. Don't be surprised. A man with a serious wound begins by applying one ointment, and then in the course of its healing another, and at the end still another. Thus, in the beginning of my way one kind of remedy was necessary; a little later a different one does me no harm. If I saw that it did, I would not look for a second or a third. It is not strange that I should have had this experience, seeing that St. Paul said, shortly after his conversion: "There was given me a sting of my flesh, an angel of Satan to buffet me";[1] and elsewhere, "I see another law in my members, fighting against the law of my mind";[2] "the flesh lusteth against the spirit: and the spirit against the flesh."[3] And so great was the rebellion in his soul that he went so far as to say: "For the good which I will, I do not; but the evil which I will not, that I do,"[4] "for that which I work, I understand not."[5] Later, on another occasion: "For I am sure that neither death, nor life, nor angels, nor things present, nor things to come, nor any other creature shall be able to separate me from the love of God, which is in Christ Jesus our Lord."[6] At the begin-

[1] 2 Corinthians 12:7.
[2] Romans 7:23.
[3] Galatians 5:17.
[4] Romans 7:19.
[5] Romans 7:15.
[6] Romans 8:38-39.

ning of my way I was very much like him. Throughout my life and at its end may it please the Supreme Goodness not to deny me His abundant and most holy grace, that I may be like all who are His true servants and imitate and serve them. I would ask Him even to take away my life rather than grieve Him in anything or grow slack in His service and praise.

But to come to the point. I should have written you more frequently during the last five or six years but for two reasons. The first, my studies and my constant association with others, which, however, had nothing to do with temporal interests. The second was that I did not have sufficient reason for thinking that my letters would redound to the praise and service of God our Lord or so comfort my kindred according to the flesh as to make us kindred according to the spirit and to help us both in the things that last forever. The truth is, I can love a person in this life only so far as he strives to advance in the service and praise of God our Lord; for he who loves anything for itself and not for God does not love God with his whole heart. If two persons serve God equally, and one of them is a relative of mine, God wishes us to cherish a greater affection for our natural father than for another. He would have us prefer a benefactor and a relative to one who is neither; a friend and acquaintance to one who is unknown to us. For this reason we revere, honor, and love the apostles more than we do the other saints, since they loved God our Lord more perfectly and served Him more faithfully. For charity, without which no one can attain eternal life, is the love with which we love God our Lord for Himself and everything else for Him. And we must also praise God in His saints, as the psalmist teaches us.[7]

I have a great desire, a very great desire indeed, if I may say so, to see a true and intense love of God grow in you, my relatives, and friends, so that you will bend all your efforts to the praise and service of God. Doing this, you make it possible for me to love you and serve you ever more and more, because in this service of the servants of my Lord there is for me both victory and glory. It is with this solid love and honest desire that I speak, write, and advise you just as I should honestly wish and desire you to advise, urge, and correct me in terms of sincere humility without any thought of worldly or profane glory. It is none of my business to condemn a man who in this life lies awake with plans for adding to his buildings, his income, his estate, in the hope of leaving behind him a great name and reputation. But neither can I praise him; for according to St. Paul we ought to use the things of this world as though we used them

---

[7] Psalm 150:1.

not and own them as though we owned them not, have a wife as though we had her not, because the fashion of this world passes and in a moment is gone.[8] God grant that it may be so.

If any of these truths have in the past made any impression on you, or if they do so now, I beg of you by God's reverence and love to make every effort to win honor in heaven, fame and renown before the Lord, who is going to be our judge. For if He has given you an abundance of this world's goods, it is to help you earn those of heaven by giving a good example and sound teaching to your sons, servants, and relatives. Converse spiritually with some, impose a proper punishment on others, without anger or harshness. Share with some the influence of your family and help others with money and goods. Deal with an open hand with poor orphans and the needy. The man with whom our Lord has been so generous should not be close. One day we shall find in heaven as much repose and delight as we have dispensed in this life; and since you can do so much where you are, I beg of you again and again by the love of our Lord Jesus Christ to make every effort not only to give this matter some thought but to put it into practice, because for those who love, nothing is hard, especially when done for the love of our Lord Jesus Christ.

I have written at this great length to answer once for all the detailed questions set down in your letter and to make you fully acquainted with the situation.

To the lady of the house and all the family, together with all those who you think will be glad to hear from me, my sincerest regards in the Lord, who must judge us. Begging Him by His infinite and perfect goodness to give us the grace to know His most holy will and the strength perfectly to fulfill it, I remain, . . .

I received your letter on the twentieth of this month of June; and as you were very urgent about an answer, I am writing this and two copies, in the hope that what you decide in our Lord may not be without effect. If this letter reaches you in time, it will be all the better if your son arrives three weeks in advance of the Feast of St. Remy, or even earlier if possible, as he would then be able to make some preparation before beginning the course. A nephew of the archbishop of Seville wishes to do this, having registered here in the College of St. Barbara for philosophy this coming Feast of St. Remy. They could both take advantage of this introduction, as there will be no lack of opportunity. May the Perfect Goodness be pleased to ordain all to His holy service and continued praise.

[8] 1 Corinthians 7:29-31.

¶ TO ISABEL ROSER
1, 83-89, Letter 4

Isabel Roser was a noble and well-known matron of Barcelona. Her husband, John Roser, was a businessman of some means and of holy life, and both he and his wife were busy with good works. One day Isabel, listening to a sermon in the Church of Santa Maria del Mar, saw St. Ignatius seated on the altar steps among the children, his face all aglow. Struck by his grave and modest demeanor, she called him to her home and invited him to dinner. The saint accepted the invitation and spoke to her and her husband of the things of God with such warmth that from that moment they both remained very much attached to him and helped him considerably with their alms. Ignatius is answering three letters he had received from Isabel. He first thanks her for an alms she had given him, comforts her on the death of another pious woman named Canillas, and accepts the excuses of others who were then unable to help him. He goes on to show that God frequently heals the soul by afflicting the body. Lastly, he exhorts Isabel to practice virtue even in the face of difficulties.

Paris, November 10, 1532

IHS

May the grace and love of Christ our Lord be with us.

I received from Dr. Benet your three letters and the twenty ducats with them. May God our Lord be pleased to give you credit for this on the day of judgment and repay you for me, as I am sure He in His divine goodness will do in new and sound money. I hope that He will not have to punish me for ingratitude, if in some way He makes me worthy of giving some praise and service to His Divine Majesty.

You speak in your letter of God's will being fulfilled in the banishment and withdrawal of Canillas from this life. In truth, I cannot feel any pain for her, but only for ourselves who are still in this place of endless weariness, pains, and calamities. I knew that in this life she was dearly loved by her Creator and Lord, and I can easily believe that she will be well received and entertained. She will have little desire for the palaces, the pomps, the riches, and the vanities of this world.

You also mention the excuses of our sisters in Christ our Lord. Indeed, they owe me nothing, and it is I who am eternally indebted to them. If they see fit to employ their means otherwise for the service of God our Lord, we should rejoice. But if they are unwilling or unable, I should really desire to have something to give them so that they could do much for the service and glory of God our Lord. As long as I live I cannot but be their debtor, and I am thinking that, after we have finished with this life, they will be well repaid by me.

In your second letter you tell me of your long-drawn-out pain in the illness you have undergone and of the great stomach pains that still remain. Indeed I cannot help feeling the liveliest sympathy with you in your sufferings, seeing that I desire every imaginable happiness and prosperity for you, provided it will help you to glorify God our Lord. And yet when we reflect, these infirmities and other temporal privations are often seen to be from God's hand to help us to a better self-knowledge and to rid ourselves of the love of created things. They help us moreover to focus our thought on the brevity of this life, so as to prepare for the other which has no end. When I think that in these afflictions He visits those whom He loves, I can feel no sadness or pain, because I realize that a servant of God, through an illness, turns out to be something of a doctor for the direction and ordering of his life to God's glory and service.

You also speak of my forgiving you if you can no longer help me, since you have many obligations to meet and your resources are not sufficient for all. There is no reason for you to speak of forgiveness from me. It is I who should fear; for when I think of failing to do what God wishes me to do for all of my benefactors, I begin to fear that His Divine Justice will not forgive me, and all the more so, that I have received so much from you. Finally, since I am quite unable to fulfill my duties in this respect, my only refuge is to consider the merits I shall gain before the Divine Majesty—that is, with the help of His grace, which the same Lord will distribute to those to whom I am indebted, to each one according as he has helped me in His service, and especially to you, to whom I owe more than to anyone else I know in this world. As I recognize this debt, I hope that our Lord will help me to repay it. Be sure that your solid and sincere affection for me will bring me as much spiritual joy as if you sent me all the money in the world. Our Lord insists that we look to the giver, and love him more than his gift, and thus keep him ever before our eyes and in the most intimate thoughts of our heart.

You also suggest that I write, if I think it good, to our other sisters and benefactresses in Christ to ask help for the future. I would rather be guided in this by your judgment than by my own. Even though La Sepilla offered in her letter and shows a desire to help me, I do not think for the present that I will write her for help in my studies.[1] My reason is

---

[1] A lady of Barcelona with something of a shrewish disposition. Her name was Eleanor Zapila Rocaberti or, according to other commentators, Anna de Rocaberti. Ignatius' first meeting with her is narrated in Dudon, *Loyola*, p. 72.

that there is no certainty of my remaining here for a whole year. And if I do, God, I hope, will give me the light and judgment to do all for His greater service and always carry out His will and desire.

In the third letter you speak of the enmities, the intrigues, and the untruths which have been circulated about you. I am not at all surprised at this, not even if it were worse than it is. For just as soon as you determined to bend every effort to procure the praise, honor, and service of God our Lord, you declared war against the world and raised your standard in its face, and got ready to reject what is lofty by embracing what is lowly, to accept indifferently honor and dishonor, riches and poverty, affection and hatred, welcome and repulse—in a word, the glory of the world or all the wrongs it could inflict upon you. We cannot be much afraid of the reproaches of this life when they are confined to words, for all the words in the world will never hurt a hair of our heads. As to words of double meaning, even when they are vile and hurtful they will give neither pain nor satisfaction except insofar as they are willfully admitted. But if we wish absolutely to live in honor and to be held in esteem by our neighbors, we can never be solidly rooted in God our Lord, and it will be impossible for us to remain unscathed when we meet with affronts. Thus, the satisfaction I once took in the thought of the insults the world offered you was balanced by the pain I felt at the thought of your having to seek a remedy against this pain and suffering. May it please the Mother of God to hear my prayer for you, which is that you may meet with even greater affronts so that you may have the occasion of greater merit, provided that you can accept them with patience and constancy and without sin on the part of others, remembering the greater insults which Christ our Lord suffered for us. If we find that we are without this patience, we have all the more reason to complain, not so much of those who hurt us as of our own weakness and sensuality and our failure to be mortified and dead as we should be to the things of the world. For these people make it possible for us to gain a more precious treasure than anyone can win in this life and greater riches than anyone can amass in this world. . . .

Thus, I would rather fix my attention on one fault that I had committed than on all the evil that might be said of me.

May the most holy Trinity grant you all in all your trials and in everything else in which you can serve God all the grace that I desire for myself, and may no more be given to me than I desire for you.

Please remember me most sincerely to Master Roser, and to any who you think will be pleased to hear from me.

¶ TO AGNES PASCUAL
I, 90-92, Letter 5

Ignatius answers a letter that he has received from Agnes and thanks her for her interest in him. An entire year has passed since he received the letter from her. In the course of that year he has taken his master's degree. The resulting expenses have left him greatly in need of money. He gives the names of a few ladies who are inclined to help him and asks Agnes to commend him to them. His letter also includes a thoughtful greeting to the boy John, Agnes' little son.

Paris, June 13, 1533

The grace and love of our Lord be ever our help and support.

It is a year now since I received a letter from you through Dr. Benet (may he rest in glory) when he brought alms and support from Barcelona. From your letter and from sources of information here I learned of the efforts you have made in my behalf and the great amount of good will you have always shown. You likewise offer to make the same efforts and take the same interest in the future. It seems that you have not only laid me under obligations for the past, but that you would like to do so for the future as well. May it please God our Lord that that true Master, for whose love and reverence you do this, repay you.

Although I have already answered your letter, I thought of writing this, not only because of your great kindness, as for the fact that my studies have become more expensive than hitherto. This Lent I took my master's degree and in doing so paid out in unavoidable expenses more than my position or resources warranted. As a result I find myself very short of funds and in much need of help from God our Lord. For this reason I am writing to La Sepilla.[1] She made me a very generous offer in a letter she wrote, in which she showed an intense desire to help me and asked that I write and let her know my needs.

I am also writing to Isabel Roser but say nothing to her on this point. She wrote me a letter telling me not to be surprised if, because of her own needs, she could not help me as much as she might wish. I readily believe her; and if I may venture to say so, I say that she has done more for me than she really could. Indeed, I owe her more than I can ever repay. It would be better not to say anything to her that would give her an inkling of my need, as I would not wish to sadden her for not being able to help me. When I left Barcelona the wife of Mosén Gralla manifested a great

---

[1] See Letter 4, note 1.

desire to help me throughout the course of my studies and has done so all along. Others also have helped, Doña Isabel de Josa has offered, and so has Doña Alduncia de Cardona, the latter having given me some support. I am not writing to any of the last three for fear of appearing importunate; but do you commend me to them and their prayers. As to Doña Gralla, I always feel that, once she is informed, she will wish to contribute to the alms that may be sent me. With regard to her and the others do what you think best, and that will be best in my eyes. I shall always be satisfied because I am always their debtor, and it is not possible for me to be anything but your eternal debtor.

The bearer of this letter will give you fuller information of what happens here, and you can trust him in everything as you would trust me.

I have a great desire of news of your son, John, my old friend and true brother in the Lord, who is to be our eternal judge. Tell me how things are going with him, for you know that I cannot help but rejoice in his happiness and be pained at its absence. May God our Lord be pleased to give him the grace always to know himself perfectly and be aware of the Divine Majesty in his soul, for, thus captured by His love and His grace, he will be freed from all creatures in this world.

I close, asking God our Lord in His infinite goodness to do with both of you in this life as He did with that blessed mother and her son Augustine. Be sure to remember me cordially to the circle of your friends and loved ones.

The person who was to have brought this letter has been detained by some business matter. He is sending in his place the man who will deliver this and who is returning here at once.

¶ TO JAMES CAZADOR[1]
I, 93-99, Letter 6

This letter is an answer to one which Ignatius received from James Cazador. In it he discusses several matters about which James had

[1] James Cazador was a native of Vich. At the time of this letter he was archdeacon of the cathedral of Barcelona. He took possession of the see as bishop on June 20, 1546. He was among Ignatius' benefactors in Barcelona and sent help to him at Paris. Ignatius had left Paris in 1535 to return to Spain. After three months at Azpeitia and several errands in northern Spain in the interest of his companions, he returned to Italy and finally arrived at Venice to finish the studies he had interrupted at Paris. At Venice he awaited his companions from Paris, who were to join him for their pilgrimage to the Holy Land, and while waiting for them he pursued his theological studies.

written him. Ignatius tells him that he will have sufficient funds for the coming year. He gives him some sound advice concerning a will which Mosén Claret was to make. Next he says that, unless God ordains otherwise, he plans on going to Barcelona after finishing his studies. Finally, he expresses his willingness to help the pious women of whom Cazador speaks, and would also like to help the religious of the Convent of Santa Clara to lead a more regular life. The nun of whom Cazador speaks should not lose heart. Ignatius does not understand her case clearly, but she must realize that our Lord wishes her only good.

Venice, February 12, 1536

IHS

The grace and love of our Lord be ever our protection and help.

On reading your letter of January 5 I experienced a feeling of joy, mingled with considerable pain because of the bad news it contained. Joy with sadness, two contrary feelings; joy on beholding the zeal our Lord gives you to weep with those who weep, not only in their corporal infirmities but even to a greater degree in their spiritual trials as well; and pain when I think of the misfortunes you describe in your letter. I have thought of five or six points on which I might have something to say in answer. I will begin with the least in order and which are least likely to quench the thirst of our souls, so that we may not end up with a relish and taste for things which have less to do with our eternal salvation.

First. You say that you will not fail with the usual contribution; I am only to let you know when. Isabel Roser has written that the coming April she will supply me with sufficient funds to carry me to the end of my studies. That will be better, for she should be able to take care of my expenses for a year, both with regard to books and other necessities.

Meanwhile, although the cost of living here is high and present arrangements do not put me beyond want, and manual labor makes demands on my time over and above what is needed for study, I am well enough supplied because Isabel Roser has advanced me twelve scudi on her account in addition to the other help and alms which you have sent me from Barcelona for the love and service of God our Lord, who I hope will repay you in sound money, not only for what you are doing for me but also for the great care and interest you are always taking in my poverty. Really, I do not think that parents could show their own children greater.

Of the fortnight before Christmas, when I was in Bologna, I spent a week in bed with stomach pains, chills, and fevers. I then made up my mind to come to Venice, and have been here a month and a half with much better health on the whole. I am sharing the home and the society of a very good and learned man. I do not think that I could possibly be better off than I am here.

Second. I am not much worried to learn that the three nephews are away from Marable, although I should like to know something of the reason why they are. I suppose I shall soon know, as I have written to one of my Paris friends, asking him to look them up and call on them for me. I say I am not worried because, unless I am mistaken, they are modest and highly respected young men. I feel that, wherever they are, they will give a good account of themselves. While I was there I noticed that Losada was very quiet, and with the example of the two elder brothers, especially of James, I trust that in our Lord they will be faithful to their duty. May it please Him in His complete and perfect goodness to keep them under His guiding hand.

Third. You have asked me—and your mere requests are a command in our Lord—my opinion about the illness of Mosén Claret.[2] There is but little for me to say here and now, as you have seen what I said in another letter. My sole desire is that you help him to manage for the health of his soul, and whatever else our Lord has given him in this life, since I do not think he would take advice from anyone else as well as from you. If he has no children or near relative to whom he could leave his property by law, it would seem to me to be better beyond doubt and sounder to leave his property to Him from whom he has received it; that is, to the great giver of all, our ruler and Lord. This he could do by remembering pious, just, and holy causes. As far as possible, it would be better to do this while he lives than afterwards. I cannot at all approve a man's leaving his property to another for the maintenance of horses and dogs merely for hunting or to bolster a social position or for worldly display. Besides several other degrees of perfection, St. Gregory lays down these two: one, when a man leaves all his possessions to his relatives and follows Christ our Lord; and the second, which he notes is higher, when he leaves everything to the poor according to that text in the Gospel, "If thou wilt be perfect, and so on."[3] I mean, it would be better to give to the poor when relatives are not so poor as those who are not relatives. But, other things

---

[2] John Claret was a man of means whom Ignatius had known during his stay in Barcelona. He recovered from this illness and was visited in 1539 by Araoz on his way from Rome to Barcelona, who brought him Ignatius' greetings.

[3] "If thou wilt be perfect, go, sell what thou hast, and give to the poor and thou shalt have treasure in heaven" (Matthew 19:21).

being equal, I have more obligations to my relatives than to others who are not relatives.

Fourth. Concerning the desire you manifest of seeing me in Barcelona and hearing me preach, be assured that I find the same desire in my own heart. Not that I find any satisfaction in doing what others cannot do or in repeating the success of others; but I should like to preach in a minor capacity on subjects that are more easily understood and of less importance, with the hope in God our Lord that, if I take up these humble subjects, He would add His grace, so that in some way I might be able to advance in the praise and service I owe Him. Thus I have hopes that, when my studies are finished, which will be in about a year from this coming Lent, I will not tarry in any other part of Spain to preach His word before we see each other there, as we both desire. For I have no doubt that I owe more to Barcelona than to any other city in the world. But all this with the understanding, *clave non errante*,[4] that God our Lord does not employ me outside of Spain in tasks more painful and humiliating for me. I will, however, preach as a poor man, and certainly not with the embarrassing abundance I now enjoy by reason of my studies. However that may be, as a pledge of what I here say I am going to send you when my studies are finished the few books I now have, or may have then, as I promised Isabel Roser.

Fifth. You say that you have written to the *beata*,[5] and that you would like to have us meet, thinking that our meeting would be a source of pleasure. I am certain it will be, for I make it a general rule to treat of the things of God when I enter into relations with anyone, even though he be a great sinner. I find that it is always I who am the gainer. How much should I profit in every way when these persons are chosen servants of God!

Indeed, ever since Dr. Castro[6] spoke to me at length about this soul, I have been very much drawn to her, as I knew she was under your direction; and I have thanked God for what He has accomplished in her. It is my hope that, if it be for His praise and service and our greater advantage, He will bring about a meeting before long.

---

[4] This might be translated "if the key fits." But that St. Ignatius uses the phrase in an extended meaning may be gathered from the context.

[5] We do not know the identity of this devout woman.

[6] De Castro was one of the first to whom Ignatius gave the Exercises in Paris. He later became a Carthusian in the Monastery of Val Christi in Valencia. Ignatius had visited him there en route from Azpeitia to Venice. He always had great confidence in De Castro's prudence, and even recommended Peter Faber to make a general confession to him when he was tormented by scruples during his studies in Paris (*Epistolae et instructiones*, I, 96, note).

Sixth. To come to what you say about the Monastery of Santa Clara,[7] I certainly could hardly consider him a true Christian whose heart would not be pierced at the thought of so much harm done to the service of God our Lord. That a single individual should fail in judgment is not so regrettable as the harm that results to so many of both sexes who might devote themselves to God's service. Indeed, such is our misery that we find the greatest difficulty in overcoming ourselves; and even where the spiritual profit is greatest, the slightest occasion is enough to bring us to naught. Really, I should be very glad to visit these religious if it were possible for me by doing so to give some substance to their exercises and manner of life, especially for her who apparently finds herself in such trouble and peril.[8]

I cannot easily be convinced that anyone who is given to worldly pleasures, or at least less devoted to God our Lord but still preserving some sense and judgment, should be reduced to such a state of despair because of her determination to give our Lord a better and more intimate service. I am only human and weak, and if someone were to come to me to serve me and love me more, I would not allow him to come to such a pass if I had the power to prevent it. How much more, then, will God, who, being divine, became human and died merely for the salvation of all, prevent such a disaster. Therefore I cannot easily believe that this soul should incur such suffering and misfortune for the sole reason of having given herself to God's service unless there be some interior or future cause. For it is God's way to give understanding, not take it away; to give hope rather than mistrust. I say "without some other interior cause" because it is possible that her soul at the time she made the Exercises was wounded by sin; and there are so many different kinds of sin as to exceed all number. Or it may be that she went about making the Exercises in the wrong way, because not everything that seems good is good, and in this person,[9] although good and grace seemed to be present, they really were not, because they do not dwell peaceably with sin and evil which were really there. This may be able to account for the enemy's unusual activity.

---

[7] This convent was founded by Berengarius Palou, bishop of Barcelona, in 1233. It continued as a Franciscan convent until the end of 1327, when it passed into the hands of the Benedictines. Some of the members of the community were women of conspicuous holiness, among them Teresa Rejadell, to whom the following letter in this collection is addressed. But there were others who did not share this fervor. The more fervent were anxious to have the Society undertake their direction, but Ignatius never allowed himself to be moved by their entreaties.

[8] Perhaps this refers to Teresa Rejadell, from whom the saint was soon to receive a letter.

[9] The editors of the *Monumenta* find this passage very obscure. Our text reproduces what they offer as a clarification (*Epistolae et instructiones*, I, 98, note).

I also said "without a future cause" because God our Lord disposes all things with order, weight, and measure. It is possible that our Lord sees that, although for the moment that soul is in grace, it is not going to make a good use of the graces and gifts and, not persevering, would fall into greater sins and finally be lost. Our Lord, seeing this, in His kindness rewards her for the slight service she has given and permits these fears and continual temptations to afflict her, but prevents her from perishing entirely. For we must always suppose that whatever the Lord of the whole world does in the souls of men is either to give us greater glory or to lessen our evil if He does not find better dispositions in us.

Finally, since we do not know the roots and the causes, we cannot be sure of their effects. And therefore it is always very good for us to live in love, but also very prudent to live in fear, since the judgments of God are entirely inscrutable, and we should not demand reasons for what He wills. There is nothing left for us to do but to weep and pray, asking for greater soundness of judgment in matters of conscience for her and for all others of that monastery. May His Divine Goodness arrange it thus, and never permit the enemy of our human nature to gain so great a victory against the souls whom He has so dearly bought and redeemed with His most precious blood.

I close with the prayer that His infinite goodness grant us the grace to know His holy will perfectly and completely fulfill it.

¶ TO SISTER TERESA REJADELL
I, 99-107, Letter 7

In the Monastery of Santa Clara, Barcelona, this religious of noble family reached a very high degree of sanctity. Ignatius frequently gave her spiritual guidance and the present letter to her is a precious commentary on the Rules for the Discernment of Spirits and on Scruples, which are given by him in his book of the Exercises.

Venice, June 18, 1536

May the grace and love of Christ our Lord be our never-failing protection and help.

Your letter, which I received a few days ago, brought with it much joy in the Lord, whom you are serving and whom you desire to serve even more earnestly, and to whom we must attribute all of the good that we see in creatures.

You said that Caceres would inform me at length about your affairs. He has done so. And not only that, but he has given me an account of the direction he gave you in each particular. Reading over what he tells me, I do not find anything to add, although I should like further enlightenment from your letter because no one can give an account of another's experiences that will be as accurate as that given by the one undergoing them.

You ask me for the love of God our Lord to undertake the direction of your soul. It is many years now since His Divine Majesty, without any merit on my part, has given me the desire to give as much pleasure as I can to those men and women who walk in the way of His will and to be of help to those who labor as they should in His service. I have no doubt that you are of their number, and I am therefore very desirous of being in a position to practice what I preach.

You also are very earnest in asking me to tell you what our Lord may have to say to me and to tell you frankly what I think. I will be very glad to give you a frank opinion; and if at times I appear severe, it will be rather against him who is trying to upset you than against you yourself. The enemy is leading you into error in two things, but not in any way to make you fall into a sin that would separate you from God our Lord. He tries rather to upset you and to interfere with your service of God and your peace of mind. In the first place he proposes and leads you on to a false humility. And in the second, he gives you an exaggerated fear of God, with which you are altogether too much occupied.

In the first place, then, the enemy as a rule follows this course. He places obstacles and impediments in the way of those who love and begin to serve God our Lord, and this is the first weapon he uses in his efforts to wound them. He asks, for instance: "How can you continue a life of such great penance, deprived of all satisfaction from friends, relatives, possessions? How can you lead so lonely a life, with no rest, when you can save your soul in other ways and without such dangers?" He tries to bring us to understand that we must lead a life that is longer than it will actually be, by reason of the trials he places before us and which no man ever underwent. He fails to remind us of the great comfort and consolation which our Lord is wont to give to such souls, who, as new recruits in our Lord's service, surmount all these obstacles and choose to suffer with their Creator and Lord. The enemy will then try his second weapon, which is pride and vainglory. He will endeavor to make the individual see that there is a great deal of goodness and holiness in him, and puts him in a position high above his merits. If the servant of God is proof against these darts, humbling and abasing himself and refusing consent to the suggestions of the enemy, the enemy draws his third weapon, which is false humility. When he sees that the servant of the Lord is so good and humble and, obedient to all the Lord's commands, regards his own uselessness and weakness without any thought of self-glorification, he is ready with the suggestion that, should he happen to speak of the graces our Lord has bestowed upon him in actual deeds or merely in resolve or desire, he sins by another kind of vainglory in speaking favorably of himself. In this way he tries to prevent him from speaking of any of the blessings he has received. His purpose is to prevent him from producing fruit in others as well as in himself. For he knows that, when such a person recalls to mind what he has received, he is always helped in regard to greater things. One ought, however, to be very reserved, and speak only with the motive of helping others or himself: others if he sees that they are in the proper dispositions and likely to believe him and draw some profit from what he says. Thus, when the enemy of our salvation sees that we are humble, he tries to draw us on to a humility that is excessive and counterfeit.

What you say makes this very plain; for after you speak of weaknesses and fears, which are very much to the point, you continue: "I am a poor religious, and I think I have a desire of serving Christ our Lord." You don't venture to say "I have a desire of serving Christ our Lord," or "Our Lord gives me the desire to serve Him," but you say "I think I have a desire." And yet you see and you understand that these desires of serving Christ our Lord are not your own, but come to you from our Lord. If you were to say that our Lord gives you great desires of serving Him, you would be giving praise to the same Lord because you are making known His gift, and you glory in Him, not in yourself, because you do not attribute that grace to yourself.

Hence we must examine the matter closely; and if the enemy uplifts us, we must abase ourselves by recounting our sins and miseries. If he keeps us down and depresses us, we must raise ourselves up in true faith and hope in our Lord by recalling the blessings we have received and with how much love and affection He is waiting to save us. The enemy does not care whether he speaks the truth or whether he lies. His sole purpose is to overcome us.

Consider attentively how the martyrs declared that they were Christ's servants when they were arraigned before their pagan judges. Now, when you find yourself in the presence of the enemy of human nature who is tempting you, trying to rob you of the strength which our Lord gives you and to render you so weak and timid with his snares, won't you have the courage to say that you desire to serve our Lord? Rather, you must answer him by a forthright and courageous declaration that you are His follower and that you would rather die than fall away from His service. If he puts justice before my eyes, I will think of mercy. If he suggests mercy, I will think of justice. We must in this way keep to our road without perturbation, leaving the mocker to be mocked, and placing all our reliance on the authority of Holy Scripture: "Beware that thou be not deceived into folly and be humbled."[1]

To come to the second point. The enemy, having instilled a fear in us that has some appearance of humility—a false humility—aims to prevent us from speaking of good, holy, and profitable things. He will then confront us with a much worse fear, the fear that we are separated and estranged from our Lord. To a great extent this is the result of what precedes. For, as the enemy was successful in his first attempt, he finds it easy to attack in this second stage. To explain this in some way I will point out another line of thought which the enemy follows. If he finds one whose conscience is easygoing and who falls into sins without a thought of their gravity, he does all he can to make venial sins appear no sins at all, and mortal venial, and a very serious mortal sin a mere trifle. In this way he takes advantage of the failing he perceives in us, I mean this excessively lax conscience. If on the other hand he comes upon one whose conscience is delicate (a delicate conscience being in itself nothing faulty, however) and sees that such a person avoids not only all mortal and all venial sin (as much as the latter is possible, for we cannot avoid them all) but even tries to keep from himself the very appearance of slight sin, imperfection, and defect, he tries to darken and confuse that good conscience by suggesting sin where there is none, changing perfection into defect, his only purpose being to harass and make one uneasy and miserable. When, as frequently happens, he cannot induce one to sin, or even hope to do so, he tries at least to vex him.

For a clearer understanding of this fear and its origin I will call your attention briefly to two lessons which our Lord usually gives, or permits. The one of them He gives, the other He permits. The first is an interior consolation which casts out all uneasiness and draws one to a complete love of our Lord. In this consolation He enlightens some, and to others He reveals many secrets as a preparation for later visits. In a word, when this divine consolation is present all trials are pleasant and all weariness

---

[1] Ecclesiasticus 13:10.

rest. He who goes forward with this fervor, warmth, and interior consolation finds every burden light and sweetness in every penance or trial, however great. This consolation points out and opens up the way we are to follow and points out the way we are to avoid. It does not remain with us always, but it will always accompany us on the way at the times that God designates. All this is for our progress.

But when this consolation is absent the other lesson comes to light. Our ancient enemy sets up all possible obstacles to turn us aside from the way on which we have entered. He makes use of everything to vex us, and everything in the first lesson is reversed. We find ourselves sad without knowing why. We cannot pray with devotion, nor contemplate, nor even speak or hear of the things of God with any interior taste or relish. Not only this, but if he sees that we are weak and much humbled by these harmful thoughts, he goes on to suggest that we are entirely forgotten by God our Lord, and leads us to think that we are quite separated from Him and that all that we have done and all that we desire to do is entirely worthless. He thus endeavors to bring us to a state of general discouragement. We can thus see what causes our fear and weakness: it is a too-prolonged gaze at such times on our miseries. We allow ourselves to be laid low by his misleading suggestions. For this reason it is necessary for us to be aware of our opponent. If we are in consolation, we should abase and humble ourselves and reflect that soon the trial of temptation will come. And when temptation, darkness, or sadness comes upon us, we must go contrary to it without permitting ourselves to pay any attention to the unpleasant impressions caused in us, and hope patiently for the consolation of our Lord, which will cast out all our uneasiness and scatter all the clouds.

It remains for me to speak of how we ought to understand what we think is from our Lord and, understanding it, how we ought to use it for our advantage. For it frequently happens that our Lord moves and urges the soul to this or that activity. He begins by enlightening the soul; that is to say, by speaking interiorly to it without the din of words, lifting it up wholly to His divine love and ourselves to His meaning without any possibility of resistance on our part, even should we wish to resist. This thought of His which we take is of necessity in conformity with the commandments, the precepts of the Church, and obedience to our superiors. It will be full of humility because the same divine Spirit is present in all. But we can frequently be deceived, however, because after such consolation or inspiration, when the soul is still abiding in its joy, the enemy tries under the impetus of this joy to make us innocently add to what we have received from God our Lord. His only purpose is to disturb and confuse us in everything.[2]

At other times he makes us lessen the import of the message we have received and confronts us with obstacles and difficulties, so as to prevent us from carrying out completely what had been made known to us. Right here there is more need of attention than anywhere else. We may often have to control the desire we feel and speak less of the things of God our Lord; at other times we may speak more than the satisfaction or movement we feel prompts us to. We act thus because in this matter we should give more heed to the good of others than to our own desires. When the enemy thus tries to magnify or diminish the communication received, we must proceed for the purpose of helping others, like a man who is crossing a ford. If I find a good footing—that is, some way or hope of profiting the neighbor—I will pass right on. But if the ford is muddied or disturbed and there is danger that scandal may be taken from what I say, I will rein in and seek an occasion more favorable to what I have to say.

We have touched on matter that can hardly be dealt with in a letter, at least without a much longer treatment. Even then there could be matters that could better be felt than put into words, let alone written down in a letter. If it please our Lord, I hope to see you there soon, and then we can come to a clearer understanding of some things. In the meantime, since Castro is close at hand, I think it would be good to communicate with him. No harm can come of it and possibly some good. Since you tell me to write what I think in the Lord, I will say that you are fortunate if you know how to keep what you have.

---

[2] To avoid all misunderstanding three things should be noted: (1) St. Ignatius is speaking of the operation of God in the soul, not of the efforts that the soul, moved by divine inspiration and supported by grace, makes of her own free will, interiorly and exteriorly, to merit everlasting life. (2) That what he says is this, that God sometimes communicates Himself to the soul with such power and dominion that the soul of itself cannot impede the divine operation, nor fail to perceive God's presence or see what He reveals or hear what He says or understand what He teaches or feel herself powerfully drawn to His love; and this seeing, hearing, understanding, perceiving (now taking place in the highest part of the soul, the mind and the understanding, and some of it in the imagination), is the *operation* to which the saint says that God moves and *urges* the soul, and is the *meaning* which the soul *takes without being able to resist even should it wish to*. (3) As the demon is able to counterfeit the divine inspirations and consolations without its always being in our power to rid ourselves of his suggestions, and although we are always (with God's grace) masters of ourselves and can refuse our consent to them, the saint places in his third point a very easy, clear, and safe rule by which we can distinguish true inspirations from their counterfeits. It is that they contain nothing, or urge us to nothing, that is contrary to what the Church teaches in matters of faith and bids us practice in the matter of morals. He gives the fundamental reason: that one and the same Holy Spirit is author of true inspirations from God and the teacher of the Church, who cannot contradict Himself, telling the Church one thing and us another (*Monumenta*, I, 105, n. 5).

In closing I beg the most holy Trinity to bestow upon us all plentiful grace to know God's most holy will and perfectly to fulfill it.

¶ TO SISTER TERESA REJADELL
I, 107-09, Letter 8

In the direction of souls it is necessary to speak with exactitude. Efforts at meditation should be gentle and not tire the body. Good health is an assistance to prayer. It is important to realize that God loves us in order to grow strong in His love and to despise thoughts opposed to His service. The soul that conforms itself to the divine will is mistress of the body.

Venice, September 11, 1536

IHS

May the grace and love of Christ our Lord be our never-failing help and support.

I have received two letters from you at different times. The first I think I answered at some length, and you should have received my answer by this time. In your second letter you add only a few words to what you had to say in the first, and I will now answer these briefly.

You say that you find in yourself great ignorance and great cowardice, and so forth. To know this alone is to know much. But you go on to add that this condition is produced by the many and vague directions you have received. I agree with you that, when one is indefinite, one does not understand, and helps less. But the Lord, who sees this need, will Himself come to your aid.

Every kind of meditation in which the understanding is engaged wearies the body. There are other kinds of meditation, orderly and restful, which are pleasant to the understanding and offer no difficulty to the interior faculties of the soul, and which can be made without interior or exterior expenditure of effort. These methods do not weary the body but rather help to rest it, except in the two following instances. The first is when you withdraw the natural nourishment and recreation which you should give to the body. By nourishment I mean when one is so taken up by such meditations that he forgets to give the body its proper nourishment at the proper hours. By recreation I mean to allow the understanding to roam at will, provided only that the subjects it deals with be good or indifferent, or at least not bad.

The second instance is this, and it is of frequent occurrence in those who are much given to prayer or contemplation. They find trouble getting to sleep because just before bedtime they exercise their minds on the matter of their meditation and keep thinking about it, and consequently find it difficult to fall asleep. It is the enemy who chooses this moment to present good thoughts to the mind. He has but one purpose, to make the body suffer by robbing it of its sleep. This must be avoided entirely. With a healthy body you will be able to do much. I don't know what you can do with one that is infirm. A healthy body is a great help either for good or evil: evil for those whose wills are depraved by evil habits, but good in those whose will is entirely given to God and trained to habits of virtue.

If, however, I do not know what meditations and exercises you make and the amount of time you give to them, I cannot say more than what I have written, unless Caceres has told you otherwise. And here once more I insist especially that you think of God as loving you, as I have no doubt He does, and that you correspond with this love and pay no attention whatever to the evil thoughts, even if they are obscene or sensual (when they are not deliberate), nor of your cowardice or tepidity. For even St. Peter and St. Paul did not succeed in escaping all or some of these thoughts. Even when we do not succeed fully, we gain much by paying no attention to them. I am not going to save myself by the good works of the good angels, and I am not going to be condemned because of the evil thoughts and the weaknesses which the bad angels, the flesh, and the world bring before my mind. God asks only one thing of me, that my soul seek to be conformed with His Divine Majesty. And the soul so conformed makes the body conformed, whether it wish it or not, to the divine will. In this is our greatest battle, and here the good pleasure of the eternal and sovereign Goodness. May our Lord by His infinite kindness and grace hold us always in His hand.

¶ TO THE CONFESSOR OF THE QUEEN OF FRANCE

I, 109-11, Letter 9

According to the plan adopted in 1535 the companions of Ignatius at Paris were to have left the city on January 27, 1538 after taking their examinations in theology. Political events, however, forced them to anticipate the date. Spanish troops had advanced into Picardy and Provence, and feeling in the capital was aroused. The friends of Ignatius, rejecting the counsel of their professors, left the city on November 15, 1536 and took the road to St. Nicholas du Port. Ignatius, being advised of their plan, wrote to the Dominican priest Gabriel Guzman, confessor of Queen Eleanor of Austria, sister of Charles V, to request her assistance.

Venice, toward the end of 1536

Remembering the kindly interest and affection which for God's service you have always shown me apart from any merit of mine, I made up my mind to write you this letter. It is not my thought to repay you—that is quite beyond me—but rather to ask fresh favors in the praise and service of His Divine Majesty. I had always been aware of your charity, but I came to know it in its fullness when in my absence you arranged an interview for me with that great religious to whom I ask you now to remember me most cordially.[1] For this I shall be grateful to you as long as I live, and I am very glad to be thus obliged to you. If ever I can, whether present or absent, be of any service to you, I shall consider myself honored if God makes me worthy in His supreme and divine goodness to repay my great indebtedness.

Master Peter Faber with a few companions is about to undertake a journey[2] that may prove to be fraught with danger, about which you might have more information from him. I am very much afraid that he and his companions, in the spreading disorders and terrible wars from which Christendom is suffering because of our sins, may find themselves in great and even extreme need. I ask you by the reverence and service we owe to God to give them whatever help you possibly can and in any way that God shall inspire you. Over and above your doing it for the love and glory of His divine and sovereign Goodness, I will consider anything you do for them as done for me personally.

Our dear friend Dr. Castro has written me several times from the Charterhouse of Val de Christo at Segorbe, where he is now a monk. He made his profession on the Feast of St. John last. May God give him abundant grace ever to go from good to better in His holy service and praise. I ask to be cordially remembered to Padre Fray John[3] and good

---

[1] The allusion is to Matthew Ori, inquisitor of France. Ignatius had a long talk with him on his return from Rouen, where he had gone to visit a sick Spanish student who had stolen his money. He heard that he had been denounced to the Inquisition because of his responsibility in inducing De Castro, Amador, and Peralta to adopt a life of voluntary poverty. Father Gabriel Guzman must have intervened on that occasion to exculpate Ignatius.

[2] A lively description of this journey is given in Dudon, *Loyola*, p. 184.

[3] John de la Pena, Ignatius' professor of philosophy.

Master John.[4] His servant, Master Michael,[5] is here leading an entirely new life. I am writing [to Faber] about him and other matters you will be glad to learn of.

¶ TO MANUEL MIONA
I, 111-13, Letter 10

Miona was confessor to St. Ignatius at Alcala and Paris. The saint urges him to make the Spiritual Exercises for a month. Miona agreed, and made them at Paris under the direction of Father Jerome Domenech. As a result he entered the Society of Jesus.

Venice, November 16, 1536

IHS

The grace and love of Christ be our protection and help.

I am very eager to have some news of you. And no wonder, seeing how much I am indebted to you as your spiritual son. It is only right that I make some return for the great love and affection which you have always felt for me and shown me in your actions. But in this life I do not know of any other way of paying even the smallest part of this debt than by having you make the Spiritual Exercises under the man I shall name. You have already offered to make them, and I beg of you by the service of God our Lord to write me and let me know whether you have tried them and liked them. If you have not, I beg of you, by the love and the bitter death He suffered for us, to begin them. If you ever regret it, I not only accept whatever penance you may wish to impose on me, but you may look upon me as a mocker of the spiritual persons to whom I owe everything.

I have not written to you before this because I felt that in writing to one I was writing to all. If you read the letter I am addressing to Faber, you can find in it any news you may wish to have of me. Once again, and again, and as often as I can, I beg of you by the service of God our Lord, take my advice for fear that some day the Divine Majesty reprove me for not having exerted myself to the utmost, knowing as I do that the Spirit-

---

[4] Very likely Father John Benoist, who is named in other letters of St. Ignatius.
[5] Michael Landivar, a Navarese. He once tried to kill Ignatius at Paris, joined him at Venice, belonged for a time to the small band of apostles, but was sent away. In 1538 we find him associated with a group of calumniators whom Ignatius forced to acknowledge their lies in court (Polanco, *Chronicon*, I, 67-69).

ual Exercises are the best means I can think of in this life both to help a man to benefit himself and to bring help, profit, and advantage to many others. Even though you felt yourself to be in no special need, you will see how they will help you to serve others beyond anything you ever dreamed of.

I have nothing else to add, and so close, begging of the divine mercy of God our Lord the grace to know His most holy will and perfectly to fulfill it, according to the talent entrusted to each of us, lest some day He apply to us the words, "Thou wicked servant, thou knewest, etc."[1]

¶ TO JOHN PETER CARAFFA
I, 114-18, Letter 11

This letter to the Theatine archbishop, John Peter Caraffa, who later became Pope Paul IV, was almost certainly written some time in 1536, shortly after Ignatius had returned from Spain and before his ordination. Ribadeneira tells us that Ignatius was on familiar terms with the archbishop, who had given up his titles and possessions to found the order of the Theatines. It seems that the frank observations of Ignatius, which were given in all sincerity, were not well received by the retired dignitary, who looked upon such language coming from so unknown and supposedly inexperienced a person as daring, not to say impertinent.

Some time in 1536

IHUS

The life and everlasting happiness which we all desire so much is founded in an interior and genuine love of God our Creator and Lord. And this life that we desire binds us all together in a firm bond of sincere, true, and unfeigned affection in the same Lord, who desires to save us if it were not for our weakness, our faults, and our accumulated misery. These reflections led me to make up my mind to write this letter. One will not find in it the bombastic style affected by so many, and which I do not condemn if it is well ordered in our Lord. I realize that, when one has left the world and cast aside its dignities and fleeting honors, we can easily believe that he has no longer any relish for the empty honor and esteem of mere words. For he will understand that he who makes

---

[1] "He saith to him: Out of thy own mouth I judge thee, thou wicked servant. Thou knewest that I was an austere man, taking up what I laid not down and reaping that which I did not sow" (Luke 19:22).

himself less in this world will be greater in the next. Every consideration, therefore, being set aside which might incite to disturb or undo true interior and enduring peace, I ask, by the love and reverence of Christ our Creator, Redeemer, and Lord, that this letter be read in the same spirit of affection in which it is written. So true is this affection that I beg and beseech His infinite goodness with all the strength that He has so graciously given me to bestow on you both in this life and in the next as many blessings both for body and soul as He will bestow on me in the most holy service which we are bound to render Him.

With a purpose, therefore, that is prompt and ready to be of service to all those whom I know to be servants of my Lord, I will touch upon three points, and I will be as simple and sincere as perfect candor and frankness require. Not that I wish to lay down an opinion or offer advice, but it is my purpose to persuade and urge that we take care always to lay our petitions before our Lord, from whom comes all enlightened opinion and sound counsel.

In the first place I think I have sufficient reason, founded on arguments that are sound and conjectures that are sufficiently probable, to be afraid of even entertaining the thought of loosening in any way the bonds of the community which God has given you. In speaking thus I am moved by a feeling of true peace, love, and charity. I think it would be for the greater praise and service of God our Lord for it to remain even more firmly compact. Indeed, I do not give full expression to my thought on this point. I wondered what might be the source of this feeling of assurance; and after commending the matter earnestly and often to God our Lord, I thought I would write as lesser people do with those in higher station if they can be of service in giving good advice in something which concerns the service of God our Lord. The chances are that they will not make use of any direct or indirect occasion of doing so.

Secondly, I am not scandalized or disedified when a person in such a position as yours makes his noble origin or the dignity of his station in life a reason for indulging greater elegance in dress or the furnishings of his apartment, especially if he does so with a thought of those externs who may come to deal with him. For even this can be done with a view to one's needs or the circumstances of time and place. And yet we should keep before our mind only that which is perfect. And for this reason I think it would be the part of wisdom to call to mind saints like the blessed Francis and Dominic and others of the long ago, and consider especially their manner of life in dealing with their associates and the example they gave at the time they were forming their orders. We should have recourse to the true and sovereign Wisdom to ask for greater light and to obtain that clearness of vision which will order everything to His greater service and praise. Many things are lawful which are not expedient, as St. Paul says of himself; and we must not give others the occasion of indulging a weakness but should serve as an example for their advancement, especially those of our own household, whose eyes and ears are more attentive to the words and actions of their superior.

Thirdly, I hold it as an established truth that God our Lord has created everything in this present life for the service and good of men, and this is true with all the greater reason in regard to those men who are more perfect. Now, since your pious and holy congregation is a way to perfection—in fact, is the state of perfection—I have no doubt, indeed I firmly believe, that even though they do not preach or engage in any of the corporal works of mercy, they are justified in expecting food and clothing according to the order of divine charity. They are leading a blameless life under obedience and have, therefore, more time for occupations that are more spiritual and more important. They can thus accept this support which will help them to increase their praise and service of their true Creator and Lord. It seems, therefore, to be very good and a much safer procedure to place everything in the hands of Christ our Lord, for whose sake we do everything for the greater edification of all, and because this will be the best way of preserving and enlarging the pious and holy community which you have already begun.

But we must weigh well the reasons which others who are not so courageous or who find themselves in greater solicitude for the things of this world or the necessities of life may allege in an opposite sense, and who base their stand on apparently solid arguments. They assert that it would be very difficult for them to continue for any length of time in such an order for three reasons which stand out very clearly. First, they are without the bare necessities of life, and yet they do not beg; second, they do not preach; and third, they do not practice the corporal works of mercy, such as burying the dead, saying Mass for the dead, and so on. Even if they did not beg, as I have said, but performed some of their works in public, such as preaching and so on, they would awaken an interest in other members of the clergy, moving some to repentance and others to help them to preserve and increase their numbers. If they had neither facilities nor opportunities for such works, they should take the trouble to ask some parishes to call upon them for help in burying the dead and in praying for them and offering Masses gratis. I should think that, if they were thus to serve our Lord in pious works, the people would feel more inclined to support them with great charity. I might say that, even though they did no begging but put all their trust in the Supreme Goodness, this would be enough to guarantee their support. Men of weaker faith, or those who bear the responsibilities of authority, might object to this and say that St. Francis and others of the blessed who thought they had as much confidence and trust in God did not for this reason neglect to take proper means to see that their houses were preserved and grew in number for the greater service and praise of the Divine Majesty. To do otherwise would have seemed to them rather to tempt the Lord they aimed at serving and to act in a way that would not be in keeping with His service.

I omit other reasons of greater moment, as I do not wish to commit them to writing, since they were not conceived by me originally but were raised and suggested by others. It is enough for me to offer you these reasons which I have weighed and examined, and do this with perfect candor and frankness. Instead of harm, only profit can result from always having recourse to God our Lord, to ask that in His infinite and sovereign goodness He grant new remedies for new ills. May He be pleased in His usual kindness and sovereign grace to lay His most holy hand on all, so that all will turn out to His greater service and praise, just as I desire, and always pray and beseech Him in the interest of my own undertakings.

¶ TO PETER CONTARINI[1]

I, 123-26, Letter 13

The original of this letter is in Latin. Ignatius assures Contarini that God will provide sufficiently for those who for His sake have left all. They who have an abundance of temporal possessions should be careful not to become enmeshed in the love of them. Ignatius and his companions have taken refuge in the deserted Monastery of St. Peter near Venice.

Venice, August 1537

IHS

As I have written to Martin Sonorza at greater length about our affairs and touched on some points dealing with your domain, I will be very

---

[1] Peter Contarini was a Venetian and had made the Exercises under Ignatius. Later he became bishop of Paphos. He was the nephew of Cardinal Gaspar Contarini and the brother of Lawrence, ambassador of Venice at the Diet of Ratisbonne in 1541. Ignatius writes from Venice, where he had gone with Lainez and Faber after their ordination to the priesthood, June 24, 1537. His other companions had gone to other cities of upper Italy.

brief here. It is not that I think there is any need of writing to you, but we would not wish to be thought forgetful of you.

So far, by God's favor, we have enjoyed good health, and daily experience the truth of having nothing yet possessing all things;[2] all the things, I mean, that the Lord promised to those who seek first the kingdom of God and His justice.[3] Now, if everything will be added to them who first seek the kingdom of God and His justice, can they who seek nothing but the justice of the kingdom and His kingdom be lacking in anything—they whose blessing is not so much of the dew of heaven and the fatness of the earth but of the dew of heaven alone? I mean, they who are not divided, they who have both their eyes fixed on heaven. May He grant us this grace, He who, when He was rich in all things, stripped Himself of all for our instruction; He who, although in the glory of omnipotence and omniscience and infinite goodness, made Himself subject to the power, the judgment, and the will of the lowliest of creatures, man. But enough of this, especially when speaking to those whom Christ keeps in a condition of life different from ours; for it rather behooves you to reflect that, if you have possessions, they should not possess you, nor should you be possessed by anything temporal, but should refer them all to the Master from whom you have received them. For the man who cannot be all taken up with the one thing necessary should be eager at least to set in order all those things about which he is much concerned. But I am straying from my original purpose, and I return to ourselves.

We have found a monastery near Vicenza, about a mile from the Santa Croce gate, called San Pietro in Riccasolo. Nobody is living there, and the monks of Santa Maria delle Grazie are quite willing to allow us to stay there as long as we like. We have accepted and will be here for several months, God willing. Thus we have nothing else to do but be good and perfect, because God on His part will never fail us. Do you join us, therefore, in asking our Lord to give us all the grace of doing His holy will, which is the sanctification of us all. And may Christ Jesus our Lord keep you in health and direct us all in the way of peace, which is in Him alone.

As to Gaspar, I beg of you, if his affairs which he has left to you are not attended to, to see to it that he will not be able to say, or even to suspect, that we are the cause of his being detained at Venice.

---

[2] 2 Corinthians 6:10.   [3] Matthew 6:33.

PART II

1538-1540

¶ TO JAMES DE GOUVEA[1]
I, 132-34, Letter 16

Ignatius is glad to have news of Don James. The saint and his companions are at the orders of the pope; many good people would like to use them in the Indies but the pope wants them in Rome. They are ready, however, to go to the Indies if the pope sends them. Caceres will give Don James any news from Rome. Don James should try to train for the Church men who are holy as well as learned.

Rome, November 23, 1538

IHS

May the grace and peace of our Lord Jesus Christ be with us all.

A few days ago your messenger arrived with your letter. From him we had news of you and from your letter we learned of your kind remembrance of us, as well as your ardent desire for the salvation of the souls that are whitening to the harvest in the Indies. Would that we were able to give you some satisfaction and appease our own desires, which are aflame with the same zeal! But there are at present obstacles which stand in the way of our satisfying the desires of many others, let alone yourself. You will understand this from what I am going to say.

All of us who are mutually bound in this Society have given ourselves to the supreme pontiff, since he is the lord of the worldwide harvest of Christ our Lord. In thus offering ourselves we have pointed out to him that we are ready for any duty he may wish to assign us in Christ. Should he, therefore, send us where you would like to see us, we shall go gladly. Our reason for thus placing ourselves at his disposal is that we know that he has a better knowledge of what will be profitable for the universal Church.

There have not been lacking some who for some time have been trying to have us sent to the Indies, which the Spaniards are daily adding to the realms of the emperor. A Spanish bishop and the envoy of the emperor

---

[1] James de Gouvea was one of the many Portuguese who were sent to Paris by John III for studies. He there became acquainted with Ignatius. In 1538 the king of Portugal wrote to ask him to take a missionary interest in the Portuguese Indies. Mascarenhas, the king's ambassador at Rome, was informed of this step (*Epistolae et instructiones*, I, 738). James de Gouvea, remembering Ignatius, let him know of the desire of John III and entrusted to him the letter to Mascarenhas. For his answer to De Gouvea, Ignatius makes use of the pen of Faber, who writes in Latin. The refusal was not definitive. Mascarenhas carried on the negotiations and succeeded in 1540 in having Francis Xavier sent to the Indies (*ibid.*, I, 739). According to Polanco (*Chronicon*, I, 86), John III's request for Jesuit missionaries was suggested by De Gouvea. Dudon (*Loyola*, p. 149) relates an incident which would lead us to believe that the relations between De Gouvea and St. Ignatius had a rather stormy beginning.

have been especially approached on this project. But they have learned that the supreme pontiff is not in favor of our leaving Rome for the present, since the harvest here is abundant. To be sure, we are not afraid of the great distance at which the missions lie nor of the labor involved in learning the language, if only the will of Christ be accomplished. Pray for us, therefore, that He make us ministers of the word of life. "Not that we are sufficient to think anything of ourselves as of ourselves,"[2] but our hopes are in the abundance of His riches.

You will find an abundance of news of us in the letter which we have written to our very special friend and brother in Christ, James Caceres,[3] the Spaniard, who will show it to you. There you will see what trials for Christ we have had to undergo at Rome and how we have come through them unscathed. Even at Rome there are not wanting those who have no love for the light of truth and life which the Church teaches. Be you, therefore, wide-awake, and teach the flock of Christ by the example of your holy living as earnestly as you have hitherto exerted yourself in defense of the Church's teaching. For how can we believe that our good God will preserve us in the truth of our holy faith if we refuse to lead good lives? It is much to be feared that the main cause of false teaching is to be found in vicious living; and if the vices are not corrected, the errors will not disappear.

As we bring this letter to a close, it only remains for us to beg you to be kind enough to remember us to our most reverend teachers, Bartolome, Cornet, Picard, Adam, Wancob, Lawrence, Benoist, and all the others,[4] who are glad to be known as our teachers as we are to be their pupils and sons in Christ Jesus, in whom we wish you health.

¶ TO PETER CONTARINI

I, 134-36, Letter 17

At this time Ignatius was attempting to put an end to certain opposition which had developed against him and his followers in Rome. To do this, he had presented his case to the governor of Rome and the pope. Peter Contarini and his uncle, Cardinal Gaspar Contarini, had both made

---

[2] 2 Corinthians 3:5.
[3] Caceres later left the Society (*Epistolae mixtae*, I, 64, 69, 90, 593).
[4] Of the teachers mentioned here John Benoist and Lawrence were Dominicans, Peter de Cornet a Franciscan, and Picard a secular priest.

the Exercises and were deeply interested in the welfare of Ignatius and the Society. This letter is one of thanks for a letter of recommendation. Ignatius gratefully recalls the service rendered him and speaks of the favorable sentence given him and his companions by Benedict Conversini, governor of Rome. The original letter is in Latin.

Rome, December 2, 1538

IHS

May the grace and peace of our Lord Jesus Christ be with us all.

We received your recent letter to us, and together with it the letter of recommendation you sent in our behalf to Most Reverend Gaspar Contarini. We are grateful to your kind interest for both of them. In the one we behold the kind recollection you have of us, while in the other we have experience of your generous service. Your most reverend uncle had no more than read your letter when he sent one of his attendants to the governor with the request that he dismiss our case, which had come before him. A few days later the whole incident was brought to an end, and in a way which we thought would especially redound to God's honor and the good of many souls. Sentence was passed declaring that after a diligent inquiry nothing was found either in our life or our teaching that justified suspicion. But the sentence just as it stands, if you have any inclination to see it, is in the hands of the imperial ambassador at Venice. Some friends of Ours sent it to him.

We know that this document is not going to be proof against blame in the future. We have never wished for such an exemption. All we wished to do was to safeguard our honor, the soundness of our teaching, and the innocence of our lives. God grant that we shall never be uneasy about being called ignorant, uncultured, unskilled speakers, or even if we are called wicked, fickle, deceivers. But we were grieved that our teaching itself was declared unsound, and also that the way in which we were walking was thought bad, because neither the one nor the other was our own but Christ's and His Church's. But enough of this.

All those whom in your letter you said you wished to greet through us now return your greetings through me. All are well. May they likewise be strong in spirit through Jesus Christ our Lord, who is our peace, our repose, our fullness and consolation, and altogether that good for which we have been made and reborn, and for which we have been preserved in this world up to the present.

With every best wish in Him, we hope that you will continue to protect us as you are doing.

¶ TO THE LORDS OF LOYOLA
1, 145-47, Letter 19

Martin Garcia de Onaz, brother of the saint, having died November 19, 1538, his son Bertram succeeded to his title and estates. But when Ignatius wrote this letter he had received no news of his brother's death. He sends a copy of the acquittal which Benedict Conversini, bishop of Bertinoro and governor of Rome, had issued in an accusation which had been brought against Ignatius and his first companions. The acquittal dated November 18, 1538, declared false and groundless the rumors that had circulated against them. Ignatius adds some spiritual advice and tells of his first Mass celebrated in the Church of St. Mary Major on Christmas Day. A photographic reproduction of this letter by D. Fernandez Zapico is in Archivum Historicum Societatis Jesu, *I, 100-04 (1932).*

Rome, February 2, 1539

JHS

May the grace and love of Christ our Lord be our never-failing help and support.

As I have already written to you within the last few days in the letters which Rojas[1] and Magdalene de Sendo are bringing, I will be brief here. Because of the great interest Rojas has in Ours and because they will be long delayed on the way, this letter, I surmise, will reach you about the same time they do. I am therefore sending along with it a copy of the verdict or declaration which was issued here in our regard, so that you can give it to them should they wish to take it along with them. There is no lessening of their good desires for having associated with us or of the good desires of others in our Lord, who is to be our eternal judge. Happy they who in this life prepare themselves for the judgment and salvation by His Divine Majesty. For His love and reverence I beg of you not to put off setting your consciences aright. Your souls will thus be without uneasiness in that moment of extreme and ultimate need. My greetings and best wishes to all. Let all those who wish to have word of us and to benefit their consciences consider this letter as addressed to them. I close, asking God our Lord, by His infinite and supreme goodness to give us all His abundant grace to know His most holy will and perfectly to fulfill it.

---

[1] Francis Rojas later entered the Society and led a rather checkered life in it. In a later letter to Araoz, who was then provincial (September 1, 1547), directions are given for the dismissal of Rojas. But he managed to survive until 1556, when he left the Society of his own accord.

The bachelor Araoz[2] is staying here. If God our Lord grants only part of my desire, he will be rich in this life and in the next. Last Christmas Day, in the Church of St. Mary Major, in the chapel which preserves the manger in which the Child Jesus was laid, with His help and grace I said my first Mass.[3] I earnestly desire and beg of you by the love and reverence of His Divine Majesty that we remember each other in our prayers. Let us not lose sight of the fact that we are at the very end of our days and about to give a strict account of our lives.

¶ TO BERTRAM LOYOLA
I, 148-51, Letter 20

Ignatius exhorts his nephew to try to bring about a reform in the clergy of Azpeitia, the parish of which was under the patronage of the family of Loyola. He advises him to send his brother Millan to the University of Paris, and tells him that the supreme pontiff, Paul III, has given a viva voce *approval of the Institute of the Society of Jesus, September 3, 1539. He recommends Anthony Araoz, who is on his way to Spain, and encourages Bertram to promote the growth of the new religious order.*

Rome, September 24 [?], 1539

IHS

The grace and love of Christ our Lord be ever our help and support.

I beseech you by His love and reverence, do not disappoint my hopes. It has pleased God our Lord that the place your father (God rest him) once had in my confidence should now be held by you. It is my hope in God our Lord that His Divine Majesty has preserved you to this moment for the purpose of pacifying and reforming the clergy, especially of your town. If you do this, you will be showing them a love that is real and true, but if you refuse, one that is carnal and harmful. Again I beg of you for the love and reverence of God our Lord to recall how often I touched upon this subject,[1] and to devote all your efforts to it. Our fore-

---

[2] Araoz was a nephew of Doña Magdalene Araoz, wife of Martin Garcia de Onaz, elder brother of the saint. He was born in Vergara in 1515. After his studies in Salamanca he went to Rome in 1538, apparently intent on making his way in the world. He did better and entered the Society and became the first provincial of Spain. He died in Madrid in 1573.
[3] Ignatius had been ordained priest in Venice June 24, 1537. Concerning his first Mass see Father Pedro de Leturia, *Manresa*, Vol. 12, 63-74.
[1] During the three months of the summer of 1535 which Ignatius spent in Azpeitia.

fathers tried to signalize themselves in other respects—and please God, their efforts may not have been altogether in vain. But you should signalize yourself in the things that are to last forever, and should take no step that should have to be repented later. I have every confidence that my hope in our Lord and in you as His instrument cooperating with His grace will not be disappointed. But enough of this.

We have learned here of the talent of your brother Millan and of his interest in study. I should be very glad to see you give some thought and consideration to this. If my opinion has any weight with you, I would send him to Paris and nowhere else. He will make greater progress there in a few years than he would make at another university in many. Besides, the students in that country are more upright and virtuous. I cannot help taking a lively interest in his greater progress, and should be very glad to see him follow this path. May I ask you to let his mother know this? If Araoz does not happen to be there, others will be, men of weight and reputation who will take good care of him.[2]

Regarding our affairs here, you will be glad to know that we have seriously determined in our Lord, after weighing the matter again and again, that it will be advisable and even necessary to lay a firm foundation and take deep root if we are going to build for the future. It has pleased our Lord in His infinite goodness to lend His most holy hand to our undertaking. We have every hope that through His unlimited and customary grace He will have a special providence over us and our affairs—or better, over His own affairs, as we do not seek our own in this life. He has done so in the face of so much opposition, misadventure, and conflicting opinions that the vicar of Christ our Lord has approved and confirmed our whole manner of proceeding, our work, our living in community, and so forth. He has granted full faculties for drawing up constitutions which according to our judgment will be adapted to our way of life. Anthony Araoz, the bearer of this letter, will be able to give you much more detailed information on this and the other points I have touched on. I could not do more if I came in person, for we of the Society look upon him as one of us. In fact, he has been in our house here for close on to ten months, and we are now sending him to Spain on business of his own as well as ours. After he has carried out his mission, he will return to us here. Therefore, besides giving him credit, I ask you for the love of God our Lord to give him the welcome you are accustomed to

---

[2] Millan studied in Salamanca, which he left for Rome in 1541. There he was admitted to the Society and was sent to Paris in 1542 by St. Ignatius to continue his studies.

give to the servants of the Divine Majesty or which you would give to me if I came myself. In him you will have a living letter. I shall not write more of this.

I ask a special remembrance in your prayers and those of our devoted friends, now especially since I have been given so heavy a task.[3] I have no confidence in my own strength to carry this burden successfully, but I have every hope in the infinite power and goodness of God. I count on your prayers and the prayers of all who love me in the Divine Majesty to help me never to refuse any labor in His holy service.

I close, asking His Divine Majesty to dispose of all of us to His greater service, so as always to give Him greater glory in all things.

POSTSCRIPT. It seems to me in our Lord that this undertaking which I am going to explain should more properly be yours. There are many reasons; and once you have weighed and considered them, you will find them to be sound. I remember that, when I was at Loyola with you, you begged me to let you know something of the Society which I was hoping to begin. I also believe that God our Lord was waiting for you to take a prominent part in it, so that you could leave behind you a greater memory than others of the family have left. To come to the point, I have tried in spite of my unworthiness to lay with God's grace a firm foundation for this Society of Jesus. We have given it this name with the pope's approval. It devolves on me, therefore, to exhort you again and again to build on the foundations thus laid, for you will have no less merit in the superstructure than I in the foundation, and all by the hand of God our Lord. I mean, of course, when the opportunity offers, and circumstances seem right and just to you, and His Divine Majesty gives you His most holy grace for it.

I am writing in the same vein to Doña Mary de Vicuna,[4] as I think that she can be of some help in this matter. Share this letter with my sister, Doña Magdalene, and the lord of Ozaeta, as in my letter to them I have referred them to you. If you know of any others who would be willing to help, they will be doing it for the Lord, who well knows how to repay them with interest. My deepest respects to the lady of the house.[5] She should consider this letter as addressed to her.

---

[3] The care of the newly born Society.
[4] Mary de Vicuna was a prominent and very pious matron whose noble family is mentioned in local histories. Magdalene Loyola was a sister of St. Ignatius, and Bertram Lopez de Gallaiztegui, lord of Ozaeta, a nephew.
[5] Joan de Recalde, Bertram's wife. Bertram de Onaz y Loyola succeeded his father, Martin Garcia, to the title and estates of Loyola. In 1538 he married Doña Joan de Recalde, daughter of John Lopez de Recalde, knight of Santiago and quartermaster general of Spain.

¶ TO BERTRAM LOYOLA
I, 155-56, Letter 23

A letter of recommendation for Francis Xavier, on his way to India, and Peter Mascarenhas, ambassador of the king of Portugal. Francis remained in Lisbon preparing for his expedition until April 7, 1541. He spent the next eleven years in India and Japan. He was planning his first missionary expedition to China when he died in 1552.

Rome, March 20, 1540

IHUS

May our Lord be always our help and support.

Owing to the extreme pressure I am under in suddenly having to send some of our men to the Indies, some to Ireland, and others to different parts of Italy, I will not have the time to write at length as I should wish. Master Francis Xavier of Navarre, son of the lord of Xavier, one of our Society, is the bearer of this letter. At the request of the king of Portugal and at the command of the pope he with two others are going overseas in the interests of the same king. Master Francis will give you full details and will speak to you about everything in my name as though I myself were present.

The ambassador of the king of Portugal, in whose company Francis is traveling, is, you must know, one of our dearest friends, one to whom we are very deeply in debt, and who in the service of our Lord can do us many favors with the king and with all with whom he deals. I beg you therefore, for the service of God our Lord, to show him every courtesy and treat him with all the honor you can.

Araoz, if he is there with you, should consider this letter as written to him. As regards Master Francis, I would have you take his word for everything that concerns me as though I myself had uttered it. Remember me very especially to the lady of the household and all the family.

¶ TO THE TOWNSPEOPLE OF AZPEITIA
I, 161-65, Letter 26

Ignatius urges his fellow townsmen to remember his preaching to them during the three months he spent with them in 1535. He assures them of his desire to serve them and exhorts them to lead a Christian life, which is the source of all peace. He recalls to their minds the good prac-

tices established among them in 1535. These practices included the ringing of the bells and the helping of the poor. He again asks that they do away with card playing and reminds unmarried women that they should not wear headdresses. He recommends that they establish the Confraternity of the Blessed Sacrament of the Minerva with monthly confession and Communion for the members. He encourages them to communicate frequently and commends himself to their prayers.

Rome, August-September 1540

IHS

May the perfect grace and love of Christ our Lord be our never-failing help and support.

His Divine Majesty well knows how much and how often He has given me the sincere wish and earnest desire to be of some spiritual service, even though it be slight, and to do what kindness I can in the Divine Goodness to all the men and women of my native land, where God in His usual mercy bestowed on me the very beginnings of this natural life, without any merit on my part, and for which I have never been able sufficiently to thank Him. These desires, which come from the Lord and Creator of us all rather than from any natural cause, led me five years ago from Paris to your city. Although I had little health at the time, He who brought me there with His usual heavenly kindness supplied me with enough strength to do a little work, as you then saw. What I failed to attain must be blamed on my faults, which still bear me company.

Let me repeat that there is no desisting in my earlier desires that you continue to enjoy in this life peace and quiet of heart in the true peace of our Lord, not in the peace of the world. In the world there are many princes, great men and little men, who make truces and treaties in their external lives but in whom true interior peace never enters because they entertain animosities, envy, and many other evil desires against the very persons with whom they have come to terms. But the peace of our Lord, which is interior, brings along with it those other gifts and graces that are necessary to salvation and to eternal life. The reason is that this peace makes one love one's neighbor for the love of one's Creator and Lord, and with this love one keeps all the commandments of the law, as St. Paul says: "He that loveth his neighbor hath fulfilled the law,"[1] because he loves his Creator and Lord and his neighbor for his Lord's sake.

The thought has occurred to me that I might accomplish my desires in some other way, as my absence is now unavoidable. A great work pre-

---

[1] Romans 13:8.

sents itself, which our Lord has brought about with the help of a friar of St. Dominic, a great friend of Ours, one whom we have known for many years.[2] The purpose of this work is to honor and promote devotion to the Blessed Sacrament, and I made up my mind to offer your souls some consolation in the Holy Spirit with this bull which Anthony Araoz[3] has with him. The indulgences enumerated in the bull are so many and so precious that I could not even begin to estimate their true value. I can only beg and beseech you for the love and reverence of God our Lord that you all hold it in the highest esteem and do all you can to promote and extend this devotion by having it preached to gatherings of the people, by processions and other ways of moving the people to devotion. I well remember the time I spent with you and the determination of the people to carry out certain proposals after they had been laudably and holily drawn up into constitutions. The ringing of bells,[4] for example, for those in mortal sin; that there should be no poor who have to go begging but that all should receive the help they need; the doing away with card playing and forbidding the sale of playing cards; the wiping out of the abuse of women wearing the headdress of the married when they were unwed and offending God.[5] I recall that the observance of these holy rules and constitutions was begun and continued during all the time I spent with you, and that with no little grace and blessing from God to help you in carrying out such salutary designs. But here I cannot be certain of your perseverance, seeing that your constancy may weaken in undertakings that are so upright and so pleasing to the infinite and supreme Goodness. But whether you have persevered and developed further or whether you have given up and returned to your former state, I beg and beseech you by the love and reverence of God our Lord to do your best to make every effort to honor, support, and serve His only-begotten Son, Christ our Lord, in so great a work as the Blessed Sacrament, in which His Divine Majesty is present both in His divinity and His humanity as entirely, as powerfully, and as infinitely as He is present in heaven. This you can do by adopting constitutions in the confraternity which will

---

[2] Fray Thomas Stella, who founded the Confraternity of the Blessed Sacrament of the Minerva, which was approved by Paul III, November 30, 1539.

[3] Araoz was a nephew of Magdalene Araoz, wife of Martin Garcia Loyola, brother of St. Ignatius, who sent him to Spain toward the end of September 1539.

[4] This ringing took place at noon. Martin Garcia Loyola founded this custom in his will, and left means for the payment of the ringers. St. Ignatius had destined a part of his inheritance for the same purpose.

[5] The girls of the country usually went bareheaded. Married women wore a headdress, which also was affected by women living in irregular unions, to which the headdress gave a semblance of legality. See Dudon, *Loyola*, p. 160.

oblige you to monthly confession and Communion. This should be done voluntarily and without any obligation under pain of sin should it be omitted. I have no doubt, rather I firmly believe, that by doing this you will be making considerable spiritual progress.

In the early Church members of both sexes received Communion daily as soon as they were old enough. But soon devotion began to cool and Communion became weekly. Then, after a considerable interval of time, as devotion became cooler still, Communion was received on only three of the principal feasts of the year, each one being left to his own choice and devotion to receive oftener, either every three days or every eight days or once a month. And finally, because of our weakness and coldness, we have ended with once a year. You would think that we are Christian only in name if you can calmly and quietly contemplate the condition to which the greater part of the world has come.

Let it be our glory, then, out of love for so good a Lord and because of the immense benefit to our souls, to restore and renew in some way the holy practices of our forefathers; if not entirely, at least in part, to the extent of monthly confession and Communion, as I have already suggested. Should one wish to go oftener than this, there is no doubt that he would be acting in conformity with the wish of our Creator and Lord, as St. Augustine and other holy doctors assure us. For, after saying "I neither praise nor condemn daily Communion," he added, "but I do exhort you to communicate every Sunday."[6]

I have every hope that God our Lord, in His infinite goodness and His customary mercy, will pour out in abundance His grace on the souls of all of you, to bring about a service so becoming and of such clear and unmistakable profit to souls. I close, therefore, begging by the reverence of God our Lord that you give me a share in your devotions, and especially in your devotion to the Blessed Sacrament, as you always have a large share in mine, poor and unworthy as they are.

---

[6] In the time of St. Ignatius it was usual to attribute this text to St. Augustine. And yet Father Cristóbal de Madrid in his little *Opus de frequenti usu sanctissimi sacramenti eucharistiae* (1574) calls attention to the fact that the work *De ecclesiasticis dogmatibus* is attributed to the learned Alcuin. The passage cited is found in Chapter 53 of this work.

PART III

1540-1548

¶ TO BERTRAM LOYOLA
1, 165-67, Letter 27

Ignatius rejoices that Bertram is faithful to his duty and that he gives good example to all. He has received this news of Bertram from another companion, Araoz. He thanks God for this, sends various letters to be delivered, and finally expresses the wish that Millan set out for Rome.

Rome, October 4, 1540

JHS

May the sovereign grace and love of Christ our Lord ever be our help and support.

I have heard from Araoz of the great grace which His Divine Majesty gives you in His service, of the good reputation you enjoy, and of the good example you give throughout the province. For all this I give ceaseless thanks to God our Lord, in the hope that you will always continue to advance from good to better until you actually fulfill all the hopes I have had for you all the time I have known you. I wrote you at length a few days ago when I sent the bull concerning the Blessed Sacrament, and so I will be brief here.

If Araoz is not there, you may open and read the letters addressed to him. In them you will find more detailed news of us. If Stephen de Guia is not there with you, I ask you for the service of God our Lord to send a reliable person with the package for him. If you send it in any other way, take every precaution that the package be delivered to him personally, as it is very closely concerned with the service of God. If Stephen is no longer among the living, open the package and see that its contents are sent to the person to whom it is addressed, a certain Rojas who I think lives in Alava, or nearby in Piedrola. Sometimes he is to be found in Bilbao, and is called I think Fanste de Rojas.

I have let you know in other letters how great is my desire of seeing Millan here in Rome. As I think it will be greatly to the service of God our Lord and that his relatives and friends will be much honored, I repeat my request, and ask you to trust me on this point.

Señor de Ozaeta and all our relatives should consider this letter as written to them. I should like to have an answer to my other letters, and to this. Remember me to the lady of the house, and to all the family of Doña Mary de Vicuna.

My greetings to any others who you think would be glad to hear from me in our Lord. May He in His infinite and supreme goodness ever be our protection and support.

¶ TO MAGDALENE LOYOLA

I, 170-71, Letter 29

Ignatius exhorts his sister to signalize herself in God's service by means of good works and frequent confession and Communion. He sends her some blessed rosaries which had been enriched with indulgences, for an explanation of which he refers her to the young Jesuit, Anthony Araoz, and ends with a request for prayers.

Rome, May 24, 1541

IHS

May the perfect grace and love of Christ our Lord be our never-failing protection and help.

I received your letter a few days ago. It gave me much satisfaction in the Lord to see therein the good and holy desires you have conceived for God's glory. May it please our Lord by His infinite and supreme goodness to increase these desires of yours to love Him above all things, so that you will place not only a part but the whole of your life in the same Lord, and in all creatures for His sake. By dealing with persons who speak and work for the glory of His Divine Majesty and by the reception of the sacraments of penance and holy Communion as frequently as possible, your soul will become united with Him by true hope and you will grow in a lively faith and a very necessary charity, without which there is no possibility of salvation.

For the reason that the soul who is desirous of serving her Creator and Lord in all things seeks to do so by every means possible, I have thought I could be of some help to you. Confident that you will receive them with the reverence and affection due to the things of our Creator and Lord, I am sending you a dozen blessed rosaries which have many graces attached to them, and three more which have other favors, and three others still which have all the graces the others have. What these graces are you will be able to see in the memorandum which I am enclosing in this letter and sending with the licentiate Araoz. You will find there the conditions under which you may make use of these treasures. Having received this special grace, you will give me much pleasure in the Lord if you write me of the spiritual progress you make with it to the greater glory of His Divine Majesty.

Remember me most cordially to all those who love you in our Lord and to those who you think would in His Divine Majesty like to hear from me. May He in His infinite goodness deign to give us ample grace to know His most holy will and strength perfectly to fulfill it.

¶ TO FATHERS SALMERON AND BROET
I, 179-81, Letter 32

Salmeron and Broet were sent by the pope as papal legates to Ireland. The following is part of the instructions given them by St. Ignatius. The instructions are entitled "How to negotiate and deal with others in our Lord."

Rome, early September 1541

In your dealings with all be slow to speak and say little, especially with your equals and those lower in dignity and authority than yourselves. Be ready to listen for long periods and until each has had his say. Answer the questions put to you, come to an end, and take your leave. If a rejoinder is offered, let your reply be as brief as possible, and take leave promptly and politely.

In dealing with men of position or influence, if you are to win their affection for the greater glory of God our Lord, look first to their disposition and accommodate yourselves to them. If they are of a lively temper, quick and merry of speech, follow their lead in your dealings with them when you talk of good and holy things, and do not be too serious, glum, and reserved. If they are shy and retiring, slow to speak, serious and weighty in their talk, use the same manner with them, because such ways will be gratifying to them. "I became all things to all men."[1]

Do not forget that, if one is of a lively disposition and deals with another who is like him, there is very great danger of their failing to come to an agreement if they are not of one spirit. And therefore, if one knows that one is of such a lively disposition, he ought to approach another of similar traits well prepared by self-examination and determined to be patient and not to get out of sorts with him, especially if he knows him to be in poor health. If he is dealing with one of slower temper, there is not so much danger of a disagreement arising from words hastily spoken.

Whenever we wish to win someone over and engage him in the greater service of God our Lord, we should use the same strategy for good which the enemy employs to draw a good soul to evil. He enters through the other's door and comes out his own. He enters with the other by not opposing his ways but by praising them. He acts familiarly with the soul, suggesting good and holy thoughts which bring peace to the good soul. Later he tries, little by little, to come out his own door, always suggesting some error or illusion under the appearance of good, but which will

---

[1] 1 Corinthians 9:22.

always be evil. So we with a good purpose can praise or agree with another concerning some particular good thing, dissembling whatever else may be wrong. After thus gaining his confidence, we shall have better success. In this sense we go in with him his way but come out our own.

We should ingratiate ourselves with those who are sad or tempted, speak at length and show great satisfaction and cheerfulness, both interior and exterior, so as to draw them to the opposite of what they feel, for their greater edification and consolation.

In everything you say, especially when you are trying to restore peace and in spiritual exhortations, be much on your guard and remember that everything you say may or will become public.

In business matters be generous with your time; that is, if you can, do today what you promise for tomorrow.

On the supposition that you hold jurisdiction, it would be better if Master Francis took charge of contributions or offerings. You will thus be better able to accept or decline obligations in respect of all if none of the three of you touch money but rather send it by another to the person in charge of it. Or it would be better that the person seeking a dispensation give the fee to the person in charge and take a receipt for it to show that the dispensation was given. If any other way be more convenient, use it, but see to it that none of the three of you even touches any of the money connected with the mission.

¶ TO ISABEL ROSER
I, 186-87, Letter 35

Ignatius explains that his letter will be short because at present his poor health forbids a longer one. He writes a word of praise for Father Anthony Araoz, who is about to set out for Spain. Ignatius is returning a letter from the archdeacon Cazador. He realizes that Cazador has not understood his letter in the spirit in which it was written.

Rome, February 1, 1542

May the sovereign grace of Christ our Lord be our unfailing help and support.

The little health I am now enjoying does not encourage me to write at length. May His Divine Majesty be blessed, exalted, and glorified that He thus visits us both, and at last gives us a breathing space so that we may serve Him the better.

As I promised you in a longer letter, one of the Society will leave for those parts about Easter, ten days before or after we have baptized a Jewish woman. He will leave here about twenty days from now, either by land or sea. As danger will not be lacking however he goes, especially the times being what they are, be sure to keep him in your prayers and in the prayers of our other devoted friends. If he arrives safely and in good health, I am sure that you will be quite satisfied and consoled in our Creator and Lord, because here among Ours he is very highly thought of for the many graces and gifts which His Divine Majesty has bestowed on him.[1]

Cazador writes, and it is clear from his letter that he has not understood mine in the spirit in which it was written. I am returning his letter for greater clarification with another which Master Lawrence wrote me, and am writing him another letter in which I abase and humble myself as much as I can, as I should like to do with everyone, and offer some explanation which I hope will make me better understood. Read all these letters, then seal only the one I have written to Cazador, and have all three delivered to him in one packet, please. I recommend myself to you, to your sisters and mine in our Lord. May He ever be our unfailing help and support.

¶ TO BERTRAM LOYOLA
I, 188-90, Letter 36

Ignatius announces the departure of Millan from Rome for Paris, where he is to study, and urges Bertram to supply a youth of such high promise with all that he needs.

Rome, beginning of February 1542
IHUS

May the sovereign grace and love of Christ our Lord always be our help and support.

Having written you at length on the subject of this letter, because of my poor health I will be content today with recalling briefly what I have

---

[1] Father Anthony Araoz had just been ordained, and made his profession in the hands of Ignatius, the first after the original ten. He, with James de Eguia, was being sent back to Spain. Lawrence is evidently the Lawrence de Garcia who had left the Society and who later bemoaned his inconstancy to Faber, begging to be readmitted even as a "hired servant" (*Epistolae mixtae*, I, 15-17).

already written. First of all, I will announce the departure of your brother Millan, who, with God's grace and his health permitting, will leave Rome this present month before the beginning of Lent, bound for Paris. He will travel in excellent company with a passport from the French ambassador. As the ambassador is always very well disposed toward us, he always gives us a safe-conduct for travelers whenever we need one. Father Araoz will also travel with Millan for a distance of about two hundred miles and then, parting company with those who are bound for Paris, will go straight to Barcelona, God permitting, where he will tarry for several months to give some exhortations. If you write him, you can direct your letter in care of Isabel Roser, who lives opposite the Church of St. Justus.

If you have not made provision for your brother in Paris by the time this letter reaches you, I beg you by the reverence due our Lord to do so as promptly and as carefully as possible. He ought to find his allowance there when he arrives, by Easter or earlier. You can make use of the method you used at Salamanca, or any way you think better. In France students have much to suffer when their allowances are not promptly forthcoming, as Mary de Vicuna will have learned by this time from her son who is there. You could send the allowance to this latter, and he can deliver it to Millan on his arrival, or you could send it to Jerome Domenech, a canon from Valencia, who is at the Lombard College. I have directed Millan to apply to him, as he will profit more from associating with a man of his learning. Judging from what I have seen of him here in Rome and from the way in which he made the Spiritual Exercises, which you once had such difficulty with, your brother has reaped such great fruit that, if our Lord gives him some space of years, I hope to see him become a shining light, to the great satisfaction of all of you who sincerely love him and for the enlightening of many souls whose vision is darkened by love of the perishable things of this world which is passing away. If, therefore, you wish to have this consolation in the future, do your best to make provision at once by sending him enough now to meet the year's expenses. As times are, I fancy that you might find some difficulty in getting bankers to make the advance you need. I have made inquiries, therefore, and set down in the enclosed memorandum the means you can employ to secure it.

We have reason to give increasing and unending thanks to God our Lord for the news that comes to us of the Society in different places. May He always be our unfailing help and support.

Remember me to the lady of the household and to all the family, and to all those who you think will be glad to be remembered by me.

¶ TO FATHER SIMON RODRIGUES
1, 192-96, Letter 38

The present letter to Simon Rodrigues gives striking evidence of the prudence for which St. Ignatius was noted. Rodrigues, a Portuguese and a companion of Ignatius from his Paris days, had introduced the Society of Jesus into Portugal in 1540. He enjoyed great influence with the king, John III. Because of his regard for the monarch, he might be led into some indiscretion should a controversy arise between the king and the pope. A difference had occurred. The king was displeased with Paul III because, against the wishes of·the Portuguese court, he had raised to the cardinalate Michael de Silva, former ambassador to different pontiffs and present bishop of Viseo and prime minister of the kingdom. The king brusquely recalled his ambassador, Don Christopher de Sousa, from the papal court and seized the temporalities of the bishop, who, after the king had refused him permission to go to Rome, went without it. Ignatius wishes Rodrigues to be convinced that Jesuit headquarters in Rome would do their best to achieve a reconciliation. With great tact Ignatius quotes the cardinal of Burgos, who said that reports that John III was refusing obedience to the pope were ridiculous. Ignatius refrains from telling Rodrigues what to do but declares that gratitude to the monarch requires the Society to do everything possible to bring about peace.

Rome, March 18, 1542

IHS

May the perfect grace and eternal love of Christ our Lord be our never-failing protection and help.

It seems to me in the light of the Divine Goodness, although others may think differently, that ingratitude is the most abominable of sins and that it should be detested in the sight of our Creator and Lord by all of His creatures who are capable of enjoying His divine and everlasting glory. For it is a forgetting of the graces, benefits, and blessings received. As such it is the cause, beginning, and origin of all sins and misfortunes. On the contrary, the grateful acknowledgment of blessings and gifts received is loved and esteemed not only on earth but in heaven. I thought it would be well, therefore, to remind you that from the time we came to Rome we have been continually favored in many things by the pope and have been the recipients of special favors from his holiness. On the other hand, it is known to the whole Society, and to you more clearly than to others since you are there present, that we are under the greatest obligations to the king, your lord and ours in our Lord.

First. For the many spiritual graces which God our Creator and Lord has been so good as to bestow on us, His wish being to raise everything to His greater service and praise through His ordinary grace, as Creator looking with an infinite love upon His creature, and although infinite, made Himself finite and willing to die for him.

Second. Who are we, or whence are we that God our Lord should have ordained that so outstanding a prince should have taken notice of us? For acting on his own initiative or at the suggestion of others, but certainly not because of any thought or effort of ours and even before the Society was confirmed by the Holy See, he asked the pope with such insistence for some of Ours for his service in our Lord and showed us such special consideration at a time when our teaching was under no little suspicion.

Third. Since your arrival there, you will be much more familiar with the situation—not that we are kept in the dark. In fact, we are treated with much love and affection, even with temporal assistance, such as cannot be expected from all princes. For from the abundance of his heart and out of affection for us, he has offered to found a college and to build some houses for the Society[1] despite its unworthiness before our Creator and Lord in heaven and so great a prince on earth. And this is not all, for he has taken under his protection those whom we have sent from here to Portugal for studies.

I wished to remind you of all this because if you in Portugal and we in Rome have one and the same end of always serving our Creator and Lord in all respects ever more and more, and are faithful and grateful to those to whom under the Divine Goodness we owe so much, we shall try with all the strength that heaven gives us to carry our share of the spiritual and corporal labors and trials, many of which the enemy of our human nature for quite the contrary end has endeavored to sow between these great and important personages.

Now, since you as well as we are quite aware, not only of what has taken place but of what is actually going on, it only remains for us as bounden debtors very diligently to take up our spiritual arms, you in your position and we here in ours, having forever abandoned those of time, and be instant daily in prayer, continuing to make a special memento in our Masses and begging our Lord to deign to lay His hand and bestow His grace on a matter which is so worthy of being commended to His infinite and supreme goodness. Although I am quite convinced that with

---

[1] He is referring to the foundation of the College of Coimbra and of the residence of San Antonio in Lisbon.

God's grace the enemy will never prevail over this work, no small harm and confusion can come to many souls if this situation were to continue even for a few days.

I had a long conversation on the subject with the cardinal of Burgos,[2] who in all such matters is a very special supporter and adviser in our Lord, and the few words he spoke to me not only confirmed me in my opinion but gave me also no little consolation. He said: "Someone has told me that there was a report that the king of Portugal is refusing obedience to the pope." The good cardinal would not hear of it, and answered with some spirit: "Who says that? Even if the pope trampled the king of Portugal under foot, he would not do so. Think you that the people of Portugal are like these Italians, or that the king is like the king of England, who was already half out of the Church before he declared himself so? Do not think that of so conscientious a Christian as the king of Portugal."

I have entertained the thought of writing to the king, but have held back, partly because of my insignificance and unworthiness and partly because I am excused by your presence there at court. It is your duty to pay the king due reverence and to speak for all of us as well as for yourself. And yet, if you think I should write, I will abide by your judgment, as I have no desire of falling short even in the slightest detail, in our Lord.[3]

Afterwards, on a mandate from the pope, Master Faber left Spain, Master Bobadilla the legation of the English cardinal [Pole], and Master Le Jay the diocese of Cardinal Carpi [Faenza], all bound for Germany. We have received letters from the last two dated February 15, six days after their safe arrival in Spires, describing their preparations to enter the desert. We have had no letter from Faber as to his arrival in Germany. Although the nuncios to Ireland have embarked, we have no news of their passage or landing. As I have written at length elsewhere concerning the dispersed Society and the spiritual fruit which our Lord deigns to gather through them, there remains nothing to add here. May He in His infinite and supreme goodness be our protection, favor, and help.

A week ago today the king's ambassador left for Portugal.

---

[2] John Alvarez de Toledo, O.P., who at the pope's command examined and approved the book of the Exercises. The cardinal had taken the Roman College under his protection and had founded that of St. James of Compostella.

[3] This conflict between the supreme pontiff and the king came to an end when both agreed that the administration of the Diocese of Viseo be given to Cardinal Farnese, who secretly agreed to hand over the income, less a pension for the coadjutor bishop whom the king was to present, to the bishop, Don Michael de Silva, to whom the pope had insisted that the king restore it.

¶ TO FRANCIS BORGIA, DUKE OF GANDIA

XII, 217-19, Appendix I, Letter 3

This is not a letter, but a summary of a letter found in an unpublished manuscript life of St. Francis Borgia. Borgia had apparently asked the advice of Ignatius concerning frequent Communion to which inquiry Ignatius gives a prudent answer.

Rome, middle of 1542

Father Ignatius answered the viceroy that, although he could not give a general rule that would apply equally to all, still frequent Communion would be profitable for some and pleasing to God, and might be harmful for others and displeasing to His Divine Majesty. But of itself the frequent reception of the blessed Sacrament of the Altar is a good and holy practice, and it should be encouraged when there are present in the soul of the recipient that disposition and preparation which this celestial and divine food demands. This disposition of soul can be recognized after an honest examination of conscience in a soul that has been enlightened and swept clean of all self-love. One should not be mistaken about dispositions and think they are present when they are not, nor should one fear when there is no reason for fear and by an indiscreet timidity deprive oneself of this sweet and precious bread of life. It is a mistake to presume to take our seat at this heavenly banquet unless we are invited by our Lord, and it is no less a mistake for the soul to reject health and life when it sees itself in need of them and God is inviting it. The first sins by arrogance and the second by cowardice, because through human respect and to be spared the trouble of preparing one deprives oneself of the grace of the most holy sacrament. He went on then to give some rules and regulations to guard against a mistake. The first rule was that the intention must be pure and upright if one wishes to receive frequently; the second, the advice of the spiritual father or ordinary confessor; the third, the progress which the soul sees itself making in virtue, especially in charity, humility, kindliness, and devotion. For if frequent Communion brings a growth in these virtues, the soul must not through timidity deprive herself of so great a blessing. He ends his letter by saying that, if at such a distance his judgment of the character of his lordship had any weight, relying on what he had heard from so many of the life, good example, good works, and prayer of his lordship, he would venture to advise him to trust in God's mercy and, taking courage from the gifts he had already received from His blessed hand, approach the holy table frequently. He hoped that this would result in no little fruit for his own soul and the souls of others who would be led to imitate him and encouraged to practice the same virtue. As he himself was prevented by his many occupations from journeying to Spain, he offered to send one of his companions, a spiritual man well versed in divine things, by whose counsel his lordship could be guided in this matter and in any other that should happen to occur.

¶ TO FATHER SIMON RODRIGUES
I, 211-12, Letter 44

Father Rodrigues felt called upon to complain that the two scholastics, Francis Rojas and Francis Villanueva, had failed in proper humility and submission of judgment. Ignatius' reply is couched in words of the greatest import.

Middle of the year 1542

✝

If Rojas[1] is willing to be humble and to take the proper means to insure this, there is still time for leniency, and I would not wish any change made at all. If, however, you see that such is not the case for reasons which are better known to you than to me, I leave everything to your judgment and I will consider best whatever you shall decide. If it is impossible for him to remain with you, he will be welcome here until we see to what extent he has improved and whether his amendment is lasting. I cannot say that of Carvajal. It is some six weeks since he arrived from Paris, and although he wishes to belong to this community, he has not yet spent a night in it.

I wish the same to be understood of Villanueva[2] if he is willing to abase and humble himself. But if he is headstrong and refuses correction, even though he were my father he should have no part with me. I beg of you for the love of our Lord Jesus Christ to see above all that your subjects are all completely obedient and humble. If they fail in this they

---

[1] Rojas continued to give trouble, and when later he was sent to Portugal, his dismissal was seriously considered. He must have weathered the storm, however, as he later became rector of the college in Saragossa, where he rendered signal service for a few years. His former restlessness, however, revived and he later left the Society (*Chronicon*, VI, 537 and *passim*).

[2] Francis Villanueva. Ignatius had the greatest confidence in Villanueva, who richly repaid this confidence. Later, according to Father Astrain, he came to enjoy as much authority in Spain among his fellow Jesuits as did St. Ignatius in the whole Society.

cannot go on with you, nor will they last long here. So deeply have I felt what you have written that I am not writing to either of them, and have not the heart to write more now.

¶ TO JOHN BAPTIST VIOLA
1, 228-29, Letter 52

St. Ignatius takes exception to a representation made by John Baptist because he finds it lacking in candor. John Baptist had not followed directions when he was sent to the University of Paris. For that reason he suffered some disappointment in the matter of studies. He wrote a letter which has not been preserved, but we can guess at its contents.

Rome, August 1542

IHS

May the sovereign grace and love of Christ our Lord be our never-failing help and support.

I received your letter but fail to understand it. In two different places you speak of obedience. In the first you say that you are ready to obey me, and in the second you say: "Because I would rather die than fail in obedience, I submit to the judgment of your reverence." Now, it seems to be that obedience seeks to be blind in two ways; in the first it belongs to the inferior to submit his understanding when there is no question of sin and do what is commanded him; in the second it is also the inferior's duty, once the superior commands, or has commanded, anything, to represent to the superior whatever considerations or disadvantages may occur to him, and do so humbly and simply, without any attempt to draw the superior to either side, with the result that afterwards he will be able with peace of mind to follow the way that shall be pointed out to him or commanded.

Now, applying this to your obedience, I cannot manage to understand it. For after you have given me many good arguments to persuade me to approve another teacher, you tell me elsewhere in your letter: "It has seemed good to me to write your reverence to ask you kindly to let me know whether I should change teachers or go on wasting my time." You yourself can judge whether you are seeking obedience or whether you submit your judgment to accept any decision I may make. If you have so much judgment and are satisfied that you are wasting your time, where is your submission of judgment? Do you think, forsooth, that I must tell you to waste your time? May God our Lord never permit me to harm anyone when I cannot be of help to him!

In another place you say: "I am truly sorry to have wasted these last eight months under this teacher, but if notwithstanding you think I ought to go on wasting it, I will continue with him." I recall, when you left here, that I told you that the course of the *Sumulas* would be advanced two or three months when you reached Paris, and that you should study Latin to give you a start for four or five months and then for three or four take the elements of the *Sumulas,* so that you could enter the regular course with some preparation the following year. But, following your own ideas rather than mine, you saw fit to enter a course already two or three months advanced. Judge for yourself who is the cause of your wasting time.

I close, asking our Lord by His infinite goodness to give us the fullness of His perfect grace, so that we may know His most holy will and perfectly fulfill it.

¶ TO SIMON RODRIGUES

1, 234, Letter 56

Ignatius gives a humble answer to some thinly veiled complaints from Rodrigues that he shows little interest in Portugal.

Rome, November 1, 1542

I am very much pleased with the great charity and the holy zeal by which you would have me believe that, if I really knew the whole truth of all that is being done in Portugal, I would not excuse my feet from making the journey nor my tongue from singing the praises that are called for.

If I have not done, nor am now doing, the very little I am able to do, I roundly condemn myself. You can rest assured, therefore, that there is no need of convincing me on this point. All you need do is explain matters clearly. I must yield to many when it comes to deeds of prowess, as I know how weak and frail I am. But weak as my efforts may be, I am convinced that they have been employed to the full satisfaction of all who have anything to do with this matter. As I have told you on other occasions, it will be sufficient to propose a matter in which you are interested, and leave it to me to judge and to decide whether to speak or keep silent as really the person who is in charge.

¶ TO PETER FABER
1, 236-38, Letter 58

St. Ignatius explains to Faber the plan and care which members of the Society should employ in their letters. He asks that each one of them write a principal letter every two weeks which can be shown to other members of the Society. This letter should describe their spiritual activities. Ignatius complains of the neglect of this practice and admonishes Faber to avoid it in the future.

One wonders whether we cannot envisage in this institution the very modest beginnings of what later developed into such imposing productions as the Jesuit Relations *and other similar publications fostered in the other provinces of the Society.*

Rome, December 10, 1542

IHS

I recall having frequently spoken to you, and when you were away of having often written, to the end that each of the members of the Society should, when they write to us here, write out a *principal* letter which can be shown to others; that is, to anyone at all. We do not dare show some letters to friendly eyes who wish to see them, because of their lack of order and the irrelevant things they contain. Now, these friends know that we have letters from this one and that one, and feel hurt if we refuse to let them see their letters, with the result that we rather cause disedification than otherwise. Even recently it happened that I was put to considerable inconvenience. I had to show some letters of two of Ours to the cardinals who were personally concerned with the contents of the letters. But because the letters also contained matters that were irrelevant to their business and were set down without order, it was no easy task to withhold what did not concern them.

I needs must repeat again what I have said before, so that we may all understand one another on every point. I beg of you, therefore, by the love and reverence of God our Lord, to see to it that your letter writing be directed to the greater service of His Divine Goodness and the greater advantage of our neighbor. In the *principal* letter put down what each one is doing in the way of preaching, hearing confessions, giving the Exercises, and other spiritual activities, as God makes use of each for the greater edification of our hearers and readers. If the soil you are working be unproductive and there be little to write about, put down briefly something about health, your dealings with others, or such matters. Do not include irrelevant details but leave them for separate sheets in which you can write of letters received and the spiritual consolation they have given you, items of news, especially of the sick, business matters, and even some words by way of exhortation.

I will set down what my own practice on this point is, and I hope will continue to be, in our Lord, about writing to members of the Society. It will help to keep me from making mistakes. I write the principal letter once, putting down what will be edifying, and then I reread and correct it, keeping in mind that all are going to read it. Then I write it out a second time, or have someone else do it, for what appears in writing needs a closer scrutiny than what is merely spoken, the written word remaining as a perpetual witness which cannot be amended or explained away as easily as is done in talk. Even with all this I am sure that I make some mistakes and am afraid of doing so in the future. Other details which would be irrelevant in the principal letter, or which might not be edifying, I leave for the separate sheets. In these sheets one may write hurriedly out of the abundance of the heart, with or without a predetermined order. But this should not be true of the principal letter, which should always show signs of care, so that it can be passed about for the purpose of giving edification. Everyone seems to have failed in this regard, and so a copy of this letter is being sent to all. I beg and beseech you in our Lord to write out the main or principal letter as I have here indicated and then, after looking it over, rewrite it; that is, it should be written twice, as I do with mine. In this way I am convinced that the letters will show greater order and distinction. In the future, if I notice that this is not done for the greater union, charity, and edification of all, I shall be obliged to write you and command you under obedience to reread, correct, and rewrite every principal letter you send me. I do not want to have to answer to God for any negligence of my own in this matter, and I shall be satisfied with that, having done all that I could, although I should much prefer that you give me no occasion for writing you so. I exhort you, then, as I am bound to do for the greater glory of God our Lord, and I beg of you by His love and reverence to improve your writing and to conceive some esteem for it and a desire to edify your brethren and your neighbor by your letters. Be assured that the time you spend at it—it can be put down to my account—will be well spent in our Lord. It costs me an effort to write a principal letter twice, to give it some appearance of order, to say nothing of many sheets besides. Even this letter I have written twice with my own hand; how much more, then, should each member of the Society do likewise? You indeed have to write to one person only, but I to all. I can say in all truth that the other night we counted the letters that we were sending out to various places and found that the number reached two hundred and fifty. If some of you in the Society are busy, I am convinced that I am not less busy than any of you, and with less health than you. Up to the present I cannot praise a single one of you in this matter, though neither do I wish to find fault. If the copies of the letters from others which I send you seem to be arranged in some order and contain little that is superfluous, it is because, at no little loss of time, I have selected what is edifying, rearranging the very words they use and cutting out those that are irrelevant, so as to give all of you some pleasure in our Lord and edification for those who hear them for the first time. So, again I beg of you, by your love and reverence for the Divine Majesty, put your heart in this matter and get to work with all diligence; it will contribute so much for the spiritual progress and consolation of souls. Every two weeks write a principal letter, revised and corrected, which, all told, will be really the work of two letters. In the sheets you may be as long as you like, where you have to write only to the individual who is to use them. With God's help I will write you all once a month without fail, but briefly; and more at length every three months, when I will send all the news and transcripts from all the letters I receive from Ours. Let us all, therefore, for the love of God our Lord, help one another. And do me the favor of bearing with me, and lighten in some way the heavy burden you have placed on my shoulders, to say nothing of other things which are not lacking here: I mean works of piety and other spiritual investments. If I could do the work of ten or if we were all together here in Rome, we should have more than we could do. In case your memory fails, as mine does often enough, keep this letter before you, or some substitute reminder of it, while you are writing your principal letters.

¶ TO JOHN III, KING OF PORTUGAL
I, 243-46, Letter 60

Ignatius addresses the king, John III, with a deep sense of gratitude and humility. He thanks the king graciously for the many and great favors he has bestowed on the Society of Jesus. Ignatius felicitates him on the marriages that had been arranged between Mary and John, his daughter and son, and Philip and Joan, the son and daughter of Charles V. Mary married the prince Don Philip on the thirteenth of November, 1543, but Joan, being under age, did not marry until the year 1552. He appreciates the request of the king for additional companions but at present is unable to fulfill it. He offers his services and those of the Society, ending with a eulogy of the king's representatives at the papal court.

Rome, March 8, 1543

IHS

My Lord in Christ Jesus.

May the perfect grace and infinite love of Christ our eternal Lord attend and abide with your highness, preserve and prosper you in His greater service, praise, and glory.

It is now many days since I first wished to address this letter to your highness, but my little significance and less merit have prevented me. I now find some strength in the Lord, and encouraged by Francis Botello,[1] who I may say in parenthesis is an eager and careful servant of your highness, not only in matters of greater importance but in those of less in illness and health alike, I find occasion to write this letter. I cannot help but rejoice in our Lord and give His Eternal Goodness infinite and ceaseless thanks when I reflect on how much, through His infinite and supreme goodness, He does for us, unworthy as we are of any mention. He has shown this continual interest by choosing your highness as the distinguished and faithful instrument to fulfill His purpose. If on the one hand Paul planted and Apollo watered, it seems on the other that your highness both plants and waters, so that, having performed a complete work, you would have the complete merit in our Lord. When did we merit to have your highness be mindful of us, most unworthy as we are, in the time of our greatest trials in Rome, when being considered traitors, you ask for us as true and loyal? By whose merit does it happen that, abject and discouraged as we are, some of Ours should be so well received by your highness on their arrival in Portugal and raised to a position of such esteem? Whence comes it, in a word, that this least Society, so useless and unknown for any service either in heaven or on earth, should be favored with such an abundance of manna? It is truly a great comfort to me, and I find it a real delight, to be forever beholden to you. For the knowledge and recognition of so inestimable a debt as we owe to God, and to your highness as His representative, seems to me to be an assurance against the possibility of our ever failing in gratitude. So, with-

---

[1] Botello was John III's business agent at Rome in the preliminary negotiations for the establishment of the Inquisition in Portugal, and was in charge of the case dealing with Michael de Silva, cardinal and bishop of Viseo.

out the least hesitation, I firmly believe and hope in our Lord that in His supreme and infinite goodness He will fully repay your highness in heaven as well as on earth and that He will give us His usual grace. And this not only to us who now make up the present Society, but to those who are to come after us, so that, if any sacrifices of ours or prayers or good works of any kind have any weight with His Divine Majesty, as we hope in the sovereign and perfect Goodness they will have, your highness will have and hold a complete share in them in return for all that your highness does for the Society. May His Divine Majesty thus repay your highness with most holy consolations and spiritual blessings, and thus help your highness to make ever greater progress in His service, praise, and glory. For with His favor and help no enemy in this life or in the next will be able to prevail against us, and so you can look forward to perfect peace both here and hereafter.

To make sure of this end, just as evil companionship can be an obstacle and an impediment, so good and holy companionship is no small help. For this reason we have felt an intense satisfaction in our Lord to learn of the advantageous marriages which your highness has succeeded in arranging. In this there is more of God's hand than man's, seeing the blessings that will redound to many and the peace and security of your kingdoms, in which it would seem that our Lord becomes more visible the more He passes into eclipse elsewhere. May it please the most holy Trinity in its infinite and supreme goodness to give to your highness the grace of relishing spiritually what you have so holily planned and achieved, and may He by His infinite mercy deign to cast an eye on this Christian people which was so dearly bought, and bring fair weather after storm and spiritual joy after so many calamities, for His greater honor, praise, and glory.

As to the request of your highness for one or several of Ours for the increase of the divine service, unworthy as we are, we appreciate your continued kindness; but by the time your highness' letter arrived the pope had left for Bologna, and we were able to make only some temporary arrangements to facilitate the obtaining of your request and our desire.

With regard to the matter of the holy Inquisition and related affairs, we can dispense with any thanks, which we do not in any sense deserve, partly because our services are so feeble and so few in our Lord and partly because we are already under such heavy obligations to your highness that, if in anything we can be of service, we look upon it as an additional favor and a mark of your kindness, even when all that we can offer is our desire to serve.

Thanks without end be to His Divine Majesty that matters today are moving on with such good order. They have had excellent guidance and direction, and it would seem that our Lord Himself lays His hands upon instruments of His own, necessary or suitable, such as the representatives your highness has chosen and sent to this country. The one in the short time he had at his disposal, the other, working to the best of his ability, have arranged everything with such skill and diligence that they both move forward with great security at every step.

I close, asking God our Lord by His infinite and supreme goodness to give us plentiful grace always to know His most holy will and perfectly to fulfill it.

¶ TO FATHER JAMES LAINEZ
1, 246-47, Letter 61

After Ignatius was elected general, he set to work writing the Constitutions. He first worked out a number of unconnected points. In this letter he instructs Lainez to put into practice two points of the Constitutions, one of which was concerned with the teaching of catechism to children. On this matter Lainez, like all the other professed of four vows, had made a special promise. The second point is concerned with dress.

Rome, March 13, 1543

JHUS

I am sending you herewith those points of the Constitutions which deal with the teaching of boys and were subscribed to by the six who were present and who acted with the authority of those who were absent.[1] These points, then, are to hold until they are further explained and put into some appropriate form. Therefore, in conformity with the Constitutions and their declarations, I am obliged to command you, and I do command you in virtue of holy obedience, two things. The first is that you teach boys or men for forty days each year. The year may be reckoned from the day you left Rome or from the day of your arrival at your destination, and should include twelve whole months. If you have already fulfilled a year according to this reckoning, or after you have fulfilled it, you

---

[1] See *Constitutiones Societatis Jesu, latinae et hispanicae,* 309-10 (Madrid, 1892). The six fathers who were present in Rome in 1541 were Ignatius, Lainez, Le Jay, Broet, Salmeron, and Codure. Those absent were Xavier and Rodrigues, who had gone to Portugal; Faber, who had gone to Germany; and Bobadilla, who had gone to the Kingdom of Naples.

may begin with the calendar year—1543, for example—and do the teaching any time you please. You may do the same in the year 1544, teaching any time you please, and so on for the following years, not reckoning by the twelve-month period, but from year to year.

The second point is that your clothing and footwear should conform to what is said in the enclosed chapters of the Constitutions which deal with the matter of clothing and footwear. I exhort you to keep exactly the fifth and sixth chapters; and if this admonition does not suffice, I command you in virtue of obedience. However, if I can do so with a clear conscience, considering the promise and vow I made to God our Lord on the day of our profession, as far as I am empowered to do so by virtue of the Constitutions, I grant you a dispensation to be used at your discretion in our Lord.[2]

¶ TO ASCONIUS COLONNA
I, 254-55, Letter 63

A letter of recommendation for Father Araoz, who was going to Naples to preach. Ignatius touches on the mutual advantage which spiritual persons draw from associating together and speaks of seeking our last end by imitating Christ crucified. Asconius Colonna, duke of Palliani and Tagliacozzi and constable of the Kingdom of Naples, was the son of Fabricius Colonna. His wife was Joan of Aragon. They were the parents of Mark Anthony Colonna, who with Don John of Austria won a victory over the Turkish fleet at Lepanto. Ignatius reminds him with marks of great affection that only those blessings are to be valued which help in the attaining of eternal salvation.

Rome, April 15, 1543

May the sovereign grace and everlasting love of Christ our Lord greet and abide with your excellency.

The licentiate Araoz, a member of our Society and bearer of this letter, will have to spend some time in Naples. Besides being enlightened in the spiritual things that interest your excellency, it is my desire that you enjoy

---

[2] There seems to be an apparent discrepancy or inconsistancy on the part of Ignatius thus giving a command in virtue of obedience and immediately dispensing from it. His action may be better understood if we reflect that he might have been safeguarding the Constitutions against the introduction of anything like a religious habit. This giving a command and allowing the individual to apply it according to circumstances of time, persons, and place was his usual practice.

each other's company by an interchange of spiritual gifts, with your usual kindness and great charity in our Lord and the true Spirit. For souls that are inflamed with a desire for His greater service, praise, and glory, whetting each other's appetites, are always roused and helped by an unfailing solace and spiritual progress. As the object is infinite and the potency finite,[1] there will always be room for improvement.

God our Lord, who is my judge for eternity, knows how deeply rooted in my soul is the intense desire I have of serving your excellency in our Lord and of promoting your complete prosperity and happiness in heaven and on earth, to the greater glory and praise of His divine and eternal Goodness. In this life a thing is good for us only insofar as it is a help toward life eternal and evil insofar as it is an obstacle to it. Thus the enlightened soul, its understanding clarified by dew from heaven, when it suffers contradictions places its nest on high and desires nothing but Christ and Him crucified, so that, if it is crucified in this life, it will rise in the next.

I close, begging Him by His infinite and supreme goodness to grant us in all things His perfect grace, so that we may know His holy will and always fulfill it.

¶ TO MARGARET OF AUSTRIA
I, 271-73, Letter 71

Margaret of Austria, at the time duchess of Parma, was a person of no small influence at the papal court. Ignatius wishes to induce her to intercede with the pope in behalf of a priest who because of some serious offense had served three years in prison and who after a number of years spent in penance desired to obtain a dispensation to celebrate Mass again. Peter Codacio, the bearer of Ignatius' letter, was the first Italian to enter the Society. He became a member in 1539.

Rome, August 13, 1543

JHUS

Most excellent Lady in our Lord.

May the sovereign grace and everlasting love of Christ our Lord greet and visit your excellency.

---

[1] The object is God, the finite potency is the effort of the soul to seek and unite itself with Him by knowledge and love.

As our Peter Codacio, procurator of our own house and the new House of Refuge, is going to court to obtain a document which turns out to be necessary for the house and its inmates, I gladly take this occasion to write to your excellency. A father of the order of St. Dominic brings me a letter in which he is recommended by persons to whose sentiments, in matters that are just and proper, I think I have every reason in conscience to defer and whose request I should not think of refusing. For God's greater glory, therefore, I have determined to write this letter to your excellency, especially since God, according to the father's own statement, has bestowed upon him the great favor of having some report of his trials and sufferings come to the ears of your excellency. Now, as among the spiritual works of mercy it is an outstanding act of virtue to comfort a soul that is weighed down with pain and sorrow, I cannot resist humbly interceding with your excellency in behalf of this father. And this the more, as I know from experience that your excellency is readily disposed to all works of mercy in our Lord. And yet, fearing that I prove importunate in asking for something that cannot be granted or that may not appear to you as just and proper, I will tell your excellency that, in order to avoid the disappointment of a refusal, I have myself examined the matter in our Lord and consulted with others, learned men of the Sacred Penitentiary. They are all one in thinking that the request is worthy and deserving of support, especially as the poor man has served three years in prison for his offense, has done much penance through the space of eight or nine years, and now comes with the permission of his superior and the approval of learned men of his order. If he obtains the desired permission, he can comfort his soul with the offering of the Holy Sacrifice. It is understood that, to avoid scandal, he will not celebrate in the place where the fault was committed but elsewhere, either in public or private, as superiors of his order judge to be for the greater glory of God our Lord. In this way and with these reservations it will be much easier for His Holiness Pope Paul III to grant the dispensation that will give so much consolation to this soul.

But as I refer your excellency in this matter as in all else to Peter Codacio, who will act in my stead just as though I were present in person, I will bring this letter to a close, asking and humbly beseeching of the goodness of God our Lord to guard and rule your excellency in all your actions by His divine and eternal goodness.

The lady countess of Carpi shows some improvement in health, although she is not entirely well. Endless thanks to the Giver of all life, whether of soul or body, and praise and glory to His greater service.

¶ TO SISTER TERESA REJADELL
I, 274-76, Letter 73

Ignatius consoles her on the occasion of the death of her sister Louise by assuring her that her sister is in heaven. He settles some doubts concerning the habit and the rules of the order to which Teresa belongs, and goes on to explain the principles concerning daily Communion. He shows that it is not forbidden either by the Church or the theologians and tells her that, if the love of God grows in her soul with the practice, it will not only be lawful but even preferable to receive daily.

Rome, November 15, 1543

IHS

May the perfect grace and love of Christ our Lord continue to help and favor us always.

1. I have heard that it was God's will to remove your sister Louise, and ours in our Lord, from the trials of this present life. I have every reason to believe with certainty that she is in a better life, a glorious and eternal life, where I hope that she will favor and reward us with holy usury, seeing that we have not forgotten her in our own poor and unworthy prayers. Were I, therefore, to attempt to console you at length, I should feel that I were doing you wrong, as I must judge that you conform yourself as you should to the perfect and everlasting providence of God, which is entirely concerned with our greater glory.

2. As to the habit and observance of rule, if you have a judgment in your favor, and even if you did not have one, you have a confirmation from the Apostolic See, and so should have no doubts that you are surely in conformity with the service and the will of God.[1] For a rule of any saint can oblige under pain of sin only insofar as it is approved by the vicar of Christ our Lord or by someone else who speaks with his authority. Consequently the rule of St. Benedict, of St. Francis, or of St. Jerome has no force of itself to oblige under pain of sin, but can do so only when it has the confirmation and authorization of the Apostolic See, because of the divine efficacy which it can impart to such a rule.

3. As to daily Communion, we should recall that in the early Church everybody received daily, and that up to this time there has been no written ordinance of Holy Mother Church nor objection by either positive or scholastic theologians against anyone receiving daily Communion should

---

[1] Ignatius is alluding to a jurisdictional dispute instituted by the Franciscans and settled by a bull of Leo X, which handed over the visitation of the Monastery of Santa Clara to the Benedictines.

his devotion move him thereto. It is true that St. Augustine said that he would neither praise nor blame daily Communion, but he did on the other hand exhort everyone to receive on Sundays.² Further on, speaking of the most sacred body of Christ our Lord, he says: "This bread is our daily bread. So live therefore as to be able to receive it daily." Now, this being true, even if the indications are not so good or the inclinations of the soul so wholesome, the witness on which we can always rely is that of our own conscience. What I mean is this. After all, it is lawful for you in the Lord if, apart from evident mortal sins or what you can judge to be such, you think that your soul derives help and is inflamed with love for our Creator and Lord, and you receive with this intention, finding by experience that this spiritual food soothes, supports, settles, and preserves you for His greater service, praise, and glory, you may without doubt receive daily; in fact, it would be better for you to do so.³

On this point and on some others I have spoken to Araoz, who will deliver this letter. Referring you to him in everything in our Lord, I close, praying God our Lord by His infinite kindness to guide you and govern you in all things through His infinite and supreme goodness.

¶ TO FATHER NICHOLAS BOBADILLA
I, 277-82, Letter 74

St. Ignatius insisted much on regularity in the correspondence he carried on with his sons throughout the world. To this end he had Polanco send out a detailed instruction.¹ But this instruction was only a codification of practices already introduced by Ignatius. He himself was very exact in sending news to his sons. As he wished the letters coming from a distance to be such as might be shown to others, either in the houses of the Society or to friends and benefactors, he wished letters which he called "principal" and which dealt with their apostolic labors to be well thought out, orderly, and edifying. Everything else could be set down on separate sheets with greater freedom and ease. He had made some very pointed

---

² The opinion attributed by St. Ignatius to St. Augustine was actually expressed by Gennadius, whose *De ecclesiasticis dogmatibus* was at the time thought to have been written by Augustine.
³ St. Ambrose, in a sermon attributed to St. Augustine, says: "Accipe quotidie, quod quotidie tibi prosit. Sic vive, ut quotidie merearis accipere. Qui non meretur quotidie accipere, non meretur post annum accipere."
¹ *Epistolae et instructiones*, I, 542-49.

observations to Faber² on his failure to observe these directions. The same thing happened to Bobadilla. But Bobadilla, an excellent man indeed but a bit forthright and outspoken, answered that he considered his time too valuable to be writing with such care or even to read these famous "principal letters." Ignatius stuck to his demands in a fatherly way, and with touching humility added a few further observations.

Day and month uncertain, 1543³

IHS

May the perfect grace and love of Christ our Lord be always in our help and favor.

As I find myself by His infinite grace more disposed to humble myself on all points rather than defend myself on a few and as I think it will be to His greater glory, I have decided to make the most of the opportunity.

1. Concerning the fraternal correction between us which I have had a mind to make for God's greater glory, you say that you understand my mind but that all will not accept it with your understanding and sincerity. I have all in mind—that is, all the members of the Society—because it is for them alone that I have written. If, however, you should feel that some of them on receiving word on this point will not take what I have to say with your sincerity and simplicity of mind, I hope in our Lord that I will agree completely with each of them, to your and their complete satisfaction.

2. You say that it is one thing to put something in writing and another to say it by word of mouth, and you insist that it would be impossible to make my palate the standard of taste for all. I remember having written that the principal letter should be gone over twice; that is, written once and corrected, then rewriting it or having it copied to avoid the untidiness of hurried writing, a fault into which I think some of Ours have fallen. If all of us were to do this—and myself the first, as I think I have greater need—we should be a greater help to one another in the Lord. I did not want to say, nor do I say now, that, if one has used a certain expression, he should change it to another, nor that he should try to write with greater ability than he has. If I cannot add to my own low level of understanding, I could ill afford to try to raise that of others, seeing that it belongs to our Creator and Lord to give much or little. But I mean that each one should

---

² See Letter 58.
³ The date of this letter is unknown. The editors of the *Monumenta* place it some time in the year 1543 (*Epistolae et instructiones*, I, 277). There is a very genial and pleasing account of Bobadilla in Father James Brodrick's *Origin of the Jesuits*, pp. 237-42.

write the principal letter once, correct it and rewrite it or have it rewritten, and thus each one of Ours will be aided by the other. For neither I myself nor any other can give to another more than we have ourselves. But with this attentiveness and care each one gives in a better way what he has received from His Creator and Lord. It does not seem from this that I am aiming at exercising so widespread and detailed an authority as you think.

3. You think it good enough to draw up a brief summary of your letter and have copies made of this, but not to send us a full account as we desire. You are well aware that I wrote to you, and that there is a general agreement among us, that in the principal letter there will be news of some edification, according to what God our Lord works in each for the spiritual good of souls; but if one wishes to give other information, such as bits of news, illnesses, or needs, he may write it at as great length as he wishes, but on separate sheets or in another letter.

4. You observe that in the copy of my letter to you I had said "Procuro de expedir mi tiempo" when I should have said "expender mi tiempo." If you will look well at that letter, you will see in my own hand "expender" and not "expedir." That may be explained by the fact that the one who transcribed my letter here wrote "expedir" in place of "expender," which I, relying on another, did not correct, as it was not a principal letter which could be shown to others. I am willing to acknowledge myself as guilty as you judge me to be in our Lord.

5. With regard to the fault you find in the address on the letter I wrote you, which runs, "En el palacio del rey de los romanos," I admit writing that, thinking that you would be better known in the palace where you are a frequent caller than in the court at large, since that is coextensive with the city or town. But if there was a fault in writing "de los romanos," I will say hereafter, "En el corte del rey de romanos." If everybody laughed at that, as you say they did, I should think that, when you saw that some laughed, you would not have shown it to everybody. I will be very grateful to you in our Lord if you show them this letter also, for if I correct the one, I can also correct the others. This will be my lifelong desire, to be directed and corrected for my faults in the hope that the correction extend to all of them and be given with brotherly affection. I recall that I made this earnest request of all the Society from the time you made your profession. It was that, whenever any of you saw me in any fault, you would after prayer to God our Lord and, conferring with His Divine Majesty, inform me of my faults and thus help me to correct them in our Lord.

6. You think that I should not be losing time in correcting details of so little importance, and that some who do not know me might think that I have nothing to do with my time. Do not lose sight of the fact that this matter of correspondence has been agreed upon among us after long discussion. Recall too that I have already written you at length, begging you to rewrite your principal letters twice in the manner I have described and to avoid the inconveniences I have already enumerated, and that, if you did not do so, I should be compelled, although much against my inclination, in view of the spiritual profit in general and the obligations of my conscience, to command you in virtue of holy obedience. You received my letters and answered with sufficient edification and contentment; but later, after the first few letters, you disregarded entirely the requests I had made so earnestly in our Lord and included in your principal letter much that was merely local news, all of which, coming in another letter or on separate sheets, would have given us all much gratification as being news of you. But the fact that you were suffering from a touch of skin irritation which was tormenting you should have been put on a sheet by itself, as we had often agreed, so that we could give to each a morsel according to his taste, and everything be for the good. Many friends and acquaintances who know that we have letters from some of the Society wish to see them and find a great delight in them. If we don't show the letters when they ask, we estrange them; if we show them a disorderly letter, they are disedified. I am not so eager to correct the wording of your letters as I am for your perfection in general, and some part of that consists in humbling yourself and in obeying him in whose hands you made your vow of obedience, especially in things that are in themselves good, or indifferent, or without sin. Hence I am of the opinion up till now that giving a part of my time to this would be to the greater glory of God our Lord, and to the greater spiritual benefit of the Society. If you think otherwise, I will be able to conform to what you judge to be better in our Lord, because I do not think that I should be less the gainer in your company, in the eyes of His Divine Majesty, than I would be with anyone else in the Society.

7. You say: "You think that everybody is edified with these copies of yours. I don't show many of them, nor do I read many of them. I haven't the time. Two letters could be made out of the superfluous matter in your principal letter." Indeed, I never thought that you would show them to everybody or that everybody would be edified. But I did think that you would show them to a few and that they for the most part would get some good from them, as up to this all those to whom I have written this

same principal letter think they have benefited, unless I deceive myself from what they say in their letters. This holds true even of Dr. Ortiz and his brother Francis and Dr. Picard at Paris. As to your thinking my letters not worth reading for lack of time, I have by God's grace time and to spare and the inclination to read and reread all of yours. If it will make you read mine, I will make a real effort to follow your advice as best I can in the Lord and remove from my letters everything you think superfluous. This I will do also for the others to whom I have written who share your disapproval, if only you will let me know. For it would be a great mistake on my part to spend so much time and labor and succeed only in displeasing, without advantage to anyone.

Therefore I beg of you by the love and reverence of God our Lord to let me know the best way of writing you, whether I do it myself or with the help of a secretary, so that I may be sure to please you in every respect. In the meantime, as I do not know what course to take, I will await your letter, or I will have someone else write who will know better how to meet with your requirements.

Moreover, since you know my earnest desire, I beseech you by the same love and reverence of His Divine Majesty to do your very best in your letters to me, as I have so often asked you and do now once more beseech you in our Lord. If I cannot obtain what I so earnestly ask of you, it will be because I am wholly unworthy, or for any other reason you may entertain. On condition that the Society, or the half of it, approves, I give you my vote, whatever it may be worth, and gladly and sincerely offer to turn over to you the office I now hold. Not only do I choose you, but if you think otherwise, I am perfectly willing to choose anyone you or any of the others may name. I am convinced that whatever would be thus decided would be for the greater praise, reverence, and service of God our Lord and to my own greater peace of soul in His Divine Majesty. For it is the very truth that, absolutely speaking, my desire is to have a lowly station and be without this weight of responsibility as long as I live.

Thus always and in everything I wish to set aside my own poor judgment. I hold now, and hope that I shall always hold, as much better whatever you or the Society, or a part of it, shall determine. And this determination I here and now with my own hand approve and confirm.

In the meantime I return to the subject of your own personal needs. You know that it is our profession to offer ourselves to be sent wherever the vicar of Christ shall think good and as he shall decide, without asking even for any provision for the journey. In speaking for others, I did not see anything wrong in calling attention to your needs there, so that in providing, or not, for your needs, they might do as seemed to them more for God's glory. Guided therefore by the contents of your letter to me, I spoke to Cardinal Santa Croce and also to Cardinal Morone. If I were in your place, I would be quite satisfied with this, and accept relief for my needs from any who offered as coming from God's hand. If occasionally I was left in want, I would think that God was pleased to try me, to give me an opportunity for more merit in His greater service, praise, and glory. But I don't see why I should enlarge on this point, as I think I have long known your spirit in our Lord.

If I have delayed in writing you, it is because I did not know where you could be found. You spoke to me of taking the baths, and I did not know where you were going to stay.

May it please God that this letter find you in perfect health, wherever you may serve Him best and praise His most holy name.

¶ TO JAMES CRESCENZI
1, 291-92, Letter 77

Ignatius encourages him to settle a family misunderstanding and to set his affairs in order. He urges him to accept a sum of money which he had sent him.

Rome, June 14, 1544

IHUS

My Lord in our Lord.

May the sovereign grace and love of Christ our Lord visit and greet your lordship.

I know that your lordship will not be surprised at the delay which matters of business meet with here in spite of one's care and attention. Just how much that care has been your lordship can see from the document which accompanies this letter and which was drawn up by the Most Reverend Monsignor Crescenzi and represents his views. Nevertheless, as it is my desire to see perfect peace between persons who are so closely related, I cannot refrain from urging your lordship to come to the completest possible agreement. This will leave your children in perfect peace, which is far more valuable than any other merely apparent advantage. In the name of the piety which animates you, give me an early answer and let me know what you think will be more to the glory of

God our Lord. I will then make every effort, however weak, to carry out your decision.

The morning of the same day that your lordship left here, I sent Don Elpidius with the money for distribution to the poor. He did not find your lordship and wished to leave the money with the Señora Joan, but she refused and still refuses to accept it. As soon as you have determined on how this money is to be distributed, please bid this lady accept it and tell her how she is to dispose of it. Otherwise I will send it to you by a reliable messenger. With my vow of poverty, I do not want any money clinking in my pockets when I come to die. When I bequeath my body—or better, this earth—to the earth, I do not want to be found with even a farthing either of my own or anyone else's.

I close, asking God our Lord in His infinite and sovereign goodness to deign to give us His abundant grace to know His most holy will and perfectly fulfill it.

¶ TO A MAN WHO WAS TEMPTED
I, 294-95, Letter 79

The recipient of this letter is unknown. He apparently had some connection with the community in Padua. He wished to return to his homeland or remain in the house at Padua, without, however, being a member of the community. This St. Ignatius refused to permit. In words that breathe of affection for the tempted man, Ignatius persuades him to leave the Society's house but not to return to his home. He should devote himself to good works and take up some study at Padua, and not omit proper recreation.

Rome, November 28, 1544

JHUS

May the perfect grace and love of Christ our Lord always be our protection and support.

I could not at all fail in the affection my heart feels for you, and so I will briefly answer your letter and that of Master Lainez, as God grants me understanding.

First, with regard to your going back home and living there, I do not think that anything could be worse for you. Because, as past experience proves, it is the last thing you should think of, as I have explained at length in other letters.

Second, I do not think that I could approve of your remaining in the house with Ours, nor can I feel satisfied that it would be a good thing; partly because you would not find the fruit you are looking for and which you have every right to expect, and partly because of the disappointment both Ours and you would feel at their inability to help you in body and soul as they desire. All things considered, I always thought that it would be safer in our Lord and better for all concerned if you took lodging apart from Ours in Padua, with some good companions, paying what you would expect to pay at home, and try that out for a year. You should go to confession frequently and have a talk with some of Ours several times a week. For the rest, you could attend several lectures, but with the purpose rather of strengthening and clearing your mind than of acquiring academic learning for the sake of others. See that your associations are pleasant and take some innocent recreation that will leave the soul unsullied, for it is better to keep the soul unsullied than to be made lord of all creation. By means of these interior consolations and the spiritual relish they will give you, you will attain to that peace and repose of conscience, and then, as your strength of body and soul allows, you can better give yourself to study for the sake of others and be sure of better results. But above all, I beg of you for the love and reverence of God our Lord to remember the past and to reflect not lightly but seriously that the earth is only earth.

May God in His infinite and perfect goodness be pleased to give us His perfect grace, so that we may know His most holy will and entirely fulfill it.

¶ TO JOHN III, KING OF PORTUGAL
1, 296-98, Letter 81

False accusations had been noised abroad in Rome against Ignatius and his companions, and there was some possibility of difficulties arising in Portugal in spite of the favorable judgment passed by the governor of the city. To obviate these difficulties the saint recounts to the king, with great sincerity and humility, the persecutions he had undergone in Alcala, Salamanca, Paris, Venice, and finally Rome. He points out to the king that he had emerged from these experiences without taint on his character or teaching. Ignatius hopes that with this information his majesty will know how to tell the false from the true. For the rest, Ignatius glories in the persecutions of the past and desires even greater for himself and his Society, whose sole desire is to be clothed with the livery of Christ our Lord. He ends by asking the king's permission for Rodrigues to come to a meeting of the older fathers to be held in Rome. Permission had already been granted by the pope.

Rome, March 15, 1545

IHS

May the perfect grace and everlasting love of Christ our Lord come and abide with your highness. Amen.

From more than a few tokens and indications I am convinced, our Lord knows, that, if certain experiences of mine have not already come to the ears of your highness, they soon will. They concern our Lord more than they do me; may His be the glory forever. I could desire always to glory in them, not for myself but for our Creator and Lord, and as we are under such obligations to your Christian highness, I thought that I should acquaint you with them sooner or later, even though briefly.

On my return from Jerusalem my superiors in Alcala de Henares subjected me to three different trials. I was arrested and kept in custody for forty-two days. The same thing took place in Salamanca, where I was not only confined to jail but also put into chains for twenty-two days. I underwent another trial at Paris, where I was pursuing my studies. In all these five trials and two imprisonments, by God's grace I never wished to have, nor did I have, any other advocate or attorney than God, in whom, by His favor and grace, I have placed all my confidence for the present as well as for the future. Seven years after the first trial in Paris another was held in the same university, another in Venice, and the last in Rome, which involved the whole Society. In the three trials last mentioned, because of my connection with others of the Society, which is your highness' even more than it is ours, we wanted to let justice have its course to prevent God's being offended by the defamation of its members. It happened, when the final sentence was passed, that there were present in Rome three persons who in the quality of judges had heard the indictment against me, one at Alcala, one at Paris, and the other at Venice. In all these eight trials, by God's grace and mercy alone, not a single proposition, not a syllable even of mine, was condemned. Nor was I punished or banished for any more serious charge.

And if your highness wishes to know why there was so much indignant investigation of my case, you should be advised that there was never any question of being involved with schismatics or Lutherans or Illuminati, for I never knew any of them or had anything to do with them. The reason, particularly in Spain, was that I, being without education, should venture to speak at such length on spiritual subjects. People were surprised at this. The fact is—and our Lord, who is my Creator and judge, will be my witness—that not for all the power and wealth under heaven could I wish not to have gone through this experience. It is my desire to have as much and ever more to suffer in the future for the greater glory of His Divine Majesty.

If, therefore, some report of these happenings should reach your highness, I am sure that, with the perfect grace and gentleness which His Divine Majesty has bestowed on your highness for His greater service and praise, your highness will take time to recognize His graces and will be able to distinguish what is good from what is bad, to your own advantage. You will understand that, the more we desire to succeed, apart from offense on the part of our neighbor, in clothing ourselves with the livery of Christ our Lord which is woven out of insult, false witness, and every other kind of injustice, the more we shall advance in spirit and earn those spiritual riches with which, if we are leading spiritual lives, our souls desire to be adorned.

In view of the great desire which Ours have here of seeing Master Simon and because of the need we have of taking thought in matters which touch the Society closely, we humbly beg your highness, for God's glory, graciously and affectionately to give the permission, which his holiness has already given. I have the greatest confidence that his coming here together with the others from whom we expect such help will be for the service of His Divine Majesty and of your highness, to whom the Society belongs more than it does to us.

I pray that her majesty will consider this letter as addressed to herself, and to her kindness and prayers I humbly commend myself in our Lord, begging that He in His infinite goodness will give us His perfect grace to know His most holy will and perfectly to fulfill it.

¶ TO CARDINAL MARCELLUS CERVINI
1, 300-02, Letter 83

Marcellus Cervini, the future Pope Marcellus II, was one of the most prominent of the reforming cardinals in the court of Paul III. He had submitted to the pope the outline of the Institute drawn up by Ignatius in 1539. He always strove to protect the newborn Society and lavished all his affection on it. At the Council of Trent he became the pope's legate. In the present letter the saint expresses the desire that the Council be attended with every success. He sends the cardinal news of Simon Rodrigues and recommends him. He also recommends Le Jay, who will be at Trent as theologian. Le Jay was one of the first companions of Ignatius. From 1541 to his death he was an apostle in Germany.

Rome, April 15, 1545

IHS

Most reverend Monsignor and Father in Jesus to whom I owe all respect.

May the sovereign grace and everlasting love of our Lord Jesus Christ greet and visit your lordship with the abundance of His mercies, as He is wont to visit always and instruct and console the souls for whom He has a special love, especially in times of such urgent need and supreme importance as the present.

May it please His Divine Majesty that all things be accomplished according to your lordship's desires, as well as our own (unworthy of mention as we are), for His greater praise and everlasting glory.

Within the last four days I have received three packets of letters from Portugal, each bearing a different date. In one of them there was a letter from Araoz for your most reverend lordship, which I am sending along with this. I believe it is old, judging from the other letters which came with it. Later, in another packet of March 3, he wrote me that Master Peter Faber and he had already got the king's permission to go to the princess in Castile and that they were on the point of setting out.[1] By God's grace, if my understanding of all that has taken place in Portugal is correct, the members of our Society there, which Society is more yours than ours, are walking in the right path, rather with a great deal of filial respect and not at all in the way that rumor had it there. Moreover, Master Simon, who is the superior of Ours in Portugal, about whom most of the rumors circulating here had to do, writes us to urge us to talk with his holiness or to write to the king to allow him to come here to Rome, as he has a great desire to be here with us. As we are of one mind on this point, I have sent him the kind permission of his holiness. If he leaves Portugal this coming September, we have every hope of seeing him here in November. When he arrives your most reverend lordship will deign, I am sure, to take him under your protection and have him at your service, in our Lord.

---

[1] The Princess Mary, daughter of John III, the first wife of Philip II.

May God in His infinite and sovereign bounty keep your most reverend lordship and enlighten and instruct you to His greater praise and glory.

POSTSCRIPT. I have news of Master Le Jay, who is with the most reverend cardinal of Augsburg. His most reverend lordship is so satisfied with Le Jay that he wishes to have him go to the council. Le Jay says that, if no other command is sent him from here, he will do as the cardinal wishes. I would never have sent him to the council, although I am quite satisfied with him. And yet I do not wish to stand in the way. I recommend the matter to God. Should your eminence go to the council, may you deign to look upon Le Jay, in my stead, as your ever-faithful and affectionate servant in our Lord.[2]

¶ TO FRANCIS BORGIA, DUKE OF GANDIA

I, 339-43, Letter 101

Ignatius exalts the saintly duke and, humbling himself, gives him admirable direction on the perfect union of man with God, the value of God's grace, the obstacles which souls oppose to it, and the fruit of frequent Communion. He ends with a courteous plea for the College of Gandia.

Rome, end of 1545

My Lord in our Lord.

May the perfect love and everlasting favor of our Lord visit and abide with your lordship.

On the last of October I received your letter of July 24, written in your own hand. It has given me more than a little joy in our Lord to learn from it of matters that are drawn rather from an interior experience than from anything external—an experience which our Lord in His infinite goodness usually gives to those souls to render themselves entirely to Him as the beginning, middle, and end of all our good. May His holy name be praised and exalted in all and by all creatures, which are created and ordained to an end that is so just and proper.

---

[2] As a matter of fact, Le Jay accompanied Cardinal Otto Truchsess, bishop of Augsburg, to the Council of Trent, arriving there in December 1545. He was received with great kindness, especially by Cardinal Cervini.

But to come to particulars, I will take some of the points about which you write, as they come to mind. You ask that I be not unmindful of you in my prayers and that I give you the consolation of writing you. I have remembered you in my prayers and do still daily, and I hope in our Lord that, if they win you any favor, it will be entirely from on high, descending from His infinite goodness. Were I to consider only God's eternal and perfect liberality and the devotion and holy purpose of your lordship, I should be convinced that, in seeing you so spiritually minded, I have not failed you in the past. As to the consolation of my letters of which your lordship speaks, I find it easy to persuade myself that your lordship will find consolation not only in these letters but in all things, seeing that, when men abandon themselves to belong to their Creator, they gain an intimate knowledge which is full of consolation of how our eternal good persists throughout all creation, giving each creature existence and preserving it in His own infinite being and presence. These considerations, I am sure, and many others will provide you with an abundance of consolation. For we know that all creatures are at the service of those who love God entirely and that they help them to even greater merit, joy, and union through an intense charity for their Creator and Lord, despite the fact that the creature often opposes obstacles, as your lordship so well observes, to the effects our Lord wishes to produce in the soul.

Not only does man set up these obstacles before receiving these graces, gifts, and consolations of the Holy Spirit, but even after he has received them; graces of consolation in which all darkness and restless worry are removed from the soul, and the soul itself is adorned with the spiritual blessings that bring it contentment and cause it to fall in love with the things that continue in endless glory. Even then we allow ourselves to be distracted with thoughts about trifles, without knowing how to keep so heavenly a blessing. In fact, we set up obstacles before our Lord lavishes His graces upon us and after He has done so, with the result that we fail to retain them.

Your lordship mentions such obstacles, more to lower yourself in our Lord and to exalt us who wish to abase ourselves, when you say, relying on what you hear from Araoz in Portugal, that this Society places no obstacles to what our Lord desires to work in it. For my part, I am convinced that I am nothing but obstacle, both before and after, and I find this a source of greater satisfaction and spiritual consolation in our Lord because I can thus attribute nothing to myself which has any appearance of good. I am convinced of this one thing, with due regard for the opinion of others who are better informed, that there are very few in this world—nay, I will go further and say that there is no one—who during this mortal life can properly judge how far he is an obstacle and to what extent he resists the workings of God's grace in his soul. I am quite satisfied that, the more advanced and experienced and perfect one is in humility and charity, the more one will be aware, even in the most insignificant thoughts, of the slightest things that stand in his way and oppose him, even though they may appear to be of little or no importance. And yet we shall never, in this life at least, have a full knowledge of our obstacles and faults, as the prophet asks to be freed from the faults he knows not,[1] and St. Paul[2] admitting that he is ignorant of them, adds that he is not for that reason justified.

As I understand from your letters, our Lord, who is to be my judge, makes you in His infinite mercy a scholar in so holy a school. This is a fact which you cannot deny if you look into your own soul. It is my earnest wish in our Lord that you do your very best to recruit as many fellow scholars as possible, beginning with the members of your own household (to whom we are most obligated), and bring them by the surest and most direct way to His Divine Majesty. Now, since this way is none other than Christ our Lord, as He Himself says,[3] I give many thanks to His Divine Goodness because your lordship approaches the altar frequently to receive Him, according to what I have heard here. Besides the many rich graces which the soul gains in the reception of her Creator and Lord, there is one that is particularly outstanding, since it is one that will not permit a man to remain long and obstinately in sin. But as soon as one falls into what we call little sins—if any can be called little when the object[4] is the infinite and the supreme good—He raises him up again with renewed and increased strength and a firmer determination to serve his Creator and Lord.

As you advance in this way with the help of God's grace, and make use of the gifts which the Divine Majesty has mercifully bestowed upon you in order to win your brethren and your neighbors, you make me your debtor, without merit on my part, because of the desire I feel to imitate your lordship.

You write that you desire to have some share in the business affairs which weigh so heavily upon me here in the governing of our Society, a task which has been laid upon me by God's will, or permitted by His

---

[1] "From my secret ones cleanse me, O Lord" (Psalm 18:13).
[2] "For I am not conscious to myself of anything, yet am I not hereby justified; but he that judgeth me is the Lord" (1 Corinthians 4:4).
[3] "I am the way, . . ." (John 14:6). [4] Object; that is, God, who is offended.

eternal goodness as a punishment for my great and fearful sins. I beg your lordship by the love and reverence of God our Lord to help me with your prayers, and also to be good enough to help me by taking charge of the government and seeing to the completion of a house or college that is desired in Gandia for the scholastics[5] of the Society which is not only your lordship's but also the lady duchess'[6] and the Lady Joan's,[7] her sister. It was at the request of your lordship, which for us is a command, that these scholastics were received, and we hope that you will continue to help the establishment with your favor and protection in our Lord, as you may judge to be to His greater glory. We are now all the more delighted in the Divine Goodness that a relative[8] of the lady duchess has entered, as your lordship writes me, and that her ladyship is so pleased. I beg your lordship to recommend me to the favor and prayers of her ladyship and to those of the Lady Joan. In closing, I ask the Divine Majesty to grant us the fullness of His grace, so that we may know His holy will and perfectly fulfill it.

¶ TO FATHER LE JAY

I, 343-44, Letter 102

Father Le Jay was in Dilligen (Bavaria), defending the Catholic faith against the violent attacks of the Protestants. St. Ignatius writes to suggest expedients to prepare the return to the bosom of the Church of the unfortunate Father Bernard Ochino,[1] who was first a Franciscan, then a Capuchin and general of his order, and finally a Lutheran heretic.

Rome, December 12, 1545

✠

The purpose of this letter (which must be kept confidential) is to give you information which will help you to understand and handle this im-

---

[5] November 16, 1545 five young Jesuits had come from Portugal to Gandia.
[6] Eleanor de Castro, wife of Francis Borgia.
[7] Joan de Meneses. This placing the Society in the possession of its friends is an expression of courtesy common in Spain. A host will assure his guest that the house is his. St. Ignatius makes frequent use of such expressions.
[8] Ignatius is apparently referring to the Portuguese Anthony de Muniz. His name will recur in the letters, especially Letter 121.
[1] Bernard Ochino was born at Siena in 1487 and died at Schlakow in Moravia in 1564. He was first an observant Franciscan, but passed to the Capuchins in 1534, among whom he acquired a great reputation for religious observance, and became master general of the order. In September 1542 he left Italy, went to Geneva, and became a Lutheran.

portant work of charity, the success of which will mean so much for God's glory. Briefly, then, a very charitable person who is familiarly acquainted with Father Bernard came to speak to me and make me acquainted with the affair. It was his design to take a middle course and to provide some satisfactory means whereby a pardon could be obtained. I answered him that, if I had a letter from him, without which I did not think it possible to approach the pope or anyone else, I would do everything in my power. Thereupon this person offered to write and ask for such a letter. Taking advantage of this, you might try to visit Ochino in some way or other, without letting him know of this request of mine. As you say, you are close at hand, and I think it would help to make such a visit, if you think it proper, and learn what you can from him. Assure him that we should be glad to help him, in all charity, in any way possible, if he would only grasp the opportunity of making use of our help in the Lord. Besides this, you might try to move him, by asking him what he is about and what he can hope for, and tell him that everything can be arranged, and offer your services to see to it that the matter is favorably arranged here at Rome. If he shows signs of fear, promise him the good offices of the Society, for besides myself Master Lainez and Master Salmeron are also here. As to his person and all his concerns, he should think of us as of one mind with himself. Whether you get a letter from him, or whatever else you do in our Lord, he should not know that we have written you from here. Write us very briefly whatever happens.

By no means should he know of our letter.

¶ TO DOCTOR PETER ORTIZ

I, 354-56, Letter 109

This learned doctor, a close friend of St. Ignatius, held a benefice with the care of souls in Galapagar (Madrid), and was thinking of turning it over to the Society if the latter would agree to supply an incumbent to assume the obligations of the benefice in perpetuum. *In the part of the letter that follows Ignatius thanks him for the offer but declines the benefice and gives his reasons for so doing.*

Rome, beginning of 1546

IHS

As to the benefice, it could be held only by a professed member of the Society. I realize that, by reducing expenditures to a minimum, this benefice would make a good provision for the house or college which might be founded in Alcala. I should be very glad in our Lord if I could accept it because of some other fruit that might accrue for the general good of souls or even of this Society, which is wholly yours, and thus cooperate with your good intention and devotion to me personally. But as we profess to have neither communal nor individual incomes—a profession which has been confirmed by several bulls of his holiness—we would not venture to turn our back on a more perfect practice to one that is less perfect. Rather we should ask our Lord for His greater praise and service, to take us out of this life sooner than that we should give such an example to those who must come after us. And while the episcopacy and the care of souls supposes perfection already achieved and the entrance into religion only the beginning of perfection, it is always more perfect in religion to be without sources of revenue, whether they belong to individuals or to the community. Even supposing benefices which provide for individuals in religion were for the great advantage of the Church in general, as is probable, and certain, if the beneficed persons suffer no loss of spirit after accepting their benefices, yet, as there are many different ways in which Divine Providence could reform the Church universal, we have deemed it safer and better for us to make our way with as little encumbrance as possible in our Lord, following the divine example which He Himself has given to us. It is His example which we in all humility are most eager to understand more clearly.

Consequently, when we received word of your holy and most charitable intention and your determination to translate it into action, we received it as we were wont to, with a sense of increased indebtedness, just as if your project had issued in the effect you desire. To come to a decision, which seemed to be a foregone conclusion, we took three days during which all the priests of the house—and we are twelve—celebrated Mass, and the nonpriests, twenty in number, were asked to offer prayers for our intention. It was our intention that our own opinion and inclination should be in no detail at variance with God's will, but that His greater service and praise be accomplished in all of us. The result was a unanimous approval and confirmation of our first opinion, which was to exclude entirely all revenues, both those held in common and those held by individuals, and render ourselves safe from strife and litigation of every kind.

I have discussed this point and several others with Señor Salazar, and I think from all that he has told me that he intends to write you a detailed explanation.

¶ TO FATHER PETER DE SOTO
1, 363-65, Letter 115

Father De Soto, a Dominican, was confessor and unofficial adviser to Charles V and had accompanied him to Germany. Ignatius asks him to use his influence in behalf of Francis de Lasso, who had incurred the enmity of a Hungarian noble. There were wrongs on both sides, and these gentlemen had carried their quarrel to the extent of exchanging blows. Francis' slap was returned with the blow of a club. Ignatius, who was always a man of peace, hoped that Father De Soto might use his good offices for a restoration of peace.

Rome, February 20, 1546

IHS

May the sovereign grace and everlasting love of Christ our Lord and Creator greet your paternity and bring an increase of His gifts and graces for His greater service, praise, and glory.

Although I am quite unknown to your paternity, being a man of little substance and less influence, an occasion of doing a good and holy work offers itself, to which I should like to call your paternity's attention. John de Vega thinks that I should intervene and advises me to do so. In all things I look upon him as my lord in our Lord; and as his lordship is also writing, I cannot help writing myself. I have the greatest hope in your charity, that you will obtain the favor I ask, although I am aware that I can offer you no merits of my own.

The case is this. In order to get creatures to break away from their Creator and Lord, it happens, as your paternity may have heard, that the enemy of our human nature has done and is now doing his very best to foment a bitter enmity between Señor Francis de Lasso and a nobleman of Hungary. He is trying to make the enmity grow ever worse and has brought them to the point of losing soul and body and all they own, which is little enough, unless God our Lord apply some remedy with His own hand or make use of other means that are pleasing to His Divine Goodness. A memorandum, which I enclose, will give you full details.

I am convinced of your great zeal for God's greater glory and that no remedy will be so efficacious, especially in a matter of this kind, as your intervention with his imperial majesty. His majesty will take the matter under advisement and do something about it in that same Christian spirit which he has so often displayed on other occasions of greater importance. He can easily put a stop to these bitter quarrels, especially as there is little to choose between the two interested parties, one being about as bad as the other. I have therefore thought it my duty to call your attention to this holy opportunity as one most worthy of your paternity. And I am all the more convinced because the undertaking itself, without any urging in our Lord on my part, is one to appeal to your paternity as likely of its nature to meet with success.

He who can do all things will reward your paternity, and I will remain ever beholden to you. I may never be able, because of my little influence or authority, to make you any practical return, but I shall cherish at least an ever-growing desire of being of service to you. To love and serve the true servants of our Lord is really loving and serving the Lord of all; and this I will do on every occasion that will be within my means, to the greater glory of His Divine Majesty.

May He deign in His infinite and supreme goodness to give us His abundant grace to know His most holy will and perfectly to fulfill it.

¶ TO ANDREW LIPPOMANI[1]
I, 366-67, Letter 117

The fathers are of one opinion, that Lippomani should retain the management of his property and that he decide at his convenience what help he is to give to the College of Padua. The Society will be grateful for anything he decides to do. The text of the letter is in Italian.

Rome, February 22, 1546

✠

Very Reverend Sir.

We are aware of the great readiness and the ardent desire with which God our Lord has inspired your lordship, especially as to helping the scholastics of our order, and up to the present we have felt the effects of this desire. We know too that His Divine Majesty loves gratitude and is displeased by ingratitude, and that is why I and all the professed brethren of the Society—those of us who are present in Rome and in the name of those who are absent—humbly beg your lordship to be good enough to keep in your own hands the administration, not merely of half

---

[1] Andrew Lippomani had given half of the revenues of his Priory of the Holy Trinity, a possession of the Teutonic order, as a foundation for the college in Padua. A bull of Paul III authorized this grant. Ignatius, the better to signify his thanks (*Chronicon*, I, 172), begs the prior to be good enough to keep in his own hands the administration of all these revenues.

of the revenues of the priory, according to the concession of his holiness, but even all of them, during all the time that our Lord will give you in this life. We hope that there is still many a long day remaining to you in God's service. Your lordship will be able to preserve, increase, and even diminish the part that belongs to the scholastics at Padua, with all the liberty that was yours before you made this sacrifice to our Lord. We ourselves will look upon your acceptance of this task as a very great favor. For in this way you will not only be offering us goods that are external but your own person, which is a great deal more, since you are good enough to take this fatherly care of us, so many proofs of which you have given us up to this in such abundance.

In witness of this decision, I sign and seal this letter with my name and the seal of the Society of Jesus.

¶ TO FRANCIS BORGIA, DUKE OF GANDIA

1, 379-82, Letter 121

An answer to a letter of Borgia's. He is awaiting the dean from Gandia, and will treat of Borgia's college with him. He commends to the duke and duchess the task of restoring discipline to some of the monasteries of Catalonia. He writes that Anthony de Muniz gives many signs of repentance, and tells him that some of the members of the Society are destined for Trent.

Rome, April 23, 1546

IHS

My Lord in our Lord.

May the sovereign grace and everlasting love of Christ our Lord greet and visit your lordship.

It is some fifteen days since I received your lordship's letter dated January 16. May it please our Lord, who is waiting to judge and redeem us by means of His infinite mercy, always to give your lordship a full understanding of the great spiritual joy we received along with your letter and all the letters that we receive from you.

To give an answer that will cover everything, or at least what is more important, where everything is spiritual that has to do with the greater thirst for those ever-living waters, it seems to me—not to put a hand in another's harvest—that it belongs to Him who gave such a thirst to bring it to full fruit after having planted and watered. In like manner, since He can do everything and since He wishes to do everything in favor of souls who are disposed and desirous of His greater service, praise, and glory, I am persuaded that His Divine Majesty will throughout provide for and console those, as He is wont to do, who walk in purity of heart. There is no need of my enlarging on this point.

As to the affairs of the college, we shall talk about them, please God, when Dean Rocca comes. I trust that in His divine goodness He will not permit me to be mistaken in matters that concern His service and that of your lordship, and that everyone will in all respects be content spiritually, and that the great love and confidence your lordship entertains for us, unworthy as we are, will not be in vain.

As to the fresh desires which God our Lord has given us (as I am able to see and understand in His Divine Majesty) to help in the reform of the nunneries of Catalonia, your lordship will have more information in the memorandum which I am enclosing. The more difficult and laborious the project seems, the more worthy it appears of your lordship and of those persons who are filled with fervor and zeal for the honor of God our Lord. And therefore, by His love and reverence, I beg your lordship and her ladyship the duchess[1] (who according to the information we have is very skilled and practiced in applying the proper spiritual remedies to ordinary affairs) to take very much to heart this holy enterprise of the Divine Goodness, and to be as vigilant and as earnest as possible about it, according to the more detailed instructions that are enclosed.

Muniz, who I hear is related to my lady the duchess, become pilgrim and wearing a heavy and strange garment, barefooted and penniless, arrived in Rome on the twelfth of this month and took shelter in the Hospital of St. Anthony of the Portuguese. From there he wrote me a letter which I am sending along with this. I had him leave the hospital at once, and received him as a guest in a house that belongs to us, and supplied all his needs. He did not, however, sleep or eat with us, so there was no killing of the fatted calf on finding him who was lost. I have not yet made any attempt to speak with him in order the better to help him. And so, deeply moved and regardless of being recognized, he made the stations in Rome, stripped to the waist and taking the discipline. He was not gentle with himself but, as I am told, scourged himself till the blood ran. On other days he tried to preach, and begged alms from door to door throughout the city. When I heard of these doings I sent him word that he was

---

[1] The duchess mentioned here by St. Ignatius was Francis' wife, Eleanor de Castro.

to stop them, and tomorrow or the next day we would have a talk together.² I hope in our Lord (I still retain something of a natural feeling of affection, or better, a certain devotion toward my lady the duchess, since in a sense the matter bears some relation to her), that the Divine Majesty bring this acquaintance which has just begun to a happy growth in the future.

As to her ladyship's wish that the licentiate Araoz return to you some time, there should be no difficulty. These last few days his holiness has given orders that some of Ours should attend the council, and has put the responsibility of the appointment on me. After having had recourse for several days to God our Lord in our prayers and Masses, I have appointed Masters Peter Faber, Lainez, and Salmeron, besides Master Le Jay, one of Ours who is already at Trent. I have written to the prince to this effect and to the new Archbishop of Toledo and to Faber himself. It is believed that he is at the moment nearer Rome than Gandia. Consequently nothing should stand in the way of Araoz' visiting your lordships. But being alone in Spain, I am sure that he will have more than enough to do. As far as I can to God's glory, I will always be at the service of her ladyship, and I will be glad to write her and to my lady Doña Joan, who should consider this letter as written to her also.

I close, asking the Divine Majesty by His infinite and sovereign goodness to give us His bountiful grace to know His most holy will and perfectly to fulfill it.

¶ TO THE FATHERS AT THE COUNCIL OF TRENT

I, 386-89, Letter 123

Fathers James Lainez and Alphonse Salmeron were present as papal theologians at the first session of the Council of Trent. They arrived

---

² Anthony de Muniz was a Portuguese noble who had entered the Society in 1544 and who was sent with Father James Miron to Gandia to found the college there. On his return to Portugal, acting on the suggestion of a brother, his early fervor having cooled in the meantime—or as Father Balthasar Tellez reports, deceived by the enemy with desires of greater penance and prayer—he fled from the College of Coimbra with the purpose of spending his life as a pilgrim, wandering about from shrine to shrine. But he could not silence the reproaches of his conscience; and after he had first made the pilgrimage to Santiago in Galicia and later to Montserrat, our Lady opened his eyes and changed his heart. He then went to Rome, where, repenting the past, he carried on as the saint relates, and died shortly after of grief.

at Trent on May 18, 1546. Father Claude Le Jay had been there since December 1545 as representative of Cardinal Truchsess, bishop of Augsburg. Ignatius addressed the following excellent instruction to these three priests. He offers them some ideas for dealing effectively with others. He advises them to continue preaching, hearing confessions, and performing their other priestly duties while in Trent. Finally, he points out ways in which they can help themselves to work more effectively.

Rome, first months of 1546

IHS

Instruction on dealing with others

1. As associating and dealing with many people for the salvation and spiritual progress of souls can be very profitable with God's help, so on the other hand, if we are not on our guard and helped by God's grace, such association can be the occasion of great loss to ourselves and sometimes to all concerned. In keeping with our profession we cannot withdraw from such association and therefore, the more prepared we are to proceed according to a common plan, the more we are likely to succeed in our Lord. In the following notes, which may be modified or amplified at need, we may be able to offer some assistance.

2. Be slow to speak. Be considerate and kindly, especially when it comes to defining matters which are being discussed or likely to be discussed in the council.

3. Be slow to speak, and only after having first listened quietly, so that you may understand the meaning, leanings, and desires of those who speak. You will thus know better when to speak and when to be silent.

4. When such matters are being discussed, I should rather consider the reasons on both sides without showing any attachment to my own opinion, and try to avoid causing dissatisfaction to anyone.

5. I should not cite anyone as supporting my opinion, especially if they are persons of importance, unless the matter has been well considered. And I will deal on an equal basis with all, without taking sides with any.

6. If the matters discussed are of such a nature that you cannot or ought not to be silent, give your opinion with the greatest possible calmness and humility, and always end with the words, "salvo meliori iudicio—with due respect for a better opinion."

7. Finally, if some point of human or divine science is under discussion and I have something to say, it will be of great help to be unmindful of my own leisure or lack of time—that is, my own convenience. Rather

I should accommodate myself to the convenience of him with whom I am to deal, in order to influence him to God's greater glory.

In the ministry

1. While in Trent, Ours should try to remain together in some reputable district. And what they should especially seek to accomplish for God's greater glory is to preach, hear confessions, lecture, instruct children, give good example, visit the poor in the hospitals, exhort the neighbor according to the amount of talent which each is conscious of possessing, so as to move as many as possible to prayer and devotion. Pray and induce others to pray particularly to God our Lord, beseeching His Divine Majesty to deign to pour forth His Holy Spirit on all those who take part in the discussions of the august council, so that the Holy Spirit should descend in greater abundance with His grace and gifts upon the council.

2. In your sermons do not touch on subjects on which Catholics and Protestants are at variance, but simply exhort your hearers to virtue and devotion, devotions approved by the Church. Awaken in souls a thorough knowledge of themselves and a love of their Creator and Lord. Speak frequently of the council, and always end your sermons, as we have said, with a prayer for the council.

3. In lecturing follow the same rules as you do in preaching, and thus try to enkindle in souls a love of their Creator and Lord, explaining the meaning of the passage read, and have your hearers pray as has been indicated.

4. When you hear confessions remember to tell your penitents what you taught in public. Let the penance imposed consist of prayers for the council.

5. In giving the Exercises also, and in other conversations, remember that you are practically speaking in public. Recall that only the Exercises of the first week are to be given to all in general, unless you are dealing with very special persons who are prepared to dispose of their lives according to the manner of the elections. Even such persons should not be allowed to make any promise, either during the Exercises or at the end; nor should they be sent into retirement, especially at the beginning. Later on, if time allows, they might do so, but always with moderation, and especially if the Exercises are to be given in their entirety. Prayers for the council should also be said.

6. You should teach little boys for some suitable time according to convenient arrangements, which will vary in different places. Begin with the first rudiments, and explain them in keeping with the needs of your

hearers. When you finish with such instruction recite some prayers for the council.

7. Visit the hospitals at a convenient hour, one that will not be injurious to health. Hear the confessions of the poor, and console them, and even bring them some little gift if you can. Have them pray, as I have suggested when speaking of hearing confessions. If you are at least three, each should take his turn, a day at a time, twice a week.

8. Exhort those with whom you come into contact to frequent confession and Communion, or the celebration of Mass. Have them make the Exercises and perform other works of piety. Encourage them also to pray for the council.

9. Here also, as in the matter of discussing doctrines to be defined, it will be better to be slow to speak and to speak little, as I have said. But on the other hand, if you wish to urge souls to make progress in the spiritual life, it will be better to speak at length, methodically, and with kindness and affection.

Some self-helps

Take an hour at night in which each can share with the others what has been done that day and discuss plans for the morrow.

We should agree on matters, both past and future, by vote, or in some other way.

One night, let one of you ask the others to correct him in what he may have done amiss. And he who is corrected should make no answer unless he is asked to explain the matter about which he has been corrected. Another night, the second will do likewise. And thus each one in turn, so that all can be helped with greater charity and will enjoy better esteem everywhere.

Make resolutions in the morning and twice in the course of the day make the examen.

This order should begin within five days of your arrival at Trent. Amen.

¶ TO PETER CANISIUS
I, 390-94, Letter 124

Peter Canisius, the son of a wealthy burgomaster, pledged himself to celibacy shortly after his graduation from the University of Cologne in 1540. Three years later he visited his friend, Peter Faber, made the Exercises under him, and was admitted into the Society. He and several other companions built the first German house of the order at Cologne. During this time Peter also preached, debated, and taught at the university. In 1546 he was admitted to the priesthood and shortly afterwards was sent on a mission to obtain assistance against the apostate archbishop, Hermann von Wied. Ignatius rejoices in the triumphs of Peter.

Rome, June 2, 1546

JHESUS

May the grace and peace of our Lord Jesus Christ be with you and all of Ours. Amen.

It is a great joy to me when I see that the name of our Lord Jesus Christ is made manifest to all in His Church by virtue of His blood, and that it grows and produced fruit in so many. We give thanks to God for this ineffable mercy and kindness with which He overwhelms us through the power of His glorious name. I am deeply moved when I hear or behold with my own eyes the work which you and others who are called to the Society are accomplishing in Christ Jesus.

Courage, then, courage! Be comforted in the Lord and in the strength of His power,[1] which is Christ Jesus our Lord and God. He died for our sins[2] and rose for our justification.[3] And He has quickened us together with Him and He has caused us to sit with Him in heaven,[4] in God. Study and ponder the vocation to which you have been called. Make use of the grace which in Christ has been given you,[5] keep close to it, trade with it, never allow it to remain idle in you, never resist it. The same Lord it is who worketh in us both to will and to accomplish, according to His good will,[6] which is in itself infinite and all-glorious and ineffable for us through Christ Jesus. For the Spirit of Jesus will give thee in all things understanding[7] and fortitude, to the end that through you the name of Jesus will be glorified and bear much fruit in many souls, with the hope of a better life.

I write this to you with the idea of giving spurs to the willing horse, as the proverb goes. For the rest, you have won all our love in the Lord by your fearless activity in the Lord's vineyard and have led me to form the great hope that Jesus Christ will be glorified in you right to the end.

By order of the Reverend Father Master Ignatius.

---

[1] Ephesians 6:10.
[2] 1 Corinthians 15:3.
[3] Romans 4:25.
[4] Ephesians 2:6.
[5] Romans 12:3.
[6] Philippians 2:13.
[7] 2 Timothy 2:7.

¶ TO THE FATHERS AND BROTHERS AT COIMBRA

1, 405-07, Letter 131

An account of the death of Peter Faber, written at the wish of St. Ignatius by Bartholomew Ferrao.

Rome, August 8, 1546

May the sovereign grace and everlasting love of Christ our Lord ever be our help and support.

The greater a good is, the readier we should be to choose it; and once chosen, the greater should be our delight in it. And when this relish and delight is spiritual and eternal, there can be no reason for finding sadness or uneasiness in it. And this is true whether the joy belong to us or to our neighbor. Union of will between the creature and the Creator is the greatest good in this life, but it becomes much greater and a possession without end in the vision of the life to come. A good such as this last must be the object of our choice, preference, and desire, and must be accepted when it is offered by the Giver of all good, because it means the end of all our ills, the endless plenitude of grace and glory, and the ultimate expression of God's will. This Giver of all good, who is in the highest degree the provider of all things, has no need of anyone, except him whom He wishes to choose for a service. What He most wishes is to bring all men who are good to Himself, this being the end for which He created them. And then, too, since the Ultimate Good has the power and the wisdom to dispose all things as He pleases, even His infinite power setting no limit, it is man's duty constantly to desire all this, since, after all, we can do nothing of ourselves but incur displeasure (does not the just man fall seven times a day?).[1] God on the other hand preserves and bestows grace. It was the knowledge of this that prompted such reserve in the prayer of St. Martin when he added the condition, "But if I am still necessary to Thy people, Lord . . ."[2]

Now this necessity, it would seem, is pleasing to His Divine Majesty just now, because it will promote His greater glory. There are some whom God has in mind who will have to practice patience, even Father Master Ignatius; he because he must tarry here, and we because we cannot go on. And yet there is much joy withal because while we live here we have so good a guide and because a second representative of the Society and faith-

---

[1] Proverbs 24:16.
[2] "But if I am still necessary to Thy people, O Lord, I do not refuse the labor" (*Breviarium Romanum*, Office of St. Martin, bishop, Lesson V).

ful intercessor should go on and be there now, the Reverend Master Peter Faber, of happy memory, who on the Feast of St. Peter, August 1, God so willing, was freed from the bonds of this death, and took leave of us happily in the Lord, just as Master John Codure, our first representative, died on his own name's day, the Feast of the Decollation of St. John Baptist. Their souls are now united in heaven, and their bodies here, in Our Lady of the Wayside, here in Rome, to keep us company.

The Divine Goodness so arranging it, he died as I shall recount. After an absence from Rome of eight years, more or less, and traveling through many lands under holy obedience, he returned to Rome in perfectly good health on July 17. For a week we and his friends all enjoyed his company in our Lord. But in another week he was taken down with an intermittent fever of more than ordinary violence and finally, on the first of August, as I said, the Feast of St. Peter in Chains, being Sunday, he heard Mass, received Communion, having confessed the preceding Saturday night, and extreme unction. And then between noon and the hours of Vespers, in the presence of the whole community and a number of friends who had come to see him, he rendered up his soul to his Creator and Lord.

Everywhere we have need of the intercession of friends and saints, and we all hope that in the Divine Majesty—His will being now fulfilled—Peter will now be no less a source of help to us than he would be if he were living among us. In all things and always may His divine and sovereign Goodness be praised and glorified. Amen. Amen.

By commission of Father Master Ignatius, Bartholomew Ferrao.[3]

¶ TO DOIMO NASCIO

I, 408-09, Letter 132

This letter is addressed to Master Doimo. His name appears in a variety of forms in the correspondence of the Society of which he was a warm friend: Doimus, sometimes Doymus, with greater freedom in the surname, Nascius, Naucius, Nascio, and Naggio. In 1556 he presented the Society with a house in Ameria, and even wished to make a gift of himself. After he had been in probation for a few days in 1555, it was decided

---

[3] Bartholomew Ferrao was of Portuguese origin and was Ignatius' secretary before Polanco took over that work. It speaks volumes for Ignatius' editorial patience for allowing his long-winded introduction to stand. He did not even delete one of his supposedly vigorous Amens! Father Ferrao wrote another long letter to Father Michael de Torres, which will be found in this collection.

that it might be better for him to serve God without the obligation of obedience. This letter is an answer to a religious who had threatened to burn every Jesuit that he found between Perpignan and Seville. For Ignatius this was a familiar threat. A similar incident had occurred in Alcala.

Rome, August 10, 1546

JHS

Master Doimo.

Tell Father Barbaran that, as he says he will have burned all of Ours to be found between Perpignan and Seville, it is also my desire that both he and all his friends and acquaintances, not only between Perpignan and Seville but throughout the whole world, should be enkindled and inflamed by the Holy Spirit, and that by thus reaching a high degree of perfection they will be distinguished in the glory of His Divine Majesty.

Tell him also that a trial is in progress before their lordships, the governor and the vicar of his holiness, in which our fortunes are at stake, and that they are about to pass judgment. If he has anything against us, I invite him to come and submit his proofs before the above-mentioned judges. Should the sentence go against us, I should rejoice the more if I alone were to suffer, and thus save all those between Perpignan and Seville from being burned.

¶ TO MICHAEL DE TORRES[1]
I, 421-23, Letter 136

About the time this letter was written there was something of an epidemic of feminine vocations to the Society. Isabel Roser set the example. She went to Rome in 1543 and obtained permission from Paul III and Ignatius to make her profession in 1545, together with two companions, Frances Cruyllas and Lucretia Brandina.[2] Other generous women dreamed of the same ideal of life; women of rank, such as Anna Coutinho, Eleanor Mascarenhas, Joan de Meneses, and Joan de Cardona. Fathers

---

[1] Michael de Torres was an Aragonese by birth, had known Ignatius at Paris, and was one of the glories of Alcala. He spent some years at Rome as the representative of that university in a suit against Tavera, archbishop of Toledo (*Chronicon*, I, 169, 185). He was a theologian of solid learning and an experienced man of affairs. He entered the Society at Rome itself, and thereafter enjoyed the complete confidence of Ignatius, who entrusted important missions in Spain to him, and especially this matter of the Jesuitesses of Gandia. The present memorial was placed in the hands of this trusted agent.

[2] *Epistolae et instructiones*, I, 382; *Epistolae mixtae*, I, 109, 117, 125, 245, 268, 282, 311, 322, 335; *Scripta de S. Ignatio*, I, 11.

Araoz and Oviedo, who received their confidences at Evora, Gandia, and Valencia, were in favor of the project.[3] *Joan de Cardona sent burning appeals to Ignatius,*[4] *as did Sebastiana Exarch.*

If the affaire Roser *had not taken such an unfortunate turn, the saint would have been quite embarrassed. But Isabel Roser was a woman of little poise. She and her nephew, Francis Ferrer, spread the report in Rome that Ignatius was out for their fortune. Ignatius insisted on an official examination of their financial relations, which revealed that they were in debt to him and not he to them. He had Isabel Roser's retractation and that of her nephew entered on the official record.*[5] *His experience dictated his conclusion to break with the idea of an order for women. First an oral decision of Paul III and later an official brief liberated him from all care, present and future, of congregations of women. He had annulled the resignation of property made by Isabel Roser to Michael de Torres*[6] *and released her from all vows to the Society, October 1, 1546.*[7] *It was in the midst of these happenings that he gave the following instructions to Michael de Torres.*

September 10, 1546

IHS

A foundation of religious women subject to the Society is not to be made at Gandia. The Society, if it is to remain at the disposal of the pope, must be unhampered in its movements. As it is, the religious of St. Dominic and of St. Francis have had their tribulations in this respect. Neither should confraternities be made at Gandia.

1. It does not seem timely to establish at Gandia a convent of nuns who are to be bound and subject to the Society of Jesus. This, the least of the orders, is but beginning; the members are few in number and beset by contradictions. We cannot bring ourselves to believe that such an establishment would be opportune until the Society has shown signs of greater growth.

2. The Society has an express vow to be ready to move to any part of the world at the wish of the supreme pontiff.

3. At Gandia there is already a good and holy convent in which there are some relatives of the duke. As the city is not large, the establishing of another convent of nuns might result in harm for one or the other, or even both.

---

[3] *Epistolae mixtae*, I, 201, 215, 219, 287, 297.
[4] *Epistolae et instructiones*, XII, 367, 371, 377.
[5] *Scripta de S. Ignatio*, I, 655-58.
[6] *Ibid.*, 647.
[7] *Epistolae et instructiones*, I, 424.

4. As we see the matter here, what we ought to do in our Lord is to leave the Society free in its movements so as to be able to undertake tasks of more general import, which we cannot do if we are tied down to particular works. When all is said, if we are advancing in the way of the Lord, we should look upon ourselves as altogether unworthy even to untie the shoestrings of those blessed men, Saints Francis and Dominic. As we see that these orders are embarrassed and disturbed by the disputes which arise in these convents of women, as we have occasion to see daily here in the Roman Curia, we are justified in thinking that we shall have to deal with similar trials and scandals were we to undertake the special care of monasteries of women. It is a fact that we do have special care of three women here, by special commission of his holiness, but we entertain the hope of freeing ourselves as a special favor from the pope. Everything here at least seems to indicate such a conclusion.[8]

For this reason I am convinced that to fulfill the intentions of the duke and Lady Joan,[9] to win a larger number of souls, and to serve God more completely through both sexes, with greater spiritual profit all around, it would be a good and holy plan to form a society of women beginning with those who seem suitable and holy in our Lord, according to the enclosed memorandum, or as you there at Gandia will judge better.[10]

¶ TO ISABEL ROSER
I, 424-25, Letter 137

Isabel, known from earlier letters addressed to her by Ignatius, came to Rome to take up her residence and there to enjoy the direction of the saint. With two or three other pious women who formed a little community, she placed herself under the direction of Ignatius, as did her

---

[8] The brief of Paul III is dated March 19, 1547 (*Epistolae et instructiones*, I, 517). But as we have noted, Ignatius had received a word-of-mouth answer to the same purpose in March or April of 1546. Once restored to liberty by a word of Ignatius (October 1, 1546), Isabel Roser returned in high dudgeon to Barcelona (*Epistolae mixtae*, II, 54). Time, however, brought about an appeasement. She returned to the convent called Jerusalem, and finally (1547, 1550, 1552) wrote letters of repentance to Ignatius, and of confidence (*Epistolae mixtae*, I, 449; IV, 148, 150; *Epistolae et instructiones*, XII, 398, 399). The letter of 1550 is in Catalan. Ignatius approved her entering religion (*Epistolae et instructiones*, III, 168). He learned later in a letter from Araoz of the death of this good woman, which must have taken place toward the end of November 1554.
[9] Joan de Meneses, sister-in-law of Francis Borgia.
[10] The text of this memorandum is lacking. The society of women of which there is question here should be understood as nothing more than a pious confraternity.

companions, and took a vow of obedience to him. God permitted the holy founder to learn from his own experience that such direction was incompatible with the ministry of the Society and entirely opposed to its spirit. Ignatius therefore asked the pope to free the Society for all time from the ordinary direction of religious women, no matter to what order they belonged. This privilege being granted by the pope, Ignatius told Isabel that he could not henceforth undertake her direction. Later, in the Constitutions, the saint forbade his religious by an express law from undertaking the ordinary direction of religious women. From time to time the Society may exercise an extraordinary ministry with religious women of various orders, but it has no special bond with any order of nuns.

Rome, October 1, 1546

The truth is that I do have a desire, for God's greater glory, to comply with your good desires and keep you under obedience, as you have been now for some time, and bestow on you that care which is proper for the greater perfection and salvation of your soul. And yet I have not sufficient health and strength, owing to my continued attacks of illness, to say nothing of being occupied with matters of prime obligation in the sight of God and with his holiness, God's vicar. At the same time I cannot see how this least Society of Jesus can conscientiously assume the responsibility for ladies who are under a vow of obedience. Besides, it is about six months since I explained at length my views on this matter to his holiness. It was that I should completely withdraw, for God's greater glory, from this care of you as a spiritual daughter, and look upon you as a good and pious mother to me, as you have been now for a long time, to God our Lord's greater glory. Hence for the greater service, praise, and glory of the Eternal Goodness, as far as I can, with all due respect to higher authority, I release you to the most prudent judgment and decision of his holiness, for the greater peace and quiet and comfort of your soul and for God's greater glory.

¶ TO FATHER MICHAEL DE TORRES

I, 433-37, Letter 143

Ignatius has a brief concerning the restoration of discipline to some of the convents of Barcelona. He suggests that it should go directly to the prince and the bishops in order to expedite the reform. The Abyssinians are eager to choose a patriarch and Ignatius has refused to allow some of the princes to bestow the episcopal dignity on a member of the Society. He says that Master Lainez is among the first bishops, priests, or religious that have been asked to preach at Trent. Finally, he describes the efforts of Charles V against the Lutherans.

Rome, October 9, 1546

IHS

My very Reverend Father in our Lord.

May the sovereign grace and everlasting love of Christ our Lord ever be our help and support.

On John de Vega's arrival in Rome, I spoke to him about expediting the brief concerning the reform of the convents in Barcelona. His lordship thought that it should go directly to the prince, and that he himself would write to his highness, suggesting that he send the brief to the two bishops of Barcelona and Alger, together with an urgent letter for each, and that he himself, John de Vega, would also write to each of the bishops. Thus the task falls to me to have the secretary write the letters, and also to have the prince write to the viceroy of Catalonia. I have given Ximenez[1] the reminder to write, and I think that everything will be dispatched in this post.

The pope has returned, but the individual in charge of the register has not yet arrived, as he remained behind at Foligno, sick. I have been expecting him daily, so as to get a copy of the brief from the register. If this cannot be done here, do the best you can where you are according to the terms of our talk here, to God's greater glory.

After his departure the king of Portugal wrote me a letter, a copy of which I enclose. After speaking to Señor Balthasar de Faria, I was shown a letter which the king had written him in which he tells how Prester John has sent him a nuncio with the view of having the king send a true patriarch in return, since he is quite pleased with the ways of Portugal. He goes on to say that Prester John is in a mood to give obedience to the Apostolic See; that in his lands both men and women are circumcised, and that they observe the Sabbath as do the Jews. They receive Communion every Sunday, whether they have been to confession previously or not, and are baptized every year, and do many other things of that nature. He would have Señor Balthasar de Faria speak to the pope with a view to have Master Peter Faber (of happy memory) chosen as patriarch, and that he be commanded to accept under obedience. But his majesty, learning that Peter is beyond all the trials of this miserable life,

[1] Peter Ximenez, secretary to John de Vega.

is now bending every effort to have one of Ours sent with the same office to Prester John. It seems that all our friends are condemning us to this undertaking, even Señora Doña Eleanor Osorio. When she first heard that Master Bobadilla refused a bishopric and then that Le Jay was unwilling to accept the bishopric of Trieste, where there are many sheep and a thousand ducats income, and this in spite of the strenuous efforts of the king of the Romans, who has sent his confessor, the archbishop, to have an interview with Le Jay and induce him to accept, she told me in an affectionate outpouring of the heart that she would rather lose all her possessions than that one of the Society should accept a bishopric. And yet, in spite of this, she thought that, to succor so many souls that were being lost, we should not refuse, since this was not the same as accepting a bishopric. Master Bernard Maffei was of the same opinion, although he himself had refused a bishopric. May God our Lord dispose our wills to accept what is for His greater glory. If we were to believe Cardinals Burgos and Carpi, they would set aside some of Ours for this undertaking. We cannot take Master Lainez from the council before the first session, in which they have to decide on the decree on justification. It seems that here at Rome, just as at Trent, his holiness is having the learned examine the decree, for Master Bernard Maffei has told me that he would send the decree to me here to be examined in our house.

A fresh favor has been shown to Ours at Trent, for up to the present neither bishops nor religious nor other preachers have been permitted to preach in Trent, but the legates have ordered Master Lainez to preach. He was to have begun the next Sunday. It seems from another letter, a copy of which I am sending you, that they have already begun to preach and to give exhortations, as you will see from the letter.

Our friend Matthias[2] has been to speak with the Señora Doña Eleanor Osorio, asking her not to take sides against him, and that he will undertake to see that the sentence is signed. He offered to ask my pardon, and to speak in our favor whenever she desired, even in the Flower Market. The day before yesterday her ladyship called upon me, and told me that both she and John de Vega were of the opinion that we should accept Matthias' offer. I submitted my reasons against doing so, and finally came

---

[2] The editors of the *Monumenta*, quoting Ribadeneira and the Bollandists, speak thus of Matthias: ". . . the papal postmaster . . . a meddlesome, officious person, loose of tongue and violent of temper. Ignatius had induced a woman with whom he maintained an irregular union to leave him. He reacted by spreading many calumnies against the saint and his companions. Later he repented, recognized his mistake, changed his hatred into friendship and his insults into favors" (*Epistolae et instructiones*, I, 436, n. 6). See also Dudon, *Loyola*, p. 385.

to the opposite conclusion. I told her that I did not think we should make any bargain with Matthias. Neither did I want him to ask my pardon, nor that the sentence be given through his intervention and support. I felt confident that the sentence would be given, and in terms that would be to God's greater glory. Finally her ladyship agreed that this would be the better way. Yesterday Matthias went to speak with the pope's vicar, and had much to say in our favor publicly and to his own condemnation. He is going about making friends for fear that things may turn out badly for him, which could easily happen. May our Lord be pleased to bring about that which will be more for His glory.

According to what Master Bernard Maffei tells me, it is thought here that Cardinal Morone and Cardinal Sfondrato are going to the council instead of Cardinal Pole and Cardinal Monte, with no change regarding Cardinal Santa Croce. It seems that the council depends on the outcome of this battle between the emperor and the Lutherans. Up to now, since his departure from here, things are going well for him, and every day he makes some gain against them. He and his army are now only about a mile away from the Lutheran army.

May it please the Divine Majesty that all come to pass for His greater praise and glory, and may He in accordance with His infinite and usual mercies ever be our protection and support.

¶ TO FRANCIS BORGIA, DUKE OF GANDIA

I, 442-44, Letter 146

With paternal affection Ignatius admits Francis Borgia into the Society and tells him how to arrange his affairs before making his religious vocation known to the world.

Rome, October 9 [?], 1546

Illustrious Lord.

The Divine Goodness has consoled me in the decision which He has placed in the heart of your lordship. May His angels and the holy souls who rejoice in Him in heaven give Him infinite thanks, for here on earth we shall never be able to thank Him sufficiently for the loving-kindness with which He has favored this least Society in bringing your lordship into it. I have hopes that from your entrance His divine providence will gather abundant fruit and spiritual good for your own soul and for innumerable others who will be edified by your example. We who are already in the Society will take courage to begin anew to serve the divine Father of families, who bestows such a brother on us and has chosen for us such a fellow workman for the cultivation of this newly planted vine, of which He has given me some care, unworthy as I am. Therefore from this hour, in the name of our Lord, I accept and receive you as our brother, and as such I will cherish that love for you in my soul that is owing to one who gives himself so generously to the household of God, there to serve Him perfectly.[1]

To come to the particular point on which you wished to hear from me—the time and manner of your entering—I have given much thought to the matter and recommended it to our Lord through others. It seems to me that, the better to comply with all obligations, the change should be made gradually and with much reflection, for the greater glory of God. You will thus be able to dispose of your affairs in such a way that seculars will not know what you are about, and in a short time you will find yourself free to carry out your desires to the full in our Lord.

And coming even to greater particulars, I would say that your daughters are now old enough to be put at the head of their own households, and that your lordship should see that they are honorably married in keeping with their station as your daughters. If the occasion presents itself, let the marquis also marry. As to your other sons, they should not merely enjoy the support and protection of their elder brother, who will inherit the estate, but they should have moreover a substantial settlement which will enable them to attend some first-class university, as befits their rank, and follow up the studies in which they have already laid such solid foundations. It is also to be hoped that the emperor, should they turn out as they ought—and I hope they do—will show them the favor which your services deserve and which the love which he has always shown for you makes almost certain.

The buildings that have been begun should be finished with dispatch,[2] for it is my desire that all your affairs should be attended to fully by the time our Lord will be pleased to have you make known your change of life.

---

[1] Orlandini and Astrain give details about the vocation of St. Francis Borgia. From them we learn that Ignatius, long before Borgia asked admission to the Society, even while his wife was still living and he was governing Catalonia in the name of Charles V, knew by a divine illumination that Borgia would enter the Society and become its general (Orlandini, VI, 74-76; Astrain, *Historia,* t. I, lib. II, c. 6).

[2] The saintly duke had a number of projects on hand, principally a convent for the Dominicans in Lombay.

And while these affairs are being brought to a conclusion, I should be very glad, and I think that God would be served, if you gave yourself to the serious study of theology. Your lordship has already a sound foundation in the liberal arts as a preparation for further studies in the sacred sciences. If it is possible I should like to see you take the degree of doctor in your University of Gandia, but secretly for the present, as the ears of the world are not ready for such an announcement, until, with God's favor, time and circumstances leave us complete liberty.

Other problems can be met day by day as they come up, and I will now say no more than that I will look for frequent letters from your lordship. I too will write regularly, and I will beg of the divine and sovereign Goodness, by His favor and grace, to continue the loving favors He has begun in your lordship's soul.

¶ TO FATHER MICHAEL DE TORRES
1, 445-48, Letter 147

Ignatius complains of the slowness of the delivery of letters and speaks of ways of obtaining better service. He speaks of Benedict Palmio's wish to enter the Society. A letter must be written about restoring discipline in some convents and how the business with Isabel Roser is to be carried on. Matthias de Sancto Cassiano, papal postmaster, wishes to be reconciled with Ignatius and condemns himself. A certain Barbaran aims at bringing suit against St. Martha, but has no case. The supreme pontiff shows his kindliness toward the Society. The wishes of Francis Borgia are carefully attended to.

Rome, October 13 and 18, 1546

IHS

My Lord in our Lord.

May the sovereign grace and everlasting love of Christ our Lord ever be our help and support.

Today, October 13, I received two letters, one from Master Jerome Domenech dated September 25, in which he tells me that the letters of John Paul[1] and my own did not arrive at Bologna, and that I should write to Barcelona in duplicate. The fact is that on the very day on which we took leave of each other at the villa, although only for a short time,

---

[1] John Paul Borrell, a coadjutor brother, whose home was in Barcelona.

I wrote two letters before going to bed and put them in the mail. My letters then left here under the same heavenly influence, or better, earthly influence, as those of Master Jerome's to me, which were written at Bologna on the twenty-fifth of September, and reached here on the thirteenth of October, together with the other letter from Master Baptist Pezzano, dated the twenty-eighth of September, and along with it one for you. He acts as mediator between Benedict and his mother, and shows himself very generous to the mother. I am quite satisfied with all that he has offered, and will do my best to carry out my part. I hope, and in fact am quite convinced, that he is readier to withdraw from his mother than Benedict is from his.[2] While I am writing this I am told that he has gone through Rome making a collection everywhere. He went about begging alms without my knowing anything about it. He seems to be a youth who, if he perseveres, will do great things.

Since John de Vega's return with the pope there has been no mail or express leaving for Spain. One should have left a week ago, to whom I have given a long letter, but he has not left yet. Señor John de Vega thinks that the brief for Barcelona should be sent directly to the prince—I believe, with this mail. I have not been able to send you a copy to Barcelona because the person who keeps the register has stayed behind sick at Foligno. I am making two copies of this letter, one for Barcelona and the other for Valencia, with the hope that one or other will come into your hands.

I do not think that it will be good to give the letter that John Paul has written to Barcelona to his uncle, because what has happened here is such that it must be seen at close range. I mean that the Señora Roser wanted two things. First she wanted to remain on friendly terms with me, and asked that I give her a letter which would make it clear that she was not being dismissed for any fault. In the second place she made some objections to the arrangements regarding temporalities. This whole affair was arranged in the presence of Doña Eleanor Osorio and Isabel herself, of John Bosch, myself, and another party from outside. I say that she made some objection because, three or four days after these arrangements were concluded, she cast up her accounts, so she thought, and claimed according to her calculations that our house owed her a considerable sum of money. In a word, I did not want to agree to the first part until the second had been cleared up, as I am entirely convinced that right is on our side. I asked that she name one to represent her while I named an-

---

[2] Benedict Palmio. See *Chronicon*, I, 169.

other to represent me, and it was with difficulty that she brought herself to agree to this. It was my suggestion that if these two could not come to an agreement, we should abide by the judgment of some person of standing and learning, such as one of the auditors of the Rota, and so on. Once this was done, the pope's vicar was to settle the case so as to avoid scandal, which would be considerable here, to say nothing of what could be expected in Barcelona, some speaking in her favor and others in ours. In this way, if God so pleased, all this business of money, wills, and donations would be settled, and many offenses against His Divine Majesty avoided which could not be avoided in any other way. We should have besides a good precedent for future reference.

Matthias[3] has presented a judgment in our favor to the pope's vicar, condemning himself and declaring that he wishes to make peace with us.

Barbaran[4] has lodged a long complaint against the house of St. Martha, and his holiness has commissioned Cardinal Crescenzi to look into it. I was speaking with him yesterday, and he told me that the complaint was without foundation. Going into particulars, Barbaran said that we were conducting this house of St. Martha without apostolic authority (his most reverend lordship knew the contrary), and that we were bent on reforming the whole world; that we drew up statutes for expelling from Rome all married women who were guilty of adultery, and other such charges which have not the slightest foundation. The cardinal, being aware of all this, told me how we must proceed when talking with his holiness in order to bring these matters to light, so that they will be regarded at their real worth. I am convinced in our Lord that this will be the outcome.

After turning this complaint over to the cardinal, his holiness has done us a fresh favor with regard to the bulls for Padua, in this way. First, the writing of the bulls: we were granted the favor of drawing them up ourselves although this is usually done by his holiness. And now, by expediting the bulls in secret, which would otherwise belong to the officials of the Chancery, the college has been saved, so Master Peter Codacio tells me, the sum of at least two thousand ducats.[5]

I have given Dean Rocca the petition for the indulgences which his lordship the duke is asking for the Exercises, and also for the college and university which his lordship wishes to found. In giving him these petitions I asked the dean to speak to his holiness. I believe he will do so in

---

[3] Matthias appears in a former letter, No. 143.
[4] This is the Barbaran to whom St. Ignatius refers in Letter 132.
[5] The Priory of the Magdalena which, was held by Andrew Lippomani, was transferred to the College of Padua, the expenses of the transfer being waived.

the course of this week, and later leave for Milan, whither his holiness was preparing to send him, as he told me the day before yesterday.

Remember me to Master Christopher.[6] I close asking God our Creator and Redeemer to give us His Holy Spirit for ever and ever.

This was already written when Cardinal Crescenzi last Friday informed the pope that the complaints lodged by Barbaran against the house of St. Martha had no foundation whatever. Moreover, as the vicar Archinto must first propose the matter in the Signatura and as the dean is in a hurry, we have given him the petitions for the erection of the college and university so that he can present them.

¶ TO FERDINAND, KING OF THE ROMANS
I, 450-53, Letter 149

This good sovereign wished to oblige Father Claude Le Jay to accept the bishopric of Trieste. Ignatius tried to dissuade the king by showing him by very sound reasons that the Society would come to ruin by accepting such dignities.

Rome, December 1546

IHS

We are aware of the good and holy dispositions which your highness has always manifested toward this least Society and especially toward certain of its members. And now your highness would wish to show this concretely, apparently doing God a service and us a favor by choosing Father Master Claude for promotion to the episcopal dignity. That the intention of your highness is holy is plain to all, since it is your desire to make provision for the spiritual welfare of the souls entrusted to your care for God's glory and to show us, unworthy as we are, the great kindliness and charity you entertain for us in our Lord. We shall never cease thanking your highness in the Divine Majesty, and may God in His infinite mercy be pleased fully to reward your highness and impress deeply upon your heart (as I hope He will), how you can be of even greater help to us in progressing in the perfection of our humble calling. This will never be better done than by making use of us without bestowing on us any dignity at all. This is our earnest desire, for we are conscientiously

---

[6] Father Christopher de Mendoza.

convinced that to accept dignities would be a severe blow to the Society—so great a blow in fact that, if I were to try to fancy or imagine some means of ruining the Society, I should look upon the accepting of a bishopric as one of the best, if not the best of all. Besides many other reasons, I will submit the following.

First. This Society and its members have been joined together in one and the same spirit; namely, to travel to various places in the world, among the faithful and the infidel, as we are sent by the supreme pontiff. Indeed, it is the spirit of the Society to go in all humility and simplicity from city to city and place to place, without taking root anywhere. This spirit of the Society has been approved by the Apostolic See, as can be seen in its bulls, where it is said of us, "as is piously believed, by the inspiration of the Holy Spirit, etc."[1] To abandon this simplicity of Ours would be the undoing of our spirit, of our profession; and this done, the Society would be utterly destroyed. So we see that doing good in a particular place would involve greater harm to the whole body.

Second. As the Society makes progress in this spirit, God our Lord manifests Himself to it by great spiritual profit to souls. If the soil of parts of Germany has proved barren, in Portuguese India one of Ours has in one year baptized eighty thousand souls. Another[2] in Portugal itself, besides reaping a rich harvest in the kingdom, has guided more than twenty to renounce the world and go to India, and another hundred students who have made up their minds to go there, or elsewhere, if they will be able to be of some service to God our Lord. I have no wish to be tiresome, otherwise I could say much of Castile, Barcelona, Valencia, Gandia, and other places, especially in Italy, and of the good our Lord has deigned to work through this Society while it continues in the spirit which His Divine Majesty has imparted to it.

Third. Up to the present we are only nine professed, and as four or five of them have already been presented for various bishoprics, we have had to be firm in refusing them. Now, if one accepted, another would soon do the same, and the others would all follow suit. The result would be not only the loss of our spirit but the complete ruin of the Society, the greater being thus lost for the sake of the less.

Four. If any of Ours were to accept a bishopric, especially in these days and in a place where the Society is established (however remote be the place they have reached), and enjoys a good reputation to the edifica-

---

[1] Paul III in the apostolic constitution *Regimini militantis ecclesiae*.
[2] St. Ignatius is referring to Simon Rodrigues, whom John III wanted to make bishop of Coimbra, and to James Lainez, Paschase Broet, Nicholas Bobadilla, and Claude Le Jay.

tion of the faithful, this reputation would turn sour, to the disedification and even scandal of those who cherish us and are advancing in the way of the spirit, to the regret of those who are indifferent but desirous of advancing, and to the great disedification and scandal of those who are ill-affected toward us. These would be provided with excuses for their faultfinding and detraction, to the scandal of many souls for whom Christ our Lord died on the cross. For so far gone in corruption is the world that, the moment one of Ours sets foot in the pope's palace or the palace of princes or cardinals or of people of influence, we are thought to be motivated by ambition. If now we were to accept a bishopric, it would be the easiest way to start talk, criticism, and consequent offense to God our Lord.³

¶ TO FATHER JOHN POLANCO
1, 457-60, Letter 152

Ignatius is surprised that Polanco should write in another sense about withdrawing Lainez from Trent. He also gently but shrewdly warns him about his imprudence in attempting to correct the rulers of Florence, and urges him to set about repairing the losses inflicted on the good works they had hoped to begin by the public example of Christian humility.

Rome, February or March 1547

IHS

May the sovereign grace of Christ our Lord be our ever-present help and support. Amen.

On February 21 I received a letter from Master Lainez at Trent, and with it another from you dated the first of the month. I gather from it that you wrote to Master Lainez that other and more important undertakings should not be dropped in the hope of making a foundation at Florence, as this was a project that had almost come to naught. I am surprised and worried over two points, and wonder whether your great zeal and charity prompted you more than your experience and prudence. It would give me much spiritual consolation if you were able to free me from this doubt.

---

³ To understand how much to heart St. Ignatius took his opposition to Le Jay's promotion to a bishopric, see José Manuel Aicardo, *Comentario à las Constituciones de la Compañía de Jesús* (IV, 14 ff.).

As to the first point, I do not see what good can come from my plans to send Master Lainez to Florence if you send him directions to the contrary without first letting me know.

As to the second, before the project came into such straits I gave the matter prolonged thought and wrote you through Master Andrew [Frusius] a whole month ago to have you change your method of approach with those gentlemen; because with men like them of such exemplary conduct to be constantly on the watch to see who are favorably disposed and who are not, and to be giving them correction and advice by means of notes for the reform of their conscience or their state without first having won their affection and established your credit and authority is rather to spoil everything than to insure success in the plan proposed.

Besides, you had word from Bologna about the manner of dealing with the bishop[1] and the duke, and you were told in case they called you to be guided in everything by their judgment, so as to reap greater fruit among the people. And now, with your efforts to reform the duke and the duchess[2] all at once, you see to what a pass matters have come. I am quite satisfied, considering the great charity and ability which God our Lord has bestowed upon you, that you will profit from the past to improve the future, and that His Divine Majesty is going to accomplish much for His greater glory through your instrumentality if you are true and faithful. Do not then be discouraged, but try in the Lord of all to profit from this experience.

Here in Rome, especially among a few who do not succeed in attaining the truth, we have the reputation of wanting to rule the world. If Matthias, the papal postmaster, or some one of his followers in ignorance has passed through Florence, it would not be surprising if he has spoken against us to the duke, and this circumstance would help to throw this project for the service of God our Lord into great confusion.

For the love of our Lord, please write as soon as possible and in duplicate, but at length, and tell me in detail what you think are the occasions and causes that led to the failure of this project. In the meantime I desire that in those places where the disedification given by you personally or by all of Ours has been greater, you should now practice some acts of greater humility, to the greater confusion of the world, the flesh, and the devil. For some hours in the day you could serve the poor in the hospitals, and give their souls a little consolation by means of confessions and exhortations. Even if the situation were much worse than it is, I think

---

[1] Alexander Compeggio.   [2] Cosmo de Medici and Eleanor of Toledo.

Master Lainez should leave the council if he can be spared, and go to Florence as soon as possible, as I have already written you (in other letters) or others of Ours. If you have occasion to write him soon, urge him to come rather than otherwise. I hope in our Creator and Lord that we can repair our losses to God's greater glory and to the great spiritual good of many souls. I am sure that, if Ours there act with great humility and bring the help of humility to arrange matters, I do firmly hope with the help of God's grace that the Divine Majesty will so dispose the matter for his own greater praise and glory, since by the grace of His Divine Majesty that is all we ask.

May He by His infinite and sovereign goodness give us abundant grace to know His most holy will and perfectly to fulfill it.

¶ TO FATHER MICHAEL DE TORRES
I, 460-67, Letter 153

Ferdinand I, king of the Romans, offered the bishopric of Trieste to Father Claude Le Jay, but the good father at once politely refused the proffered dignity. He looked upon it as a danger, containing a threat of drowning in a sea of honors. The king and other powerful intercessors had recourse to the supreme pontiff and his court to oblige Le Jay to accept. St. Ignatius was very anxious to remove the danger of this miter from the Society, as a reading of the letter that follows will show in part. It was written by Bartholomew Ferrao (his secretary at the time) by order of the holy founder.

Rome, March 2, 1547

May the grace and everlasting love of Christ our Lord be ever in our favor and support. Amen.

In this letter it has been my thought in our Lord to give you an account, scene by scene, of a secret persecution which the enemy of human nature has these days been waging against the Society. You are one who loves it dearly and will not be misled by this campaign. I know that the Society itself holds your worship in affectionate esteem.

The gist of the matter is, as I believe you heard before leaving here, that the king of the Romans sent his confessor, the bishop of Laibach,[1] to deliver a letter to Father Claude Le Jay of the Society, who was attending

---

[1] Urban Weber.

the Council of Trent. To share the journey with him, the father joined the bishop in Venice, where they conversed together for two or three days. Father Claude, opening the king's letter, saw that it contained nothing more than a request to accept the vacant bishopric of Trieste. It breathed of charity and showed a purpose that was full of love. Trieste is on the borders of Venice and Slavia, a thickly inhabited region, and yields an income of two thousand ducats a year. But the father, despite all the urging of the king's confessor, was convinced that it was to God's greater service to refuse it, and wrote the king to excuse himself as best he could.

Three months later we heard here one day from Master Bernard Maffei, secretary to his holiness, that another attempt was being made to make the same father bishop, and the next morning our Father Ignatius went to the palace and spoke with the secretary, who read him a very warm letter which the king of the Romans had written to the pope, touching on three points principally. The first was that he had chosen Master Claude Le Jay for the vacant see of Trieste. As a perfect pastor was essential for that land full of errors and vice, he could think of no one better fitted for the post, since he recognized in him a man of much learning and virtue, having dealt with him and heard many of his sermons in Germany, and he praised him very generously. The second point was that, as he had written to the said father through his confessor asking him to accept the bishopric, the father had in his humility excused himself. The third point was that, therefore, his holiness should command him in virtue of obedience to accept the post, since the matter was just and necessary, and because of the great spiritual fruit that would result from a man so outstanding in virtue and learning. He amplified these three points to such an extent that the letter seemed to be one of the really important petitions which are issued in the Signatura.

When Father Ignatius saw how matters stood, he betook himself to the home of the ambassador of the king of the Romans, Don James Lasso, who showed him a letter he had received from his lord the king, part of it written in the king's own hand, in which he was most insistently charged to forward to the pope the dispatch concerning the bishopric just as it was sent to him, and to do this with all care and diligence. Our father told the ambassador that he could satisfy his duty to the king without carrying the matter through, since in that event the Society would suffer less harm than it would have suffered had it accepted the bishopric. After a few pleasant remarks, however, he answered that, if Master Claude refused to accept the post and the pope did not excommunicate him, he himself would leave Rome.

Seeing, then, that matters were getting serious, he returned to talk with Master Bernard Maffei, and learned that three of the cardinals who are taken up with such official business had seen the king's letter to the pope and had, with a right and holy intention, made up their minds to see the matter through in another way. The supreme pontiff, at the request of the ambassador, had given orders for the drawing up of a brief in which he commanded Father Claude to accept the bishopric, but the cardinals suggested that, in order to avoid further legal steps, it would be better if his holiness first made him bishop and afterwards sent the brief. The secretary said he thought that all the cardinals would be opposed to this and that, if any were in our favor, they would be the cardinal of England [Pole], and the master of the Sacred Palace,[2] as they had themselves recently refused bishoprics.

Our father spoke to one of them and to some others but, not getting what he wanted, he decided to go straight to the pope lest his conscience accuse him of not having tried all possible means. This he did. Very humbly he gave a long account of the whole matter to his holiness, and showed him that such an appointment was good neither for the Society nor for the welfare of souls.

His reasoning concerning the Society was like this. The Society began with the spirit of lowliness and humility, and with this spirit it is abundantly manifest how much our Lord has deigned to accomplish by it. And therefore, if it were now to abandon its beginning and first devotion and proceed in a contrary spirit, such as accepting dignities, it is clear that it would no longer be able to preserve itself in peace and good works but that it would come to ruin.

His second reason was that the professed of the Society were so few. Considering their small numbers, it was plain that by accepting this dignity it would put itself on the road to destruction. For if Father Claude were to take this bishopric, another professed would do the same, and a third would follow him, *et sic de caeteris,* until none were left. This is confirmed by the fact that in the last seven years four bishoprics have been offered to four of Ours. If only one had accepted, the others would have easily followed, which God forbid.

The third reason pertains to the good of souls. Much harm would come to souls and to the more universal good of the neighbor, for when all is said, should Master Claude accept the bishopric, he would not be able to help more souls than were in his diocese. But as things are, he

---

[2] The reference is apparently to Cardinal Badia, O.P.

will be able to gather much fruit in the Lord in many cities, provinces, and kingdoms. For if in one the word of God is not received, it is well sown in another and yields a hundredfold, as is seen from the experience of individuals in the Society, *Domino cooperante,* throughout Italy, Spain, Germany, Hungary, Portugal, and the Indies.

The fourth reason. Throughout all these regions the Society is held in great esteem and veneration in our Lord because it proceeds in the spirit of humility and simplicity and is far removed from the spirit of greed. There is no doubt that, if it were now to accept dignities, it would be the cause of greater scandal, disedification, and complaint, wherever it became known, than any good it could produce in a single bishopric.

The fifth reason. The acceptance of this dignity could cause another notable damage to the Society in this way. There are about two hundred novices and scholastics who have left all things in the world and who have deliberated about entering the Society in poverty, chastity, and obedience, many of whom might be scandalized at seeing us accept bishoprics and thus change our purpose and give up their vocation. Others might find this a pretext of staying on, or of entering the Society, with the thought that in time they could become bishops.[3] And thus the spirit of the Society could be turned into the spirit of rivalry and ambition.

Our father laid great stress on this reason and on many others. He was alone with his holiness in the first audience, and in the camera after dinner, until the pope (Ignatius thinking that he had done all he could) answered him with great kindness, approved his reasons and his lengthy discourse, and praised the Society. But he clung to one point which was firmly settled in his mind: that what the king of the Romans did in settling the bishopric on Master Claude had been the work of the Holy Spirit, alleging such authority as "Cor regis in manu Domini est—The heart of the king is in the hand of the Lord."[4] And his holiness was in agreement with this thought.

Finally, at the end of this long conference, Father Ignatius told his holiness that, if this bishopric were accepted, there would be such scandal and complaint that the members of the Society would no longer be able to speak with his holiness or the cardinals or other lords without having

---

[3] From St. Ignatius himself we know that an attempt was made to make bishops of Fathers Lainez, Broet, Bobadilla, and Rodrigues. Later the same thing happened to Canisius. St. Ignatius always equally opposed these promotions, judging them to be supremely harmful to the Society. But when these dignities were offered in mission lands, he had no difficulty in accepting them, as he saw in them, not a spur to ambition or greed but an abundant harvest of suffering and privation.

[4] Proverbs 21:1.

it said of them that they came in search of such dignities; and that even Señor John de Vega and Madama[5] had both sensed the same scandal, and therefore had to talk about it to his holiness.

The pope then told him to go and pray over it, and that he himself would look into it. After asking a few favors, which his holiness granted, our father began a fresh search for every possible means of preventing the threatened dignity. He could find no rest until he had achieved his desire. He then spoke with Señor John de Vega, and succeeded in having the secretary of the emperor try his hand in our favor with the pope. But although he carried out his errand with the greatest possible warmth, he got no other answer from his holiness than what had been given to our father. Rather he found him even more disposed to give Master Claude the bishopric. When Father Ignatius saw this, he enlisted Master Peter Codacio and as many others as he could to make the rounds of the cardinals. They were to visit and talk with as many as possible, because it was thought that the consistory would be held within three or four days, at which the question would be sure to come up.

It is hardly believable what diligence he used in this matter. The day was not long enough for his efforts, and he spoke to the three cardinals at night, one living a good mile from another, as in the instance of Cardinal Gaddi, who lives in Montesitorio, and Cardinal Salviatti, who lives in the Borgo near the palace. So great was his diligence, *Domino cooperante,* that half of the cardinals were of our opinion, and all of these on our side. Apart from these, the others who were in favor of accepting the bishopric took their stand on the ground that good bishoprics should be given to good men who had sufficient learning, a qualification which they said Ours fulfilled. For that reason they were against our refusing. A large number were of this opinion, even of those who were most devoted to us in the Lord.

All the cardinals had been approached in our behalf except two; one of these because it was his duty to propose the matter in the consistory and there was no use seeing him; the other, having renounced a bishopric out of devotion, later changed his mind and accepted it.

Seeing us thus encircled, and that the consistory would take place on the following day without any change of mind on the part of the pope, our father hit upon the expedient of going to Madama to have her write a note to his holiness in which she begged him not to deal with the case in the consistory but to wait until she and Señor John de Vega had writ-

---

[5] Margaret of Austria, daughter of Charles V and wife of Octavius Farnese.

ten to the king. Then, if the king continued to insist and demanded the appointment from his holiness, the Society would accept the bishopric. The note was sent that same Thursday, the eve of the consistory, and the pope answered Madama that he would do as she asked. The cardinal, however, who was to make the proposal did not know this, and on the following day went through with his proposal. He did not, however, get very far with it, as he was met with counter reasons by one of those who sided with us. It was then that Father Ignatius had a letter written in the name of the whole Society to Señor John de Vega, Madama, Cardinal Carpi, our protector, and the king, giving such a wealth of reasons and so much bemoaning that we have right along entertained good hopes of a favorable outcome.

At the same time he took good care that Ours who were at the council, and Master Bobadilla wherever he was, should have written and have others write to his majesty. But because of the wide divergence of opinion on the subject there, they were able to get only one of the prelates to write.

In the face of all these efforts here, Don James Lasso was still as urgent as he could be in his endeavor to further the petition of the king his lord; and in a subsequent consistory which was held eight days later he succeeded in having the aforesaid cardinal propose his cause. By God's grace it was defeated like the first proposal, his holiness declaring that he wished to keep his word to Madama and wait for the king's answer. This arrived in the last few days. It ordered the ambassador to let the matter drop, as he had come to judge this the better course. Masses in thanksgiving and a Te Deum were ordered here in the house for the successful issue of this trial and scourge, for we all thought that we should be tainted or besmirched had the bishopric been accepted. Infinite and unending thanks to God for that.

¶ TO THE FATHERS AND SCHOLASTICS AT COIMBRA

I, 495-510, Letter 169

At the time this letter was written there was a flourishing college of eighty Jesuit scholastics at Coimbra in Portugal. The fervor of these young men led them to such extremes as to discipline themselves through the streets of the city, to preach half-clothed, and to raise penitential cries in the silence of the night. St. Ignatius was well informed "by letters from Simon Rodrigues, who was the inspirer of these acts of fervor, and from Santa Cruz." To these was added information coming from Fathers Faber, Araoz, Villanueva, and others. Illumined by the Holy Spirit, he saw in these "holy follies" the danger of singularities, of pride and vainglory, of loss of health, and of other serious inconveniences, and decided to put a stop to them. To this end he sent them this remarkable letter. It is divided into two parts. In the first he develops a series of pointed considerations which would kindle the most dejected soul to fervor, and in the second he moderates indiscreet excesses and brings them within the safe control of obedience. In the final part of his letter Ignatius recommends union and mutual charity. He calls attention to motives for consolation that scholastics have during their years of study: the worthiness of present labor, the attainment of virtue, and helping one's neighbor.

Rome, May 27 [?], 1547

May the grace and everlasting love of Christ our Lord be ever our protection and help. Amen.

Master Simon's letter and those of Santa Cruz bring me continued news about you, and God, from whom all good things descend, knows what comfort and joy it gives me to see that He so helps you, not only in your studies but in your pursuit of virtue as well. Indeed, the good odor of these virtues has carried to very distant lands, to the encouragement and edification of many. And if every Christian should rejoice because of the common obligation we all have of seeking God's honor and the welfare of His image, which has been redeemed by the blood and death of Jesus Christ, I have an especial reason for rejoicing in our Lord, seeing that I have a distinct obligation of keeping you in my heart with a special affection. May our Creator and Redeemer be ever blessed and praised for all, since it is from His liberality that every blessing and grace flows, and may it please Him to open more and more every day the fountain of His mercy to increase and advance what He has already begun in your souls. I have no doubt concerning that Supreme Goodness, who is so eager to share His blessings, or of that everlasting love which makes Him more eager to bestow perfection on us than we are to receive it. If this were not so, our Lord Jesus Christ would never encourage us to hope for what we can have only from His generous hand. For He tells us, "Be you therefore perfect, as also your heavenly Father is perfect."[1] It is certain then that for His part He is ready, on condition that we have a vessel

---

[1] Matthew 5:48.

of humility and desire to receive His graces, and that He sees that we make good use of the gifts we have received and cooperate diligently and earnestly with His grace.

On this point I will not fail to put the spurs even to those of you who are running so willingly. For I can tell you that you must be persistent both in your studies and in the practice of virtue if you are to come up to the expectations which so many entertain of you. There are persons, not only in the kingdom of Portugal but in many other countries, who, considering the helps and advantages of every kind, both interior and exterior, that God gives you, rightly hope for more than ordinary results in you.

No commonplace achievement will satisfy the great obligations you have of excelling. If you consider the nature of your vocation, you will see that what would not be slight in others would be slight in you. For not only has God called you out of darkness into His marvelous light, and translated you into the kingdom of His beloved Son,[2] as He has done with the rest of the faithful, but because you have better preserved your purity and are more united in His service in the love of spiritual things, He thought it good to withdraw you from the perilous sea of this world to preserve your consciences from the dangers of the storms which the gusts of passion are wont to raise—the desire now of possessions, now of honors, now of pleasures—and on the other hand from the fear of losing all such things. Another reason over and above this is that, if these earthly concerns have no place in your thoughts or affections, you will be preserved from distraction and dissipation, with the result that you will be able to direct your thoughts and affections and employ them in attaining the end for which God created you; that is, His own honor and glory, your own salvation, and the help of your neighbor.

It is true that all the orders in the Church are directed to this end. And yet God has called you to this, in which His glory and the salvation of the neighbor are set before you, not as a general end but one toward which all your life and its various activities must be made by you into a continuous sacrifice. This requires a cooperation from you that should not stop with example and earnest prayer, but includes all the exterior means which His divine providence has provided for the mutual help we should give one another. From this you can understand how noble and royal is the manner of life you have chosen. For not merely among men, but not even among the angels, is there a nobler work than glori-

[2] 1 Peter 2:9; Colossians 1:13.

fying the Creator and bringing His creatures to Him as far as their capacities permit.

Therefore take serious thought of your vocation, so that on the one hand you can give many thanks to God for so great a favor, and on the other ask Him for that special help which is needed if you are properly to correspond with it with the courage and diligence you must have in large measure if you are to attain the end you have in view. Sloth, tepidity, weariness in study and in the other exercises which you have undertaken for the love of our Lord you must recognize as the sworn enemies of your vocation.

For his encouragement each one should keep before his eyes, not those who he thinks will accomplish less but rather those who are active and energetic. Do not ever permit the children of this world to show greater care and solicitude for the things of time than you show for those of eternity. It should bring a blush to your cheek to see them run to death more unhesitatingly than you to life. Hold yourselves as little worth if a courtier serve with greater care merely to have the favor of an earthly prince than you do for the favor of the King of Heaven, and if a soldier for the honor and glory of a victory and a little booty gets himself ready and battles more bravely than you do for the victory and triumph over the world, the devil, and yourselves, with the kingdom of heaven and everlasting glory as your prize.

For the love of God, therefore, be not careless or tepid. For if tautness breaketh the bow, idleness breaketh the soul; while on the contrary, according to Solomon, "the soul of them that work shall be made fat."[3] Try to maintain a holy and discreet ardor in work and in the pursuit of learning as well as of virtue. With one as with the other, one energetic act is worth a thousand that are listless, and what a lazy man cannot accomplish in many years an energetic man usually achieves in a short time.

In the matter of learning the difference between the earnest and the careless student stands out clearly. And the same holds true in the mastering of passion and the weaknesses to which our nature is subject, as in the acquiring of virtue. It is certain that the negligent, because they do not struggle against self, never win peace of soul, or do so tardily and never possess any virtue in its fullness, while the energetic and industrious make notable advances on both fronts.

Experience proves that in this life peace and satisfaction are had, not by the listless but by those who are fervent in God's service. And rightly

---

[3] Proverbs 13:4.

so. For in the effort they make to overcome themselves and to rid themselves of self-love, they rid themselves of the roots of all passion and unrest. And with the acquirement of habits of virtue they naturally succeed in acting easily and cheerfully in accordance with these virtues.

By this means they dispose themselves to receive His holy consolations from God our faithful consoler, for "to him that overcometh I will give the hidden manna."[4] On the other hand, tepidity is the cause of a lifetime of uneasiness, for we never get rid of its cause, which is self-love, nor do we deserve God's help. For this reason you should animate yourselves to work earnestly at your commendable tasks, since even in this life you will see the advantages of holy fervor, not only in the growth of perfection in your souls but even in the peace of mind it gives you with this present life.

But if you look to the eternal reward, as you should do often, St. Paul will easily convince you that "the sufferings of this time are not worthy to be compared with the glory to come that shall be revealed in us,"[5] because "that which is at present momentary and light of our tribulation worketh for us above measure exceedingly an eternal weight of glory."[6]

If this is true of every Christian who serves and honors God, you can understand what your crown will be if you correspond with our Institute, which is not only to serve God for your own sakes but to draw many others to His honor and service. Of them Holy Scripture says that "they that instruct many to justice [shall shine] as stars for all eternity."[7] And this is to be understood of those who employ themselves in the discharge of their duty, not only later in the exercise of arms but even before that, while they are getting themselves ready. If this were not so, we certainly could not apply to works that are in themselves good the words of Jeremias, "Cursed be he that doeth the work of the Lord deceitfully [that is, carelessly],"[8] and of St. Paul, "Know you not that they that run in the race, all run indeed, but one receiveth the prize?"[9] and, "For he also that striveth for the mastery is not crowned except he strive lawfully,"[10] and that means a good worker.

But more than anything else I should wish to awaken in you the pure love of Jesus Christ, the desire for His honor and for the salvation of souls whom He has redeemed. For you are His soldiers in this Society with a special title and a special wage. I say special because there are many motives of general import which likewise oblige you to work for His honor and service. His wage is everything you are and have in the natural order,

---

[4] Apocalypse 2:17.
[5] Romans 8:18.
[6] 2 Corinthians 4:17.
[7] Daniel 12:3.
[8] Jeremias 48:10.
[9] 1 Corinthians 9:24.
[10] 2 Timothy 2:5.

for He bestows and preserves your being and life, and all the perfections of body and soul, as well as blessings that are eternal. His wage is also the spiritual gifts of His grace with which He has so generously and lovingly anticipated you and continues to offer even when you oppose Him and rebel against Him. His wage is also those incomparable blessings of His glory which, without any advantage to Himself, he has promised you and holds in readiness for you, actually sharing with you all the treasures of His happiness, so that you may be by a remarkable participation in His divine perfection what He is by His essence and nature. Finally, His wage is the whole universe and everything material and spiritual it contains. For He has placed under our ministry, not only all that is under heaven but even the whole of His sublime court, not excepting even any of the heavenly hierarchy: "Are they not all ministering spirits, sent to minister for them who shall receive the inheritance of salvation?"[11] As though this wage were not enough, He has made Himself our wage, becoming a brother in our own flesh, as the price of our salvation on the cross and in the Eucharist to be with us as support and company. Oh, what an unworthy soldier he would be whom such a wage would not induce to labor for the honor of such a prince! We know indeed that, to oblige us to desire and labor for this glory, His Majesty has anticipated us with these inestimable and priceless favors, in a sense stripping Himself of His own possessions to give us a share in them; taking upon Himself all our miseries to deliver us from them; wishing to be sold as our redemption, to be dishonored to glorify us, to be poor to enrich us; accepting a disgraceful and painful death to give us a blessed and immortal life. How extremely ungrateful and hardhearted is he who after all this does not recognize his obligation to serve our Lord Jesus Christ diligently and to seek His honor!

If, therefore, you recognize this obligation and wish to employ yourselves in promoting God's honor, the times you are living in make it incumbent indeed on you to make your desire known by works. Can you find a place where the Divine Majesty is in honor today, or where His infinite greatness is worshiped, where His wisdom and infinite goodness are known, or His most holy will obeyed? Behold rather, with deep grief, how His holy name is everywhere ignored, despised, blasphemed. The teaching of Jesus Christ is cast off, His example forgotten, and the price of His blood lost in a certain sense as far as we are concerned because there are so few to profit by it. Behold likewise your neighbors, images of

---

[11] Hebrews 1:14.

the most holy Trinity and capable of enjoying His glory whom all the world serves, members of Christ, redeemed by so much pain, opprobrium, and blood. Behold, I say, the miseries that surround them, the darkness of ignorance that envelopes them, and the whirlwind of desires, empty fears, and other passions that torment them, set upon by so many visible and invisible enemies, with the peril of losing, I do not say their property or their earthly lives, but an eternal kingdom and its happiness by falling into the insufferable misfortune of everlasting fire.

To sum up briefly, if you were to examine carefully the great obligation you have of seeking the honor of Jesus Christ and the salvation of your neighbor, you would see how fitting it is for you to get ready by diligently striving to make yourselves fit instruments of God's grace, especially since in these days there are so few real laborers who do not seek the things that are their own, but the things that are Jesus Christ's.[12] And the more that others fall short, the more you ought to endeavor to make up for them, since God bestows so especial a grace on you and one so proper to your vocation.

What I have said up to this for the purpose of awakening the drowsy and spurring on those who may be loitering on the way should not be taken as a justification for going to the other extreme of fervor. Spiritual infirmities such as tepidity are caused, not only by chills but even by overwarmth, such as excessive fervor. Let your service be a reasonable service, says St. Paul,[13] because he knew the truth of the words of the Psalmist, "and the king's honor loveth judgment,"[14] that is, *discretion;* and what was prefigured in Leviticus, "Whatsoever sacrifice thou offerest, thou shalt season it with salt."[15] It is thus, as St. Bernard says, that the enemy has no more successful ruse for depriving the heart of real charity than to get her to act rashly and not in keeping with spiritual reasonableness. "Nothing in excess," said the philosopher.[16] And this principle should be our guide even in a matter pertaining to justice itself, as we read in Ecclesiastes, "Be not over just."[17] If one fails to observe this moderation, he will find that good is turned into evil and virtue into vice. He will also learn that many inconveniences follow which are quite contrary to the purpose of the one who so acts.

The first is that God is not really served in the long run, as the horse worn out in the first days does not as a rule finish the journey, and thus it happens that someone must be found to care for it.

---

[12] Philippians 2:21.
[13] Romans 12:1.
[14] Psalm 98:4.
[15] Leviticus 2:13.
[16] Pittacus, one of the seven sages of Greece.
[17] Ecclesiastes 7:17.

Second, gains that are made with this excessive eagerness are not usually kept, as Scripture says, "Substance got in haste shall be diminished."[18] Not only diminished, but it may be the cause of a fall: "And he that is hasty with his feet shall stumble";[19] and if he stumbles, the further he falls, the greater the danger, for he will not stop until he has reached the bottom of the ladder.

Third, there is the danger of being careless about overloading the vessel. There is danger, of course, in sailing it empty, as it can then be tossed about on the waves of temptation. But there is also danger of so overloading it as to cause it to sink.

Fourth, it can happen that, in crucifying the old man, the new man is also crucified and thus made unable through weakness to practice virtue. St. Bernard tells us that because of this excess we lose four things: "The body loses the effects of the good work, the soul its devotion, our neighbor good example, and God His honor."[20] From this we infer that whosoever thus mistreats the living temple of God is guilty of sacrilege. St. Bernard says that the neighbor is deprived of good example, because the fall of one and the ensuing scandal are a source of scandal to others; and he calls them, in cause at least, disturbers of unity and enemies of peace. The example of such a fall frightens many and makes them tepid in their spiritual progress. In the fallen there is danger of pride and vainglory, since they prefer their own judgment to the judgment of everyone else, usurping what is not their own by setting themselves up as judges in their own cause when the rightful judge is their superior.

Besides these, there are also other disadvantages, such as overloading themselves with weapons which they cannot use, like David with the armor of Saul. They apply the spurs to a spirited horse rather than the rein. Therefore there is need of discretion on this point to keep the practice of virtue between both extremes. St. Bernard gives this advice: "Good will is not always to be trusted, but it must be bridled, regulated, especially in beginners,"[21] if one wishes to benefit others without disadvantages to himself, for "he that is evil to himself, to whom will he be good?"[22] If discretion seems to you to be something very rare and hard to come by, make up for it with obedience, whose counsel is certain. Hear what St. Bernard says of those who wish to follow their own opinion: "Whatever is done

---

[18] Proverbs 13:11.   [19] Proverbs 19:2.
[20] St. Bernard, *De vita solitaria ad fratres de Monte Dei*, lib. 1, c. 11, n. 32 (PL 184, col. 328).
[21] *Ibid.*, lib. 2, c. 2 (PL 184, col. 339-47).
[22] Ecclesiasticus 14:5.

without the approval or against the wish of the spiritual father should be set down as vainglory, and not as something worthy of reward." We should remember that "it is like the sin of witchcraft to rebel, and like the crime of idolatry to refuse to obey,"[23] as is said in Holy Scripture. Thus if you wish to hold the middle way between the extreme of tepidity and indiscreet fervor, discuss your affairs with the superior and keep within the limits set down by obedience. If you have a great desire of mortification, use it rather in breaking your wills and bringing your judgments under the yoke of obedience rather than in weakening your bodies and afflicting them beyond due measure, especially in these years of your studies.

I should not wish you to think from what I have here written that I do not approve of what I have learned of some of your mortifications. I know that these and other holy follies have been profitably used by the saints and that they are useful to obtain self-mastery and bring down richer graces on us, especially in the beginning. But for one who has acquired some mastery over his self-love, what I have said about reducing to a discreet moderation I consider best, provided one does not withdraw from obedience. It is this obedience that I recommend very earnestly to you, joined with that virtue which is a compendium of all the others and which Jesus Christ so earnestly recommends when He calls it his especial commandment: "This is my commandment, that you love one another."[24] And I wish that you preserve this union and lasting love, not only among yourselves, but that you extend it to all, and endeavor to enkindle in your souls the lively desire for the salvation of your neighbor, gauging the value of each soul from the price our Lord paid of His life's blood. This you do on the one hand by acquiring learning and on the other by increasing fraternal charity, making yourselves perfect instruments of God's grace and colaborers in the sublime work of leading God's creatures back to Him as their last end.

Do not imagine that in this interval given to your studies you are of no use to your neighbor; because, besides the profit to yourself which well-ordered charity requires—"Have pity on thy own soul, pleasing God"[25]—you are serving God's honor and glory in many ways.

First, by your present labor and the intention with which you undertake and regulate everything for your neighbor's edification, just as soldiers waiting to get supplies of arms and munitions for the operation about to be launched cannot say that their labor is not in the service of

---

[23] 1 Kings 15:23.   [24] John 15:12.   [25] Ecclesiasticus 30:24.

their king. Even if death should overtake one before he begins to work exteriorly for his neighbor, he shall not for that reason have failed in the service of his neighbor, having helped him by the mere fact of his preparation. But besides the intention for the future, he should each day offer himself to God for his neighbor. As God is willing to accept the offering, he can serve as an instrument for the help of his neighbor no less than he would have done by preaching or hearing confessions.

The second way is to attain a high degree of virtue, because you will thus be able to make your neighbor such as you are yourselves. For it is God's will that the process of generation observed in material things be observed in things spiritual, *mutatis mutandis*. Philosophy and experience teach us that in the generation of man or animals, besides the general causes such as the heavens, another cause or agent of the same species is required which possesses the same *form* as that which is to be transmitted, and for this reason it is said that "the sun and man beget man." In like manner, to transmit the *form* of humility, patience, charity, and so forth, to others, God wills that the immediate cause which He uses as instrument, such as the preacher or confessor, be humble, charitable, patient. With the result, as I said, that, when you benefit yourselves with a growth in virtue, you are also of great service to the neighbor. You are preparing an instrument that is not less, but better, fitted to confer grace by leading a virtuous life than by leading a learned one, although both learning and virtue are required if the instrument is to be perfect.

The third way of helping the neighbor is by the example of a good life. In this respect, as I have told you, the good odor of your lives has spread abroad and exerts a good influence even beyond the limits of Portugal. I trust that the author of all good will continue His gifts and increase them in you, so that, as you daily grow in perfection, the fragrance of your virtues and the resulting edification will likewise grow, even without your seeking it.

The fourth way of helping your neighbor is very far-reaching indeed, and consists in holy desires and prayers. The demands of your life of study do not permit you to devote much time to prayer, yet you can make up for this by desires, since the time you devote to your various exercises is a continuous prayer, seeing that you are engaged in them only for God's service. But in this and other matters you have close at hand those who can advise you as to details. Indeed, for the same reason part of what I have written might have been omitted, but it is so seldom that I write you that I thought I could give myself the consolation of writing at some length.

This is all for the present, except to beg God our Creator and Redeemer that, as it has pleased Him to bestow so great a grace on you as to call you and give you the firm desire of being employed entirely in His service, so He would be pleased to continue and increase His gifts in all, so that you will persevere unwaveringly and grow in His service to His greater honor and glory and the help of His Church.

¶ TO FATHER SIMON RODRIGUES
XII, 630-31, Appendix VI, Letter 1

Ignatius advises caution in dealing with the world, and warns Rodrigues to be guarded in his speech.

Undated

IHUS

I have been thinking in our Lord of telling you of my desire to be reminded hourly and to live with the recollection of how the good angels in matters of extraordinary importance are wont to be very much alert to strengthen and build up, and the evil spirits to weaken and destroy. The same thing is true of good and evil men, as can be seen in the instance of an enmity here between two gentlemen, and others of the kind. I have not always felt safe either in spiritual conversations or in other chats of a friendly nature or on matters that are quite indifferent. In such cases many are intent on the things of earth, their honor, their temporal interests, and would pass themselves off as our friends without really being so. Even in the matter of confession or spiritual conferences, they will act thus in order to learn where we stand, whom we favor, and for what reasons and under what terms. Their only purpose is to destroy later what the servants of Christ our Lord are striving to build up, "for the children of this world are wiser in their generation than the children of light,"[1] especially when they notice that we are not careful and speak with a loose tongue. We are forced, therefore, to be very much on our guard in our friendships, confessions, and spiritual conferences. You should reflect that whatever you might let slip unguardedly is going to be known here and there, and as often happens, with additions and comments given in bad faith. As we are ceaselessly opposed to him, it is my hope that in the infinite and sovereign goodness he will always be overcome and reduced to confusion.

[1] Luke 16:8.

¶ TO MANUEL SANTOS
I, 513-15, Letter 171

Ignatius is answering a letter from the good bishop, who in all probability had shown a desire to resign his episcopal office. He was bishop of Targa and auxiliary bishop to the archbishop of Lisbon, Cardinal Vasconcelhos. Ignatius thanks the bishop very sincerely for his affection for the Society and exhorts him to the purest love of God our last end.

Rome, May 18, 1547

May the grace and everlasting love of Christ our Lord be ever our protection and help, for His honor and glory and our own salvation. Amen.

I have had much comfort and consolation in our Lord from your lordship's letter. I find in it a proof, not only of the kindly remembrance of your lordship but also of the great charity with which you desire our spiritual advancement and the advancement of God's glory in us, that glory for which all creatures were created and ordered by His eternal wisdom. I beg the same Creator and Lord, for whose love every other love should be embraced and governed, to take upon Himself the rewarding with very especial graces the affection which your lordship has shown me and the work of this Society of His name. For my part I do not know what I can do to make a return for such remembrance and affection, except to correspond with deepest remembrance and affection, praying that God, the author of all good, will increase in you those desires for His honor and service, with the continual increase of His grace to carry them into effect, and that He may be pleased to relieve your lordship of those burdens which in your letter you rightly judge to be a great embarrassment for one who has to ascend to so lofty a throne as is paradise.

And while we should not give up tasks which we have received and are fulfilling for God's honor, it is possible that the greatness of love which overwhelms the soul should find relief, even in things that are earthly and base, when one does not make oneself earthly or base but loves them all for God our Lord and insofar as they are directed to His glory and service. This is something which necessarily has to do with our last end, which is itself perfect and infinite goodness, which must be loved in all other things. To this end exclusively the whole weight of our love should be directed. And indeed, He is entirely deserving of that love, since He created us all, redeemed us all, and thus gave Himself without reserve. It is with reason that He will not have us withhold a part of ourselves, since He has so completely given Himself to us and desires to give Himself to us forever.

As to the rules and statutes, I think that you would get more satisfaction from Master Simon, who, being close at hand, can speak to you personally, than you would from me at a distance and by means of a letter. Therefore, in this matter I will leave the task of answering you to Master Simon.

My most respectful greetings to the most reverend lord cardinal.

No more for the present, except to ask the Divine Goodness to keep us who belong to Him by so many titles and to increase in your lordship all of His most precious gifts and graces. Your lordship's most humble servant in our Lord ...

¶ TO FATHER JAMES LAINEZ
1, 519-26, Letter 174

This letter written by Polanco to Father Lainez is primarily a defense of the classics. Lainez believed that excessive devotion to classical studies could deter a student from more profound subjects, such as philosophy and theology. Polanco expresses the views of Ignatius clearly and in an organized and thorough manner.

Rome, May 21, 1547

IHS

May the grace and peace of Jesus Christ our Lord be ever present in increasing measure in our souls. Amen.

It is not a small favor your reverence has done me with your letter. Writing me, as you do, in the midst of your discussions and other duties, you give me reason to be grateful for the remembrance you have of me, and I hope that the same charity which causes you to write me will cause you to remember me in your prayers, which I need so much. I shall eagerly look forward to the summary you promise when there is a lull in the occupations you undertake for the common good, and I will receive it with great affection. For this and other kindnesses may He reward you who is wont to do so for his poor, for everything that is given and received in His service.

With regard to Master Louis and Peter Ribadeneira and Fulvius,[1] I have laid your views and those of Master Claude[2] before our father master

---

[1] Among the scholastics who were studying at Padua are named Fulvius Cardoli and Peter Ribadeneira. The name of Louis does not occur.

[2] Father Claude Le Jay.

Ignatius. He has given me no definite answer with regard to individuals. It is possible that during the rest of the summer he might come to a decision to make some change in matters that will be worth considering.

As to Peter, I am certain that Father Ignatius loves him with an affection beyond that which he entertains in general and in particular for the members of the Society. He is anxious for him to have every possible advantage, for his progress in studies as in other things which will be of use to him in God's service. But thus far he has not shown much inclination either to change him or to keep him where he is. He may possibly be waiting for something to turn up before making a decision in his regard.

Your reverence thinks that excessive devotion to classical studies usually makes the mind so dainty and refined that it neither can nor cares to give itself to profounder studies, especially if their researches lead them to authors who are without the attractions of style. I agree with your reverence on the point of excess in these studies, both because of the authority with which you write and because of the examples we have of those who, having begun higher courses, wore themselves out before they had worked very hard. It is a kind of daintiness to get accustomed to the study only of those things that are easy and entertaining, or if they became frightened or annoyed by those subjects of contrary qualities, subjects that are difficult and uninteresting such as we find in philosophy and scholastic theology. But notwithstanding the difficulty I see in tarrying too long in these studies, I should not think that it would be too long, speaking again in general, to remain long enough to master the humanities, especially languages, in the case of students who are fitted by age and talent to pursue them. My reasons are as follows.

1. There is the authority of those who advise this study of languages as very necessary for Scripture. I say authority, ancient as well as modern; and I must admit that what has weight with me is to see that on this point Master Ignatius feels as I do, for he is very desirous of having members of the Society excel in Latin. Over and above the human prudence and experience in which he excels, I believe that God especially inspires him with such ideas and convictions, for His providence is wont to bestow a special flow of grace on those who have the responsibility of governing for the common benefit of those they govern.

2. We have the example of the ancients, such as Jerome and Augustine and others of the Greek and Latin fathers, for whom the study of the classics in no way blunted the fine point of their minds to prevent them from penetrating into the heart of things; not to mention the Platos and Aristotles, for example, and other philosophers.

3. It is a common practice. In subjects that are not very profound and in which the sensitive appetite cannot mislead or offer violence, there will be no common error that is general. It seems that from times long ago right up to our own it has been a common practice to begin with classical literature, with the exception of those years when barbarism not only in literature but in society reigned in the place of study. With the exception of these years we gather that this method of beginning with a good foundation in literature before going on to other studies prevailed in Greece and Italy, and I think other places as well.

4. Experience teaches us that many great and learned men, because of their lack of training, have to keep their learning to themselves and are balked of the main purpose for which they should have acquired their learning, which was to be of benefit to their neighbor. If there are others who do share the benefits of their learning, it is not with that authority and success they would have if they were as able to explain themselves as they are to understand, and to throw as much light upon their ideas when they give them forth as they had within their minds to understand these ideas themselves. This I think can be seen even in scholastic doctors. For if a part of their shrewd and learned acquisitions could be exchanged for a skillful way of explaining the remainder, they could with what remained achieve a more widespread good than they now do with all their learning.

5. Another motive for keeping the humanities as a foundation, is a whole list of reasons of which the following are a few.

(a) As in the training of the body exercises are taken up gradually beginning with those that are easier and going on to those that are more difficult, so, it seems, to make headway with those subjects which demand a severe mental effort, such as philosophy and scholastic theology, it is necessary that the understanding get accustomed to work, especially in subjects that are neither difficult nor uninteresting. Such subjects are found in the humanities, which are better adapted to minds that have not yet been trained and are less robust. Such subjects will open the mind gradually and prepare it to take subjects of more consequence with greater ease.

(b) It seems that time spent in acquiring this weapon of humane letters is well employed. For as a man advances in years and begins filling his head with impressions of greater import, such as various activities, it is with difficulty that he will come back to take up languages. Experience and reason would seem to indicate this, since the memory is no longer as ready as it was in early years to take impressions from the fancy, even of slight things. Men are not able to apply themselves to the study of conjugations and other elementary exercises in the way that those who have not yet come to deal with greater matters can do, since the understanding, accustomed to operations on a greater and nobler scale, disdains those that are elementary and refuses to lower itself to them. Imagine one who was accustomed to govern the affairs of a kingdom occupying himself with the direction of a village!

(c) Languages are undoubtedly helpful in obtaining an understanding of the Scriptures, and therefore the time spent in mastering them will be usefully employed.

(d) Languages, especially Latin, are very necessary if one wishes to share with others what God has given to him, to say nothing of giving luster to knowledge and all the natural, acquired, and infused gifts of God. The times in which we live are so trying in this respect that, as everyone wants to have a knowledge of languages, it would seem that one who did not know them would exercise but little authority.

(e) This learning seems to be especially necessary in our Society, both for dealing with men who speak different languages, either in conversation or by letter, and to give satisfaction both in preaching and in conversation to ordinary people who are more capable of appreciating humane learning. It will be a means of helping them.

(f) Although they are studying subjects that will be useful in the future, such as history, geography, figures of speech, and rules of rhetoric, even these, I have no doubt, will work together unto good for those who love God, and that more than a little.

(g) Even in these studies there will be opportunity to exercise talent and intellectual muscle, especially when a student takes part not only in rhetorical disputes, if he is engaged in that study, but by means of original compositions, either in verse or prose, speeches, or letters.

(h) I think it is very important to master a language once for all if one is to make use of it later as he should. No one can get this mastery who does not devote sufficient time and effort to it once for all. It happens that many carry the rock of Sisyphus to the brow of the hill and then let it roll down, and have to begin the climb all over again. I have had some personal experience of this, having begun Greek three different times and having borne the weight and trouble of the grammar and just begun to understand the authors a little. But because I did not continue my study long enough to be able to say that I had mastered the language and trained myself by exercise in the use of it, I have got little good out of it. I have much less Hebrew, of which I retained hardly enough to forget, and now I seem to be entirely relieved of all that I had. And all this for not having once for all made the effort to master the language. If I had, it would not later have taken such prompt leave of me.

In addition to these reasons there is the answer given to the opponents which I mentioned at the beginning. For we can say that to stay at the study of Latin and Greek long enough to master them is no reason for all not wanting to study more serious subjects. Because, even if some predisposition of the kind is left in the mind and the will, no habit is left which is easily moved and inclines us with the force of an instinct. And this will be true especially of one who does not allow himself to grow old in these studies, since he stops them when he has attained the end desired. Now, although there may be some probability that such a disposition makes for laziness in many when they come to higher studies, a really good will can overcome such an inclination, just as many overcome it for worldly ambition and dispose themselves to study subjects for which they have little or no taste or inclination.

And therefore, if there should be some in the Society who have such an inclination in a slight degree, this could be overcome with a like serious effort of the will for the love of God. For this they would have three helps which men of the world do not have. The first is the purpose for which these humanistic studies are undertaken, and that is the greater service of God and the help of our neighbor. The second is obedience, which will not allow them to dillydally over the grammar even if they want to. The third is God's grace, which, because of the authority of the two preceding reasons, can rightly be expected to be more abundant. There are reasons that have a more general application.

Speaking of Peter Ribadeneira, there are additional reasons for keeping him a little longer at these studies. The first is that it will do him no harm to know more Latin, although he is well advanced. He should see more of the authors, exercise himself in writing, and, as I said, master the language. Second, there will be plenty for him to learn in rhetoric and history. And third, having begun Greek only a short time ago, he could not make much progress in that language in the little time that remains of this year. If he takes another year, he can make himself a good Greek scholar, as I have hope in his ability. Fourth, I think it will improve his understanding of other subjects when he takes them up, and keep him from being afraid of any difficulty he might encounter. Fifth, I am inclined to think that the prior of the Most Holy Trinity will take it amiss if we remove the better students, or those at least who seem to be. Sixth, at the moment I do not see where he could go. Master Ignatius does not think it would be good to send him to Spain. The duke of Gandia and others have written to ask that some students be sent there, and our father answered that it would be better to provide themselves with students in Spain. This seemed best to them also. It might be better, therefore, not to send anyone now, to say nothing of the difficulty of travel and so on. Neither is there any accommodation in Paris. If we wait a year, I am sure that the way will be clearer.

No more of these reasons. It would be unreasonable to multiply them to such an extent as to tire your reverence, even though my letter comes to you in a moment of leisure.

If you are still busy with the articles,[3] there is no reason why you should be in a hurry to read this. It will keep fresh for reading until after the feast. I might indeed have placed this warning at the beginning of the letter, where it would be more opportune.

No more for the present, except humbly to commend myself to the prayers of your reverence and to those of all my reverend fathers in Christ, and of all those in the community. May Christ Jesus add to His grace in all, so that the honor and service of His Divine Majesty may be increased in all.

¶ TO FRANCIS BORGIA, DUKE OF GANDIA
I, 528-31, Letter 176

Ignatius answers a letter from Francis and expresses his joy at Francis' recovery from an illness. The exact nature of the illness is not mentioned, but it was probably another one of those attacks that caused Ignatius on a number of occasions to urge Francis to have more regard for his health. Francis, who was far from being a robust man, added to his natural weaknesses by prolonging his prayers beyond reasonable limits, by indiscreet fasting, and by the most severe penances and mortifications. His indomitable spirit compensated for the infirmities of his body, but he nevertheless died at the early age of forty-eight.

Ignatius asks the date on which the children of Borgia are to be married, so that he can recommend them to God and have prayers said for them by his companions. He observes that the Spiritual Exercises have

---

[3] Allusion is here made to the fourteen heretical articles on the sacrament of penance. In a letter to Polanco, Lainez had said that they were then being debated.

been highly approved by the cardinal of Burgos. He speaks of obtaining indulgences from the pope for those making the Exercises or confessing to Jesuit confessors, and intimates that he will take the matter up with Dean Rocca. He speaks of the College of Gandía, of establishing the Society at Saragossa and at Seville, as Borgia thinks best, of Borgia's profession, and of Father John Tejeda.

Rome, middle of 1547

I received two letters at the same time from your lordship, one dated the end of April and the other May 7, with the usual pleasure and spiritual joy in our Lord in increased measure, for I perceive that His Divine Majesty looks with more favor every day on your lordship by advancing your thoughts and desires in His greater service, praise, and glory. With one hand, it seems, He imparts these desires and with the other, with ever-growing diligence, labors in them and with them for His greater honor and glory. May it please His divine and supreme Goodness ever to advance and preserve you in His perfect service and praise by daily increasing His most holy graces, gifts, and spiritual visitations in your beloved and chosen soul.

As to your lordship's recent illness, I learned from a letter received at the same time of your recovery. I find, therefore, no occasion for regret. I should rather rejoice, I think, supposing that the experience has not been without some spiritual benefit. But seeing that this visitation and profit began on the feast day of the glorious St. Ignatius, I find more reason for rejoicing in our Lord, under the persuasion that your lordship will grow in devotion to the name of this blessed saint, to whom I have, or at least wish that I had, a very special reverence and devotion in our Lord.

As to the arrangements for the marriage of your children, son and daughter, with the daughter and son of the marquis of Comares, considering the care and devotion you give the matter—sentiments which I seem to experience in my own soul—I find it easy to believe that they are in the hand of Him who can never fail and that it will be a good and holy alliance, entirely for God's greater praise and glory. The blessing which your lordship asks of us here in the name of our common Lord and Creator of all things, your lordship may impart.

If I seem in any way reluctant to be the instrument, it is because I feel myself to be so unworthy of any good. And so I give your lordship all my powers, which your lordship may use in God's service as you see fit. All I ask is that we be notified here of the date on which the marriages will take place, so that all the priests of the house may say Mass and the others offer their prayers that these nuptials, which are made on earth, may be celebrated spiritually in heaven and that, being thus spiritual in heaven, they may become spiritual also on earth. If we cannot be notified in time, at least let it be soon after their conclusion, and we will then do the same and so be able to satisfy the devotion we all feel in our Lord.

The Exercises have been examined and approved by the Cardinal of Burgos, and even the Roman authorities are quite satisfied with them.[1] With regard to obtaining greater graces for those who confess to one of the Society, we shall see what can be done in our Lord when Dean Rocca returns. May He in His infinite and supreme goodness direct and accomplish all in conformity with His greater praise and glory.

As to what concerns the university and related matters which your lordship entrusts to me, both personally and through others, I will see that the proper people are approached, and I will keep the matter carefully in mind until I can manage such affairs with greater ease.

I have written to Araoz in Portugal several times and to Master Andrew[2] regarding the brothers your lordship desires for Saragossa and Seville, and I think that we shall hear favorably from there. Do you arrange matters as you judge best to God's greater glory; I am quite ready to approve whatever arrangements you make. I give your lordship whatever jurisdiction and authority I have over these brothers, so that you can act without the necessity of referring to me in all that you think will be to God's greater glory.

What your lordship asks with reference to Master Andrew seems to me to be just and holy[3] and to God's greater glory, and that this is a very special favor which God our Lord is bestowing on all of us. May He be pleased in His infinite and supreme goodness to confirm it all for His greater service, praise, and glory. For the rest I refer you to Master Andrew and to what I am writing to him.

Father John Tejeda is here in the house, your house as well as ours, and we have induced him to remain because of the heat. After the weather gets a bit cooler he will leave for Spain. His affairs have turned out according to your wishes, to God's greater glory. He leaves with us and carried away with him a good impression in our Lord, to whom be glory forever.

---

[1] *Chronicon*, I, 249.
[2] Father Andrew Oviedo, rector of the College of Gandia.
[3] This is a reference to Borgia's intention of entering the Society and binding himself by vow to do so. See *Epistolae mixtae*, I, 385.

Let the Lady Joan receive this letter as though it were really her own. I beg your kindness to remember me especially to her ladyship, and to my lords in our Lord, your sons. May He keep them always in His fear and love, to live always and die in the greater love and service of His Divine Majesty.

¶ TO THE COLLEGE OF GANDIA
I, 551-62, Letter 182

Ignatius offers both examples and arguments of great weight to prove that in every gathering of men one should preside over the others, whom all should obey. He goes on to show the members of the Gandia community what course they should follow in choosing a rector.

Rome, July 29, 1547

May the grace and love of our Lord Jesus be ever alive in our hearts and increased. Amen.

There are several reasons which impel me affectionately to make what provision I can in those matters which I judge in our Lord to be for the greater good of the Society. I have a particular obligation which grows from the heavy burden which has been laid upon me, and I feel a loving desire in keeping with this obligation, a desire which God our Lord bestows upon me, to see it increase. This leads me to consider by what means we can advance the interests of the Society and its members, to God's honor and glory.

One of these means which I consider very important is that, wherever a number of the Society are living together in community, they should have a superior or head by whom they are ruled and governed just as they would be by the general if he were present among them. As such provision has been made in Portugal and in Padua and must now be made in Louvain, I think it should also be made at Gandia, Valencia, and in other places where there are students of the Society. I shall first tell you why I think in the Lord that a superior should be placed over you for God's greater honor and glory and the greater good of the individuals and the community living at Gandia, as well as of the body of the Society in general. Then I shall go on to speak of the manner of choosing and obeying the person thus chosen, as it seems best to me in the Lord.

First, let me give the reasons I have for thinking that a superior should be had. I am afraid that I shall exceed the bounds of what is strictly necessary to convince you on a point that is so holy and essential. But it is not my intention merely to prove that what is now ordained is well ordained. Rather, it is to exhort you to accept such obedience and thereafter persevere in it cheerfully and devotedly.

To come at once to the point, one of the many reasons I have is the unfailing example given us by all men who live in community under rule of some kind, such as we see, not only in states and cities but even in particular communities and their houses. This is true not only of the past but of the present as well. Their government is commonly united in a superior, confusion and disorder being thus avoided in the proper ruling of the multitude. For it is certain that, where men of judgment and reason are commonly in agreement, it will be on what is fittest, most natural, and proper. But much more convincing is the living example of Christ our Lord, who, living a common life with His parents, "was subject to them."[1] Our Lady and common mother, the Virgin Mary, was subject to Joseph, to whom, as head of the household, the angel addressed himself, "Take the child and his mother."[2] The same Jesus Christ our Lord deigned to be the superior of the disciples while He lived in their midst, and when it was time for Him to withdraw His bodily presence, He left St. Peter as superior of the others and of the whole Church, entrusting its entire government to him: "Feed my sheep,"[3] was His commission. And he remained their superior even after the apostles were filled with the Holy Spirit. Now, if a superior was necessary for them, how much more necessary will it be for any other group to have one? We also learn that the early Church in Jerusalem made St. James the Less its head, and in the seven churches of Asia there were the seven superiors whom St. John in the Apocalypse calls angels. Under the direction of the apostles the same arrangement is found in all the other communities. Obey them, is St. Paul's exhortation: "Obey your prelates, and be subject to them."[4] What was then established is observed today. And this is true most of all in regard to religious, beginning with the anchorites and the first founders of religious orders down to our own day. The same practice has been observed; wherever any number of men live together in communities, there is always one who, vested with authority, rules and governs the others as their head.

But reason, even unsupported by examples, would urge the same procedure. If we must consider as better that manner of life in which God

---

[1] Luke 2:51.
[2] Matthew 2:13.
[3] John 21:17.
[4] Hebrews 13:17.

is given more acceptable service, we must consider as better service the life in which all are under the obligation[5] of obedience, since obedience is preferred to all sacrifices: "Obedience is better than sacrifices, and to hearken rather than to offer the fat of rams."[6] And not without reason; for in offering one's own judgment, will, and liberty, which is the principal part of man, one offers more than anything else. Moreover, this way of life aids in the attainment of every virtue, for according to St. Gregory "obedience is not so much a virtue, as the mother of all the virtues."[7] And there is nothing surprising in this, since it obtains whatever it asks of God, as the same saint says: "If we are obedient to superiors, God will be obedient to our prayers."[8] Before him Holy Scripture had said, speaking of Josue, who was most obedient to Moses his superior, that not only the sun obeyed him, stopping at his command, "Move not, O sun, toward Gabaon,"[9] but even almighty God, who created the sun and all things, "the Lord obeying the voice of a man."[10] There is a great advantage for subjects in this, insofar as an increase of the virtues is concerned, seeing that the author of them is made obedient to their prayer, and also because, according to the saying of the Wise Man, "You can count as virtue whatever you take from your own will."

This manner of life also makes it possible for us by following the will of the superior to avoid many errors of judgment and defects or sins of one's own will, not only in particular instances but even in one's whole state of life, as each one obliges (in our way of speaking) Divine Providence to rule and direct him. And this the more as one resigns oneself into the divine hands by means of the obedience which one pays to God's minister; by which we should understand every superior to whom one submits for the love of God.

Add to what has been said the further advantage of success in resisting all temptations and overcoming all weakness which the presence of the superior renders possible, with whose opinion we may conform our own and by whom we may be directed, for "an obedient man shall speak of victory";[11] that is, victory over himself, which is the noblest of all triumphs. It is certain that this road goes very straight, for it leads to the subjection of one's own judgment and will by means of holy obedience. This practice would come to an end if the superior were not at hand. This

---

[5] *"Obligacion."* Another reading, perhaps preferable, *"oblacion,"* an offering.
[6] 1 Kings 15:22.
[7] This is the teaching of the fathers. See Espinosa Pólit, *Perfect Obedience*, p. 271, n. 7.
[8] This thought of St. Augustine (PL 40, col. 1344) was once attributed to St. Gregory.
[9] Josue 10:12.   [10] Josue 10:14.   [11] Proverbs 21:28.

way of life is also of singular merit for those who know how to profit by it, as it is something of a martyrdom which continually decapitates one's own judgment and will by setting Christ's will and judgment, manifested through His minister, in place of one's own. It decapitates not only the single desire of life, as does martyrdom, but all desires taken together.

Merit is also increased by the value added to all good works when they are done through obedience. You should also recall that you will thus proceed without weariness and advance in shorter time in the way to heaven, as when one makes use of other feet than his own; that is, of his own understanding and will. In this way he will travel with continuous merit in all things, even in such actions as sleeping, eating, and so forth, just as those on board a ship advance while they rest to their journey's end, which is what they have most at heart. It helps us to gain and retain a firmer possession of the key which opens heaven to us, just as disobedience has been and continues to be the cause of our losing it. As long as the toil and exile of our present pilgrimage last, this manner of life gives us a great taste for the repose of the fatherland, not only by freeing us of perplexities and doubts but also by unburdening us of the heavy weight of our own will and all care of ourselves, to place them upon the superior with the resulting peace and rest. If one who lives under obedience does not experience something of this peace, he should examine himself well, lest it be through his own fault, by resuming some authority over himself after having left himself in the hands of the superior. Let him hear what St. Bernard has to say of him and others like him: "Why do you thus resume charge of yourselves, after having once and for all committed that responsibility to him?"[12] Thus it is a great relief for one who is aware of the favor God does him in giving him someone at hand whom he can obey. This not only supports him but ennobles him, and in a large measure elevates him above the state of man, making him divest himself of self to clothe himself with God, the highest good, who will fill the soul in the measure that He finds it empty of self-will. Such men may say of themselves, if they are sincerely obedient, "And I live, now not I, but Christ liveth in me."[13] Although one may say that whoever obeys in the Lord the general of the Society may share in this, I hold it for certain that he does not share as much—the difference in fact being considerable—as those who living in community have one whom they can obey in the Lord near at hand.

---

[12] St. Bernard, *Sermo 19 in Cantica* (PL 183, col. 866).
[13] Galatians 2:20.

Besides the spiritual advantages already enumerated, which are of more concern to individuals, this manner of life has a very close relation to the preservation of your community as a body. For no group can preserve itself intact unless it is united, and there can be no union without subordination, without a head to whom the other members should be subordinate through obedience. Therefore, if you desire the continued existence of your community, you must desire to have someone as your head.

But over and above your preservation, it is still quite important for good government that there be someone in Gandia easily available with an understanding of conditions who can make provision for them as I would if I were present among you. For experience has already proved to us that it is impossible from this distance to deal properly with matters which may be of some importance: partly because of the impossibility of keeping us informed by writing of what goes on there, since everything cannot be committed to writing; partly because, in many instances at least, the occasion would slip away in the interval between asking direction and receiving an answer from here.

Such a superior would be a great help, proper and even necessary, to anyone who has to bear the weight of such responsibility as mine. For while he is under obligation to attend to so many details, he cannot do so personally, and should attend to them at least with the help of others.

Besides what has been said, there will be no small advantage resulting from the election of a superior for the preservation of the true spirit of the Society throughout the whole body. For this it will be very useful if the scholastics and others among its members be very well trained in obedience. It should make no difference to them who the superior is, but they should recognize Christ our Lord in each of their superiors and be careful to obey Him in His representative. The reason for this advantage is that, while this virtue of obedience is very necessary for every congregation, it is especially so in this Society, which is made up of highly educated men, some of whom are sent on important missions by the pope and other prelates, others scattered in remote places far from any superior, associating with great personages—and for many other reasons. Now, if their obedience is not of a very high quality, such men could hardly be ruled at all. And therefore I hold that there is no duty more opportune and necessary for the common good of the Society than a constant and careful obedience.

Moreover, in order to know how to lead and direct others it is necessary first of all to have mastered the lesson of obedience. And as it is most profitable for the Society to have experienced superiors, so it is also in having some method in learning to obey. For this purpose we have here in this house two ministers, one working under the other. All who are in the house must obey them both, even though one of them should happen to be a lay brother, as they would obey me or anyone in my place. Finally, if the failures and successes of others should serve as a guide for us, we see that in not a few congregations many faults of no little importance have been committed because they did not have superiors with sufficient authority to govern. On the other hand, in those places where all obey a single superior, the advantage is evident.

Enough has been said touching this first part to show how reasonable and prudent it is to make provision for a superior, a measure at once useful and necessary, and how willingly and devoutly you ought to accept it. It remains to deal with the second part, the manner of choosing such a superior and of obeying him.

With regard to the election, all of you who reside at Gandia should make a retreat of three days and have no communication with one another on any matter pertaining to the election. The priests should celebrate Mass with the special intention of the success of the election, and the others should recommend it earnestly to God in their prayers. They should all consider who is best fitted for the responsibility, with no other thought than the better government and the greater good of your community in Gandia and God's honor and glory, as though they took the election upon their conscience and had to give an account of it to God our Lord on the great day of judgment. On the third day each one shall write out his vote and sign it. The votes shall then be placed together in a box or urn and shall not be touched for another day. Then, in presence of all, the votes shall be taken out, and he who shall have the greater number of votes shall be your superior or rector. Him I already approve until you shall have heard otherwise from me. You may use this method as long as there is no professed among you there and until the Constitutions are finally promulgated.

As to the manner of obeying the superior of your choice, it seems to me that you should deal with him as you would with me were I present, or with whosoever had my office. For all the authority I should wish to have were I present with you to help you to the greater honor and glory of God, all that I desire your rector to have for the same end. Therefore you should look upon him no otherwise than you would me—rather neither him nor me, but Jesus Christ our Lord, whom you obey in both of us and for whose sake you obey His ministers. He who is not ready to obey and allow himself to be ruled, as I have indicated, whether he be now present in Gandia or is to come later, and whether the rector be this one or another who shall succeed him by the ordination of the father general of the Society, let him think of following another way and leave your community and way of life, in which there should be no one who is not able or willing to submit to the obedience I have here described.

This letter shall stand as a witness to all those who are living in your community of my decision in our Lord. It is my wish and desire that this plan be carried into execution for the greater spiritual profit of the scholastics of the Society who are now with you, to the greater service, praise, and glory of God our Creator and Lord.

May He by His infinite and sovereign goodness grant us abundant grace to know His most holy will and perfectly to fulfill it.

¶ TO THE MEMBERS OF THE SOCIETY IN PADUA[1]

I, 572-77, Letter 186

The prior of the Trinita in Venice, Andrew Lippomani, who had renounced the income of his priory to endow two colleges of Jesuit scholastics, one in Padua and the other in Venice, kept putting off from day to day the actual surrender of the benefice. Meanwhile the Jesuits of the newborn college of Padua were suffering from the poverty and want spoken of in this letter. It was drawn up by Father John Polanco, secretary to St. Ignatius, but the ideas were probably suggested by the saintly founder.

Rome, August 7, 1547

Dearly beloved Fathers and Brothers in Christ.

May the grace and true love of Jesus Christ our Lord be ever in our hearts and increase from day to day to the very end of our lives. Amen.

---

[1] For a better understanding of this letter we must note that many in Padua were sick with fever that year. Some were suffering from the effects of unhealthy marsh gas not far from the house and others because of the poor quality of the meals that were served. Young Ribadeneira, who was studying there at the time, gives us a full account of it, in which there is the following paragraph on the meals:

"First, as to our table. It is usually this: at noon a little vegetable soup and a little meat, and that's all. When fruit is in season, we get a few grapes or something else according to the season. At night it is the same, a hodge-podge cooked with chicory or something similar, and a little meat. Master Polanco can tell you better, as there has been no change since he left. Although the doctor says that the scholastics must have veal or mutton, this cannot be done, for veal is very high here as in Rome and mutton is not butchered in winter, so we must do the best we can with beef" (*Epistolae mixtae*, V, 649-50).

A letter addressed to Father Master Lainez in Florence has come to us through the hands of our and your friend Peter Santini. In it we learn, among other things, of the love of poverty, of that poverty which you have chosen for the love of the poor Christ, and the opportunity you sometimes have of suffering some lack of necessities owing to the inadequacy of the help offered you by the kind and charitable prior of the Trinita. It is not necessary to exhort to patience those who are mindful of their state and who keep before their eyes the naked Christ upon His cross. And this is especially true since it is clear from the aforementioned letter what a welcome this poverty is given by all of you when you experience its effects. And yet since our Father Ignatius, who has a true father's affection for you, has entrusted me with the task of writing you, I will console myself, while consoling all of you, with this grace which His Infinite Goodness allows both you and us of feeling the effects of that holy poverty. I have no means of knowing how high a degree of this grace is yours, but with us it is in a very high degree, quite in keeping with our profession. I call poverty a grace because it is a very special gift from God, as Scripture says, "Poverty and riches are from God."[2] How much God loved it His only-begotten Son has shown us, who, coming down from the kingdom of heaven, chose to be born in poverty and to grow up in it.[3] He loved it, not only in life, suffering hunger and thirst, without any place to lay His head,[4] but even in death, wishing to be despoiled of everything, even His clothing, and to be in want of everything, even of water in His thirst.

Wisdom which cannot err wished to show the world, according to St. Bernard,[5] how precious a jewel is poverty, the value of which the world did not know. He chose it for Himself, so that His teaching, "Blessed are they that hunger and thirst, blessed are the poor, etc.,"[6] should not be out of harmony with His life.

Christ likewise showed us the high esteem He had of poverty in the choice and employment of His friends, who lived in poverty, especially in the New Testament, beginning with His most holy Mother and His apostles, and continuing on with so many Christians through the course of the centuries right up to the present, vassals imitating their king, soldiers their captain, and members their head, Jesus Christ.

So great are the poor in the sight of God that it was especially for them that Jesus Christ was sent into the world: "By reason of the misery of the needy and the groans of the poor, now will I arise, saith the Lord."[7]

[2] Ecclesiasticus 11:14.
[3] See Wisdom 18:15.
[4] See Matthew 8:20; Luke 9:58.
[5] Sermon I for the Nativity.
[6] Matthew 5:3, 6; Luke 6:20.
[7] Psalm 11:6.

And elsewhere, "He hath anointed me to preach the gospel to the poor,"[8] words which our Lord recalls when He tells them to give an answer to St. John, "The poor have the gospel preached to them."[9] Our Lord so preferred the poor to the rich that He chose the entire college of His apostles from among the poor, to live and associate with them, to make them princes of His Church and set them up as judges of the twelve tribes of Israel—that is, of all the faithful—and the poor will be His counselors. To such a degree has He exalted the state of poverty!

Friendship with the poor makes us friends of the eternal King. Love of poverty makes kings even on earth, kings not of earth but of heaven. And this can be seen from the fact that the kingdom of heaven is promised in the future to others. To the poor and to those who suffer persecution for justice' sake the Immutable Truth promises it for the present: "Blessed are the poor in spirit, for theirs is the kingdom of heaven."[10] Even in this world they have a right to the kingdom.

And not only are they kings, but they share their kingdom with others, as our Lord teaches us in St. Luke, "Make unto you friends of the mammon of iniquity, that when you shall fail they may receive you into everlasting dwellings."[11] These friends are the poor, particularly the voluntary poor, through whose merits they who help them enter into the tabernacles of glory. For they, according to St. Augustine, are the least of all, of whom our Lord says, "As long as you did it to one of these my least brethren, you did it to me."[12]

In this, therefore, we see the excellence of poverty which does not stoop to make a treasure of the dunghill or of worthless earth, but with all the resources of its love buys that precious treasure in the field of the Church, whether it be our Lord Himself or His spiritual gifts, from which He Himself is never separated.

But if you consider the genuine advantages which are properly to be found in those means that are suited to help us attain our last end, you will see that holy poverty preserves us from many sins, ridding us as it does of the occasion of sin, for poverty has not wherewith to feed its love, *non habet unde suum paupertas pascat amorem.*[13] It slays the worm of riches, which is pride; cuts off the infernal leeches of lust and gluttony, and many other sins as well. And if one should fall through weakness, it helps him to rise at once. For it has none of that attachment which, like a band, binds the heart to earth and to earthly things and deprives us of

---

[8] Luke 4:18.
[9] Matthew 11:5.
[10] Matthew 5:3; Luke 6:20.
[11] Luke 16:9.
[12] Matthew 25:40.
[13] Ovid, *De remedio amoris*, 749.

that ease in rising and turning once more to God. It enables us to hear better in all things the voice—that is, the inspiration—of the Holy Spirit by removing the obstructions that hinder it. It gives greater efficacy to our prayers in the sight of God because "the Lord hath heard the desire of the poor."[14] It speeds us on our way along the path of virtue, like a traveler who has been relieved of all his burdens. It frees us from that slavery common to so many of the world's great ones, in which everything obeys or serves money.[15] The soul is filled with every virtue if poverty is in the spirit, for the soul that is swept free of the love of earthly things shall in the same proportion be full of God, having received His gifts. And it is certain that it must be very rich, for God's promise is at the rate of a hundred to one, even in this life. The promise is fulfilled even in a temporal sense, when that is for our good. But in the spiritual sense it cannot fail of fulfillment. Thus it is inescapable that they who freely make themselves poor in earthly possessions shall be rich in the gifts of God.

This same poverty is that land fertile in strong men, *fecunda virorum paupertas*,[16] as the poet said in words which are truer of Christian poverty than Roman. This poverty is the furnace which tests the progress of fortitude and other virtues and the touchstone which distinguishes genuine gold from counterfeit. It is also the moat which renders secure the camp of our conscience in the religious life; it is the foundation upon which the edifice of perfection should rise, according to the words of our Lord, "If thou wilt be perfect, go, sell what thou hast, and give to the poor . . . and come, follow me."[17] It is the mother, the nurse, the guardian of religion, since it conceives, nourishes, and preserves it; while on the other hand an abundance of temporal possessions weakens, corrupts, and ruins it. Thus we can easily see the great advantage and the excellence of holy poverty, especially since it is poverty that wins salvation from Him who "will save the poor and the humble"[18] and obtains for us the eternal kingdom from the same Lord, who says that the kingdom of heaven belongs to the poor, an advantage that is beyond all comparison. So, no matter how hard it may happen to be, holy poverty should be accepted voluntarily.

But really it is not hard; rather, it is the cause of great delight in him who embraces it willingly. Even Seneca[19] says that the poor man laughs with greater ease because he has no cares to upset him, a truth which daily experience shows us in the instance of the wayside beggar. If you

---

[14] Psalm 9:17.
[15] Ecclesiastes 10:19.
[16] Lucan, *Pharsalia*, I, 165.
[17] Matthew 19:21.
[18] 2 Kings 22:28; Psalm 17:28.
[19] Epistola 80 ad Lucillum.

were to observe the satisfaction in his life, you would see that he is more cheerful than the great merchants, magistrates, princes, and other persons of distinction. If this is true of people who are not poor by choice, what shall we say of those who are poor because they choose to be? For, neither possessing nor loving anything earthly which they could lose, they enjoy a peace that is imperturbable and a tranquillity that is supreme. On the other hand, riches are for those who possess them like the sea that is tossed by the storm. Moreover, these voluntary poor, because of the peace and security of their conscience, enjoy an uninterrupted cheerfulness which is like a banquet without end. They prepare themselves in a very special way by means of this very poverty for heavenly consolations, which are wont to abound in the servants of God in proportion as they lack an abundance of the goods and the comforts of earth, if only they know how to fill themselves with Christ, so that He will make up for everything and occupy in their hearts the vacancy left by all else.

But I must not pursue this further. Let what I have said suffice for your consolation and mine to encourage us to love holy poverty, remembering that the excellence, advantage, and joy I have mentioned belong only to that poverty which is loved and willingly embraced, not to the poverty that is accepted because it cannot be avoided. I will add only this, that those who love poverty should as occasion offers love her retinue, which consists of poor meals, poor clothes, poor sleeping accommodations, and to be held of little account. Whoever loves poverty and is unwilling to feel want, or any of its effects, would be a very dainty poor man and would give the impression of one who loved the name rather than the reality, of one who loved rather in words than in the depth of his heart.

That is all for the present, except to ask our Lord, our Master and true model of spiritual poverty, to grant all of us the gift of this precious heritage, which He bestows on His brothers and coheirs, to the end that the spiritual riches of His grace abound in us, and at the end, the ineffable riches of His glory. Amen.

¶ TO FATHER ANTHONY ARAOZ
I, 620-22, Letter 209

Father Araoz had a considerable reputation for eloquence, apostolic zeal, and his gift of prudence in "dealing with matters connected with the service of God" (X, 248-49). Together with Blessed Peter Faber he in-

troduced the Society of Jesus into Spain. At the time of the writing of the letter which we now present the Constitutions of the Society were not yet written, and St. Ignatius instructs the new provincial on the method of naming superiors. He directs him, moreover, to choose two companions to help him and to lighten his many and oppressive occupations.

Rome, October 31, 1547

May the grace and everlasting love of our Lord Jesus Christ be always in our favor and help.

A second letter will be written you which will deal with other matters. The purpose of this is twofold. I am prompted to write by the responsibility which God our Lord has laid upon me and the need of making some provision for carrying out these purposes for the greater service and glory of our Creator and Lord.

The first has to do with those communities throughout Spain which belong to the Society and over which it has seemed good in the Lord to give you charge and jurisdiction, with the same authority which I could have over them through Jesus Christ our common Lord. You shall have seen this in the letters appointing you provincial of all Spain, exclusive of Portugal. It seems to me that, wherever these communities exceed two in number, a superior should be appointed whom the others, whether many or few, must obey. They should be directed by him as by you or me—nay more, as by Jesus Christ our Lord, for whom and to whom all must render obedience. And just as all those who live in one place must obey their immediate superior, the superiors of these places, as in the present instance, with the exception of Gandia and Valencia, such as Barcelona, Alcala, Valladolid, and Saragossa, if there or elsewhere there should be any of Ours, they must obey you and take direction from you. If a due subordination is thus well observed, the corporate unity of this Society will be maintained, and it will be ruled in all its members to the greater service of God and their own good.

I hardly think it necessary to insist with you on my reason for thinking that this appointing of local superiors is necessary and of great importance in attaining the ends of the Society. You will yourself easily appreciate it, and you may have read it in the letters I wrote to Valencia and Gandia which dealt with the election itself of the superior.

I will also explain what I judge in the Lord to be the best way of choosing such a superior. If in a given place where a superior is to be appointed you know of one who seems to you to have the qualifications for such an office, appoint him without asking the opinion of others—at least the authority of the appointment should rest with you alone. But if you doubt about the fitness for the office of a given individual, first ask the opinion of each of those residing in each place. This they should give in writing, setting forth their opinion sincerely as to what they think in our Lord will be for His greater service. They shall do this after having reflected in silence for three days and recommended the election to God, those who are priests saying Mass for this intention and thinking over which of them would be the best choice. There should be no interchange of opinion, nor should one know what the others think, let alone try to influence one another. What they have written they shall give to you sealed, or send to you or to whoever has your office. And you in like manner, recommending the matter to God our Lord and saying Mass for the same intention, after having examined their opinions, will appoint him whom you judge best able to fulfill the office to God's greater honor and glory. From that hour, by the authority given me by the Apostolic See, I will consider him superior, and the others must accept him as such.

The second point is that it seems to me in our Lord that, wherever you take up your residence and there happens to be a plentiful harvest of souls, you should have at least two companions, both of them priests, to help you in all that you have to do. If one of them, however, is not a priest, the priest should help you with confessions and more important matters, while the other will help you in those things that are less important but still necessary, such as writing for you and looking after your personal needs. If I thought in our Lord that you would not take this suggestion as though imposed in virtue of holy obedience, I would so impose it. Considering what is written to me about the multitude of your occupations and the additional burden that has been laid upon you as provincial, which likewise will add to your duties, it will be very necessary for you to have some help for the more satisfactory conducting of your affairs and to give them better attention than you could if you are alone, as also to avoid injuring your health.

I learn from your attacks of illness, and from those there who are acquainted with you, such as Dr. Torres and Santa Cruz, that you should have a little more concern for your health. You should also have someone at hand who could warn you when you neglect it more than well-ordered charity permits. The body, like the soul, is from God, and its preservation is necessary for the service of the Divine Majesty. You should therefore take sufficient care of both for love of the same Creator and Lord. Choose, therefore, two companions among those who happen to be with you, for the purposes I have mentioned and others which you may have yourself.

Trusting that what I have said will be sufficient to procure a prompt obedience, a virtue which God its author has bestowed on you, I will not delay longer on the point. Begging the Divine Majesty to make known to us all His most holy will in all things and grace to fulfill it with a prompt and true obedience, I am entirely yours in our Lord ...

¶ TO TERESA REJADELL
1, 627-28, Letter 214

This religious in her letters to St. Ignatius undoubtedly touched on the reform of her convent. In 1546 the saint attempted with fresh energy the reform of convents of nuns in Catalonia, and interested others in the project, especially the provincial, Father Anthony Araoz; the visitor, Father Michael de Torres; the bishop of Barcelona, James Cazador; the duke of Gandia, Francis Borgia; and Philip, heir to the throne of Spain and later king. In the present letter Ignatius exhorts his correspondent to recognize her own defects and disown them. He trusts that the reform, while difficult, will be successful, and refers her to others for news of the Society, for which he asks her prayers.

Rome, October 1547

IHS

May the grace and love of Jesus Christ our God and Lord live always in our souls. Amen.

Santa Cruz brought me your two letters in which, showing your dissatisfaction with the faults of the community and those of individuals, you give proof of the good desire God has given you that some means be found of correcting both the one and the other. May God in His infinite mercy hear your prayers, for it is written of Him, "The Lord hath heard the desire of the poor."[1]

Regarding the faults of individuals, it is certainly necessary that whoever knows himself should recognize the faults he has, for he will never be free of them in the state of our present misery until in the furnace of the everlasting love of God our Creator and Lord all our wickedness shall be entirely consumed, when our souls shall be completely penetrated and possessed by Him and our wills thus perfectly conformed to—or rather, transformed into—His will, which is essential rectitude and infinite good-

---

[1] Psalm 9:17.

ness. But may He by His infinite mercy grant to all of us at least daily to regret and abhor all our faults and imperfections, and participate at last in the eternal light of His wisdom and lay hold of His infinite goodness and perfection, in the clear light of which even the least of our defects will appear to be insupportable. By thus attacking them we will weaken and lessen them with the help of the same God our Lord.

As to the defects of the community for which you ask a remedy from God's hand and hope that in His goodness He will provide one, this is not only my own desire but my hope also. We may take as a sign that God will condescend to effect this reformation the fact that the prince is also desirous to see a reform and that effective means are being sought to bring it about. That there are difficulties is nothing new, but rather to be expected in matters of any importance for God's service and glory. But the more difficult the work, the more pleasing it will be, besides being also the occasion for giving God our Lord more sincere and ceaseless thanks.

As to news about our Society, you will have some one closer at hand to keep you informed. Only, I beseech you for the love of Jesus Christ, our Society's head, even though He is also our common Lord and sovereign of all created things, to remember us earnestly in your prayers to His Divine Majesty, that He may deign daily to be better pleased and glorified by our Society.

My own health isn't much. Blessed be He who by His blood and death won eternal health for us by a share in His kingdom and glory. May He grant us the grace that, whether the condition of our health be good or bad, it and all else may always be employed in His greater service, praise and glory. Amen.

¶ TO FATHER DANIEL PAEYBROECK
1, 659-63, Letter 234

St. Ignatius answers a letter from Father Paeybroeck and encourages his correspondent in the cultivation of virtue and the giving of a good example. He observes that, although one is removed from the rest of the world by his way of life, he is under the eye of men. He approves what has been done by the companions at Louvain and recommends maintaining a strict standard in admitting candidates. He promises to send James Lhoost to be their superior as soon as he can be released from his present duties in Sicily. But he finds fault with certain points in the Constitutions as they were submitted by the brethren at Louvain. He states that the Society of Jesus has been freed from the obligation of the regular direction of communities of women. He explains his thought about the communication of faculties which the supreme pontiff has granted him.

Rome, December 24, 1547

We received your letters, one dated March 4 and the other March 18. They both brought us great joy in the Lord. This joy compels us to love you and all your companions whom you have so closely united, to the glory of our Lord, in the desires of the heart and an ideal of life. It is His love alone that should be the bond which holds our whole Society together in the closest union.

I warmly approve what you tell me of your community life together, as well as of the choice you exercise in admitting applicants to our Society. It must, as I hope, all redound to the honor and praise of our Creator and to the profit of many. And it shall, if your light shall have so shone among men as to make them glorify your Father who is in heaven.[1] Others too will be moved by your example to imitate you. You have assumed a most serious obligation to live in holiness and piety; and although you are separated from the rest of the world in your dwelling and way of life, you will move about under the eye of men and be exposed to their remarks. That you will be true to your obligations, I trust in Him from whom comes every good and perfect gift,[2] to whom you have all consecrated yourselves, and from whose goodness you all have your vocation as a more than common pledge. But I also hope that in your common life you will find a great mutual help. In it you will find a brother ready to wait upon a fallen companion, to sustain the wavering, to stimulate the laggard by word and example, so that, "ministering the same [grace] one to another,"[3] you prepare yourselves to receive fresh graces from the Father, since wherever two or three are gathered together to ask a favor it will be granted, as Truth Itself has promised.[4]

Therefore, as those whom you have thus far chosen for admission to the Society have my approval, I advise you to keep to the same standard of selection for the future. I would not like to have it said of us with any truth, "Thou hast multiplied the nation, and hast not increased the joy"[5] or the strength. Be careful, therefore, that those you accept come recom-

---

[1] Matthew 5:16.
[2] James 1:17.
[3] 1 Peter 4:10.
[4] Matthew 18:19.
[5] Isaias 9:3.

mended by their upright lives. If they are not at all learned, they should have at least the ability to acquire learning, and possess a basis of good understanding and a strong will together with good health, so as to be able to bear the labors which our state of life demands of us. We are very glad to help and protect the weak and infirm outside the Society, but we have learned from experience not to admit any such into the Society, as they would be rather a drag than a help in the Institute which we have embraced for God's glory and the help of souls.

I quite agree with you when you think that James Lhoost of Geldonia would make a good superior for you. He is now in Sicily at work in the Lord's harvest, but I promise to see that he visits you without delay if he can be spared from his present occupation without notable loss. I hope that he will be no less successful there with you in his work for souls and the glory of God our Lord Jesus Christ. Only, I will add this, that I think you ought to try to win the approval and the affection of your bishop for your community, so that with your father's blessing you will grow in numbers and in virtue, to the praise of Him who created and redeemed us, our Lord Jesus Christ, who is blessed above all things forever.

I fully approve the rules and regulations you sent me, and I think they are quite suited to these beginnings of your community. As time goes on, experience will point out what, if anything, is to be added or changed. If anything occurs to me I will be glad to let you know. Meanwhile, however, I will be frank, and mention two criticisms. The first is that, as you say, in the fourth rule, "No one of either sex will be admitted to this congregation who has been under vow, and so on," you seem here to have the feminine sex in mind, although further on you rightly declare that women cannot be admitted to vows. I should here like to remind you that our Society does not and cannot accept the charge of women. Consultation, of course, is excepted, which indeed can be denied to no class, either of men or women. We used great care in obtaining this exemption from the supreme pontiff, and made provision both for ourselves and our successors, lest for the sake of minor works which are subject to many annoyances we should have to give up those of greater importance for the honor of God and the good of souls.

The second suggestion is that, while you make express mention of the vows of poverty and chastity, you do not look upon the resolve of entering the Society as a vow. Indeed, while I should not wish to entice anyone to enter the Society unless God was calling him to it, I let them know that we do not wish to rule them as committed to our care if they do not bind themselves by vow to enter. Your rule will be very weak over those who are free to withdraw from it at will. If, therefore, you are thinking of having one of Ours as superior, intimating as you do James Lhoost, I do not see how it will be possible for us to grant this without giving up a custom which we have carefully observed, unless you bolster your purpose of entering by a vow as the others do.

As to what concerns faculties and privileges granted to this Society for the good of souls, I should not want you to interpret my delay in communicating them as a lack of faith in your virtue or prudence in making use of them. My conscience is witness of the high opinion I have of you and the great hopes I entertain. But as this treasury of graces has been entrusted to me by the supreme pontiff *in aedificationem non in destructionem,* that I might share it with those of Ours whom I find apt and according to the needs of each, I am under obligation to make a very gradual and moderate use of it. I will thus keep in mind that I am to dispense it, not dissipate it. Moreover, there are many who abuse the privileges granted them, and have lately had their privileges withdrawn. I am not speaking of Ours, who by God's grace have neither abused their privileges nor been deprived of them. This of course should make us more cautious, so that, making a good and moderate use of the favors granted, we make them more permanent. As they are very exceptional, we could incur the envy of others unless we made a very temperate use of them.

From what I have said you will understand that it is not strange that I should wish to know what I am sharing and with whom. Let those therefore who wish to participate in these privileges for the edification of the neighbor write me individually, delineating their personal qualities, their desires, their progress in studies, and their reasons for thinking that they will make a proper use of the faculties. Each one should state which faculty he wants, this or that, or both. And then if I confer them (as I propose to do), I will be able to give an account of my stewardship to God, and to man should an account be asked.

I close, asking our Lord Jesus Christ to give us His abundant grace to know His will and strength to fulfill it. Yours in our Lord ...

¶ TO FATHER STEPHEN BAROELLO
XII, 226-28, Appendix I, Letter 8

This letter was written after Ignatius had sent Baroello to Sicily. Its purpose is to instruct him in the care and education of the orphans there. He reminds Baroello of the importance of humility both in his actions and in the tasks which he attempts. He says that conversation should always be moderate and edifying. He refers him to Master Florence, a French priest, who could not be admitted into the Society because of the impediment of having belonged to another order from which he was released on account of ill health. He did, however, live under the direction of its superiors and he was obedient to them. His duty was the instruction of orphans. The letter, written in Italian, was drafted by some unknown secretary under instructions from Ignatius.

Rome, beginning of January 1548

IHS

Dear Master Stephen in Christ Jesus.

Our Father Master Ignatius wishes you to keep the following advice in mind. . . .

In dealing with the neighbor pray every day especially with the intention that God give you the grace of discretion, so that you will build up and not tear down.

Try as a general rule to be alert, so as to act with all humility in matters that are within the range of your ability, and do not meddle in those that are beyond your powers. God wishes each of us to serve Him within the limits of the talents He has bestowed upon us, and He is not pleased with presumption. Our spirit should not, however, for that reason underestimate itself, so that we do not undertake vigorously what is within our capacity. . . .

As to the exterior posture, expression, and gait, try to observe a becoming modesty, and ask Master Florence[1] to admonish you. Men are quick to notice such externals, and one should try to be edifying even in these.

Keep your conversation to a mean between what is too little and too much. Out of respect for people of prominence be sure to say what is proper and likely to edify. Above all, try not to say anything that would manifest ignorance or vulgarity, but speak out calmly what the Lord will inspire you to say and what will be fitting for the persons you are talking to and the things you are talking about "to edification." May the unction of the Holy Spirit teach you all things. Amen.

Have a talk about these things with Father Master Domenech, who will consider them and give you the advice he thinks best. Amen.

---

[1] His name is given in a footnote in its Latin form as Florentius Pauletus (*Chronicon*, II, 172).

¶ TO THE COMMUNITY AT COIMBRA
1, 687-93, Letter 243

An exhortation to perfect obedience. A preliminary draft of the famous letter on obedience.

Rome, January 14, 1548

May the grace and peace of Jesus Christ our God and Lord be present in ever greater measure in our souls. Amen.

The letter I have written to Master Simon might suffice for your more pressing problems. As for others that are unessential, the poor health I have and the burden of affairs will excuse me. Yet the great affection which Jesus Christ our Lord has placed in my heart for you prevents me from wishing to avail myself of any excuse, knowing as I do that, because of your devoted obedience, you are consoled in our Lord by the letters that are written you from Rome, just as we are greatly consoled in the same Lord by the good news we hear of your spiritual progress in learning and virtue. I hope that God our Creator and Lord will augment this joy of ours from day to day by augmenting its cause, and not permit a diminution of it by permitting a diminution of its cause. It is my hope that you will be counted among those of whom the Wise Man speaks in Proverbs: "But the path of the just, as a shining light, goeth forwards and increaseth even to perfect day."[1] Therefore I beg of Him who is the author of this day, as the sun of wisdom and justice, to bring to perfection in His mercy what He has begun in you, until He brings you to discover and know "where He feedeth, where He lieth in the midday,"[2] thus glorifying Himself in all of you and displaying the riches of His omnipotent hand and the infinite magnificence of His spiritual gifts in your souls, and through you in the souls of many others.

To you also, my dear brothers in Jesus Christ our Lord and God, I send the same request in the same Lord to make yourselves ready for His visitation and spiritual treasures by purity of heart and true humility, by a complete agreement of mind and will, and by outward and inward peace which prepares a mansion in the soul and brings about the reign of Him who is called the Prince of Peace,[3] all, in a word, being made one in our Lord Jesus Christ. Because a union such as this cannot be maintained among many without some order, nor order without the due bond of obedience between inferiors and superiors, as the whole visible extent of nature, the angelic hierarchies, and the well-regulated states of men

[1] Proverbs 4:18.
[2] Canticle of Canticles 1:6.
[3] Isaias 9:6.

teach us, all of which are held together, preserved, and ruled by subordination, I earnestly recommend this holy obedience to you. It should be observed by each individual toward his superiors of whatever grade they be, and toward officials in all that regards their office; toward confessors in matters of conscience; and toward the rector in all things. In the same manner the rector as well as all others should be subject in everything to the provincial, since God has made special use of him as an instrument to inaugurate His work. He, in turn, will be subject to whomsoever God our Lord shall give him as superior general, and the general to him who is supreme over all, in whom all superiors without distinction of person recognize Jesus Christ our Lord, since it is to Him and for His sake that obedience is given to anyone at all.

Now, this obedience, if its fruit is to be union and preservation, must be concerned not only with works that are exterior, but must direct those that are interior also, such as acts of the will. For, as St. Bernard says, he who does not the will of his superior has not reached the first degree of obedience.[4] The same should be said of obedience of the understanding, for it will not last, nor can a union of wills be long maintained, if a divergence of views is fostered.

This will come to pass even if one does and wills what the superior ordains while judging the contrary and preferring his own opinion to that of the superior. Now, it is certain, supposing there is no question of sin, or the evidence being so clear as to convince the intellect, that true obedience makes subject to the superior, not only the work but the will as well. In this event the union is made firm and lasting, and peace and quiet, under this holy and light yoke, become in a certain sense imperturbable, as far as the misery of our present state allows.

They who act contrary to the intention of the superior can see from this that, even though their actions be good and praiseworthy in themselves, such as mortification, contemplation, and so forth, they have but little part in obedience, since they act contrary to what they are commanded when they do these things, follow their own will rather than their superior's, and prefer their own judgment to the judgment of him who is put over them. How little acceptable to God is a sacrifice that is offered in opposition to the mind of the superior, when the act itself is not of obligation and may even be in itself a means to perfection! Such men should understand, as St. Bernard says, that they do not make an offering that is acceptable to the Holy Spirit if they fail in a matter of

[4] *Sermo de virtute obedientiae* (PL 183, col. 656).

general obligation, which binds the subject to obey his superior. It is of him almighty God says: "He that heareth you, heareth me; and he that despiseth you, despiseth me."[5] The sacrifice of Saul seems to have been thus faulty because it was contrary to the obedience due to God our Lord which had been laid upon him by the prophet Samuel. "For the people spared the best of the sheep and of the herds that they might be sacrificed to the Lord thy God."[6] And what was the prophet's answer? "Why then didst thou not hearken to the voice of the Lord . . . and hast done evil in the eyes of the Lord?"[7] Again, when Saul appealed to his sacrifices: "Doth the Lord desire holocausts and victims, and not rather that the voice of the Lord should be obeyed? For obedience is better than sacrifices, and to hearken rather than to offer the fat of rams. Because it is like the sin of witchcraft to rebel, and like the crime of idolatry to refuse to obey."[8] So also of little value was the sacrifice of Cain when he offered the fruits of the earth and merited not the favor of God. Like them are the toils and sufferings of the body and even of the soul, or any other work whatsoever, when they are offered without the approval of obedience and charity. But on the contrary, "the Lord had respect to Abel, and to his offerings," for he "offered of the firstlings of his flock and of their fat."[9] Such is the noble sacrifice of one's own will and judgment, which is the devout offering of obedience in an odor of sweetness to the Divine Majesty through His ministers.

He who against obedience offers the sufferings or toils of his body lacks the salt which in the Book of Leviticus is required for every sacrifice. For this is not that living victim which is conformable to reason and acceptable to God our Creator and Lord, as recommended by St. Paul.[10] I should wish the truth enunciated by St. Bernard to be thoroughly understood and clearly remembered: "Whatever is done without the approval and wish of the spiritual father should be set down to the account of vainglory and not of merit." How much more so, if it is against his will! What greater pride is possible than to prefer one's own will and judgment to the will and judgment of him whom we have recognized as superior in the place of Jesus Christ our Lord? Experience ordinarily reveals such men as proud and deserving as such that the very medicines and remedies they take, such as the mortifications mentioned (when they are practiced with the approval of the superior and in accordance with reason), should turn for them into a deadly poison.

---

[5] Luke 10:16.
[6] 1 Kings 15:15.
[7] *Ibid.* 15:19.
[8] *Ibid.* 15:22-23.
[9] Genesis 4:4.
[10] Romans 12:1.

Great is the satisfaction which the enemy of our nature takes when he sees a soul traveling heedlessly, even by ways that are lofty and sublime, and without the restraint of him who knows how to rule and govern, since he then has all the more reason to look for its fall and ruin. And zeal, which would be so holy were it under the direction of obedience, becomes a weapon and a contrivance of the devil to rob the heart of true charity, and consequently of its supernatural life. See how the sons of Israel, wishing to enter even the Promised Land against obedience, were conquered by their enemies. Fear to go astray, therefore, even in spiritual things, if you disregard obedience. Observe that a very small number, when they acted through obedience, usually overcame superior forces of the enemy, while many were overcome by few when they disregarded it.

Now, since everything, as you know, is written for our instruction and edification,[11] be glad when you are ruled as far as possible by this holy and safe direction of obedience. Persuade yourselves in our Lord that you are then walking in a straight path. And you conform yourselves to the divine will when, trampling under foot your own will, you hold aloft before your eyes that of your superiors, in the belief that Divine Providence must thus rule and guide you, so that you will arrive at a higher perfection and the help of your neighbor.

May it please His Divine Majesty that in all things His most holy name be honored and glorified for ever. Yours in our Lord . . .

¶ TO FATHER NICHOLAS BOBADILLA
I, 719-21, Letter 258

Ignatius regrets that letters from Rome addressed to Bobadilla have been intercepted. He says that arrangements have been made for his support, and exhorts him to indifference regarding the scenes of his labor. If he honestly thinks that it would be to God's greater service for him to leave Germany, he should say so sincerely, without being misled by self-love. He should rather acquiesce in the will of his superiors.

Rome, February or March 1548

JHS

May the grace and peace of Christ Jesus our Lord and God be ever preserved and increased in our hearts.

---

[11] 2 Corinthians 12:19.

From two of your letters which arrived together, dated respectively December 10 and 24 last, I see that all the letters which have been written you from here have not reached you, since you make no mention of them in your letters. This letter will be rather an answer to one which you wrote to Cardinal Santa Croce[1] rather than those which you wrote to me. I called on him to talk about some other business today, and he showed me one of your letters, the one in which you speak of the arrangements you wish made for your support. With his usual charity his most reverend lordship attributed this request to the fact that you must be suffering some need, but I assured him that I really thought that you, judging it to be a matter of greater edification, refused to take what was offered you by some. The cardinal finally told me that he had spoken to Monsignor Maffei[2] and that orders would be given to Monsignor Prospero de Santa Croce, who I think is going to Germany as nuncio, to make arrangements to provide you with all that is needful. He bade me write you and tell you not to hesitate to take from the nuncio what you thought you needed, and assured me that whatever expenses you incurred would be charged to the pope. I spoke to Maffei also about the matter, and he told me that he was giving the orders referred to. You will therefore be able to have recourse to Monsignor Prospero in all your needs.

As to your recall from Germany by the authority of the pope who sent you there, it will be hard to bring it about if there is any news of the success of your stay in Germany, and I believe you have had some success, for God's service. Cardinal Santa Croce still thinks that you should remain, and Maffei, that you should not leave until you hear from Monsignor Prospero. When they inform the pope that your stay in the country is attended with but little fruit, it will not be a difficult matter to obtain your recall from him. But you can see how proper it is that you have some care of your good name, for the greater service of God our Lord.

In this matter of your recall, if you think yourself a man of obedience, as you say in your letter, you should find some other way to get my decision, such as follows. Put aside your own will, which you find to be more inclined to one side than the other, and try to keep before your eyes the one and only end of the greater service and glory of God. Consider well whether your remaining in Germany would be attended with greater fruit or whether you should come here for the same end. If it seems to you in our Lord that you would do better work elsewhere, it would be

---

[1] Monsignor Prospero de Santa Croce, bishop of Chiusi, nuncio to the emperor.
[2] Bernard Maffei, secretary to Paul III.

better for Monsignor Prospero to write me that, as far as your leaving Germany is concerned, he will have to be guided by what you write your superior. You are to write me a letter in which you profess that you are indifferent, as far as you can be, as all who belong to the Society must be, whether you remain in Germany or go elsewhere, that you desire only to be where you can be employed for the greater service and glory of God our Lord and the Apostolic See. But at the same time that you let us know what you think is God's will for you, show yourself disposed to consider that place best which holy obedience shall appoint for you. If you write in this manner, there will be occasion, should any change of place have to be made, to give more glory to God our Lord, and that with greater credit to yourself, something which is required in the ministers of God our Lord if they are to work with greater success.

May God our Lord direct you in all things and give us all the grace to know His perfect will and perfectly to fulfill it.

¶ TO FATHER ANDREW OVIEDO
II, 54-65, Letter 295

The letter begins by stating that an answer to questions concerning certain literary and spiritual exercises of the scholastics will be deferred until later. Ignatius is, however, aware of the existing situation. Meanwhile he gives many serious reasons why obedience as a special mark of the Society should be earnestly practiced. In this letter the paragraphs are numbered to facilitate comparison with the famous Letter on Obedience of March 26, 1553. It will be at once apparent that a great part of that letter was already written in 1548. Often enough not only whole paragraphs correspond as far as their contents are concerned, but there is even a very close verbal correspondence. The letter is written by a secretary under instructions from Ignatius.

Rome, March 27, 1548

IHS

My dear Father in Christ Jesus.

1. As I have already given you elsewhere the answers to your inquiry, I will here confine myself to dealing with some points on which I have special instruction from our father. His paternity has set down the principal points to be treated, and you will therefore take the contents of this letter as coming not from me but from his paternity.

2. Nothing special will be said now about the spiritual exercises and studies of the scholastics who are with you. Our father has by this time seen what is commonly done in various places by the scholastics of the Society, such as Valencia, Coimbra, Louvain, Padua, and Bologna, besides what you write of Gandia. Just now he is recommending this matter to God our Lord, and he hopes soon with God's help to finish the Constitutions which are to be put into force everywhere in the colleges of the Society, both with regard to what concerns the preservation and progress in spirit and virtue and progress in studies, and everything connected with them.

3. I have also been directed to tell your reverence to keep in constant communication with Father Araoz. As you see, the Society by God's mercy is growing, and it is hoped that with the same grace it will continue to grow daily. May the divine and supreme Goodness grant that it may not be merely in numbers and possessions, but much more in spirit and virtue, and thus His Divine Majesty be served and glorified in all.

4. With this increase of the Society just mentioned our care must necessarily keep pace. And as one man is not sufficient to attend to so many affairs, it is necessary to divide this care, so that it may be possible to direct individuals with greater satisfaction and thus make the weight more bearable and endurable for him who carries it. Because order is necessary in any large number if confusion is to be avoided, even when there is a large number of individual superiors there must be among them some rank and order, so that by this subordination the rank and unity of all may be maintained, and with it the well-being and good government of the Society.

5. Almost all creation teaches us that this must be and that it is in keeping with the dispensation of Divine Providence. For in all bodily things that are moved we see that the lower movements are made subject to the higher, and these in turn to a highest. We see the same holy subordination in the angelic hierarchy, one of which is subject to another, Divine Providence thus bringing all to their respective ends, the lowest by the middemost and the middlemost by the highest. Unity is thus preserved among them by the bond of subordination.

6. In the Old Testament we see the same subordination in secular affairs of rulers over thousands, hundreds, fifties, and tens, under one head in whom rested the supreme authority. We see the same today in well-regulated states and in the ecclesiastical hierarchy, where prelates are subordinate to the supreme pontiff. The well-being of government (or its decay) depends upon the good or ill observance of this subordination.

7. Taking all this into account, our father desires very much in our Lord that this proper subordination of some superiors to others be observed, and that private individuals show a trustful obedience to their respective superiors, and these superiors to the provincial, in the same manner as the provincial should to the general and the general to him whom God gave him as superior. For this reason he earnestly recommends that you have recourse to Father Araoz in all matters, and obey him as Jesus Christ our Lord, since he holds His place. And when Father Araoz is in doubt, write to Father Ignatius, and all will be helped in our Lord. As to writing him, you should do so as frequently and in the manner he shall point out.

8. As to the retirement and solitude of seven years which you ask, Father Ignatius thinks that, as the matter is serious and may be a dangerous precedent in the Society, it needs further thought.

9. But as to the great insistence with which you press your petition, I think that our father considers it quite uncalled for. If his paternity thought the matter to be for God's greater service and glory, he would agree to it without much urging. If he did not think so, even greater insistence than you have used would not be sufficient to move him. Speaking generally, I have often heard him say that it ought to be enough for the inferior to represent his reasons and to open his heart to the superior, without trying to draw the superior to his view or desire. For in many cases this is usually a sign of a lively self-will and of a judgment which lays down the rule by which the superior should be directed.

10. He also said that he had never read that St. Francis or any of the holy fathers had ever given any of their religious permission to retire to the desert before their profession or before they were very well known. The situation, however, is mended by the indifference you show and your readiness to accept whatever obedience shall ordain, for this is the firm anchor which will make the soul steady and secure.

11. But if a man wishes to examine himself on such indifference, as in the case of your reverence, he will ask himself in God's presence: first, whether he is seriously ready to accept or relinquish this retirement; second, whether he thinks he will be satisfied and content should he accept it or relinquish it; third, whether he thinks it would be better to accept it or give it up, depending on the decision of the superior. Whoever finds himself thus disposed can say that he has the indifference required by true obedience.

12. It is certain that, if obedience is a holocaust in which the whole man without the slightest reserve is offered in the fire of charity to his

Creator and Lord through the hands of His ministers, and since it is a complete surrender of himself by which a man dispossesses himself to be possessed and governed by Divine Providence by means of his superiors—I say that, if this is true, it is certain that it includes in the enjoining of human acts, not merely the execution which carries the command into effect but also the will which acquiesces in the command, and the judgment, which must approve the command of the superior insofar as the judgment by the energy of the will can bring itself to this.

13. This obedience, far from looking upon the superior as a man subject to errors and miseries, should behold in him the Infinite Wisdom and Goodness to whose divine providence the obedient man will submit and by which he will allow himself to be governed through the medium of His ministers, with the hope of a complete conformity with His holy will, which is the first and universal rule of all rectitude and justice. Out of love for Him he will conform himself to his superior whom he obeys in His place as the second and more immediately recognized rule, persuading himself that the two rules are identical when the superior's command conforms to the divine will, since Christ our Lord said in the Gospel: "He that heareth you, heareth me; and he that despiseth you, despiseth me."[1] St. Paul, writing in the same spirit to the Ephesians and referring to those who owe obedience to their worldly masters, says: "Servants, be obedient to them that are your lords according to the flesh, with fear and trembling, in the simplicity of your heart, as to Christ, not serving to the eye, as it were pleasing men, but as the servants of Christ doing the will of God from the heart, with a good will serving, as to the Lord, and not to men."[2] And again to the Colossians: "Whatever you do, do it from the heart, as to the Lord and not to men, . . . Serve ye the Lord Christ."[3]

14. Now, if this holds true in respect to secular masters, namely, that God's will is done in doing that of the master and that obedience to the master is obedience to Christ, what are we to think of obedience to spiritual superiors, of whom He Himself says: "Obey your prelates, and be subject to them."[4] With how much more reason can we look upon their will as the will of Christ our Lord? For he who looks upon the superior, insofar as he is superior, as Christ, will find it easy to submit his will and judgment, conforming both with that which he has taken for the rule of his actions, in the hope that Divine Providence will direct him by it, so that he shall be found conformed with the divine will alone.

---

[1] Luke 10:16.
[2] Ephesians 6:5-7.
[3] Colossians 3:23-24.
[4] Hebrews 13:17.

15. Now, to be conformed with this rule merely in the execution of a command is the lowest degree of obedience. But conforming the will, making one's own will that of the superior, is more perfect; and to conform oneself, over and above the execution, in both will and judgment, is perfect obedience, which subjects the judgment to the superior, as far as the will can bend the understanding.

16. I insist on this because, although the understanding has not the liberty which the will has, and naturally, but not freely gives its assent to the objects that are presented to it as true, yet in many instances in which the evidence does not coerce it the understanding can incline to one side or the other, representing to itself the reasons for one side rather than for the other. In such cases the obedient man ought to incline to think with the superior and seek reasons in favor of the side to which he sees him inclined, rather than the opposite.

17. There is also another method of subjecting the understanding to obedience. It is in use among the holy fathers and is easier and surer. It is to presuppose (much as is done in matters of faith, for example), that whatever the superior orders is the ordinance of God and His most holy will; and then blindly, without any inquiry, to proceed, with a kind of passion for obeying, to the execution of what is commanded. Thus we are to believe Abraham acted when commanded to sacrifice his son Isaac. Likewise, in the New Testament, some of those holy fathers of whom Cassian speaks, as John the Abbot, who did not consider whether what he was commanded was useful or not, when for a whole year with so much labor he watered a dry stick. Or whether it was possible or not, when at the command of his superior he tried so earnestly to move a rock which many men together could not have moved.

18. We see that God our Lord sometimes confirmed this kind of obedience with miracles. Maurus, St. Benedict's disciple, went into a lake at the command of his superior and did not sink. Another was told by his superior to bring home a lioness, took hold of her and brought her back with him to his superior. There are other examples with which you are well acquainted. By this I mean that the manner of subjecting one's own judgment, without further inquiry, is practiced by the saints. We suppose, of course, that the command is holy and in conformity with God's will. This example should be imitated in all things where there is clearly no sin, by all who wish to obey perfectly.

19. Would to God that this obedience of the understanding were better understood and practiced, for it is certain that it is very useful for those who live in religion, and even necessary and very pleasing to God

our Lord. Necessary, I say; for as, in the celestial bodies, if the lower is to receive movement and influence from the higher, it must be subject and subordinate, the one body being ordered and adjusted to the other. In like manner, when one rational creature is moved by another, as takes place in obedience, the one that is moved must be subject and subordinate to the one by whom he is moved if he is to receive influence and moving power from him. This subjection and subordination cannot be had unless the understanding and the will of the inferior is in conformity with the understanding and the will of the superior.

20. If therefore we consider the purpose of obedience, our understanding may be mistaken, just as our will, as to what is good for us. If we think it expedient to conform our will to that of the superior to keep it from going astray, the understanding also should be conformed with that of the superior to keep it from falling into error. "Lean not upon thy own prudence," says Holy Scripture.[5]

21. This advice is even more necessary in persons and things spiritual, as the danger in the spiritual life is greater when one advances rapidly in it without the bridle of discretion. Hence Cassian says in the conference of the Abbot Moses: "By no other vice does the devil draw a monk headlong and bring him to death sooner than by persuading him to neglect the counsel of the elders and to trust his own judgment and decision."[6]

22. Thus those who are wise judge it to be true prudence not to rely on their own judgment even in other affairs of life, and especially when personal interests are at stake, in which men as a rule, because of their lack of self-control, are not good judges.

23. This being so, if we ought to follow the judgment of another, even when he is not our superior, rather than our own in matters that are a personal concern, how much more then should we follow the judgment of the superior, whom we have taken as a guide and who stands in the place of God and interprets His will for us?

24. On the other hand, without this obedience of the judgment it is impossible for obedience of the will and execution to be what they should. For the appetitive powers of the soul naturally follow the apprehensive, and in the long run the will cannot obey against one's judgment without coercion. If for some time it obeys, misled by the general misunderstanding that it must obey, even when commanded amiss, it cannot do so for any length of time. Thus perseverance fails, or at least the perfection of obedience, which consists in obeying with love and cheerfulness. But

---

[5] Proverbs 3:5.   [6] Collatio II, cap. ii.

when one acts in opposition to one's judgment, one cannot obey lovingly and cheerfully as long as such opposition remains. Promptitude fails, and readiness, which are impossible without agreement of judgment, such as when one doubts whether it is good or not to do what is commanded. That renowned simplicity of blind obedience fails when we call into question the justice of the command or even condemn the superior because he bids us do something that is not pleasing. Humility fails, for although on the one hand we submit, on the other we prefer ourselves to the superior. Fortitude in difficult tasks fails, and, in a word, all the perfections of this virtue.

25. And on the other hand, when one obeys without submitting one's judgment, there arise dissatisfaction, pain, reluctance, slackness, murmurings, excuses, and other imperfections and obstacles of no small moment which strip obedience of its value and merit. St. Bernard, therefore, speaking of those who take it ill when they are commanded to do things that are unpleasant, says with reason: "If you begin to grieve at this, to judge your superior, to murmur in your heart, though outwardly you do what is commanded, this is not the virtue of patience, but a cloak of your malice."[7]

26. Now, if we regard the peace and quiet of mind of him who obeys, it is certain that he will never attain it who has within himself the cause of his disquiet and unrest; that is, a judgment of his own opposed to what obedience lays upon him.

27. Moreover, unity, which is the foundation of every congregation and which is secured by the proper subordination of some members to others, is sure to fail unless it is made solid by the bond of obedience, which must be complete and embrace both will and understanding. It is for this reason that St. Paul so earnestly exhorts all to say the same thing,[8] because it is by the union of judgment and will that they shall be preserved. Now, if head and members must think the selfsame, it is easy to see whether the head should agree with the members or the members with the head. From this it can be seen how necessary is obedience of the understanding.

28. But how perfect it is in itself and how pleasing to God can be seen from the value of the most noble offering which is made of the worthiest part of man, an offering in which the obedient man is made a living holocaust most acceptable to His Divine Majesty, nothing whatever being kept to himself. And what adds to its merit is the difficulty which is overcome for love of Him, by subduing the natural inclination which all men have

---

[7] Sermo III, de circumcisione.
[8] Romans 15:5; 1 Corinthians 1:10; Philippians 2:2.

of following their own judgment. From this we see that obedience, although it is a perfection proper to the will, which it makes ready to fulfill the will of the superior, yet it must also, as we have said, extend to the understanding and incline it to agree with the thought of the superior. It is thus that we proceed with the full force of the soul—of will and of understanding—to a prompt and perfect execution.

29. I have gone to some length in speaking of this holy virtue, farther than I had intended, under the direction of our father, who, while he holds it necessary in all religious orders, thinks it particularly necessary in Ours. And he desires that the members of the Society signalize themselves in it. For we cannot equal the austerity of others in the clothing we wear, in fasts and other mortifications, since our way of life is ordinary. But in this obedience and true abnegation of will and judgment he is very desirous in our Lord that we go forward and signalize ourselves.

30. I am presuming to express myself freely on this matter under the direction of our father, who had bidden me to do so, relying confidently as he does on the devotion you show for obedience. Because man offers obedience to God and not to man for himself, our father feels an obligation to safeguard what he thinks belongs to the honor and glory of God. Therefore, as he has hitherto indicated, the disposition which the obedient man ought to have with regard to the faculties which are offered to God through His minister—will, namely, and judgment and execution—so here he will propose some instances in which such obedience is rendered, so that the man who is under obedience may ask himself in God's presence about his disposition, begging God to bestow on him the proper dispositions should he find himself lacking them.

31. First. As it is a matter of obligation for every religious to obey him whom he takes for superior in those things which belong to his institute, and a matter of perfection, as the learned say, to obey in all things, even those that are difficult and opposed to one's self-will, provided there is clearly no sin, examine whether you find yourself disposed to do what is sufficient merely, or what is perfect; that is, whether you will make the superior's will your rule in certain things only, or in all.

32. Second. Given the disposition to seek what is more perfect in all things, let us suppose you judge that something is proper for God's service and you desire it as such, but you see that it is not of obligation or necessary to salvation. In that case examine in particular whether you are ready to give up the project should the superior think it better to do so, and submit both your will and your judgment to whatever the superior shows himself inclined.

33. Third. Again, if obedience should bid you do something, a doubt may arise as to whether you should obey. If there is no possibility of determining whether it would be a mortal or a venial sin, and the doubt persists, examine whether you would be disposed to take the side of obedience, in the confidence that God, whom you obey in His minister, will give this minister more light and integrity to know the divine will and to conform to it.

34. Fourth. Suppose that the superior should at one time give a command with the intention of obliging, and at another time without such an intention, but giving a clear indication of his will, or some sign that the subject will understand; examine whether you would be disposed to obey not only in the first instance which carries with it an obligation, but also in the second, which pertains to the perfection of obedience.

35. Our father would be glad to have you examine yourself in our Lord on these points of obedience with respect to Father Araoz, or anyone else whom God should give you as superior. Those who owe obedience to you should do likewise concerning their obedience to you.

¶ TO FATHER ANTHONY ARAOZ
II, 71-73, Letter 302

Scholastics of the Society who are pursuing courses at the universities may take part in public academic functions and even receive degrees, but they should not take any part in the voting.

Rome, April 3, 1548

You ask whether our scholastics should vote in elections to various chairs and offices. Do not permit this. Rather inform them that they are not to do this at all, as their own peace of mind and the spirit of our Institute will be thus better preserved. This spirit requires of us to withdraw from every appearance of ambition and to remain on terms of peace and affection with all. We will thus avoid making adversaries of those whom we do not favor. Give orders also that in Valencia, and wherever degrees are taken, they who are under your authority should occupy no special place, either first or last, but they should take part in academic functions and pass their examinations, which will show whether they have studied well or not. Should they happen to be present when others are nominated, let them withdraw, and they can pass later *extra numerum*. I consider this procedure advisable not only to free ourselves from every appearance of restless ambition, as I hope we shall be in our Lord, but also for the good example and edification of others. Although they take part in university functions and accept degrees to encourage themselves to study or to arm themselves with authority so that they can place at the disposal of others what God has shared with them, this matter of special places, because it involves more danger than profit, is, I think in our Lord, not suitable for Ours, nor in keeping with the spirit of poverty and humility by which we should be characterized. Yours in our Lord . . .

¶ TO SENOR TALPINO
II, 83-86, Letter 311

In his letter to Talpino Ignatius congratulates him on overcoming the temptations of the devil. He recounts the blessings of obedience and encourages him to embrace it. He urges him to turn over his personal affairs to a reliable person and come to Rome. Ignatius says that he will indicate the time in another letter. Talpino showed great initial fervor, for he wrote out his vow in his own blood. However, he was not equal to the sturdy demands of Ignatius, and preferred to remain in Egypt.

Rome, April 12, 1548

IHS

Dear Friend Talpino in Christ Jesus.

May the grace and peace of Christ Jesus grow in all of us. Amen.

Our father in Christ, Ignatius, received both of your letters. Explaining his thought to me, as he usually does, he lays upon me the duty of answering, a task which I am happy to undertake, since I hope in our Lord that by this interchange of letters, which your kindness initiated, I may become more closely united with you in our Lord and find a more special place in your prayers.

But to come to the task laid upon me of answering your letter, I sincerely congratulate you and give thanks to God that you have finally got rid of, as you say you have, the thoughts which were leading you away from your God whom you are serving. For I am convinced of this, that, no matter how much the demon tried to present these thoughts under the appearance of good, we understand that by God's goodness you have been freed from extreme peril in this formidable assault of the enemy. Consider the danger for you involved in the struggle against giving up a state of life which was quite properly entered on. I mean abandoning a call from

God, or one's first faith, and violating the vow by which you had bound yourself to Christ to return at last to Egypt after having crossed the Red Sea. Consider this in the light of God's truth, who once asserted that no one was fit for the kingdom of God who, having once put his hand to the plow, looked back. I repeat, the more peril in this struggle for you, the more intense should be our rejoicing over your victory through the grace of Christ, whom we should likewise entreat to make this victory sounder and firmer every day.

And yet, my dear Talpino in Christ, when you write of the anxiety you have about your health and the doctor's prescriptions, you are evidently (charity will not allow me to conceal the fact) cheating yourself of the choicest fruit of obedience. For although you are permitted by a very special gift of God to free yourself through obedience of a most annoying burden—I mean personal care and worry—you of your own accord undertake this troublesome burden in spite of your weakness, and by this action you will come to see that you not only withdraw from perfection but do yourself a distinct disservice.

If you are aware that you are denying yourself that peace and liberty and joy of spirit which they experience who, by dedicating themselves completely to God through His minister, free themselves of all personal concern, my dear Talpino in Christ, when once you offered yourself a living sacrifice to God, when you once dedicated mind and body as a holocaust to Christ and entrusted yourself to His divine providence to be started on the way to happiness through the hands of His minister, why do you now so wrongly withhold a part of yourself by this undisguised seeking of self? Why do you again usurp control of yourself by preferring your own providence to God's in thus reassuming control of yourself?

Let us admit that your health has suffered. But even if it were in a state that was deplorable, you should surely imitate Him who for your sake became obedient unto death, even to the death of the cross,[1] even should you be called upon to lose your life rather than fail in obedience. Tell me, what could be more desirable than to lay down your life in obedience to God in the person of His minister? Can you place so great a value on this poor, brief life, which sooner or later must be given up anyway, that you would not be ready to exchange it for one that is eternal and full of happiness? Do you hear Christ say, "He that loveth his life shall lose it, and he that hateth his life in this world keepeth it unto life eternal"?[2] Indeed, dear brother, cast your care upon God cheerfully and

---

[1] Philippians 2:8   [2] John 12:25.

confidently; throw all your solicitude upon Him[3] with the thought of Paul, that whether we live or whether we die, we are the Lord's.[4] Trusting that both in life and in death Christ will be glorified in your body, make ready even with eagerness for the worst.

Of course, I am all for your fighting with the weapons that become a real man. Nor do I think that I should delay in setting before you the charity and prudence of your superior in ruling those whom God has committed to his care, each to be employed according to his talents and inclinations in the different functions of our Institute, if only they give up their own wills. I hope indeed that your health will improve, but all that I pass over as hardly worthy of mention. Trust God, in whom you have believed, and make ready for the worst.

Get ready for the journey at the time indicated in another letter to Paul Anthony, according to the wish of our father in Christ Ignatius. If you have not got your affairs in order or cannot do so by summer, start the journey anyway and appoint someone to carry on for you as though you were going to die, for we must die completely to the world and the flesh. Let this be your thought, that it is better to lose some of your possessions than yourself; and therefore, if you cannot loosen your chains, break them.

My best wishes in Christ Jesus. I commend myself to your prayers.

¶ TO PRINCE PHILIP OF SPAIN
II, 149-50, Letter 382

In this letter Ignatius first sets forth his feelings of respect and reverence for the heir to the Spanish crown, and then asks him to take an interest in the reform of the nunneries of Catalonia.

Rome, middle of 1548

JHUS

My Lord in our Lord.

My lowly and humble profession does not permit me to be master of my own movements; and what I should wish with an ever-increasing desire to do in person, I thought I must do in some way to the best of my ability by means of this letter. I am speaking of the true and affectionate

---
[3] 1 Peter 5:7. See Psalm 54:23; Matthew 6:25.
[4] Romans 14:8.

reverence and gratitude which I owe to your highness in our Lord. It is a debt which I bear close to my heart and of which I have been conscious for some time past, a consciousness that makes itself keenly felt with every moment. Hence with all my strength, which I know is little enough, I beseech the most holy Trinity in its measureless and infinite mercies to console your highness in all things and to increase its most holy gifts and spiritual graces and direct them always to guide and direct your highness in this matter and in many other good, just, and holy undertakings, with the result that the splendor of the true light may be brought to shine on all possible nations, seated as they are in the shadow of so much darkness and in the enjoyment of such false security and repose of soul.

As one of these enterprises, I humbly beg your highness, by the love and reverence of God our Lord, that, when the proper occasion presents itself and tasks of greater importance permit, you deign to remember and see to it that the absence of your highness cause no remissness in the reformation of the convents of nuns in Catalonia, since your highness is well aware what a service this will be to God.

May He in His infinite and supreme goodness deign to grant your highness every grace and all success that I desire for you in this life and in the next. In my poor judgment in our Lord, there is nothing more to desire.

PART IV

1548-1553

¶ TO FRANCIS BORGIA, DUKE OF GANDIA

II, 233-37, Letter 466

The duke of Gandia was by this time a professed member of the Society of Jesus. By virtue of a papal brief he continued with the administration of his estates, and in his palace led the life of a saint. In one of his letters to the founder of the Society he had asked his opinion on his own exercises of prayer and penance. In the following letter St. Ignatius gives him rules that are full of wisdom to help him arrive at the proper mean in these exercises.

Rome, September 20, 1548

IHS

May the perfect grace and everlasting love of Christ our Lord be always in our favor and help.

When I hear how harmoniously you have reconciled your spiritual and temporal interests and directed them to your spiritual progress, I find fresh reason, I assure you, for rejoicing in our Lord; and while giving thanks to His Eternal Majesty I can attribute my joy only to His divine goodness, which is the source of all our blessings. And yet I realize in our Lord that at one time we may be in need of certain exercises, spiritual as well as corporal, and at another time we will need others. Because those which for a season have proved profitable may cease to be so later, I will tell you what I think in His Divine Majesty on this subject, since your lordship has asked for my views.

First. I should think that the time devoted to these exercises, both interior and exterior, should be reduced by half. We ought to increase these exercises, both interior and exterior, when our thoughts arise from ourselves, or are suggested by our enemy, and lead us to fix our attention on objects that are distracting, frivolous, or forbidden, if we wish to prevent the will from taking any satisfaction in them or yielding any consent. I say that, as a rule, we ought to increase these exercises, both interior and exterior, the more these thoughts are multiplied, in order to conquer them, keeping in mind the character of the individual and the varying nature of the thoughts or temptations, and being careful to measure the exercises to the capacity of the individual. Contrariwise, when these thoughts lose their strength and cease, their place will be taken by holy thoughts and inspirations, and to these we must give the utmost welcome by opening to them all the doors of the soul. As a result there will be no further need of so many weapons to overthrow the enemy. From what

I can judge of your lordship in our Lord, it would be better if you were to devote to study about half the time that you now give to these exercises. In the future, learning will always be very necessary or certainly useful; and not only that which is infused but that also which is acquired by study. And some of your time should be given to the administration of your estates and to spiritual conversation. Try to keep your soul always in peace and quiet, always ready for whatever our Lord may wish to work in you. It is certainly a more lofty virtue of the soul, and a greater grace, to be able to enjoy the Lord in different duties and places than in one only. We should, in the Divine Goodness, make a great effort to attain this.

Second. As to fasts and abstinences, I would advise you to be careful and strengthen your stomach, for our Lord, and your other physical powers, rather than weaken them. My reason is that, in the first place, when a soul is so disposed to lose its own life rather than offend God's majesty by even the slightest deliberate sin, and is moreover comparatively free from the temptations of the world, the flesh, and the devil (a condition of soul which I am sure your lordship by God's grace enjoys), I should like very much to see your lordship imprint in your soul the truth that, as both body and soul are a gift from your Creator and Lord, you should give Him a good account of both. To do this you must not allow your body to grow weak; for if you do, the interior man will no longer be able to function properly. Therefore, although I once highly praised fasting and abstinence even from so many ordinary foods, and for a certain period was pleased with this program, I cannot praise it for the future, when I see that the stomach, because of these fasts and abstinences, cannot function naturally or digest any of the ordinary meats or other items of diet which contribute to the proper maintenance of the body. I should rather have you seek every means of strengthening the body. Eat, therefore, whatever food is allowed, and as often as you find it convenient. But it should be done without offense to the neighbor. We should love the body insofar as it is obedient and helpful to the soul, since the soul with the body's help and service is better disposed for the service and praise of our Creator and Lord.

Third. Concerning the ill treatment of the body for our Lord's sake, I would say, avoid anything that would cause the shedding even of a drop of blood.

If His Divine Majesty has given you the grace for this and for all that I have mentioned (it is my conviction that He has), it would be better for the future, without reasons or arguments, to drop this penance and, instead of trying to draw blood, seek more immediately the Lord of all, or what comes to the same thing, seek His most holy gifts, such as the gift of tears. This could be (1) because of our own sins or the sins of others; or (2) while contemplating the mysteries of the life of Christ, either here on earth or in heaven; or (3) from a loving consideration of the three Divine Persons. Thus the higher our thoughts soar, the greater will be their worth. The third is more perfect in itself than the second, and the second than the first. But for a given person that level will be much better on which our Lord communicates more of Himself in His holy graces and spiritual gifts, because He sees and knows what is best for you. Like one who knows all, He points out the way to you. On our part, with the help of His grace we will learn by making trial of many methods, so that we may advance along the way that stands out clearest, which will be for us the happiest and most blessed in this life, leading us directly by ordered paths to that other everlasting life after having united us in a close embrace with His most holy gifts. By these gifts I understand those that are beyond the reach of our own powers, which we cannot attain at will, since they are rather a pure gift of Him who bestows them and who alone can give every good. These gifts with His Divine Majesty as their end are an increase in the intensity of faith, hope, and charity, joy and spiritual repose, tears, intense consolation, elevation of mind, divine impressions and illuminations, together with all other spiritual relish and understanding which have these gifts as their objects, such as a humble reverence for our holy mother the Church, her rulers and teachers. Any of these holy gifts should be preferred to exterior and visible manifestations, which are good only when they have one or other of these higher gifts as their object. I do not mean to say that we should seek them merely for the satisfaction or pleasure they give us. We know, however, that without them all our thoughts, words, and actions are of themselves tainted, cold, disordered; while with them they become clear and warm and upright for God's greater service. It is for this reason that we should desire these gifts, or some of them, and spiritual graces; that is, insofar as they are a help to us, to God's greater glory. Thus, when the body falls ill because of excessive effort, it is the most reasonable thing to seek these gifts by acts of the understanding and other more moderate exercises. For it is not the soul alone that should be healthy. If the mind is healthy in a healthy body, all will be healthy and much better prepared to give God greater service.

As to how you should act in individual cases, I do not think it wise in the Lord to speak in detail. It is my hope that the same Divine Spirit who has hitherto guided your lordship will continue to guide and rule you in the future, to the greater glory of His Divine Majesty.

¶ TO JOHN OF AVILA
II, 316-20, Letter 550

Ignatius explains that he has a twofold purpose for writing this letter. He wishes to express his gratitude to John of Avila for the support he has given to the Society in Spain, and to explain what measures he thinks he ought to take to allay the storm raised by Melchior Cano. He uses several quotations to point out the importance of defending Christ against heresy and insults.

Rome, January 24, 1549

IHS

Very reverend Sir in our Lord.

May the sovereign grace and everlasting love of Christ our Lord greet you and visit you with His most holy gifts and spiritual graces.

I have heard on different occasions and from several of Ours of the unfailing support and ardent charity which your reverence has always given to this least Society, and I made up my mind to write you for two reasons. The first is to give some sign of recognition and gratitude by way of the warmest thanks to God, and to your reverence in His most holy name, for all that you have done for the glory of the Divine Majesty in behalf of us, your reverence's devoted servants, to secure an increase in our numbers and our devotion. In this acknowledgment which I make with all possible devotion, I offer myself to your reverence as one of your associates or spiritual sons in our Lord, who am willing to comply with the utmost of the strength His Divine Majesty will give me with whatever the Lord of all may command. By so acting I am persuaded I shall be much the gainer in the Divine Goodness, both because of the return I can make for my great obligations and the service I can be to the servants of my Lord, in serving whom I feel that I am serving the same Lord of all.

My second reason is that, as your reverence will have heard reports that are favorable to Ours, it seems to me to be only just in the Divine Majesty that you also hear other reports that are not. It is my firm hope that this great spiritual trial of theirs will result in greater glory to God. The fact is, as one of Ours writes from Salamanca, they have suffered and still are suffering considerable opposition from certain Dominican fathers who are actuated, I think, more by a pardonable zeal than by trustworthy information. This opposition must have been going on for the last ten months. But now again from letters dated November 25 and December 2 last, it would seem that the opposition has increased and gone beyond all limits, so that we have been driven to adopt measures recommended by St. Augustine and many other holy doctors. In his treatise *De viduitate*[1] St. Augustine says: "Our life is necessary for ourselves, our reputation for others." And St. Chrysostom, "Let us learn from His example to bear our wrongs magnanimously, but wrongs against God we should not bear even to listen to."[2]

St. Jerome in his letter against Rufinus says: "I would not have any one put up with the accusation of heresy."[3] And St. Thomas: "We must be ready to undergo insults, should it be expedient. Sometimes, however, we should repel the insult offered, for two reasons particularly: (1) because of the good of him who offers the insult, that his boldness may be held in check, and he not repeat his attempt in the future, according to the proverb, 'Answer a fool according to his folly, lest he imagine himself to be wise';[4] and (2) because of the good of others, whose progress might be impeded by the insults offered us. Whence Gregory, in the ninth homily on Ezechiel, says, 'They who are a model for others in life should, when they can, repress the words of detractors, lest those who hear their preaching heed them not and, remaining in their bad habits, contemn virtue.' "[5]

St. Bonaventure in his *Apologeticum* says: "Although you ought patiently to put up with wrongs done you and make no complaint against them, why is it that you not only fail to do that but, not satisfied with the judgments of the bishops, you obtain judges and protectors from the Holy See and at great cost and expense summon before them whoever are a source of annoyance to you, even though it be slight, until they have given you full satisfaction? This is in open contradiction to the Apostle, who says in his Epistle to the Corinthians, 'There is plainly a fault among you, that you have lawsuits one with another.'[6] I answer: 'Religious should patiently endure wrongs and annoyances from which no other evil ensues, except what is felt for the moment, as is the case with offensive words, or

---

[1] *De bono viduitatis, epistula ad Julianam viduam*, cap. 27.
[2] *Homilia quinta super Matthaeum*, op. imperf., post medium.
[3] *Ad Pammachium adversus errores Ioannis Hierosolymitani episcopi* (Opera, edit. Basileae, 1565, II, 162).
[4] Proverbs 26:5.   [5] II, II, q. 72, a. 3.   [6] 1 Corinthians 6:7.

loss of property, or blows, and the like, since they cause no further harm. But when greater damage can result, such as serious harm to souls, patience is no longer expedient.'"[7] Cajetan says in the *Summula*: "It is a sin to disregard one's own good name which has been falsely besmirched, when such neglect can result in harm or the fear of harm to others, since reputation is necessary to us for the benefit of others. And, as St. Augustine says in such a case, 'He who, confident of his innocence, disregards his reputation, is cruel, because he kills the souls of others.'"[8]

This, we think, should be our course for God's glory. First, with all politeness and kindness send them a letter from one of the cardinals, one who seems to have some influence with them.[9] Second, present them with a patent from their general. Third, if we get no results from either of these attempts, in order to live up to our obligations to God our Lord and charity toward our neighbor and, moreover, to squelch the power of the enemy of our human nature, who in this manner prevails on people of learning and even religious created for God's greater glory, we shall proceed to a formal process with all the fulminations of a papal brief. Your reverence will see, after being thus informed, that you will have greater reason for earnestly recommending to God in your holy sacrifices and prayers our petition that His Divine Majesty may deign to bestow His favor and aid on the side which will redound more to His praise and glory. With the help of His grace we neither seek nor desire aught else.

May this and all things else tend always to His glory, and may He deign in His infinite and sovereign goodness to give us all His bountiful grace so that we may always know His most holy will and perfectly fulfill it.

¶ TO PRINCE PHILIP OF SPAIN
II, 344-45, Letter 580

In this letter Ignatius reveals the friendly relations which existed between himself and the future King Philip II. It was doubtless St. Francis Borgia who formed the first bond of union between them. Borgia had always been influential in the court and he was friendly with Prince Philip. Their first joint undertaking was the reform of the monasteries of Barcelona. This matter was dealt with in a previous letter which Ignatius

---

[7] *Libellus apologeticus in eos qui fratrum minorum adversantur*, quaest. 12.
[8] Cajetan, *Summa*, Pars I.   [9] John Alvarez de Toledo, O.P.

wrote to Philip. St. Ignatius begins his letter with expressions of respect and esteem for the prince. He shows the future king how the Divine Goodness fills with consolations the souls that prepare themselves properly. He expresses his hopes and prayers that the prince's soul will be one of those who receive the fullness of God's consolation.

Rome, February 18, 1549

JHS

My Lord in our Lord.

May the sovereign grace and everlasting love of Christ our Lord greet and visit your highness with His most holy gifts and spiritual graces.

When so chosen a soul, and one so visited and enlightened by God's inestimable graces and spiritual gifts, collects itself with so much ease and disposes of all its interior powers by resigning its understanding, its talents, and its desires to the Supreme Wisdom and Infinite Goodness; and when, thus disposed and filled with trust and resignation, is desirous of being ruled and governed by its Creator and Lord, it is quite usual for His Divine Majesty to bestow His continuous delights and His most holy consolations on it, filling the soul with Himself, so that it will produce great and genuine spiritual fruit, and that in ever-growing abundance, to the greater glory of His Divine Goodness.

I can see what is everywhere perceived, the good name and reputation for holiness which is spread abroad by your highness. It is this that gives us ground for the solid hope that they who look for the success of your plans will not be disappointed. In fact, I feel within me ever-greater reasons for desiring intensely the greatest possible prosperity and success for all of your highness' undertakings, to the greater glory of the Lord of all. In my poor and unworthy prayers I am continually begging of His Divine Goodness, and I have been doing so for many years now, the support of Him who can do all things for this success, and to keep on doing so for the residue of life which our Lord will grant me.

Your highness, if I seem too free and bold in writing, I hope that I will be pardoned for the love and reverence of God our Lord. When I visited Don James de Acevedo[1] and paid him my respects as the representative of your highness, the increase of devotion that remains with me as an effect of his presence makes it impossible for me not to write this letter and reveal to your highness the inmost feelings of my heart, the warm desire I have for the greater service and glory of our Creator and Lord.

---

[1] James Acevedo, treasurer to Philip II, was sent by the prince to his father Charles V at Brussels, whence he came to Rome as ambassador to Paul III.

May He by His infinite and supreme goodness be ever present, and pour His divine graces and spiritual gifts upon your highness, so that in all things He will guide, preserve, and give increase to your highness in the greater service and praise which is His due. Ever your highness' humble servant in our Lord . . .

¶ TO MATTHEW SEBASTIAN DE MORRANO
II, 345-47, Letter 581

Matthew Sebastian de Morrano was imperial governor of canals at Saragossa. With his usual kindness and courtesy Ignatius writes him to tell him that he cannot undertake the government of the religious of St. Clare in Barcelona.

Rome, February 22, 1549

IHS

Very honorable Sir in our Lord.

May the sovereign grace and everlasting love of Christ our Lord greet and visit you with His most holy gifts and spiritual graces.

I have heard of you from others before this, and of the special gift of charity which the Author of charity has bestowed on you, and of all the good you have done for our least Society. Consequently I feel I have a special obligation of wishing to be of service to you in our Lord. Your letter of the third of this month has added to my knowledge and to my desire. This letter, which was so full of humility and affection, reached me this week; and the more it makes clear God's gifts to you, the less reason I see in myself for your being so generous in sharing these gifts with us. I beg God our Lord, to whose glory alone all well-ordered blessings should be referred, to make some return to the charity which He has given you for us with His infinite charity and spiritual gifts which come from it. I will only say that I have been greatly delighted in the Lord by the exchange of letters between us, and I would be still more delighted if, at the very first opportunity you give me, I could show the desire which the Divine Goodness gives me, to do you every spiritual service in keeping with my profession of poverty.

But you must understand that the authority of the Holy See interferes, and prevents our Society from undertaking the task which you and the pious ladies of St. Clare would like to have it assume. The Society, according to its Institute, must, so to say, have one foot on the road, ready to hasten from one place to another. There would be serious difficulty, therefore, if it were to handicap itself with the direction of convents of nuns. Not because this is not a good work to undertake, but it is one which would be quite embarrassing and out of harmony with our manner of life. It is now a long time since we asked his holiness to be exempt from work of this kind. He has already signed the documents which exclude us, so that it would not be possible now to act against his authority and contrary to his formal decrees. But if ever the Society should have to undertake such work, I should wish, both because of your request and because of the kindly feeling we have for those religious, to have the work begin with them. Meanwhile, I have no doubt that persons so spiritual and so attached to God's will, who must have moreover a very lively faith and hope in His divine providence and so broad a view for the universal good, will finally hold the Society properly excused in this matter.

May the eternal wisdom and infinite goodness of Christ Jesus our Lord and God bestow on us all His light and integrity of mind, so that we may always know His most holy will and perfectly fulfill it. Your humble servant in our Lord . . .

¶ TO JERONYMA OLUJA AND TERESA REJADELL

II, 374-75, Letter 630

Ignatius offers a word of consolation to these excellent religious of the Convent of Santa Clara in their troubles, and tells them that it is impossible for the Society to undertake their direction.

Rome, April 5, 1549

IHS

May the sovereign grace and everlasting love of Christ our Lord ever be our protection and support.

I have received letters from different persons in Barcelona, and from them I can see that our Lord has sent you trials, and thus given you no small occasion to practice the virtues which His Divine Goodness has bestowed on you and of proving their solidity, since it is in things that are hard that one can test one's spiritual progress. I have many an occasion to see this in His service. May it please Christ Jesus, who died and suffered so much for us all, to give us abundant grace to suffer with profit for His holy love what is given us to suffer, and thus apply a remedy to all that needs remedying in the way that will be most acceptable to His Divine Goodness. But this I hold for certain, that that remedy is not the one you have been indicating up to the present. For although the Society, in keeping with the many obligations for which in our Lord it has a special affection, has every wish to console and be of service to you in accordance with our profession, yet the authority of the vicar of Christ has closed the door against our taking part in the government or direction of religious women. The Society at the very beginning asked this, as it judged that it would be to the greater service of God our Lord to be as free as possible from these ties, so as to be able to hurry to any part of the world where obedience to the supreme pontiff and the needs of the neighbor should summon them. For this reason I do not think that the remedy you suggest would be at all pleasing to God our Lord, and I hope that in His infinite bounty another more fitting means will be found to attain your ends, which we all desire in our Lord, to your peace and special consolation.

While I defer to what you, being on the spot, might think best, you will see from Master Polanco's letter how the matter presents itself to me. I will not therefore enter into details here. But I will say this, and I hope that you will believe me, that for the end we all have in view, which is the greater service of God our Lord, it would not do for us to accept the task in question. If we did have to undertake such a work for religious women, our services would be offered to you before all others.

May it please the Divine Wisdom to grant that we may always know His most holy will and find our peace and happiness in ever fulfilling it. Your servant in our Lord ...

¶ TO ANDREW LIPPOMANI
II, 445-46, Letter 743

Ignatius suggests an expurgated edition of the Latin classics which can be safely and profitably placed in the hands of schoolboys.

Rome, June 22, 1549

IHS

Very reverend Monsignor in Christ.

The sovereign grace and everlasting love of Christ Jesus greet and visit your reverend lordship with His holy gifts and spiritual graces.

I have delayed some weeks to write your lordship, as I had no special reason for writing. But I have decided to write, not only to offer you my respects and prayers that the Holy Spirit has during these days enriched you with His spiritual treasures, but to make known to you a desire which our Lord has given to me many years now. Your lordship can be a help toward its realization. I shall be glad to know what you think of it.

I have been reflecting on how young minds are by nature disposed to receive and retain early impressions, whether they be good or harmful. And these first impressions, together with the good or bad example and instructions they receive, have a very important influence on their after-lives. In the light of this truth I realize that the books which are read, especially in courses of literature, such as Terence, Virgil, and others, while they contain many things that are profitable for the learned and far from useless in the practical aspects of life, also contain many things that are profane, immodest, and harmful, even when they are no more than alluded to. Scripture tells us that "the imagination and thought of man's heart are prone to evil from his youth."[1] This will be truer still if such things are placed before young boys in books which they study, hear explained, and keep ever ready at hand.

In view of this, it has long been and still is my thought that it would be very opportune to remove these immodest and harmful passages from such books and substitute others that would have a more beneficial influence, or at least get rid of the questionable passages and keep the good, even if nothing else is added. For the last few years I have thought that something like this would be a great boon in promoting a Christian way of living and the proper training of youth. But I never saw any means of getting it done, and so the desire remained unfulfilled. Our Lord is developing His work in our Society by means of His servants, who are not only opening colleges but even universities. Two are now under the direction of the Society, one at Gandia and the other at Messina. This would make it appear that the project is becoming more practical, and could be easily realized, at least in those places where the Society is in authority.[2]

I would be very happy to know what your reverend lordship thinks about the project, because, if you agree with the view I have here expressed, you could be of great help for the glory of God our Lord, as I shall explain later.

---

[1] Genesis 8:21.
[2] Father Frusius was later commissioned by St. Ignatius to put his hand to this work. In his *Jesuit Code of Education*, pp. 55-57, Father Allan P. Farrell has a brief, clear, and capable discussion of the subject of censorship.

But this will be all for the present, except to say that we are all well, God be praised. We commend ourselves most earnestly to the prayers of your reverend lordship, and beg the sovereign and infinite goodness of God to give us all abundant grace ever to know His holy will and perfectly to fulfill it.

¶ TO FATHER JOHN ALVAREZ
II, 478-84, Letter 776

A letter of reproof. Alvarez is reprehended for writing without proper order in his letters, in too great haste, and for failing to distinguish his subject matter. He is also called to time for his unfavorable interpretation of the use of human prudence, as though acting with such prudence were "bending the knee to Baal." The letter was written by Father John Polanco under instructions from Ignatius.

Rome, July 18, 1549

IHS

It will not be a matter of surprise to you to learn that reproofs are sometimes sent out from Rome. Nor do I think that you will be displeased in receiving these which I have to send you at the order of Master Ignatius. Indeed, I think you will treasure them above rubies. If I have to dwell at some length on them, do not lay the blame on your own deserts alone, but also on the concept that has been formed here of your fortitude, in the sense that you are a man to whom can be said whatever needs saying. Besides, I am merely the pen, so that nothing should be taken as coming from me but as from our father, who has given the orders.

In the first place, you did well to observe obedience in the matter of writing every week, but it was done rather crudely in that the letters were kept in the house. What you should have done was to try to find someone, once the letters were written, to carry and deliver them. They could at least have been sent by way of Valladolid, where there are usually many leaving for here. Our father thinks that hereafter it will be enough to write every two weeks, unless some occasion demand that it be done oftener. But some means of sending them should be looked for every week.

Second. As to the manner of writing, that which is in use in the Society is, in the letter for general reading, to write only about things that can be shown to others. Matters relating to business, or items which are not for everyone's eyes, are written on separate sheets which accompany the letter that can be shown around. You failed to do this, and so your letters could not be shown here. They are being returned to you underscored, so that you can see what should be written on separate sheets—that is, all that has not been underscored. These are our father's orders. We have kept a copy of the underscored portions and will show the rest to the cardinal of Coria and others.[1]

Third. As to the terms that you use, here too you should be more careful and reserved and use Latin at the proper times.

Fourth. As to your harping on the letter of the licentiate Madrid,[2] it is true that no member of the Society has seen it. But as he is a friend of the Society, he saw your letters and others with the things they had to say about that Father Cano, which are quite well known now and which put him in the mood for writing that letter out of the abundance of his heart. If you keep in mind only his good intention, you will see that he did not deserve the lusty blows you administer in nearly all your letters.

Fifth. You say further, as can be seen from your letters, that you did not think it opportune, after commending the matter to God, to make use of the documents which we sent you. There had been a change of attitude, you said. That was all well and good. But in giving your reasons for not making use of the help sent you, you do not seem to us to have reasoned well, taking as you did so spiritual a view of the matter as to lose all touch with reality in the case. Your way of writing betrays a judgment in your mind which seems to hold that to use resources and to obtain such favors would be to act from a spirit that was base and merely human, which, to your mind, would be "bending the knee to Baal,"[3] and so forth. In another passage still, speaking of another letter for Master Gallo[4] which our father wrote at the request of Don James Acevedo, who wrote himself to his relatives, you say that they experienced the greatest joy in being without the leaven of such helps, as you can see at greater length in his letters.

There are many faults in this manner of writing, if I am to speak the truth as obedience bids me. First, you judge and condemn your superior as having a base and merely human spirit, for it was he who provided

---

[1] Francis Mendoza.
[2] Christopher Madrid, of whom Polanco speaks frequently. At the time this letter was written he had not yet entered the Society, although he was very friendly with Ignatius and his companions.
[3] Romans 11:4.
[4] On Gallo see *Epistolae mixtae*, III, 644-45.

these helps. And it would not be a slight matter even to think of his bending the knee to Baal, or what would be worse, causing others to do so. Thus by being so very spiritual you cease to be spiritual at all in a matter of great importance, such as the spirit of humility and obedience.

In the second place, one who thinks like this even to himself is wanting, I don't say in respect for his superior, but even in common courtesy. And he should not have written it to the one he condemns, at least not so brazenly, and that in a letter which was written for the eyes of all.

In the third place, you seem not to remember, or not to have known, that these helps in great part, if not altogether, were asked for there in Salamanca, partly by Father Dr. Torres himself and partly by Father Master Estrada.[5] And you yourself showed that you wanted them when you wrote how they were rising up against our very holy father, and other details of your heavy cross. The cardinal of Coria here thought that the letter was written in anger,[6] and as the intervention was to a great extent sought by your party, and also offered by God through certain devoted persons, there seems to be no justification for saying that we have been bending the knee to Baal here, or worshiping him by accepting such help and sending it on to you.

In the fourth place, if we regard the philosophy of your spirituality itself, we shall find that it is neither very solid nor very true. You seem to hold that the use of natural helps or resources, and taking advantage of the favor of man, for ends that are good and acceptable to our Lord, is to bend the knee to Baal. Rather, it would seem that the man who thinks that it is not good to make use of such helps or to employ this talent along with others which God has given him, under the impression that mingling such helps with the higher ones of grace produces a ferment or evil concoction has not learned well to order all things to God's glory and to find a profit in and with all these things for the ultimate end, which is God's honor and glory. That man might be said to bend the knee to Baal who makes capital of such human helps and puts greater hope in them than he does in God and the supernatural help of His grace. But he who has placed the foundation of all his hopes in God and who carefully makes use in His service of the gifts which He bestows, interior and exterior, spiritual and material, in the thought that His infinite power will do all that it wills, with or without these means, and who thinks that such solicitude pleases Him when it is properly turned into love of Him—this is not to bend the knee to Baal but to God, in

---

[5] Michael de Torres and Francis Estrada.   [6] See Alcazar, *Chrono-Historia*, I, 117.

recognition of His authorship, not only of grace but of nature too. He who fails to give Him unmixed thanks and to rejoice purely in Him does not seem to recognize this when means of human contriving intervene in those events that are the cause of his joy and thanksgiving. Rather it would seem that he sees one principle of grace and another of nature, when he speaks like that. God our Lord was quite able, even without the human power and influence of Joseph, to support the children of Israel in Egypt. But Joseph did not act ill in availing himself of his power and influence to do so. Again, there was little need of the power of Esther and Mardochai to secure the liberty and salvation of the same people, but they were not worshipers of Baal for having made use of it. It is true that, when God wishes to bestow His grace in abundant measure and manner extraordinary to show that He is above all nature, there is little need of human help. This was seen in the early years of the Church, when He bade His disciples not to think of what they were going to say in the presence of princes, since the Holy Spirit, whom He wished to communicate to them in a special manner, had no need of their natural abilities. But even then we see that the Holy Spirit made use of the human gifts of some in the primitive Church, as of Apollo and of St. Paul himself, who did not think that he was bending the knee to Baal when he took advantage of the prejudices of the Pharisees against the Saducees and exclaimed, in order to effect his escape from them, "Concerning the hope and resurrection of the dead I am called in question."[7] Again, when they were about to scourge him, he appealed to his exemption as a Roman citizen; or when he told King Agrippa that he considered himself happy to plead his cause before his tribunal. In the Epistles he draws on such human prudence, aided by superhuman prudence, as the author of both bestowed on him.

Even after the fortunes of the primitive Church were well founded, we see that this was the common practice of the Greek doctors, Saints Athanasius, Basil, Gregory Nazianzus, and Chrysostom; and of the Latin fathers, Jerome and Augustine, and Ambrose before them; and after them Pope Gregory and the others who followed him. All employed human talents and efforts, learning, eloquence, skill, and even the weapons of the powerful, for the holy end of God's service. They never thought that they were worshiping Baal, but God almighty, whom alone they served with natural and supernatural means. It is also a conclusion of the scholastic doctors that we should make use of human means, and that it would often

[7] Acts 23:6.

be tempting God not to use the means that God Himself puts into our hands and wait for miracles instead.

This should be enough. To summarize, therefore, at the proper times the use of human means, when they are directed purely to God's service, is not wrong, if the anchor of our hope takes firm hold of God and His grace. But not to use such means when God provides others, excuses one from blame; or when we think that they will not be of any help in His divine service. On this point we are in full agreement.

Sixth. As for the patent of the Dominicans and the two clauses which it ought to contain, it will not be difficult to have them supplied, unless forsooth this were to bend the knee . . . The truth is that not a single member of the Society spoke to the said master general,[8] nor did any one ask for a similar patent which the minister general of the Franciscans[9] issued in Valladolid, at whose request I do not know, except that it was certainly not one of Ours. Tell him that as many copies as may be wanted can be taken of both documents.

Because of what you said throughout the whole letter, or in parts of it, our father master in Christ, Ignatius, says that you are not to perform the office of secretary until you learn better how to do so, but you are to show your letters to father doctor[10] or Father Estrada, either of whom should sign the letters that are sent here.

This is what I am bidden to write by his paternity. As there was no need of greetings at the beginning, so neither is there of compliments at the end. But I do commend myself to your earnest prayers. Your servant in Jesus Christ . . .

¶ TO FRANCIS BORGIA, DUKE OF GANDIA

II, 494-95, Letter 790

Ignatius suggests that Borgia use his influence to induce Fathers Oviedo and Onfroy to reject the deceits of the evil one and return immediately to the manner of life proper to the Society. Both Oviedo, rector of the College of Gandia, and Onfroy, under the guidance of the Franciscan

---

[8] Master General Francis Romei is frequently mentioned by Polanco.
[9] According to Moroni the minister general of the Franciscans was Father Andrew Alvarez. But Waddington and others call him Andrew Insulanus.
[10] Michael de Torres.

Tejeda, were giving themselves to contemplation to such an extent as to interfere with the discharge of their duties. Ignatius is evidently determined not to compromise in the matter. A later letter from Borgia gives him the happy news that the present letter had the desired effect.

Rome, July 27, 1549

IHS

If all that is written us is true, it seems that b^1 and $c,^2$ one perhaps more than the other, have found the solitude for which they were looking, and are on the point of finding another which is greater still if they cannot humble themselves and permit themselves to be guided, each according to his vocation. The remedy which is very necessary is evident, and can be applied to them immediately, or by the intervention of one who is willing on his part and fully able. The first of these remedies invites us to prayer and sacrifice before the Divine Goodness; the second, with the help of God's favor, your lordship could achieve in some way, particularly by your presence and authority.

Therefore, in view of my obligation in conscience and because I firmly believe so without the slightest shadow of doubt, I protest before the judgment seat of Christ our Creator and Lord, who is my eternal judge, that they are misled and lost, sometimes on the right road, sometimes off of it, deceived by the father of lies. It is his way to suggest or propose a truth, or even several, in order to come off with a lie and entangle us in it. By the love and reverence of God our Lord, while commending the whole affair to His Supreme Goodness, let your lordship give the matter much thought, and diligently take such measures as will prevent the scandal which might be caused and the harm done to all parties concerned, and bring about rather a complete change, so that His Divine Majesty be served in all things, and they be restored to His greater service, praise, and glory, for ever and ever.

¶ TO FRANCIS BORGIA, DUKE OF GANDIA

XII, 632-54, Appendix VI, Letter 3

The praiseworthy desire of reforming the Church, which eminent persons had been conceiving for some years now, was the occasion of la-

---

[1] *b*: Onfroy.   [2] *c*: Oviedo.

mentable illusions to some who dreamed of angelic popes, rulers, Cyruses, and other extravagances of the kind. Among these deluded persons was Father Onfroy, who prophesied that Francis Borgia would become pope and reform the Church, and to this end would make use of the new religious order founded by Ignatius. This order had to be very contemplative, and therefore its founder was going astray in forbidding the eremitical life and long hours of prayer to those who offered themselves to this form of life. Onfroy sent a memorial in his own defense to Rome. St. Ignatius studied it very carefully, and gave the answer that the reader will examine in the following document, which contains three parts. In the first some general indication is given of the reasons for proceeding with great caution in accepting or rejecting prophecies, and some norms are given for distinguishing between them. In the second part these norms or criteria are applied to Onfroy to encourage the conclusion that his prophecies, for extrinsic reasons and because of the character of the prophet himself, offer no guarantee of being genuine. In the third part judgment is passed on the statements of Onfroy. The document is long, but is so instructive in the matter of the discernment of spirits and is of so perennial an interest that it would be a pity to abbreviate it, and worse to omit it.

July 1549

Principles concerning prophecies

Before coming to particulars, we thought it wise in our Lord to make certain statements which may help in treating of this matter to contribute to the greater glory of His Divine Majesty.

1. It is clear that we are not bound to refuse acceptance to all prophecy made after the time of Christ, as is clear from St. John, Agabus, and the daughters of Philip,[1] and St. Paul warns us, "Despise not prophecies."[2] Neither must we give credit to all who claim to be prophets nor accept their prophecies, seeing that there are so many ways in which we can be deceived in this matter, according to the warning of the apostle John: "Believe not every spirit, but try the spirits if they be of God."[3]

It is clear, likewise, that in contingent future events we should not say roundly that something is impossible when it is possible. To believe, however, that everything that is possible will actually come to pass would be silly, as the Wise Man says, "He that is hasty to give credit is light of heart."[4] Even less excusable would be the belief of those who have had

---

[1] Apocalypse 22:6; Acts 11:28, 21:9.
[2] 1 Thessalonians 5:20.
[3] 1 John 4:1.
[4] Ecclesiasticus 19:4.

experience of such deceptions such as we have in large numbers and measure today.

Thus it will be profitable, as well as quite necessary, to submit such spirits to a close examination. For this God our Lord, as in a matter of importance, gives His servants special grace, *gratis data,* for the discernment of spirits, according to the Apostle.[5] And this grace works and is helped by man's activity, especially his prudence and learning.

Keeping this in mind, we may piously accept some of the current prophecies if they fulfill these conditions: they should contain nothing contrary to reason or sound doctrine; they should be a cause of edification rather than otherwise; they should offer some probability of being genuine founded on the character of him who proposes them and on the nature of their contents. It is true that prudent and spiritual persons usually suspend judgment in such cases, even when they do not condemn them, and prefer to await the event before passing on them as genuine, because even the prophets themselves do not in every instance see everything in the prophetic light as clearly and as positively as they may say they do. For this reason Jonas said absolutely, "Yet forty days, and Nineveh shall be destroyed,"[6] because he did not see, or at least did not express, the condition which there was in that statement in the eternal disposition of God our Lord; namely, "unless they do penance."

It also happens that a true prophet can be mistaken because he does not see the matter he speaks about in the prophetic light, but merely in the light of his natural intellect and reason, and consequently may give out as true what is not true. Nathan was so mistaken when he told David in God's name that he would build the Temple. Later, however, in the true and supernatural light, he saw the contrary, and so instructed him; namely, that because he had shed so much blood he should not build it.[7] Besides this, the same Scriptures warn us that we must be much more cautious in believing those who are not aware of their prophetic office, seeing that they can so easily mistake falsehood for truth.

In such revelations or prophecies, even when they contain nothing against faith or morals but are in conflict with reason, it is not only lawful to refuse belief, but it would be good to deny them, unless they are confirmed by miracles or other higher signs of approval.

If, therefore, these revelations contain something contrary to good reason or sound doctrine and morals, and would cause disedification if they were believed, it would be certain that belief in such prophecies could

---

[5] 1 Corinthians 12:1. [6] Jonas 3:4. [7] 2 Kings 7:3-12.

come only from ignorance and lightness of mind. It is right and meritorious, therefore, to deny and discredit them in favor of truth and virtue, an act which would consequently be pleasing to the Author of truth.

Nature of the prophecies of Father Onfroy

Now to come to the point proposed, the prophecies or revelations of Master Onfroy, on which we have been commanded by obedience to pass judgment, having commended the matter to God our Lord and considering the matter in His Divine Goodness, we are of the opinion that these revelations belong to the last class enumerated above. Our reasons for this judgment are partly extrinsic, partly personal to Master Onfroy, and partly taken from the revelations themselves. Even the mere reading of them, apart from any formal examination, leaves a bad impression on the mind, in spite of the sympathy one feels at seeing such dispositions in their author, whom we love in the heart of Jesus Christ. For it often happens that falsehood and truth have of themselves a direct effect on the understanding and lead us to accept or reject a proposition even before we have reasoned about it. We have reason to think that God our Lord has given us some grace of discernment of spirits, and it is to this gift more than to other causes that we attribute this judgment. But the reasoning which later confirmed this judgment is as follows.

1. This spirit of prophecy or insight, particularly that which concerns the reformation of the Church, an angelic pope, and so forth, that has been current for many years now, should rightly be regarded with much suspicion. Through this it seems that the devil has found occasion to make fools of all those whom he finds disposed to accept such things. He takes into account the gifts, character, learning, and, according to his view, the graces of these exceptional individuals, from Amadeu[8]—not to go further back—and Fray Jerome of Ferrara [Savonarola], who was a man of great and exceptional gifts. It is really enough to strike one with terror to have anything to do with such things, when one sees a man of such prudence and learning, and as far as we can see of great virtue and devotion, misled, especially when he was willing to submit to such tests to make sure that his spirit was of God. And yet he was mistaken, as we can see, now that the time set down in his prophecies has elapsed.

Speaking of modern times, it is a cause of great wonder in our own days to see how many have become involved, among them even cardinals

---

[8] Probably the Portuguese Franciscan Amadeu, whose name in the world was John de Menezes da Silva. He was born in Ceuta in 1431 and died at Milan in 1482, author of the book *Apocalypsis nova sensum habens apertum*.

like Galatino, whose case is common knowledge, to say nothing of others not generally known and whose names I omit out of respect for their reputation, who undoubtedly held, and now hold, that there are going to be angelic popes for the reform of the Church. There was a well-known chamberlain of Pope Paul called Ambrose, who was convinced of this and would not hand over the papacy for anything but its full value.

In these days there was also a man at Urbino with similar views who went so far as to don papal vestments and create cardinals. He soon had so numerous a following that the duke of Urbino thought it would be no easy matter to rid himself of the impostor and get him out of his territory. The same thing happened in other parts of Italy, as in Spoleto, Calabria, where in these days a descendant of St. Francis of Paula has come up with the idea that there had to be an angelic pope who was to reform the Church. His election was to have taken place last May, but it did not come to pass.

William Postel[9] allowed similar ideas to take possession of him, and your lordship knows what excellent qualities he had. As a result they had to turn him out of the house here. In Venice, where he is now, he has been waiting for the time to come for the fulfillment of his prophecies. In the meantime Francis, king of France, who according to Postel was to have been the temporal monarch, has died. But despite all this he now finds means of evading the falsity of his prophecies, and says that because the king refused to believe he stood in the way of God's purposes. Now it is his son who will carry out God's plans, as did Josua in place of Moses, when he was told that it should be he who should lead the children of Israel into the Promised Land. And he actually did so. Postel is now as much attached to his opinions as ever, even more so, and is in fact beyond all hope of cure. Indeed, the poor man has fallen into other errors so intolerable that they give good proof of his state of mind. The fact is that they look upon him as beyond hope and have forbidden him to preach. Even the Inquisition would like to get its hands on him.

Just a few days ago someone came from Portugal with ideas of reforming the Church, and here in the house our father tried to bring him to his senses. Another Portuguese says that toward the end of the coming August he will infallibly be elected pope, and so he was doing his best to take over a church as his residence, a very inconvenient place in most respects, but one which he thinks will afford him a very showy exit when he is elected pope.

---

[9] Father Brodrick gives a brief account of him in *Progress of the Jesuits*, pp. 35-36.

Not to dwell on these particulars, I will mention only one more person who has come these days to speak to our father about his affairs and who gives evidence of considerable spirituality. He has come a distance of some two hundred miles, and according to himself has already been elected pope. He asserts that among others Cardinal Farnese has been present in spirit at his election, and he thinks that all he has to do now is to enter into possession of the papacy. I think our father answered him very graciously, telling him that an election of the pope is held only when the see is vacant, and that he should learn whether Pope Paul was still living to see whether his election was legitimate.

But to get back to where we started. The first reason which has great weight with me is the sight of these specimens and others like them. Matters of this kind, even when they have firmer foundations, are deservedly suspect, and this should be enough to keep us from meddling in them.

2. The second reason is that neither Dr. Araoz in Spain nor our Father Ignatius here has even a word of approval for what you propose. Rather they look upon it as an error and a trick of the enemy of our human nature. Their mere assent or disapproval has great weight with us, in the first place because they are superiors, and as such must rule as a part of their office, for which they receive a great influx of God's gifts, those gifts that are necessary for the proper government of those under their care. And second because they are such special servants of God our Lord. In doubtful matters it is much better to be on their side, even when we have no reasons, than with others who have an abundance, especially in a question of determining whether a spirit is of God or not. Our Lord says, "If any man will do the will of him [that sent me], he shall know of the doctrine whether it be of God."[10] Certain it is that an upright life is very important in such discerning of spirits. In the third place, they both apparently have this gift of the discretion of spirits as a special gift of Christ our Lord, and it seems more proper and reasonable that they should in all that concerns their own subjects than that others outside of the Society should have it. When we add to this their great prudence and experience, there seems to be every reason for believing them on points which they hold so steadfastly and with such certainty, when it is their business to be so informed as is the case, especially with our father master Ignatius.

3. When God our Lord makes such supernatural revelations, He usually does so for some good end and has in view some advantage for man-

---

[10] John 7:17.

kind. It is characteristic of these graces *gratis datae* to be directed toward the good of the neighbor, according to St. Paul[11] and the doctors. Now, if we look to the end that might be served by these prophecies and revelations, we find, instead of advantage, harm and disedification for the members of the Society should they put any trust in them, and for others as well. For to say that the Society is not well instituted and should be better founded, would surely cause whoever would believe this story to be disturbed; with his eyes on the future, he would fail in his observance during the present. And finally, as it would be a great help, if one is to make any progress in the Society, to esteem and love it, so to do anything that would weaken this esteem and love would be causing great harm. And externs would think that there was little edification to be found in it if in its very beginnings it was losing its spirit with its increase in numbers, and was in such dire straits. The damage thus stands out clearly, and we can see no advantage in making the condition public, especially when the prophets are unwilling to make known to their superiors the methods they propose to use in bringing about a reform.

Considering all things together, we say that, just as in matters that are not certain we ought to be inclined to trust in those which are a source of edification if accepted, so we should be inclined to consider those false which offer no help. And so they are. To sum up, therefore, the reasons we have advanced, we see that this sort of judgment constantly leads many astray in our days, and considering the unfavorable opinion of Father Araoz there in Spain with you and Father Ignatius here with us, both of them superiors, men of prudence and eminent servants of God our Lord, and that the consequences of such revelations are harmful rather than profitable, it is our judgment that they do not come from the good Spirit.

The character of Father Onfroy

There are also reasons for condemning the matters dealt with above stemming from the character of Master Onfroy. In the natural order the agent requires a subject properly disposed to receive its influence, and we may suppose that this will be required in the supernatural order, even though the contrary may take place on certain occasions, since the infinite power of God does not require the subject to be properly disposed. But we are speaking of the majority of cases, although even here such a properly disposed subject is not absolutely necessary. Consequently, if we were

[11] 1 Corinthians 12:7, 14:1-31.

to see a person disposed for such graces, our reason would be inclined to believe that he possesses them. And if we were to see that one was not so disposed, but rather of a disposition likely to be misled, we would incline to the opposite view. It is clear for the following reasons that Master Onfroy has this tendency to be misled.

1. From the point of view of his understanding. Considering his natural temper of mind from the way he speaks about Father Oviedo, he is not a proper subject for the gift of prophecy. There is confusion in his understanding, as Father Oviedo warns us, and for this reason he is not good at teaching. Now, an understanding to be apt for the prophetic gift should be clear and distinct, not merely for receiving such illuminations, but to distinguish in them what is revealed absolutely from what is revealed conditionally, and to discern what it knows naturally from what it knows prophetically, because if they are not kept distinct one can easily be taken for the other.

2. Another indication that he has been deceived is this—which can be seen in No. 24 and many others—that he is a man who is thoroughly satisfied with his own judgment and inordinately fixed in his own opinion. What has contributed to this firmness or hardness of head is his prolonged and irregular prayer and other mental exercises, joined with corporal mortifications. The natural result of this is that, the more a rational being withdraws from material things, the more firmly fixed the understanding becomes in what it apprehends, whether it be true or false. It frequently happens that such persons, especially if they are blinded by the fumes of some passion—which seems to have happened in the present instance—accept what is doubtful and false as truth itself.

3. Another factor contributing to his deception is the mistreatment of his person in the indiscretion with which he has practiced certain corporal and mental exercises. Word has reached us here that he has suffered from hemorrhages and other disorders. In this way, I am afraid—and it seems fairly clear—that he has upset his own imagination and done some harm to those powers of the soul where resides the judgment of particular things, by which it distinguishes the true from the false, the good from the bad. It is from the derangement of this faculty that delirium comes, and so on, and it is quite possible that by the time he reaches this stage, he may have given—which God forbid—clearer signs of even greater errors.

4. From the point of view of the will we can also see how easily this deception can happen. For the will, which may be inclined to one side or the other, draws the understanding after it and does not leave it free

to judge correctly. This is why as a rule men are not good judges in their own affairs. Now, Master Onfroy seems to have a great inclination to prolonged meditations and prayers, so much so that he wants to go to a desert, and is sore at heart, it seems, when this his self-love meets with opposition. This, apparently, is the source of those prophecies enumerated in Nos. 8, 9, 10, 26, 27, 30, and 31, in all of which this self-love seems to be clearly perceptible.

5. Walking straight before the Lord, seeking His will in all things, will help to avoid deception and will be a sign also that one is avoiding it. A failure in this rectitude of intention, such as we see in Master Onfroy, achieves just the opposite. I say failure of this rectitude, for it is certain that his will is not in conformity with God's will, the perfect rule of rectitude, since it does not conform itself through obedience with the will of the superior, as may be seen in Nos. 10 and 30 and others, where he rather sits in judgment on his superior and condemns him.

6. It is also a sign that one's spirit is good if it leads to the loving observance of all a man's obligations in the service of God our Lord, just as it seems to be an evil spirit that leads to the opposite. There is evidence of this in No. 9 and elsewhere, where he shows but little devotion to the Institute he has embraced and has promised by vow to follow. For he thinks that the Society has not been well instituted, and he wants to see it re-established to his own liking. It is plain that, when one is not very well disposed to a duty, one is not usually very careful to be perfect in fulfilling it.

7. It is a sign that the spirit is from God when it makes the soul more humble and lowly, since it has a better knowledge of itself in the light which God our Lord communicates to it. But the spirit which actuates Master Onfroy seems to come from his mind and our adversary, seeing that it inspires him with considerable pride. It is pride that makes him judge and condemn one whom he has taken as superior in place of Christ our Lord, his commands, and the Institute of the Society.

8. Moreover, the mortification of spiritual vices, such as ostentation and vainglory, is a sign of the good spirit; and when we see that these appetites are not mortified, we take it as a sign of the evil spirit. This lack of mortification appears in many of the propositions concerning him, especially in Nos. 20 and 21, where he speaks of those who are in the extraordinary way, or soon to be. Now, if he has had a revelation of these things, it does not seem proper for him to publish it abroad so readily. Persons who have received such extraordinary favors from God usually take the words of Isaias as applying to themselves, "My secret to myself, my secret

to myself."[12] And if they do make some things known, they do so with moderation, and only so far as they think God wishes them to or commands them to, for the edification of the neighbor.

9. To this reason is allied the following, which deals with the curiosity, the rashness, and the intrusion of self which will appear in the third part which here follows, all of which are striking indications of the bad spirit, as their contraries would be of the good.

Wherefore, as far as his person is concerned, there is confusion of understanding, stubbornness of judgment, and injury to certain physical functions, especially those that are mental. The will is prejudiced and not directed to obedience, nor given to the observance of his obligations. Pride and empty show, curiosity and rashness which can be seen in his words, all point to the presence of the spirit that has inspired them. It is a bad spirit, and should be opposed as the adversary, the father of lies, and the enemy of all good.

Criticism of the alleged revelations

We come now to the third division of our proofs which deals with the revelations themselves. We will examine some of the propositions in numerical sequence.

Nos. 1, 2, 3. (1) Although these numbers together with some others deal with prophecies that do not in themselves involve impossibilities, they should not be accepted for other fundamental reasons, as involving difficulties and falsities which have already been mentioned, and will be mentioned later on. If the spirit that prompted them were good it would speak well consistently. (2) If we inquire into the purpose of these revelations, we will find nothing advantageous, rather the contrary: disturbance, and so forth. (3) Taking a reasonable view of things, as matters now stand, there is no reason for trusting such novelties. For if they must be accepted as being above reason or opposed to it, every prudent man ought to be given arguments that would satisfy an understanding that is based on reason, if such things are to be received as revelations from God our Lord. For unless this is clear, it is not right to run the risk of error lightly. And this all the more so that we are not bound to believe all that even genuine prophets tell us, because in matters that have not been clearly shown to them, they can be mistaken. Sometimes they have been, especially when they spoke of matters that were not part of their prophetical message but which they understood from the natural operation of their

---

[12] Isaias 24:16.

reasoning powers, a thing which has happened to some of them, as we have already noted. Now, if this happens in the case of genuine prophets, how much more cautious must we be in believing those whose possession of the prophetic gift is doubtful, especially when they seem to be telling us of visions that come from our adversary or from their own disturbed fancies. And there are many such in our day.

Nos. 4 and 5. (1) It does not seem proper to oppose or resist the vicar of Christ. Nor is even martyrdom desirable if it is to come from this quarter. (2) Neither does it seem probable that the Creator and Lord of all things should leave the pope so embarrassed in the general affairs of the Church when He has never done so in spiritual matters. (3) Neither is it likely that He will persecute this Society which is so much His own and so devoted to His service. And yet the thing itself is possible.

No. 8. As to the Society's losing its spirit with the increase in numbers in the last three years, we believe, as far as we can reasonably judge and without the possibility of doubt in our Lord, that just the opposite is true. (1) Because experience proves, speaking of those concerning whom we have had reports, both professed and nonprofessed, that there has been a growth in spirit and virtue and the interior life. (2) Proofs of this are to be seen in the edification given at the council and in different cities of Italy and Sicily, and in the great fruit that God our Lord has produced in many souls by means of the Society in Venice, Padua, Bellum, Verona, Ferrara, Bologna, Florence, Perugia, Foligno, Rome, Naples, Messina, Palermo, and many other places, as can be seen partly from the reports that are now being sent in and those which have been sent in at other times. The same is true of Spain, which is not far away, and of the Indies, which are very remote, and the Congo and Africa, where we can readily see that the Divine Majesty is making much use of members of the Society. Indeed, it is He Himself who calls our attention to the signs by which we can distinguish different men when He says, "By their fruits you shall know them,"[18] words which provide us with good grounds for the conjecture that our interior spirit and virtue have grown, since we see such good fruit on the exterior. (3) Our father is of the same opinion, and his word ought to have weight as one who being interested has the will and the opportunity of learning for himself.

No. 9. That the Society is not well instituted and will be better founded in spirit. (1) There is no reason why we should try to convince ourselves that this pronouncement was inspired by the Holy Spirit, who

---

[18] Matthew 7:16.

is "the Spirit of truth,"[14] and "hath knowledge of the voice,"[15] and can be ignorant of nothing. In fact, the contrary spirit, so far as it manifests itself, is ignorant of the affairs of the Society which, except for what is fundamental and essential, are in the course of formation. For the Constitutions are only partly drawn up, some parts of them being still under discussion, and even in the bulls some points are being revised, after recommending the whole matter to God our Lord with many Masses, prayers, and tears. What is aimed at is not a relaxing of what has been well founded, but a greater perfection, because we can always, for God's glory, go from good to better, without waiting to see the fulfillment of the prophecy which goes on as though the prophet thought that the affairs of the Society were already settled once for all. (2) The Institute of the Society, so far as Master Onfroy can see from the bulls and briefs, contains nothing that is against the spirit, even in his understanding of it. For instance, the point of longer or shorter hours for prayer. Up to the present no limit has been set for the members of the Society, nor for its scholastics, as nothing at all has been determined. This being so, what part of the Institute is apparently so poorly conceived and in need of reformation according to the spirit? (3) The Holy Spirit does not dictate or command to be published anything that offers no advantage for the future and would even do harm in the present to those who accept the revelation. In this particular instance, acceptance would destroy our devotion to the Institute of the Society, entailing a less exact observance of it. For no one would be exact in his observance of what he disapproves, nor would he be anxious to perpetuate it.

No. 10. His unwillingness to declare even to superiors anything that concerns the reformation proposed. (1) This indicates a wrong attitude. At least it shows a very low opinion of the superior, for it holds him to be incapable of dealing with his revelations. It does not seem credible, since God has made him head of His Society, not in fancy or imagination but in the reality of truth. On the other hand, Master Onfroy shows a very high opinion of himself, as though he alone were competent, and so on. (2) It smells also of the spirit who "hateth the light"[16] and who avoids truly spiritual persons, who he knows are not ignorant of his trickery and who will make known his deceits. (3) He shows very imperfect obedience and slight respect for those whom he obeys in the place of Christ. (4) This revelation seems to be without profit, since it is not communicated to persons and places where some spiritual benefit might result.

[14] John 15:26. [15] Wisdom 1:7. [16] John 3:20.

No. 13. Besides an apparent manifestation of his old opinions and desire for solitude and affection for persons concerned with his prophecies, the matter in itself does not seem to be to the point. (1) Because when God wishes to confer the gift of prophecy, He does not usually wait to confer it until the individual gives himself wholly to Him in prayer, as can be seen in the instance of Moses, David, and the other prophets who held public office, and such like. And we can see from the case of Balaam how little God need depend on man's disposition, for Balaam was a bad man, and we are told that, although his will was bad his understanding was good enough. Did his ass have the dispositions which he [Onfroy] asks for the speaking of prophecy? (2) This disposition is either natural, as would be a great and clear understanding, and so forth (and this disposition would be greater in others than in Father Oviedo), or it is supernatural, a grace *gratum faciens,* or gift of the Holy Spirit, as would be the gift of understanding or wisdom. Now, it is not known that these were ever held to be, or were called, dispositions for prophecy. Many have had them who were not prophets, and others have been prophets without even being in the state of grace, to say nothing of these gifts of the Holy Spirit. Therefore it is not easy to see how Father Oviedo has the disposition for prophecy. In a word, it is all imagination, lightly entertained and lightly spoken.

No. 14. These also seem to be the creatures of imagination and fancy and are very improbable, although everything is possible with God. And to keep to the point without undue length here, I will only observe that it seems that, if Tejeda were to be an instrument for the reform of his order, he ought not to fail, as he does, in certain points of perfect obedience. This failure he himself did not deny here. While this dispensation of God remains hidden, it would be a bit of rashness to believe it. It is quite possible that Father Oviedo and Master Onfroy have carried away some infection from their association with him [Tejeda].[17]

No. 15. Since he doubts, it is evident that he has no revelation on these matters, but a mere opinion, in which: (1) There seems to be some irreverence in comparing men who are still living with the saints, and especially such a comparison with St. Francis. (2) There is rashness in such a judgment. For although he may know great things of Tejeda, he

---

[17] Father Andrew Oviedo was involved in the same error as Father Francis Onfroy. They were both under the influence of a Franciscan friar named Tejeda, or Texada. Tejeda had a reputation for sanctity, but his influence was withdrawing the two Jesuits from the spirit of their Institute and imbuing them with a spirit that was quite foreign to it. St. Ignatius sends them this pointed warning.

does not know all about St. Francis. (3) For all that we know about Tejeda here, and perhaps there may be much more in him, we have no difficulty in deciding the question as to which of the two has accomplished more. Indeed, it seems that only a blind attachment could find anything to doubt about.

No. 18. As to Duke Francis' being the angelic pope, the thing is possible and even very easy for the Lord of all. And here we would yield to none in our joy in the same Lord for whatever great undertaking His Divine Majesty may be pleased to employ him. And yet it would be better to keep so great a dignity entirely out of our thoughts until the time comes for it to become known, leaving Him to do all according to His Divine Goodness.

Nos. 20, 21. (1) First of all, it shows great rashness to give expression to what is said in these numbers, for only God can weigh merits. It is not credible that He has revealed, or is revealing ever so often, matters of so intimate a nature, things already past and others still to come. He says that *soon he will advance to an extraordinary state,* a man with so many conflicting qualities especially . . . (2) Even supposing them to be revealed, matters so important and secret should not be disclosed so gratuitously. (3) There is no advantage in making such things known, and consequently the seer ought to be judged guilty of vanity and presumption. The saints, when such things were revealed to them, were not wont to speak of them without a good reason. St. Paul was fourteen years without disclosing the revelation God made to him when he was rapt to the third heaven.[18] (4) What he says about the extraordinary state and the continuous presence of God seems fantastic and false, for we do not read anything like this even of the great saints, although some servants of God have a more continuous consciousness and more frequent actual thought of God than others. (5) It seems impossible, according to the common experience of very spiritual and holy persons, because such a presence requires an actual and fixed attention in the intellect, even continuous, and this is repugnant to our present condition of *viatores*. Even very devout servants of God complain about the wanderings and the instability of the mind, and we read that St. John occasionally relaxed his contemplation by bringing his attention down to the bird he held in his hand. When one of his disciples was disedified at this, he answered that, as the bow cannot always be bent, neither could the understanding.[19] It is true that

---

[18] 2 Corinthians 12:2.
[19] See Cassian, *Collationum ss. patrum, collat.* 24, c. 21 (PL 49, col. 1312-15).

occasionally, and even frequently, many servants of God have a great and vivid knowledge of eternal truths and that this knowledge is certain and fixed. However, it is impossible for us to believe that they should remain in this state continuously.

No. 22. This fear is founded on a mistake. Here we have no other information than what has come from you, some of it from Father Oviedo himself, some from Father Araoz. If, then, the spirit has told you of other tares, it is much to be feared that this information has come from that spirit who is a liar himself and the father of lies.[20]

No. 23. (1) If this liberty, which he says was taken in obedience to the superior and with the sole intention of helping Father Oviedo, did go beyond the bounds of moderation, it did not at least spring from those tares. Master Polanco knows this for certain. And if the spirit of Onfroy says that he [Polanco] was the instrument of the devil in sowing the tares, Polanco himself would see, and without doubt, that it is not the spirit of truth, because his conscience is witness before God that he sincerely loves Father Oviedo in the Lord, and always has loved him in himself, and is, and always has been, by God's grace far from doing anything like sowing tares. (2) Regarding Master Polanco, this is either a revelation or a suspicion. If a revelation, beyond what has been said, he should not fear, but know it for certain as a revelation. If it is suspicion, he should be careful lest his opinion be against charity, or that it be at least rashly entertained.

No. 24. (1) Here there is evidence of the spirit of disobedience and pride for not submitting the understanding even to the highest of his superiors. (2) There is also vanity, for he is seeking to give the impression that all of the knowledge he possesses comes to him in a supernatural way. (3) Here, as we have said previously, the sequel is considered both fantastic and false.

No. 25. Either he holds this as a revelation, and it is certain that they who have knowledge of something through their prophetic light have for themselves no other foundation for their certainty, although for the sake of others they may seek the support of reason and authority; or it is not revelation, and in this case we see that it is unreasonable in him to be obstinate, since the three authors he produces are subject to error and are not all of weighty authority. And although they all speak favorably, it may well be that they are not clearly understood or correctly interpreted by him. One of them, Henry Herp, must be interpreted in several pas-

---

[20] John 8:44.

sages to get the meaning they allege out of his words.²¹ The same is seen in an author who writes a very long preface at the beginning of a very little book. I do not recall his name, but as he is favorable to him, it is quite certain that he says this.

Nos. 26, 27, 28. Something has already been said in No. 8 that bears on the point dealt with here. When all is said, there is no doubt of the necessity of God's increasing our spirit and our virtue from day to day, and we hope that He will do so. But he is not excused of rashness in speaking of what he does not know, and it is difficult to withhold the accusation of pride, as he looks upon himself as very spiritual, even going so far as to hold the Society in contempt.

No. 29. He says that in no other order is there less prayer. If he means that the Institute of the Society limits its prayer to a shorter period than the others, he is wrong, because up to the present no limit has been set down. If he means that individuals pray less in no other order than is done with us, he says what is false, if one considers what is actually done. It will always have to be taken into consideration that life in the colleges, taken up as it is with study, is one thing, and another, life in the houses of the Society where there are no studies.

No. 30. Here he lays bare the source of his pain and the origin of so many prophecies. He is quite wrong. (1) He is ready presumptuously to condemn his superior for being wrong on a point about which he himself knows nothing. The fact is that they who are in touch with matters know that the superior is quite right. Now, it is certain that the Society does not forbid prayer—Christ commands it and it is necessary for salvation.²² But it does set limits for some individuals who are inclined to carry it too far. And this is entirely in keeping with God's will, to whom everything that is reasonable and moderate is pleasing because it is in conformity with His wisdom. (2) He shows that he has not mortified his judgment, and that he does not really know what obedience is.

No. 31. That a meditation of one and two hours is no prayer, and that more hours are required, is bad doctrine, and against the opinion and practice of the saints. (1) Consider the example of Christ, who, although He sometimes spent the night in prayer, at other times was not so long, as in the prayer at the Supper²³ and the three hours He prayed in

---

[21] Henry de Herp, O.M., of the strict observance, died in 1477. In 1555 the Carthusian Bruno Loer edited the mystical works of this author under the title *Teologia mística*, which was forbidden for reasons pointed out in the text. It was printed in 1582 with the proper corrections by Peter Felipe, O.P. See Hurter, *Nomenclator litterarius*, IV, 910.

[22] Matthew 7:7; Luke 11:9, 18:1.   [23] John 17.

the Garden. He will not deny that these were prayers, nor can he say that each of them went beyond one or two hours. They probably did not go beyond one, as there would not have been sufficient time in the night for the other mysteries. (2) Take the prayer which He Himself taught us. Christ called it prayer, even though it is short and can be said in less than one or two hours, and no one should say that it is not prayer. (3) Consider the example of the holy hermits whose prayers as a rule were not even as long as an hour, as we can see in Cassian,[24] who recited so many psalms at a time, and so forth. This is the practice in the public services and offices of the Church, unless indeed he would have it that not even these are prayers. (4) The same is seen today in the practice of the faithful in general, and even of devout persons, very few of whom indeed pray for more than two hours at a time. (5) If prayer is "asking God for what is proper," and, to give it a more general definition, "the elevation of the mind to God with pious and humble affection,"[25] and if this can be done in less than two hours, and even less than a half-hour, how can he wish to deny the name or essence of prayer to what does not exceed one and two hours? (6) Are ejaculations, which are so much praised by Augustine and the saints, no prayers?[26] (7) The scholastics who are at their studies for God's service and the common good of the Church, how much time over and above their occupations must they give to prayer if they are to keep their mental faculties in condition for the work of learning and at the same time preserve their health? It would be good to realize that not only when he prays does man serve God, because if he served God only when he prayed, prayers that lasted twenty-four hours a day, if such a thing were possible, would be short, since the whole man as completely as possible should be given to God. And indeed, at times God is served more in other ways than by prayer, so much so in fact that God is pleased that prayer is omitted entirely for other works, and much more that it be curtailed. Indeed, it is right to pray perseveringly and not to faint, but this should be properly understood, as the saints and doctors of the Church understood it.

No. 32. Whether this is true or not can better be seen where you are, if your lordship thinks it of importance.

This will suffice, I think, on the character of Master Onfroy and for the statements which are attributed to him.

---

[24] *De coenobiorum institutis libri xii*, 1. 2, cc. 2, 4, 10; 1. 3, c. 3 (PL 49, col. 78-79, 83-84, 97-99, 116-26).
[25] St. John Damascene, *De fide orthodoxa*, 1. 3, c. 24 (PG 94, col. 1090).
[26] St. Augustine, *Ad Probam*, epist. 130, c. 10, n. 20 (PL 33, col. 1075).

¶ TO THE FATHERS SENT TO GERMANY

XII, 239-47, Appendix I, Letter 18

Yielding to the entreaties of Duke William IV of Bavaria, Ignatius in 1549 sent Fathers Claude Le Jay, Alphonse Salmeron, and Peter Canisius to Ingolstadt. They were to look upon the reformation of the University of Ingolstadt as the main purpose of their mission, and, as far as possible, the reformation of all Germany. We give here only the first part of the instruction which was sent from Rome in the name of Ignatius by Father Polanco.

Rome, September 24, 1549

IHS

1. Your first and greatest asset will be a distrust of self together with a great and magnanimous trust in God. Join to this an ardent desire, enkindled and sustained by obedience and charity, to attain the end proposed. Such a desire will keep the end incessantly before your mind, and cause you also to commend it to God in your sacrifices and prayers and to make use meanwhile of all other opportune means.

2. The second means is a good life, and therefore an exemplary life. You should shun, not only evil but the very semblance of evil, and show yourselves as patterns of modesty, charity, and all the other virtues. For as Germany is in great need of good example, she will derive much help from it; and even though this example be wordless, the affairs of the Society will prosper and God will do battle for us.

3. You should cherish a genuine affection and show it for all, and especially to those who have more influence for the common good, as the duke himself, to whom you should offer your excuses for arriving so late, and to whom you must show an affection which not only the Apostolic See but our Society cherishes for him as well. Courteously promise him that you will devote every effort and endeavor for the help of his people.

4. Show your love in truth and in deed by bestowing favors on many, giving them now spiritual assistance, and again in exterior works of charity, as will be explained later.

5. Give proof that you are not seeking your own interests, but those of Jesus Christ;[1] that is, His glory and the good of souls. In keeping with this, accept no stipends for Masses or sermons or the administration of the sacraments. You must have no income of any kind.

---

[1] See Philippians 2:21.

6. Make yourselves loved by your humility and charity, becoming all things to all men.[2] Show that you conform, as far as the Institute of the Society permits, to the customs of the people there, and whenever possible see to it that no one goes away from you sad, unless it be for the good of his soul. But do not gratify others at the expense of conscience, and let not excessive familiarity breed contempt.

7. Do not take sides in faction and party strife, but follow a middle course and be friendly with both sides.

8. It will be helpful if you have the reputation, based on fact, of holding sound doctrine, and this not only in respect of the Society but of yourselves personally. This should be with everybody, but especially with the ruler and men of influence. It will be a very great help toward this authority not only to cultivate interior composure, but such as manifests itself exteriorly; namely, in your manner of walking, your gestures, clothing that is becoming, and above all in the circumspection of your speech, the maturity of your counsels, not only in practical matters but in speculative questions as well. This maturity will prevent you from giving your opinion precipitously if the matter is difficult. In such a case take your time to think the matter over, study the question, and even talk it over with others.

9. You must try to be on good terms with those in government positions and be kindly disposed toward them. It will help to this if the duke and the members of his household who have a wider influence confess to Ours, and insofar as their duties permit, make the Spiritual Exercises. You should win over the doctors of the university and other persons of authority by your humility, modesty, and obliging services.

10. Consequently, if you should learn that you or the Society is in ill esteem, especially with persons in authority, you should prudently undertake a defense, and try to get them to understand the work of the Society and your own, to God's greater glory.

11. It will help to have an exact knowledge of the disposition and character of the men involved, and to consider beforehand all possibilities, especially in matters of importance.

12. It will help if all the companions not only think and speak alike but even dress alike, and observe the same external manners and social customs.

13. Each of the companions should be careful to reflect on what is adapted to the end proposed, and they should talk matters over among

---

[2] 1 Corinthians 9:22.

themselves. The superior, after having heard what the others think, shall decide on what is to be done or left undone.

14. They should write to Rome to ask advice, to describe conditions. This should be done frequently, as it can be of no little help to all.

15. From time to time they should read this instruction and what will be stated later, and other points which they think ought to be added, so that their memory may be refreshed should it begin to grow dim.

¶ TO DON JOHN DE VEGA
III, 13-15, Letter 1145

The viceroy of Sicily and his wife, Eleanor de Osorio, together with their children, Isabel, Ferdinand, Alvaro, and Suero were tried friends of the Society of Jesus. On March 30, 1550 our Lord called to Himself the saintly lady, to the unspeakable sorrow of her husband and her children. Ignatius, who, like the truly just man, lived by faith and considered himself a pilgrim in this world always sighing after the true fatherland of the Christian, looked upon death in the state of grace as a supreme favor from God. He disclosed these thoughts in the three following letters, two of which were addressed to the viceroy and the other to his daughter, Isabel de Vega.

Rome, April 12, 1550

IHS

My Lord in our Lord.

May the supreme grace and eternal love of Christ our Lord greet and remain with your lordship together with His most holy gifts and spiritual graces.

Last night, Friday, I learned from your letter of March 30 that God our Creator and Lord had taken to Himself your most dearly beloved Lady Eleanor. Truly, He had loved and enriched her in this life with especial graces and virtues, and permitted her to send on in advance to the kingdom of heaven a great treasure of good and holy works. May our Lord be ever blessed for all the dispositions of His most holy providence! And as the death of Christ our Lord and Redeemer has canceled out our death, making of it the end of our temporal miseries and the beginning of eternal life and happiness for those who die in His grace, may it please His infinite and supreme Goodness not only to have made Lady Eleanor a sharer in the fruit of the blood and death of His only-begotten Son, but even to fill up in us who remain the emptiness which her absence might cause. For it is certain that if we look only to what concerns her ladyship, the more tender and genuine the love she inspired in us when living, the less occasion we have to grieve, as her life and works leave us no room for doubt that the most liberal and gentle rewarder has already placed her among His chosen and blessed saints.

But if we who are left behind look to ourselves, the absence of one whose presence was so good and desirable cannot fail to cause a feeling of the deepest sorrow. And yet I am convinced in our Lord that from heaven, no less, indeed much more, than when she was here on earth, will she be of help to all of us. For her charity and ability to help have grown greater the closer they are joined to the infinite charity and power of her Creator and Lord.

For the rest, as far as your lordship is concerned, I hold it certain that, with the greatness of mind and fortitude of soul with which the giver of all good things has endowed you, you will accept this visitation as coming from God's own hand.

May His Supreme Kindness be pleased so to communicate itself to your lordship and rule your house and all the affairs of your government, that you may come to experience that it is His Divine Majesty that foresaw and imposed this trial. Under His rule and direction your lordship can repose and be comforted in all your affairs.

We ourselves, more to fulfill in some part the gratitude we all owe to so great an affection and so many favors than because we think such help necessary for one who so lived and died, besides the Masses and prayers of this whole community will write to all the houses of the Society to do likewise, since our great obligations are well known in all of them, obligations which it is a joy to us to acknowledge. May He in His infinite and supreme goodness give His most holy peace and endless glory to those whom He receives from this world. And to your lordship and to us who remain in it, may He deign to grant His most perfect grace, so that we may always know His most holy will and perfectly fulfill it.

¶ to DONA ISABEL DE VEGA
III, 17-19, Letter 1146

Ignatius consoles Isabel on the death of her mother, Eleanor de Osorio. He tells her that when death is viewed merely from the human point of view it is an occasion of the deepest sorrow. In extending his sympathy he dwells on the abundance of motives for comfort. There are three letters of this nature, the present letter, the preceding one, and the one immediately following.

Rome, April 12, 1550

IHS

My dear Lady in our Lord.

The grace and love of Christ greet you and remain with you.

Having to write to tell of the arrival of the candles and other articles which Lady Eleanor had sent us with her usual great charity, we learned that God our Creator and Lord had called her from this present life to the rest and happiness of life everlasting. If we look upon this from a merely human point of view and not with the eyes of faith, it would be the occasion of the deepest sorrow for all of us, so agreeable and indispensable were her presence and company, and so great the love due to the virtue and goodness of her ladyship. But if we consider, as we should, the reward which God our Lord has prepared in His holy kingdom for those who live and die in His service, and that for them the ending of this brief and toilsome life is the beginning of another that is happy and endless, we should rather welcome the occasion of praising and blessing our Creator and Lord Jesus Christ, our life and our every good, and rejoice in the glory and happiness which He shares with those whom He takes to Himself, rather than grieve for the loss we suffer of the help and comfort which such a death inflicts upon us. For although the flesh as flesh resents it, the spiritual conviction of what is better should prevent our sense of personal loss from afflicting us so much. We should reflect on the great gain to her whom we love so much and on what has been more pleasing to our Lord, in whose service, praise, and glory life and all things else should be ordered.

May it please the Holy Spirit, true comforter of the faithful, to console you with the abundant inspiration of His grace. And thus, I think, Lady Eleanor in heaven will obtain this grace for you and will help us all to bow in worship before the Divine Majesty. The less solicitous she is of herself, having reached the term and fulfillment of all her desires, since the Infinite Good communicates itself to her with complete satisfaction, she will be all the more solicitous to help those whom she has left on earth here below to attain with her the same happiness.

Here in this community we have begun to recommend her soul to God in Masses and prayers, and we shall continue to do so, to Him who created and redeemed her and dowered her soul with so many especial graces. And the same has been ordered done in different monasteries in Rome and in all places where there are houses of our Society. It is my conviction, however, that it is we who need her ladyship's help and favor before God our Lord. May it please Him to give us His grace to spend all our life in His holy service, so that when it is ended we may rejoice as do they who arrive at their haven of rest and repose after the trials and perils of the sea. May He give us all the fullness of His grace, so that we may know His most holy will and perfectly fulfill it.

¶ TO DON JOHN DE VEGA
III, 63-65, Letter 1211

The viceroy answered Ignatius' letter of April 12, 1550. In this answer it can be seen how deeply sorrow had wounded his heart, which, however, was upheld by a feeling of humility and hope that is deeply Christian. Ignatius answers this letter with the one that follows, in which he tells his correspondent of the blessings God wishes us to receive when He sends us trials. And he thanks him for the love he offers the Society of Jesus.

Rome, May 31, 1550

My Lord in our Lord.

May the perfect grace and eternal love of Christ our Lord come to you and abide with your lordship together with His most holy gifts and spiritual graces.

From your lordship's letter of the first of the month I gather that there has been produced in your lordship one of those effects which the Creator aims at producing in His creatures by means of such visitations; namely, to lower them in their own esteem so that they will judge themselves worthy of any punishment however severe, since in the faults of human weakness there is more than sufficient cause for punishment.

I was consoled also in our Lord at seeing another fruit which the servants of God our Lord gather from their trials, and that is to replace the love of the things of this world with a desire for everlasting life. But as the world usually holds us willing prisoners in its embrace, there is need of the help which comes from a disgust with it, if we are to raise ourselves to heaven. Blessed be our most wise Father, who is so merciful when He disappoints and so tender when He chastises. May it please Him to increase daily in your lordship what He so earnestly seeks in this way, which is our increased love of Himself and of all perfection. And this will increase in the exact measure that we refuse to be taken up with some other creature. Thus I am quite certain that the means which His eternal providence had ordained by the companionship of such a blessed consort on earth, He has made much more fruitful for your lordship and your whole household by transferring her to heaven, where, having so much less to desire for herself—being filled with the Supreme Good—she will so much the more employ her charity, now made perfect, in obtaining from the most abundant fountain of all graces and blessings those graces which are necessary to attain the same end for those whom she loved so much and now loves much more and is much more able to help.

From this your lordship can understand what our Lord gives me to know of the state of that blessed image of Him, now in her felicity and glory, resting from all her trials where, all else remaining here below, her good works alone can follow her—good works which she enjoys endlessly in the divine worship of Him for whose love she performed them.

As to the rest, the affection of which your lordship gives proof in your wish to see increased in our Lord the favor of this least Society which is wholly yours, Jesus Christ our God and our Lord, who Himself has inspired you, will, we hope, in His divine love perfect it and reward it always. I make no offering on my part because, as we are entirely yours in our Lord, there remains nothing that we can offer anew, even though the desire of fulfilling our duty in the Divine Majesty increase. May He in His infinite and supreme goodness give us all His abundant grace that we may always know His most holy will and perfectly fulfill it.

¶ TO CHARLES BORGIA
III, 79-80, Letter 1228

Ignatius, in his letter to Charles, congratulates the marquis on his progress and growth in virtue. He expresses his hope that with God's grace he will achieve even greater heights.

Rome, June 13, 1550

IHS

My dear Lord in our Lord.

May the sovereign grace and everlasting love of Christ our Lord greet and visit your lordship with His most holy gifts and spiritual graces.

It is many years since I first inscribed your blessed family in my soul, and your lordship in particular as its main support, with the desire that our Lord Jesus Christ keep you all written in the book of life. But as yet I have had no occasion to write your lordship in particular. I find one now in the spiritual joy I feel in our Lord at what Master Andrew writes of the great favors which He who is the infinite and supreme good so liberally bestows on you. I am thinking especially of the disposition of heart which these holy gifts find in your lordship and which move you efficaciously to desire and carry out what concerns His service and glory. Endless blessings on him who has made your lordship his heir, not merely of his estates and temporal possessions but also of the virtues and the spiritual riches of the lord duke,[1] which is a much more precious and significant heritage. It is this, and not the former, which must make your lordship heir to the kingdom of heaven and the possessor of wealth which has no limit either in value or in term of possession, but is infinite and supreme in itself, the enjoyment of which is to be without end. Besides, I am persuaded in the same Lord that, as the good example of virtue which your lordship gives is in these times of much edification to all and offers us a great occasion to praise and bless the author of all good, so we hope that not only will He preserve but daily add to your lordship's virtue, and thus give us a fresh and greater occasion to glorify and praise His infinite mercy.

No more for the present, except to offer myself and our least Society for the perpetual service of your lordship in our Lord. May He in His infinite and supreme goodness deign to give us all His bountiful grace that we may ever know His most holy will and perfectly fulfill it.

¶ TO JOHN BERNAL DIAZ DE LUCO
III, 107-09, Letter 1263

John Bernal Diaz de Luco was a canonist of note and a doctor of Salamanca. He was first vicar-general of the Diocese of Salamanca, then of the Archdiocese of Toledo. Later he was councilor for the Indies and bishop of Calahorra, where he died in 1556. He had met Faber in 1541,

---

[1] Francis Borgia. Francis had written to Ignatius, March 31, 1550: "I should like to have your reverence write the marquis and congratulate him. You can take occasion from what Master Andrew writes about our Lord apparently beginning to prepare the soul of the marquis for great graces. I recommend him to the prayers of your reverence" (MHSI, Sanctus Franciscus Borgia, II, 569).

and from that time remained a close friend of the Society. When he was named bishop of Calahorra in 1545, he made every effort to bring the Jesuits to his diocese, and wrote to St. Ignatius to this effect. The saint thanks the bishop for his manifestations of kindness. The bishop had exhorted Ignatius to take an interest in the Basques. He replies that the Society will do all within its power to fulfill the duty of charity. He says that Dr. Araoz has been in Onate organizing the new college there. He expresses his hope that it will be able to fill the great need which that country has for spiritual teaching.

Rome, July 8, 1550

JHS

My Lord in our Lord.

May the sovereign grace and everlasting love of Christ our Lord greet and visit your lordship with His most holy gifts and spiritual graces.

I received your lordship's letter of June 4, and consider it no small favor and mercy in our Lord, and will continue to do so, that your lordship is happy to see in me one who is very willing, in spite of his meager resources, to employ himself in your spiritual interests to the glory of God our Creator and Lord.

I have spoken with his holiness about the matter your lordship entrusted to me, and enclose herewith his decision.

Concerning the deep satisfaction your lordship experiences in the success which Divine Providence gives to the efforts of this least Society in His holy service and the help of souls, I could hardly believe anything else of the zeal and holy charity of your lordship. I beseech you to remember the Society in your prayers and holy sacrifices, to the end that the infinite and supreme Goodness which has begun it may deign to accept the lowly instruments it offers, and make them daily more suitable to serve and glorify Him in the help of souls.

Of the care which your lordship exhorts me to have of the Basques, I have no doubt that, as prelate of so many of them,[1] your lordship will himself have a great care of them, and that this care will be evident in works. In this respect I hope that, as far as possibility allows, we will not fail your lordship in our bounden duty of charity.

Our Dr. Araoz has been in your part of the country these days to organize the college which is to be begun at Onate, but I do not know whether he is still there. If this attempt receives the help it deserves, as I have no doubt God through His servants will help it, there is every reason

---

[1] The greater part of the Basque provinces then belonged to the Diocese of Calahorra.

to hope that it will be for the great spiritual profit of that country, which is in dire need of spiritual teaching and exhortation, as your lordship well knows.

I am very glad to promise the prayers which your lordship asks with such insistence. May the infinite and supreme Goodness be pleased to hear them, and give us all His abundant grace to know His most holy will and perfectly to fulfill it.

¶ TO THE ARMY IN AFRICA
III, 113-14, Letter 1267

Ignatius wrote this letter to the members of the Spanish army in Africa who were fighting the infidels there. Through his intercession Julius III had extended the graces of the jubilee to the Spanish army. This army was under the command of John de Vega, and at the time this letter was written, they were besieging the city of Tunis.

Rome, July 9, 1550

IHS

Ignatius of Loyola, general of the Society of Jesus, to the illustrious lords, nobles, brave knights, captains, and soldiers, and to all Christians who are waging war in Africa against the infidels, the help and favor of Jesus Christ and lasting health in the same.

Having by commission of his excellency, Don John de Vega, viceroy of Sicily and captain-general of these holy expeditionary forces, begged in his name and in that of the whole army, of his holiness, our lord Julius III, by divine providence pope, that the treasure of the jubilee which is open to the faithful who come to Rome and visit certain churches be also extended to you, who for the glory of Christ and the exaltation of our holy faith are engaged in military operations against the infidels his holiness with ready will and apostolic kindness has granted you this grace, on condition of a contrite confession, so that when you behold the large liberality of the Most High and His spouse the Church, you may the more bravely, spiritedly, and earnestly wage battle with the enemies of the holy cross to a more successful issue of the war, and if you survive win a victory, or dying, the blessedness of heaven, having obtained pardon of all your sins.

Now to make known to you the granting of this grace, we have thought it proper to write you these present letters, sealed with the seal of the Society.

¶ TO ISABEL DE VEGA
III, 121-22, Letter 1275

Ignatius assures Isabel that he remembers her in his prayers, and hopes that she will obey the divine will. Masses have been said for her deceased mother; but because he is sure that she is already enjoying eternal happiness, he will have the Masses and prayers offered for Isabel's father and the success of the war in Africa.

Rome, July 19, 1550

IHS

My Lady in our Lord.

May the sovereign grace and everlasting love of Christ our Lord greet and visit you with His most holy gifts and spiritual graces.

As your last letter was an answer to mine, I have not been in a hurry to write again. But I have not been remiss in offering continuous prayers to God for you, as I am very desirous in His Divine Majesty to see a constant increase of His gifts in your soul. With the greater light and knowledge of spiritual and eternal things which comes from these gifts, you will not suffer so much from temporal losses. For not only will you make little of the loss of that blessed soul of Lady Eleanor, whom God has taken from this world, but you will be consoled with the thought of her ladyship's repose. You will not even think her death a personal loss, seeing that where she is she will be all the better able to help you reach the same bliss that now is hers, as her desires and prayers will be the more efficacious in the divine presence. You will even miss her presence and companionship the less, the more the thought and love of heavenly things associates you with heaven. May it please Christ Jesus our God and Lord to raise your soul to Himself and possess it completely with His holy love, so that, whatever state you choose, you will be a vessel of election filled with His spiritual treasures. Amen.

For the rest, I hope that the holy inspirations and desires which God our Lord has given you and must continue to give you will not lose their effect, and that you will always be ready to follow His divine will and summons, and render great service and glory to His holy name. May it please His infinite and sovereign Goodness to direct you with His special providence in all your ways, and especially in these which have so important a bearing for the whole of life. I will not fail to beg this constantly from His Divine Majesty.

I have taken care of the Masses which you wanted said at privileged altars, and in addition to them we have already said here at home three hundred. But as I felt almost ashamed to be praying so much for a soul who has been so long in glory and is helping us by her intercession, I arranged that all the Masses and prayers said in this house should be directed to asking God's favor for John de Vega and his naval forces. I have written in this sense to other places in the Society.

May it please God our Lord to hear our prayers so far as it will redound to His service and glory, and give us all abundant grace always to know His most holy will and perfectly to fulfill it.

¶ TO THE CARDINAL OF LORRAINE
III, 139-41, Letter 1300

Ignatius consoles the cardinal on the death of his father, the duke of Guise. The cardinal's living faith and hope, he says, will warn all not to attach too much value to the things of this life. Ignatius then wishes the cardinal every blessing in his new station, that of cardinal of Lorraine, which he attained on his uncle's death.

Rome, August 11, 1550

IHS

Most reverend Monsignor and our most respected Protector in Christ.

May the sovereign grace and everlasting love of Christ our Lord greet and visit your illustrious lordship with His most holy gifts and spiritual graces.

Some days ago I wrote a letter out of obedience to your most reverend lordship. I hope that I shall always act so. Our friend John Baptist Viola is bearing the letter, but will delay its delivery until he can find you a little less occupied, after you have finished the pious duties connected with the funeral of my lord of Guise,[1] of happy memory, whose passing from this short and miserable life to that which is happy and eternal your most reverend lordship has accepted, I am sure, from God's hand, not only with the fortitude of a true Christian, who should not be saddened by such a passing, as the Apostle says, "as others who have no hope."[2] Yours should be the fortitude of a true prelate and column of the Church, of whom Jesus Christ our Lord says, "You are the light of the world."[3] By the example of your living faith and hope and love of the life of heaven,

---

[1] Claude, father of Charles. Charles was cardinal of Lorraine.
[2] 1 Thessalonians 4:12.   [3] Matthew 5:14.

you are a warning to all not to esteem the life of earth except insofar as it is a means of obtaining the life of heaven. This has been fulfilled, with God's grace, in the instance of my lord of Guise, as we should believe from the sweet odor of his solid piety, his religious life, and his Christian virtues. The fruits he had produced in the service of God had come to maturity in this life on earth, and the sweet providence of God our Lord wished to gather him to Himself and reward him with life eternal. Although I know that the great piety and charity of your most reverend lordship will not fail to make use of the suffrages with which the Church Militant is able to help those who are on their way to the Church Triumphant, seeing that her abundance in this respect cannot but help him, I have given orders that all the priests of this house and any others who may be present in it recite special prayers for his excellency, and that all the Masses in the house be said with this intention, and that other Masses be said at the different privileged altars in Rome, to ask the Divine Mercy to bestow on him His unfailing and most blessed light, so that he may know God's eternal truth and rejoice in His infinite and most happy goodness with joy and glory unending. Over and above the common obligation of charity we owe to your most reverend lordship as our true protector and lord in Jesus Christ our Lord, we all feel under the gravest obligation in the presence of His Divine Majesty to cultivate a very special devotion and affection for the person and the family of your most reverend lordship, and we ask the Supreme Goodness to bestow on you most abundantly His most holy gifts, both in this world and in the next, for His greater service and glory.

We are also aware that, as a consequence of the passing away of the cardinal of Lorraine[4] of happy memory (may he be in glory), your own burden has been increased. We hope, however, that the giver of every blessing will add to your spiritual strength, so that you may be able to bear this burden for the profit of all and the benefit of His Church, and this we will beg of His Divine Majesty.

Master Viola will give you some news of our Society (which is entirely your most reverend lordship's) in the service of God in various parts of the world. We hope this story will be repeated in France, when the Divine Wisdom, in His own time and place, will so dispose through your most reverend lordship. May He grant us all abundant grace always to know His most holy will and perfectly to fulfill it.

---

[4] John of Guise, cardinal of Lorraine, was the uncle of Charles. On the death of John, Charles, who hitherto had been called the cardinal of Guise, began to be known as the cardinal of Lorraine (*Chronicon*, II, 89-90).

¶ TO THE JESUITS IN ROME
III, 156, Letter 1326

These directions were given personally by St. Ignatius. Obedience should be prompt and blind, leaving any occupation on the instant.

Rome, August 24, 1550

Our reverend father master Ignatius wishes for God's greater glory and the greater spiritual progress of all of Ours (as he has already partly declared in other Constitutions), that in the future, when his reverence or father minister summons anyone, whether he be a priest or not, or the subminister calls one who is not a priest, they should all answer the call at once, as though it was the voice of Christ our Lord, and practice this obedience in the name of His Divine Majesty. In this way obedience should be blind and prompt. If one is at prayer, he should leave his prayer. If he is writing and hears the voice of his superior, or rather the voice of Christ our Lord, and has begun a letter, say *a* or *b,* he should not wait to finish it. In like manner, if he happens to be with anyone at all, even a prelate (supposing he owes him no obedience), he should come if he is called by any of his superiors. Should one be called who happens to be taking some bodily refreshments of any kind, whether he be at table or in bed, or busy with an invalid, serving a drink or a medicine, or engaged in a service which could not be interrupted with harm to the patient, such as helping to bleed him, or should he be going to confession or about to receive Communion, or hearing the confessions of others in the case of a priest, in all such cases he should send word to the superior and ask whether he wishes him to leave his meal, or his bed, or whatever else it may happen to be.

¶ TO JOHN DE VEGA
III, 190-91, Letter 1392

A letter of congratulation to the viceroy of Sicily on the success of his arms in Africa.

Rome, September 27, 1550

IHS

My Lord in our Lord.

May the sovereign grace and everlasting love of Christ our Lord greet and visit your lordship with His most holy gifts and spiritual graces.

The purpose of this letter is to join with your lordship in giving many thanks to God our Lord, as principal author of every blessing, for the very successful issue that He has deigned to give this undertaking in His service under the direction of your lordship. Besides the joy which we share with all the faithful in seeing so great a wrong put to rights that came from Africa to afflict our lands and which will be, as we hope, the beginning of every blessing in the exaltation of our holy faith and the defeat of her enemies—besides this common joy, we feel one that is altogether special in the fact that your lordship was the main instrument in this work, and that you and Don Alvaro have returned safely.

May it please His divine and sovereign Goodness to preserve you, and ever add to His holy gifts, for His own service and glory, and the universal good of His Church. Please God, your lordship will be the occasion for the beginning and increase of so many good works which will weave for you both in heaven and on earth a rare and lasting crown, for the great service, praise, and glory of His Divine Majesty.

¶ TO CHARLES BORGIA
III, 216-17, Letter 1427

A polite answer to a letter received. Ignatius congratulates Charles and thanks him for help offered for the beginning of the Roman College.

Rome, November 1, 1550

IHS

My Lord in our Lord.

May the sovereign and everlasting love of Christ our Lord greet and visit your lordship with His most holy gifts and spiritual graces.

From other letters your lordship will have heard of the lord duke's safe arrival in this country and of the great joy and spiritual consolation which God gives us in his presence.[1] This letter will merely be an answer to one of your lordship's, in which you mention the great responsibility which God's gifts impose on you and the fear you have of not being able to bear the weight without special help. This itself is a good disposition in your lordship for receiving abundant help from Him who laid the weight upon your shoulders, for the great honor and glory of His holy

---

[1] Borgia entered Rome on October 25. He was received by all classes with much rejoicing. Polanco gives an account of the joy experienced by Ignatius and his friends at this official welcome.

name and the universal good. For He knows that He must take from His own house what He could not find in your lordship's, or anybody else's for that matter—I mean the gift of His wisdom and holy charity which are so indispensable for the good government of such an estate as yours. And because I have the greatest hope in the Divine Mercy, who must bestow these gifts most liberally on your lordship, I do not fear the weight of the others. Indeed, I am quite satisfied that in bearing this burden, as your lordship does others, you will have to show yourself the son of so great a father and the heir of all the virtue and grace which the author of all has bestowed upon him. May it please the Sovereign Goodness to be attentive to the desires and prayers of this least Society, which, being so beholden to that blessed house in the Lord of all, will, I hope, never permit us to be remiss in offering such prayers to His Divine Majesty for your lordship. Especially will the precept of charity oblige us to do so for the lord duke, of whose health we will take the care you ask with the view of obtaining his lordship's cooperation.

I hope that God our Lord will not permit us to be remiss if at any time the opportunity presents itself of being of service to your brother Don John.[2]

We give thanks to God our Lord, the author of all blessings, for the favor and help which your lordship extends to our work here in Rome.[3] May He make your lordship a sharer in any service that is done Him in this college and church, which with His divine favor we hope will be much. It would be superfluous for us to make a fresh offering of ourselves, being as we all are, in a sense, your lordship's inheritance.

May it please God our Lord to give us His abundant grace always to know His most holy will and perfectly to fulfill it.

¶ TO JOHN DE VEGA
III, 219-20, Letter 1428

Ignatius consoles John de Vega, viceroy of Sicily, on the death of his eldest son, Ferdinand, who died as the viceroy was returning victorious from the war in Africa. Lainez, in a letter to Ignatius, says: "We em-

---

[2] John was the brother of Charles, and had come to Rome with his father the duke.
[3] Borgia bestowed a considerable sum of money on the Roman College, and in addition certain annual revenues of his two sons, the marquis of Lombay and John. Each of the sons gave five hundred gold pieces.

barked on September 25, but were detained by contrary winds until the twenty-eighth. On the morrow the news came of the death of his eldest son whom he had left in his place in Sicily." Domenech wrote: "His death was so holy that I could wish that my own would be as happy."

Rome, November 1, 1550

IHS

My Lord in our Lord.

May the sovereign grace and everlasting love of Christ our Lord visit your lordship with His most holy gifts and spiritual graces.

The grief we should all feel that Señor Ferdinand de Vega has left us here in this world is no reason why we should not recognize the very special love and particular consideration which God our Lord has for your lordship in thus visiting your family and taking such precious pledges to Himself. Our Lord, who created him and redeemed him, has only transferred him to another life that is unending. His purpose is to detach your lordship from all earthly love, seeing that He gives you so many reasons for fixing your heart in heaven. Blessed be His boundless providence and charity which governs all our ways. May He be pleased to give your lordship the grace to see and relish the fruit of His visitation and to understand how much better off is your good Christian son now than before, and to be content with all that His divine and supreme Goodness reveals as more acceptable to Him and for His greater glory.

Here in this Society, which is so much your lordship's own, all the help for his soul that its suffrages in Masses and prayers can give is being given and will continue to be given. May it please the Lord of all to accept them and to apply to us who are still in this mortal life the suffrages of which he who dwells in life eternal will have no need, so that in all things we may know His most holy will and always fulfill it.

¶ TO ISABEL DE VEGA

III, 220-21, Letter 1429

Ignatius consoles her on the happy death of her brother.

Rome, November 1, 1550

IHS

May the sovereign grace and everlasting love of Christ our Lord ever be our help and support.

Although we have had no letters from your city, the report has reached me that God our Lord, having granted the father so great a victory on earth, has willed to give the son a more perfect one in heaven. After overcoming all the weakness of the frail body and of the soul, Señor Ferdinand de Vega will attain the enjoyment, unmixed with care, of the supreme good, and this in spite of his few years. His is a victory which all of us in this life aim at achieving, whether our years be few or many. I have no doubt that the tenderness of natural affection will have exacted its tribute of tears from you, but I also hope that the grace with which God our Lord supports and perfects the weakness of nature will have given you such conformity with His designs and so much remembrance and appreciation of the things of eternity, that you would rather be with your mother[1] and brother in our heavenly home, when it will please God our Lord, than bring either of them back to the trials of this exile and pilgrimage. We should have a firm hope that after such a life and death as his, but especially after what our Lord Jesus Christ went through, the divine and supreme Goodness must have already granted him all that the prayers poured forth by you and by us have asked for him, even anticipating to some extent the suffrages we offered.

May He be pleased to grant to all of us who remain here below His bountiful grace, so that we may also know His most holy will and perfectly fulfill it, and find our everlasting happiness in His joyous presence. I ask to be remembered to Señor Alvaro and Señor Suero.[2]

¶ TO THE MEMBERS OF THE SOCIETY
III, 303-04, Letter 1554

During the last months of 1550 Ignatius summoned the professed members of the Society to Rome to study and confer about the suitability of the Constitutions, which had been written by Polanco under his direction. Among the companions assembled were Francis Borgia, Anthony Araoz, Andrew Oviedo, James Miron, Manuel de Sa, Peter Tablares, Francis Estrada, Francis Rojas, Lainez, Miona, Andrew Frusius, Polanco, and Bobadilla. Each of them had full freedom to express his opinions. There were some criticisms offered and Ignatius continued to revise and retouch the text. It was, however, essentially finished in 1551.

---

[1] Eleanor Osorio, who died March 30, 1550. See Letter 1146, April 12, 1550.
[2] Isabel's brothers.

It was at this time that Ignatius submitted to the professed members present the following letter, in which he proposed that he should resign from his office of superior general. He considered himself completely unfit because in his great humility he was convinced that he lacked the necessary qualifications. None of the companions wished their leader to resign and they begged him for the good of the order to remain in office. He did, although shortly afterwards he became seriously ill for a time and never fully regained his health.

Rome, January 30, 1551

IHS

1. At different times throughout these months and years I have given the matter free and undisturbed thought, and I will state in the presence of my Creator and Lord, who is also my eternal judge, what I take to be the balanced results of this reflection, to the greater praise and glory of the Divine Majesty.

2. Regarding calmly and with a sense of reality what I see in myself, as a result of my many sins, imperfections, and infirmities of body and soul, I have often and at different times come to the conclusion that I really do not possess (being infinitely lacking, in fact) the gifts required for the proper discharge of the office which the Society itself has laid upon me.

3. I have a great desire in our Lord that this matter be taken under consideration, and that another who is better, or not so bad, take over the office of governing the Society which is now mine.

4. I desire that such a person be chosen and given this office.

5. And not only does my desire persist, but I think with good reason that this office should be given, not only to one who would perform it better, or not so ill, but to one who would have only equal success.

6. Considering all this, in the name of the Father and of the Son and of the Holy Spirit, my one and only God and Creator, I lay down and renounce simply and absolutely the office which I hold, and beg and beseech in our Lord with all my heart, both the professed and those who wish to join them, to be pleased to accept this resignation which is made with so much justification before His Divine Majesty.

7. If those who are to accept and pass judgment on this petition, to God's greater glory, detect any inconsistency in it, I beg of them for God's love and reverence to commend it to His Divine Majesty, so that in all things His most holy will be done to His greater glory and to the greater general good of souls and of the whole Society, understanding everything for the greater praise and eternal glory of God.

¶ TO ISABEL DE VEGA
III, 326-27, Letter 1587

A polite answer to a letter, with a few words of consolation on the death of her brother.

Rome, February 21, 1551

IHS

My Lady in our Lord.

May the sovereign grace and everlasting love of Christ our Lord greet and visit you with His most holy gifts and spiritual graces.

I received your letter of January 11 and the gifts for this coming Lent that you sent with it. May He who endows you with such remembrance and charity accept it and reward you with an increased recompense in this life and with the perfect life in eternal glory.

You speak of entertaining a kind of envy, on the one hand, of Señor Ferdinand de Vega, who is now in glory, when you see him beyond the danger of offending God our Lord in this wicked world, and, on the other, of feeling a continual concern about him for having been called at so early an age. I observe that such envy is good and holy, and the concern too, on condition that neither the envy is lacking in conformity with God's will that you are left behind in this land of pilgrimage, painful as it is, as long as it may contribute to God's greater service, nor the concern be lacking in the firm hope that God our Creator and Lord has taken to His glory Señor Ferdinand de Vega, of happy memory, or holds him very close to it. In God's presence old age of itself does not add to our merits, nor does youth, in life eternal, take away from them. Rather, he is richer who makes himself a greater sharer in the merits of Christ through that charity which is His gift. There are many who by their great good will make up for the lack of time or of good works in His service. I have every trust in His infinite kindness that Señor Ferdinand de Vega will have made up for this lack. The example he gave in life and in death make such hope reasonable. Finally, we have so good a God, so wise and loving a Father, that we should never doubt that in His kindly providence He withdraws His children from this life at the very best possible moment for them to pass to the other. Let this be sufficient.

You are quite right in saying that there is no need of letters to keep me in mind of Señor John de Vega, or to have me remember him in my poor prayers and sacrifices. May it please the divine and sovereign Goodness to lend an ear to my continual prayer for his lordship, his family, and his interests.

Master Lainez left for Florence at the time of the duke's departure. I will see that what you say in your letter is sent to him.

We are all enjoying good health, thanks be to God, although I have had but little these past few days.

May He in His infinite and sovereign goodness give us all abundant grace always to know His most holy will and to fulfill it perfectly.

¶ TO FERDINAND, KING OF THE ROMANS

III, 401-02, Letter 1721

Ignatius praises the zeal of the king in his desire to repair the losses which the Church suffers in Germany, and shows himself ready to help in so holy an enterprise by sending some fathers to Vienna to begin the university planned by Ferdinand.

Rome, after the middle of April 1551

Most serene King.

May the sovereign grace and love of Jesus Christ our Lord ever protect your majesty and perfect you with a continual increase in His gifts.

There is nothing of greater importance, or nothing that is in itself more worthy of the care and solicitude of Christian princes, than the defense and promotion of the Christian religion. With reason, therefore, does your majesty, most serene king, think earnestly of restoring this religion where it has fallen and of making it secure where ruin threatens it and of endeavoring to apply all possible and opportune remedies to it. For all this we give thanks to God, the author of all good, and we ceaselessly beg Him ever to preserve this excellent disposition of mind which He has bestowed on your majesty. We ask that He enkindle in your heart an even more ardent desire for His glory and the salvation of souls, and give you the strength necessary to carry out these plans to the end.

But among other remedies which it is proper to use against the widespread disease which afflicts Germany, that one should be sought which is to be found in the presence at the universities of men who, because of the example of their religious life and the soundness of their Catholic teaching, will endeavor to help others and to lead them to what is good. This seems to be, not only a prudent and very practical thought but one that is necessary and even inspired by God. Would that this could be in part realized, with the help of the divine clemency, by means of the college of our Society which your majesty writes he is going to establish in Vienna. We have the firmest hope in the divine goodness that it will be, and we ourselves, as we should, will try according to the measure of our weakness not to disappoint the devotion of your majesty.

At the first opportunity we will send two theologians and some scholastics to Vienna. They will be able to help in this work by their learning and example. At least, this is the opinion of your majesty's ambassador. Meanwhile, if it seems good that Master Le Jay should go ahead, he will be ready to obey your majesty, as we are all most ready so to do, in our Lord Jesus Christ. May His boundless kindness grant that your majesty may know what is pleasing to Him in all things, His perfect will, and ever fulfill it for His greater glory and the universal good of Christendom. Amen.

¶ TO FATHER URBAN FERNANDES
III, 499-503, Letter 1848

This father, who held the office of master of novices in the College of Coimbra, received his appointment as rector of that house with great repugnance. He proposed to St. Ignatius certain questions having to do with the better performance of the duties of his office. The following answers were given by Father Polanco in the name of the holy founder. He was also referred for further information to the Constitutions of the Society, which were not promulgated, however, until 1553.

Rome, June 1, 1551

IHS

In this letter you will find, dear father, an answer to yours of March 8. And first of all, regarding our father's wishes about writing, he means that he wishes to be informed not merely of edifying items of news having to do with the harvest reaped in confessions, sermons, and so forth, because it will be enough to write of these things in one letter every four months and there is no need for a monthly letter going into greater detail; but what he wants to know is everything, as far as possible, that he should know for the better discharge of the office which God has laid upon him. Things of little importance are numberless, and one could write of them without end. They can be cared for sufficiently by whatever provision has been made there through local superiors and provincials, and our father would be pleased if information were given him about things of greater moment and which involve more than usual difficulty. He wishes to be kept informed of the number in the community and the names of those who enter and leave or are dismissed, and to this end he has asked that you send every four months a list of names with their principal qualifications. When the list in our hands is complete, it will be sufficient in the next letter to touch on anything new that has occurred in the preceding four months.

1. He would also like to know what progress the scholastics are making in their studies and their spiritual life, especially if one is more than ordinarily beset by temptations, or anything else of importance, and what means are used to help him. Likewise, of those who are making solid and resolute progress in God's service. It might be well to touch briefly on the mortifications that are used to effect a cure in various attachments, and the success that attends their use. This should be rather in general; or, if details are added, they should be very brief. Mention should be made of those who are progressing more than ordinarily in solid and persuasive preaching; those who are ready to be sent to various places when they have finished the ordinary course of study; or who, without waiting to finish completely, were sent out for a time as an experiment or to satisfy some request that could not be denied. And so of other things which I have mentioned in a memorial I gave to Father Brandao, a copy of which, I think, was sent to your reverence, or which I will send along with this.[1]

As to what he wishes written about matters of greater importance in what pertains to government, and so forth, I do not think that I am qualified to speak even of those which are of least importance. But the Holy Spirit whose "unction teacheth you of all things,"[2] who instructs those who dispose themselves to receive His holy illumination, and especially in that which pertains to a man's office, will teach your reverence. I am sure that He will, seeing that He gives you so much good will to succeed in what is to His greater service. But, not to omit anything of what I have been able to understand of the mind of our father and of his manner of acting, I think that he desires members who are fit for something, who have a natural aptitude and vigor either for the study or teaching of letters or for helping in external works of the ministry. And they should not lack industry for either the one or the other. He will

---

[1] See Letter 1854 to Father Brandao, June 1, 1551.
[2] 1 John 2:27.

sooner take one who gives some hope of distinguishing himself in these external occupations, apart from learning, than one who has no inclination or no aptitude for these occupations, even though he had slight but not sufficient ability for letters.

2. He wishes that they be more than mere boys, and of a size which I here indicate, allowance being made for exceptional gifts or rare cases. As a rule they should have a pleasant exterior, which is something required in our Institute and manner of life for associating with the neighbor. Do not be satisfied with persons whose external appearance is unpleasant, unless they compensate for this drawback by other exceptional gifts from God which might even present them in an edifying light.

3. He does not wish to accept very young persons if they do not enjoy good health. If they are educated, or persons of more than ordinary foresight, he is more willing to overlook the lack of health. For such persons may be useful even if they have one foot in the grave.

4. With regard to those already admitted, I have this to remark, that what he most carefully keeps in mind, and the nonobservance of which he most keenly deplores is not serious sin, as we may suppose one to be free of that, but obedience, which should extend, not only to the carrying out of an order but even to making the superior's will and judgment one's own in everything where one can be sure there is no sin. He holds that obedience to be imperfect when the subject is satisfied with doing what is commanded, and doing it even willingly, but does not go so far as to judge that he should do it by overcoming his own judgment and making it captive to holy obedience, always understanding, of course, to the extent to which the will exercises jurisdiction over the understanding. This will always be possible as long as there is no evidence coercing the understanding. Persons who are hardheaded and disturb the peace of others, even in slight matters, he does not usually put up with.

5. With regard to mortifications, I notice that he has a decided preference for those which attack one's love of honor and self-esteem rather than those which afflict the flesh, such as fasts, disciplines, and chains. Concerning the latter, it appears that he does not ply the spurs, but rather holds a tight rein unless one experiences troublesome or dangerous temptations of the flesh. And this especially with students who, when they are making progress in their studies and their spiritual life, should be left to their studies. The period preceding their studies or that following their completion is a more suitable time for these mortifications.

6. As to prayer and meditation, if there are no bothersome or dangerous temptations, as I have observed, I notice that he rather approves the

effort to find God in all things than that one should spend a long time in prayer. It is this spirit he desires to see in members of the Society, that if possible they find no less devotion in any work of charity or obedience than in prayer or meditation. As a matter of fact, they should do nothing at all except for the love and service of God our Lord, and each one should find greater satisfaction in what he is commanded, for then he can have no doubt that he is acting in conformity with the will of God our Lord.

7. In the members of the Society he desires the surrender of the individual will and an indifference toward anything that may be ordered. This indifference is usually represented by an old man's staff, which allows itself to be moved about as the owner sees fit, or like a dead body, which offers no resistance no matter where it is carried. He is, indeed, accustomed to inquire about one's inclinations; as, for example, whether one has a preference for studies or for some other kind of service. Yet he is happier to send to studies those who have no particular preference for anything, except to do the will of God our Lord interpreted by obedience, than he would be if they had a great desire for study.

8. As to studies, he heartily wishes that all be well grounded in grammar and the humanities, especially if age and inclination are in one's favor. Then he excludes no kind of approved learning, neither poetry, nor rhetoric, nor logic, nor natural philosophy, nor ethics, nor metaphysics, nor mathematics, especially, as I said, in the case of those who are of the proper age and ability. For the Society is happy to be provided with all possible weapons, on condition that they who wield them do so for edification and are ready to use them or not as shall be judged best.

9. As to opinions to be held, he would prefer unanimity in the Society, as far as it is possible, even in important speculative questions, and all the more so in practical matters. When one gives signs of being more tenacious in his opinion than is becoming, he is accustomed to make use of this as a means to put aside one's own judgment and permit oneself to be judged by others.

10. As to purity of intention, he would have all strive to have a perfectly upright intention of seeking God's glory in all their activities, whether of body or soul. He would have them always seek to help souls, one in one way and another in another, one meeting them personally, another helping others to meet them, always keeping in view the general rather than the particular good.

11. Concerning those who may be assigned to tasks, such as studies, for which they may be personally fitted, but with certain disadvantages to

themselves, I have seen our father remove such persons from such tasks, as he considers it more important that they advance in virtue than in learning when work and worker do not harmonize. He has therefore withdrawn some from studies because they were not at peace and did not profit spiritually. He would apply the same principle to business matters.

12. I do not observe that our father is very exacting in the matter of a strict observance of house regulations; that is, where individuals are concerned who for some particular reason, such as ill health or occupations, fail to observe some of these regulations. In fact, he has at different times made exceptions as discretion suggested. They who are not excused must observe such rules, and penances are imposed on those who do not keep them, as a reminder and as a warning to others. For as there is no sin in not observing them, it is right that they should be observed and some penalty must be expected for nonobservance. In less important rules he is easier, and hardly ever harsh, unless some point of obedience is involved or the matter is of some importance.

This will be enough for this writing. The Constitutions of our father, which we hope to be able to send you soon, will have more to say on these matters.

No more, then, except to commend myself to the prayers of your reverence and of all our dear brothers.

¶ TO FATHER ANTHONY BRANDAO
III, 506-13, Letter 1854

The Portuguese Anthony Brandao, already ordained, had accompanied Simon Rodrigues on a journey from Portugal to Rome. He laid before Polanco a list of sixteen questions to be submitted to Ignatius. We reproduce both questions and answers, as they all deal with some very practical aspects of the spiritual life, the answers being very revealing with regard to direction of St. Ignatius for the scholastics of the Society.

In the houses of study in the Society study is one of the obligations of a state of life. Instead of increasing by rule the exercises of piety, one should get accustomed to seeking God in all things, to offering Him one's studies and intellectual labors, and to nourishing the holy desire of helping souls. In the matter of confession one should examine the slightest imperfections should the devil attempt to cause one to lean to laxity. If one is at peace with God, the confession should be brief without going into de-

tails, but with an effort to arouse sorrow for the offense. Make use of sacramentals. Authority and affection are a great help in the matter of fraternal correction, but in no case should one resort to rudeness in making one's observations.

Rome, June 1, 1551
IHS

Instructions which are given by our Father Ignatius, or by his direction, to those who live away from Rome, and other points worthy of notice which should not be forgotten.

For Portugal

A scholastic of the Society [Father Brandao] wishes to have our father's direction on the following points:

1. How much time should be given to prayer by a scholastic still at his studies, and how much time should he spend conversing with his brethren, supposing that the rector sets no limits to these occupations?

2. Should Mass be said daily, or only on certain days even when it seems an obstacle to study?

3. After finishing philosophy should one give more time to speculative or to moral theology, on the supposition that one does not give oneself entirely to both subjects in the colleges?

4. What is to be done when one finds oneself entertaining an inordinate ambition for learning?

5. Should one offer oneself to the superior before being asked to do a certain work, or leave the whole matter in his hands?

6. What method of meditation that is more in keeping with our vocation should be followed?

7. In confession, should one descend to particular imperfections, or be satisfied with mentioning the more general faults so as to be brief?

8. If the confession is made to a member of the community and the confessor questions the penitent, even though there is no question of sin, in what instances should he ask the penitent's permission to inform the superior on the subject matter of the confession?

9. What attitude should one take in treating with the superior concerning the difficulties of others? Should he make a complete revelation of them, even though some of them have ceased to be a trouble?

10. Should one correct any imperfection that is noticed in a member of the Society, or should it be allowed to pass, permitting the individual to be deceived into thinking it is no imperfection?

11. If before God one believes that the superior—the rector, for instance—is not right in a certain matter, should the provincial be informed, and thus of other subordinate superiors, or should one close one's eyes?

12. What rule should be followed in writing either to externs, or to Ours, when there is no real need or command of obedience, but merely for motives of charity?

13. In dealing with externs or Ours, should they use language which might appear to them to be mere civility, or should they avoid all forms of flattery?

14. What should one do about giving information concerning one of the Society, and how should it be done?

15. Or would it be lawful to counsel an extern, or one of the house without vows, to take vows?

[16.] What should they do about using or not using a privilege of the Society in dealing with a penitent?

The first question has two parts, and the answer to the first part is to remember that the purpose of a scholastic at his studies in the college is to learn, to acquire that knowledge with which he can serve God's greater glory and be of help to his neighbor. This is a task which demands all that a man has, and he will not give himself completely to his studies if he also gives a large amount of time to prayer. Hence it will be sufficient if scholastics who are not priests (supposing no interior disturbance or exceptional devotion), give one hour to prayer over and above the Mass. During Mass the scholastic should make a short meditation while the priest is at the secret parts. But at the hour of prayer he would ordinarily recite the hours of our Lady or some other prayer, or meditate, should the rector judge that to be better. If the scholastic is a priest, it will be enough for him to say his Office, celebrate Mass, and make the examens. Should his devotion move him, he could add another half-hour.

The second part of the question will be answered if we consider the purpose of conversing with others, which is to influence for good him with whom we converse. This edification is hindered by excess in either direction, and we should therefore avoid extremes and try to hold a middle course.

With respect to the last clause of this question, our reverend father made some remarks on the great esteem we should have for obedience. Some saints have excellences that are wanting in others, and the same is true of religious orders; and therefore it was his desire that in the Society there be an excellence which would put it on a footing with any other religious order, even if they had excellences which we could not aspire to equal, although we might well make the attempt in some things—poverty, for instance. But our reverend father wished that our excellence be obedience, as we have a greater obligation to excel in it because of the extra vow of obedience which the fathers have to the sovereign pontiff, which does away with every excuse we might have for not carrying out an order of obedience. And he also said that this obedience could not be perfect unless the understanding of the subject was in complete conformity with the understanding of the superior. Without this conformity life would be a continual purgatory, and with little hope of stability.

To the second question our reverend father answered that, considering the purpose one of Ours should have in his studies, he could be satisfied with two Masses a week, over and above Sundays and feast days, supposing that none of these three reasons persuade otherwise, (1) obedience, (2) common good, (3) exceptional devotion.

To the third question, preference should be given to speculative theology, because, after finishing with the colleges, one has to devote oneself to moral theology, as that is necessary for conferences and other occasions, and speculative theology is proper to the schools where fundamental truths are taken for study.

The fourth question will be answered along with the sixth.

The Fifth. It would be good once for all to offer oneself to the superior for him to dispose of one to the greater glory of God our Lord, leaving all care of self to him as having the place of Christ our Lord on earth, seldom making any representation unless something occurs which might especially require it.

The Sixth. Considering the end of our studies, the scholastics can hardly give themselves to prolonged meditations. Over and above the spiritual exercises assigned for their perfection—namely, daily Mass, an hour for vocal prayer and examen of conscience, and weekly confession and Communion—they should practice the seeking of God's presence in all things, in their conversations, their walks, in all that they see, taste, hear, understand, in all their actions, since His Divine Majesty is truly in all things by His presence, power, and essence. This kind of meditation, which finds God our Lord in all things, is easier than raising oneself to the consideration of divine truths which are more abstract and which demand something of an effort if we are to keep our attention on them. But this method is an excellent exercise to prepare us for great visitations of our Lord, even in prayers that are rather short. Besides this, the scholastics can frequently offer to God our Lord their studies and the efforts they demand, seeing that they have undertaken them for His love to the sacrifice of their personal tastes, so that to some extent at least we may be of service to His Divine Majesty and of help to the souls for whom He died. We can also make these exercises the matter of our examen.

To these exercises may be added that of preaching in the colleges. After the example of a good life, one of the most efficient means of helping the neighbor and one which is especially in order in the Society is preaching. Our reverend father was of the opinion that no little fruit could be gathered if the scholastics were exercised in preaching. He thought they should preach on Sundays, on subjects of their own choosing, and as an exercise that entailed no loss of time, two or three of them could at supper recite the formula of the tones which they had been taught, using at first the formula that is in use here at Rome. As the possibilities of this are exhausted, another could easily be taken which could be developed in keeping with local customs. The advantages of this exercise are very great, but for brevity's sake we omit them here.

The seventh deals with confession. To avoid any mistake, we should notice from which side the enemy launches his attack and tries to make us offend our Lord. If he aims at getting us to commit mortal sins easily, the penitent should weigh well even the least imperfections which lead to that sin, and confess them. If he finds himself drawn to doubts and perplexities, making sin out of what is not sin, he should not descend into minute details, but mention only his venial sins, and of these only the more important. If by God's grace the soul is at peace with God our Lord, let him confess his sins briefly, without going into detail. He should try to feel confusion for them in God's presence, considering that He who is offended is infinite, which imparts a kind of infinity to the sin. But by the sovereign goodness of God our Lord they are venial, and are forgiven by using a little holy water, striking one's breast, making an act of contrition, and so forth.

To the first part of the eighth, questions may and sometimes should be put regarding certain venial faults, for they may be the means of revealing mortal sins, and help the penitent to a clear manifestation of his conscience, by which he may be further helped.

The Second Part of the Eighth Question. For greater clearness on this point, our father insisted on the importance of the superior's being in touch with all that concerns his subjects, so that he could provide for each according to his needs. Thus, if he knows that one undergoes temptations of the flesh, he will not station him near the fire by assigning him, for example, to hear the confessions of women, and so forth. Nor will he entrust government to one who is lacking in obedience. To guard against anything like this happening, our father usually reserves certain cases to himself; all mortal sins, for example, and vehement temptations against the Institute, the superior, and other forms of instability. Keeping this in mind, the confessor, according to the circumstances of each case, may discreetly ask leave to make a manifestation to the superior. There is reason to believe that a troubled conscience will be helped more in the Lord in this way than in any other.

The Ninth. The answer to the ninth may be surmised from the preceding, and it is that the superior should be wholly informed about everything, even of things past, always taking for granted one's good will, and with every precaution for the due observance of charity toward the neighbor.

The first part of the tenth concerns the correction of another. For this to be successful it will help much if the corrector has some authority, or acts with great affection, an affection that can be recognized. If either of these qualities is absent, the correction will fail; that is, there will be no amendment. For this reason it would not be proper for everybody to undertake such correction. But in whatever manner it is done, and if one is reasonably certain that it will be well taken, one's admonition should not be too forthright, but toned down and presented without offense; because one sin leads to another, and it is quite possible that, once committed, it will not dispose the sinner to accept even a well-intentioned correction in the right spirit.

To the second part of the tenth, as to where one should be left under the false impression that there is no imperfection, our reverend father says that it might be better for the person's progress to do so; that the more one attends to the faults of others, the less he will see of his own, and thus make less progress himself. But if one is really advancing, with his passions well under control and in good order, with our Lord expanding his heart so that he is a help to others as well as to himself, such a one may correct him who is in error, provided the manner suggested in the eleventh number be followed.

As an answer to the eleventh question, our father recounted what he said to the six who were together after making their profession; namely, that they could help him to perfection in two things: the first was their own perfection; the second was to call his attention to what they thought was contrary to this perfection in him. He wanted them to have recourse to prayer before they corrected him, and then, if in the presence of God our Lord there was no change in their understanding and judgment, they were to tell him privately, a procedure which he himself follows now. Our father said that it would be a great help to success in this matter if the superior entrusted this duty to some of his subjects—priests, for example, and others who were looked up to. He who wishes only to benefit himself would do well to close the eyes of his judgment. If anyone should have something to say, let him be careful first to place himself in the presence of our Lord, so as to know and make up his mind what he ought to do. Second, he should find some acceptable manner of telling the delinquent if he thinks that he will accept the correction. But if he thinks that he will not accept it, let him tell the superior. Our father thought it would be a great advantage to have here a syndic to make these things known to the superior. Besides, he would have one or two as vice-rectors, one subject to the other, to help the rector, and with this arrangement the rector would be much better able to be of greater help to one or the other and would keep the affection of his subjects, as they could look upon him as a refuge if they thought themselves hardly dealt with by the vice-rectors.

Our father gave an answer to the thirteenth which seems rather striking to me; namely, that in dealing with another we should take a cue from the enemy who wishes to draw a man to evil: he goes in the way of the one whom he wishes to tempt, but comes out his own way. We may thus adapt ourselves to the inclinations of the one with whom we are conversing, adapting ourself in our Lord to everything, only to come out later with the good accomplished to which we had laid our hand. Our father made another remark as to how to free oneself from one whom there was no hope of helping. He suggests talking to him rather pointedly of hell, judgment, and such things. In that case he would not return; or if he did, the chances are that he would feel himself touched in our Lord.

Finally, one should accommodate oneself to the character of him with whom one is dealing, whether he be phlegmatic, choleric, and so forth. But this should be done within limits.

The remaining questions depend more on the circumstances of individual cases, which in this instance are not given.

¶ TO FATHER ANTHONY ARAOZ
III, 534-35, Letter 1882

Father Araoz was a nephew of St. Ignatius and a close friend of his. He was zealous in his work for the Society and served as provincial throughout Spain. In his letter Ignatius commands him in virtue of holy obedience to submit to the physician in all matters of health. He also asks him to stop preaching for three months, unless an exception is made by Francis Borgia or his son, John.

Rome, June 1, 1551

JHS

May the sovereign grace and everlasting love of Christ our Lord ever be our help and support.

I have been informed of the great need you have of looking after your health, something I have known in part. I do know that, although your health is slight, you allow yourself to be carried away by your charity to undertake tasks and labors which are more than you can conveniently bear. Judging that in God our Lord it would be more acceptable to His Divine Majesty to have you temper your zeal in this respect so that you will be able to labor the longer in His service, I have deemed it proper in our Lord to command you to follow the doctor's advice in all that pertains to your meals, the use of your time, what hours and when you are to take for sleep and repose. For the next three months, from now until September, you are to do no preaching, but are to look after your health. An occasional exception may be made, if in the opinion of our lord, the duke[1] or of Señor Don John,[2] you can do so once a month without injury to your health. To do away with all occasion for gratuitous interpretations, and that you may see that I really mean this in our Lord, I command you in virtue of holy obedience to do as I here direct.

I beg God our Lord to give us all His bountiful grace ever to know His most holy will and perfectly to fulfill it.

¶ TO FATHER JOHN PELLETIER

III, 542-50, Letter 1899

This is one of the most complete of the instructions which St. Ignatius gave on the manner of proceeding for the members of the Society in their ministrations to the neighbor. It was sent especially to Ferrara, but served also in its general outline for other houses.

In these instructions St. Ignatius recalls the principles which ought to direct the activity of his workers and gives some fundamental rules of

---

[1] St. Francis Borgia.   [2] John Borgia, son of St. Francis.

action. The instruction is divided into three parts. The first part deals with the preservation and increase of the Society, and the following means are suggested: purity of intention, complete subordination to superiors, regular observance, preaching, study, and conversation. The second part is concerned with the manner of edification and the gathering of spiritual fruit. To this end he goes over the principal ministries to be employed in dealing with the neighbor. The third part deals with economics. Ignatius suggests various means of winning the good will of important men. He recommends securing an endowment and a site for a house.

Rome, June 13, 1551

IHS

There are three objectives you should keep in mind. One is the preservation and increase of the Society in spirit, learning, and numbers. The second is that we should look to the edification of the city and seek spiritual fruit in it. The third is to consolidate and increase the temporalities of the new college, so that our Lord will be better served in the first and the second objectives.

The first objective

The first objective, which regards the membership of the Society, is something of a foundation for the others, because the better the workers are, the more apt they will be to be accepted by God as instruments for the edification of externs and the prosperity of the foundation.

1. To this end all should have a right intention, so that they will seek solely, not their own interests but "the things that are Jesus Christ's."[1] They should endeavor to conceive great resolves and elicit equally great desires to be true and faithful servants of God, and to render a good account of themselves in that which has been laid upon them, with a true abnegation of their own will and judgment and a total submission of themselves to God's government of them by means of holy obedience. And this, whether they are employed in important offices or in tasks of little moment. As far as possible they should be very fervent in their prayers to obtain this grace from Him who is the giver of all good. The superior should occasionally remind them of this duty.

2. As far as possible, the order and method of this college [the Roman College] should be followed, especially in the practice of weekly confession and Communion, in the daily examination of conscience and the

---

[1] Philippians 2:21.

hearing of Mass in the house, if they have a chapel, and if not, elsewhere, if it seems expedient; in the practice of obedience and the avoidance of dealings with externs, except as the rector shall direct. The latter will decide how much responsibility is to be entrusted to each for the edification of others, without danger of loss to himself.

3. In the community refectory there should be a daily exercise in preaching, one after the other, either at dinner or supper. This exercise may be either *ex tempore* or prepared, but not more than an hour should be given to the preparation. In addition to this there should be weekly exercises in the vernacular or in Latin. A subject should be proposed on which one will speak without preparation. There should also be sermons in Greek. Or they may have the *toni*.[2] This second point, however, may be varied and adapted to the capacities of the students.

4. Let each one be intent on his progress in learning and in helping his companions, and give himself to the study or lecturing which the rector shall indicate. Care must be taken that the lectures are accommodated to the capacity of the students. All should be well grounded in grammar and be trained in composition, the masters being careful to correct all themes. There should be some practice in discussions and debates. There should be sufficient opportunity to have all this done at home without having recourse to public schools. Some, however, may be sent to these schools if the superior, taking all circumstances into account, should think it proper.

5. In all these literary and spiritual associations they should try to win others to the life of perfection. With younger students this should be tried only with the greatest skill. Even the older among them should not be received into our schools without their parents' permission. Should it be thought expedient to receive one of these into our house after he has taken such a resolve, or to send him away to Rome or elsewhere, this may be done. Discretion and the unction of the Holy Spirit will point out the better course. But in case of doubt one may, to make certain, write to the provincial or to Rome.

6. The better to attain these ends it will be good to have some of the more advanced among the students carefully compose some Latin dis-

---

[2] The *toni*, or "tones," were an exercise in declaiming a fixed formula containing different feelings and affections. The purpose of the exercise was to teach the young Jesuit the various tones that are employed in different emotions, the modulation of voice, and the gestures demanded by the different kinds of oratory. The formula that was in use may be seen in MHSI, Reg. 254, n. 9. See also *Natalis epistolae,* IV, 594, and the letters of St. Ignatius, *Epistolae et instructiones,* XII, 686-88, for different judgments on the usefulness of this exercise.

courses on the Christian virtues, such as may be seen in the list of subjects that has been drawn up, and have them declaim them publicly in the presence of all, on Sundays and feast days. Young men and others, especially those who seem to have some aptitude for the religious life, could be invited to hear them. This is a suitable means of preparing those whom the Savior is calling to take the road to perfection. At the very least they will be giving good example and edification, and the members of the community will be helped in the practice of letters and of virtue.

The second objective

Regarding the second objective, namely, attending to the edification and spiritual profit of the city, besides helping outsiders with prayers and the example of modesty and virtue, you should make some effort to do so by means of the following practices which are external:

1. Teach Latin and Greek to all who come, according to their ability, and even Hebrew, and exercise the students in debates and composition.

2. Care should be taken to teach children the catechism on all Sundays and feast days, and even during the week, following the order of the Roman College or another that may be thought more suitable. This could be done in the house or in some nearby and convenient place, as you may there judge to be more to the purpose.

3. Be very careful to have the students form good habits. If possible, see that they hear Mass daily. They should hear a sermon on feast days when one is preached. They should confess once a month, and avoid all oaths and blasphemous and indecent talk.

4. If it can conveniently be done, there should be a sermon on Sundays and feast days, or one of them might explain the catechism.

5. If it can be done, a lecture on Holy Scripture or scholastic theology should be given for priests, such as something on the sacraments or some compendious cases of conscience.

6. Special attention should be given to heresies, and you should be properly armed against them. Keep in mind the subjects that are most attacked by the heretics, and try to be considerate in laying bare their wounds and applying a remedy. If this much cannot be done, their false teaching must be opposed.

7. You should try to bring people to the sacraments of penance and Communion, and be ready to administer them.

8. You will be able to help all with whom you deal if you make use of spiritual conversation, especially if you find in them some disposition to be benefited. The Exercises of the first week could be given to many;

but the other weeks only to those whom you find suitable for the state of perfection and who are truly willing to be helped.

9. You should be careful to help the prisoners and visit the jails if you can, and preach occasionally, and exhort the inmates to confession and a return to God. Hear their confessions if opportunity offers.

10. Do not forget the hospitals. Try to console and give spiritual help to the poor as far as you can. Even in these places some exhortation may be profitable, unless circumstances seem to advise otherwise.

11. In general you should try to keep informed about the pious works in the city where you reside, and do all you possibly can to help them.

12. Although many means of helping the neighbor and pious works are proposed, discretion will be your guide in the choice you must make, it being taken for granted that you cannot do all. But you should never lose sight of the greater service of God, the common good, and the good name of the Society.

The third objective

The third objective deals with consolidating and increasing the temporal goods of the new college. A great help toward this will be the daily sacrifices and the special prayers which all the members of the community ought to offer for this purpose, insofar as it will be for God's glory. Moreover, the observance of what has been said in the first and second objectives will help more than any other means we could devise. But to touch on a few means belonging properly to this third objective, we will suggest the following:

1. Try to preserve and increase the good will of the prince, and try to please him whenever possible according to God. Be of service to him in those pious works which he is especially interested in promoting, provided they offer no prejudice to God's greater service. Be careful likewise to maintain a good name and esteem and authority in his regard, and speak to him in such a way that he will come to hope that the Society is disposed on its part to help the work progress, even if it ordinarily begins in a small way, in order that later it may grow rather than fail.

2. You will also have to make an effort to win over individuals and benefactors, and talk with them on spiritual things. To help them with special care is something quite proper and acceptable to God, with whose business we are concerned.

3. The better to preserve your own authority in spiritual things, you should try if possible to have our friends rather than ourselves ask for us and manage our temporal affairs; or let it be done in such a way that

there is not even the appearance of greed. To avoid all such worries, it might be better to fix on a given amount for your support, although nothing should be said about this, except at the proper time and in the proper manner.

4. Have a special care that, although it may not be given at present, a good site be given in time that will be large enough, or which can be added to until it is large enough, for a house, a church, and a school, and, if possible, not far from the center of the city.

5. Write us every week for help and guidance.

¶ TO FATHER CLAUDE LE JAY
III, 602-05, Letter 1965

King Ferdinand wished to give a fresh impetus to theological studies in the University of Vienna. To effect a realization of the king's desires, St. Ignatius, who considered the study of sound theology one of the most important safeguards for the defense of Catholicism in Germany, suggests three ways which would lead to the firm establishment of theological studies in the university.

The first was to see that students came from all the provinces. The second was to initiate the preparatory studies with the view to preparing the students for theology. Both of these methods had their limitations. For this reason he chose a middle course: to continue with the same studies but to offer along with them some special courses for those who had the aptitude. In this way the younger of them would be prepared and subsequent courses made ready for the more thorough study of theology.

Rome, August 8, 1551

JHS

May the grace and peace of Christ our Lord ever grow in our souls.

From your reverence's letter of July 21[1] our father master Ignatius learned of the holy purpose of his majesty the king[2] to reform theological studies in the University of Vienna, and in fact to restore them, since, as we understand, they have been practically given up, as there were no students for the courses. Indeed, considering the conditions of the times in Germany, this provision seems to be most desirable and highly neces-

---

[1] See Le Jay's letter, MHSI, *Epistolae Broeti*, 369-71.
[2] Ferdinand, king of the Romans.

sary. Our father, and indeed all of us, would consider it a privilege to help his majesty in this matter if the Society were able. But I will state freely to your reverence what is here thought about the means to attain this end—that is, the restoration of theological studies in Vienna—and you can make what representation you think proper to his majesty.

If we give the matter serious thought, three courses will present themselves. The first is the one which your reverence says his majesty wishes to use; namely, that the provinces send some students for theology, that some of these students be Jesuits, and that there be frequent lectures and exercises, and so forth. This course will, it seems, be very acceptable if a large number of students could be found in Vienna, or sent on from the provinces, who are ready to take up theology and go through with it. Some such arrangement would be necessary for the success of this plan. But there is reason to fear that such a disposition is lacking, and that on two counts.

The first is, as we have learned, that there is today little inclination and interest for this study among the Germans, especially for scholastic theology. Without this interest and inclination every kind of exercise will turn cold, and in the end there will be little progress. The other reason is that such students, even though they are well disposed, will not have the proper foundation in logic and philosophy, or even perhaps in the languages. This foundation is indispensable. If some are found, they will be very few; and for these theological exercises a large number of fit and well-grounded students will be needed. Otherwise, as experience in other universities teaches, the whole thing will catch a chill. It will not be enough to establish good order if there is none to observe it, and thus we shall not attain the end we have in view. If it is claimed that our own scholastics could form a nucleus, they would not be a large enough number, and others might get the idea that they ought to leave this study to religious. Thus they will never be able to carry out the purpose of supplying the parishes with educated pastors, since Ours are not allowed to undertake such parishes. The first way would seem, then, to be beset with the difficulties mentioned.

The second way is to begin more deliberately to prepare students, keeping in mind the ultimate purpose of restoring the study of theology. This would be to have the provinces send on young men who are destined for that study. They should be first well grounded in Latin, and those who have the ability and are thought fit, in Greek and Hebrew as well. After a good foundation in the humanities a large number, say a hundred or so, should begin the course of liberal arts and be carefully trained in it. In subsequent years others in good numbers who have been well grounded in the humanities will enter the course. But they should always keep theology in mind, and the teachers of the humanities and philosophy should constantly encourage them and fill them with a love of theology. When they have finished their philosophy, of the hundred who began, fifty or perhaps more will be ready for theology. Here their progress will be notable if they have come in sufficient numbers, are well disposed to theology, and have laid a good foundation in the lower branches.

This would seem to be a very good way, but certain difficulties may be encountered. The first is that the result of so much labor will be long in coming, even though a matter of five or six years should not be considered long when we think of the permanence of the result. The second is that there are already many students in the university advanced in the languages, and some even in philosophy, who would not be disposed to give themselves to the lower branches. The third is that it would not seem very becoming in a university like that of Vienna to omit the higher branches even for a time while the students were being grounded in the lower.

A third way could be taken which would avoid these difficulties, and it is this. Let the lectures in philosophy and theology continue as they now are, but insist, as was pointed out in the second way, and make it a point to do so, on laying a good foundation for the future study of theology. The students in the lower classes of languages should be instructed and prepared, so that the students who are sent on by the provinces to study theology and all the others who are now attending the university for the study of languages see to it that they get a good foundation in the liberal arts under teachers who will try to enkindle in them a desire for sacred theology and a love of it. Once there is a goodly number of young men who have advanced in the study of the languages, they could begin a course of philosophy with good and repeated exercises, after the manner of Paris. Thus in the following years, when they have finished the course of arts or philosophy, there will be a good number of well-trained students eager for theology. This will be the time to begin a course in theology, and subsequently, as the years go by, it could be given as it is at Paris. Public lectures will then have a larger attendance and an audience able to profit from them.

In this last way the college which his majesty the king is preparing for the Society can be of no small help, because, in the first place, it will offer lecturers in humanities and languages who, besides their lectures, will have a special care to see that the students are exercised and advance in their studies and in good morals, and are inspired with a zest for the study of theology. Once the college has a competent number of well-prepared students, it can also supply lecturers in philosophy who will proceed as we have indicated, and make their students ready for theology. And these being prepared, it will be able in the same way to supply teachers of theology who will carry on their courses after the manner of Paris, where our Society first made its studies and with whose teaching methods it is acquainted.

This way seems to be free from objections. The first difficulty mentioned above, the delay, can be better put up with, especially as it is necessary and does not entail any interruption in the ordinary lectures of the university. The second difficulty, which deals with students already advanced, ceases for the same reason, because, if they do not wish to lay a better foundation, they can go on as they are doing. The third, the danger to the reputation of the university ceases for the reason that everything will continue as usual. If some lecturers leave and there are no others to take their places, one could be provided from the college for a lecture course in Sacred Scripture, and another for cases of conscience, and so on, until there are students sufficiently well prepared, as we have indicated, to begin a course in scholastic theology with a good foundation. This might seem to be laying a heavy burden on the Society, to provide lecturers in humanities and later on in philosophy and theology, but we are under such heavy obligations to his majesty the king and the public good resulting will be so great that we should in no way hold back.

Your reverence, therefore, should take up this whole matter with the bishop of Laibach,[3] and if he approves, with his majesty the king. At least, our father, by explaining his thought and offering to do what he can, is partially repaying a general debt of charity, and a special debt which he owes to the service of his majesty, to the glory of God our Lord. May He in His infinite wisdom guide us all and govern us so as to contribute to the salvation of souls and His praise and glory. Amen.

¶ TO FATHER ELPIDIUS UGOLETTI
III, 638-39, Letter 2048

On the occasion of the founding of a college in Florence, Father Ugoletti is advised as to the manner in which scholastics are usually sent

---

[3] Monsignor Urban Weber, bishop of Laibach and confessor to the king. He died in 1558.

to new colleges. *When the foundation is left in the hands of the Society, poverty should be observed. Provision that is made by the founders should be kept within the limits of propriety. The letter is entitled: "Instruction for Don Elpidius Concerning the Manner of Sending Scholastics."*

Rome, early September 1551

JHS

Hitherto our scholastics, when they go to found a college of the Society, have been sent in one or other of two ways. The first is apostolic, without money, ill-clad, like pilgrims that are seen here in Rome unless they go to be presented to the pope. In the place to which they are sent, they dress them as scholastics of the Society are wont to dress. This is done when the founders leave the matter in the hands of the Society, because she can then act in conformity with her poverty. This is what was done in the College of Padua and the College of Venice, which was founded by the prior of the Trinita.[1]

The second way is for those whom God has inspired to found colleges, to write to the general and also to the pope, or to one who will speak with him, so that the work can be begun with his blessing and from devotion to the Apostolic See, and to give good example in the court. In this second case, as they there must provide clothing, let orders be given that they dress as we do here, so that when they go to kiss the pope's foot, they may make a more presentable appearance. The place where they are going should provide some traveling expenses, so that they may travel in moderate comfort. This way has been followed by the cities of Messina and Palermo, the letters being written both by them and the viceroy John de Vega. This was also done, these last months, by the king of the Romans;[2] and from Naples his excellency the viceroy[3] writes (as does the duke of Montaleone) that the same provision will be made for the twelve who within a few days are to be sent to begin a college there.

What you should do is this. Set these two ways before her excellency,[4] either by word of mouth or in writing, so that she can make a choice, seeing that the scholastics belong to her excellency, as does indeed the whole Society. Whichever way seems to her to be best for the glory of God our Lord will seem most proper to all of us, since we do not look upon the work or the workers of the Society so much our own as her excellency's.

---

[1] Andrew Lippomani. See Letter 743, June 22, 1549.
[2] Ferdinand I.
[3] Peter of Toledo, father of Eleanor, duchess of Florence.
[4] Eleanor of Toledo, duchess of Florence.

¶ TO FATHER SIMON RODRIGUES
IV, 49-50, Letter 2300

Rodrigues is relieved of his office of provincial of Portugal.

Rome, December 27, 1551

Ignatius of Loyola, superior general of the Society of Jesus, wishes eternal salvation to his beloved brother in Christ, Simon Rodrigues, priest of the same Society.

Prudence and justice in Christ Jesus demand that those who undertake no slight labor in the government of the provinces of our Society should not expect to be weighed down with this burden without end. Therefore there should be some division of such burdens among others who are capable of bearing them. As you have lived long and labored much in the province of the kingdom of Portugal, which was entrusted to you by us and more than ordinarily prospered by God, the author of all blessings, we have thought, considering your age and infirmities, that you should be held to these tasks no longer. By the same authority, therefore, by which we laid this burden on you, we now, in order to give you opportunity for repose after so many years, release you from this office in the name of the Father and of the Son and of the Holy Spirit.

¶ TO FATHER MANUEL GODINHO
IV, 126-27, Letter 2383

The devout Father Manuel Godinho was much afflicted because he thought his office as procurator of the College of Coimbra was an obstacle to his perfection in the religious life. In this sense he must have written to St. Ignatius, who in the following letter comforts and encourages him, reminding him of the supernatural end of the Society, which sanctifies exterior occupations undertaken through obedience.

Rome, January 31, 1552

May the perfect grace and everlasting love of Christ our Lord ever be in our favor and help.

I received your letter, dear brother in our Lord, and from it I learn of your arrival at San Fins with the brethren who are under your care there, and that everything was done with due edification.

Although the charge of temporal affairs seems to be and is distracting, I have no doubt that by your good and upright intention you turn everything you do to something spiritual for God's glory, and are thus very pleasing to His Divine Goodness. For the distractions which you accept for His greater service, in conformity with His divine will interpreted to you by obedience, can be not only the equivalent of the union and recollection of uninterrupted contemplation, but even more acceptable to Him, proceeding as they do from a more active and vigorous charity. May God our Creator and Lord deign to preserve and increase this charity in your soul and in the souls of all. We rightly hold any operation whatever in which charity is exercised to God's glory to be very holy and suitable for us, and those activities even more so in which the infallible rule of obedience to our superiors has placed us. May He who gave to Eliseus this twofold spirit, which you say is so necessary, give it to you in abundance. I will not be remiss in desiring and begging it of His Divine Majesty.

If, looking only to God's glory, you still think that in God's service this office is unsuitable for you, confer with your superiors there, and they will do what is proper. Even here, as one who holds you very close to his heart, I will not fail to help you.

May Christ our Lord help us all with His bountiful grace, so that we may know His holy will and perfectly fulfill it. Yours in our Lord . . .

¶ TO FATHER FRANCIS XAVIER
IV, 128, Letter 2384

Ignatius misses a letter from Xavier, but is glad that he is back safe and sound from Japan and that he found the door open to the preaching of the gospel. The Society is prospering. He will learn more from Polanco, who has been instructed to write him in greater detail. Ignatius says that he is still moving amidst the trials of life.

Rome, January 31, 1552

JESUS

My dear Brother in Christ our Lord.

May the sovereign grace and everlasting love of Christ our Lord ever be our help and support.

I have received no letter from you this year, although I hear that you have written from Japan but that the mail has been delayed in Portugal. We are very glad in our Lord that you have returned safely, and that the door has been opened for the preaching of the gospel in that land. May it please Him who opened it to bring those nations through it out of their infidelity to find entrance to the knowledge of Christ Jesus, who is our salvation and the salvation of their souls. Amen.

By the goodness of God the Society's affairs are prospering. It is growing in numbers in all parts of Europe. He is making use of us, His least instruments, who with or without them is the author of all good.

For further details I refer you to Master Polanco's letter.[1] This letter will serve to let you know that I am still alive amidst the sad misery of this life.

May He who is the eternal life of all who are truly living give us His grace always to know His most holy will and perfectly to fulfill it.

¶ TO PRINCE PHILIP OF SPAIN
IV, 268-69, Letter 2627

A letter of thanks to the future Philip II for the support he had shown in the difficulties which arose in Toledo with the archbishop. Ignatius takes advantage of the occasion to ask him to continue his interest in the reform of the monasteries of Catalonia.

Rome, June 3, 1552

IHUS

My Lord in our Lord.

May the sovereign grace and everlasting love of Christ our Lord greet and visit your highness with His most holy gifts and spiritual graces.

Although the great indebtedness, love, and affection which I bear to the service of your highness cause me to have you daily vividly present in the sight of God our Creator and Lord, I decided to write this letter and by means of it humbly kiss your highness' hands for the favor, which in addition to so many others, you have shown us all by supporting our case, as our true protector and lord, with the lord archbishop.[1] May God, our perfect and eternal good, be your highness' unending and happy reward, since it was His service that has moved, and I hope will continue to move, the royal and Christian soul of your highness, so that you will continue to show the same favor to this least Society which belongs entirely to your highness.

---

[1] Polanco wrote a letter of eight pages [2386], giving details of the Society's activity in Italy, Sicily, France, Germany, and Belgium, together with news of a few individuals.

[1] The archbishop of Toledo, John Martinez Guijeno, ordinarily called Siliceo. There is a brief account of this incident in Dudon, *Loyola*, pp. 353-55.

Besides, I do not think that I should fail to remind your highness of the reform of the monasteries of Catalonia. When the present political disturbances give you the opportunity, as I hope in our Lord they will, I pray your highness to remember, when the time comes, to give command for the completion of so Christian and holy a work. I am sure that this will be a great service to our Lord, and I will not fail to recall it to your highness' attention at the proper time.

May it please the supreme and divine Goodness to give us all abundant grace ever to know His most holy will and perfectly to fulfill it. Ever your highness' most humble and lifelong servant in our Lord . . .

¶ TO FATHER FRANCIS BORGIA
IV, 283-85, Letter 2652

Charles V had asked the cardinal's hat for Borgia, and the pope was quite willing to bestow it. Borgia himself, merely to obey the pope's desire, was inclined to accept. Ignatius, after interesting several cardinals in the affair and discussing it with them, took time for prayer in order to learn God's will. For two days he hesitated, and on the third he came to the decision that he should resist the offer with all his might. Then, he spoke to the pope personally and pointed out the disadvantages which would follow and the advantage of leaving things as they were. He admitted, however, that others, also under divine influence, might think that the offer should be accepted. He asked Borgia to write him and tell him what he thought about it, so that he could show the letter to others.

The project was given up, but only for a time. The matter was again taken up in 1554. At that time St. Ignatius directed the saintly duke to renew publicly his profession, which had previously been made privately, adding the simple vows which the professed of the Society take in addition to the solemn vows of the profession. One of these simple vows has to do with the refusal of ecclesiastical dignities. Borgia took this vow, and wrote to Princess Joan to have Prince Philip desist from this attempt to make him a cardinal. This effort was successful, and there was no more talk of the affair.

Rome, June 5, 1552

IHS

May the sovereign grace and everlasting love of Christ our Lord ever be our protection and support.

With regard to the cardinal's hat, I thought that I should give you some account of my own experience, to God's greater glory, and speak as I would to my own soul. It was as though I had been informed that the emperor had as a matter of fact nominated you and that the pope was willing to create you cardinal. At once I felt impelled to do all I could to prevent it. And yet, not being certain of God's will, as I saw many reasons for both sides, I gave orders in the community that all the priests should say Mass and those not priests offer their prayers for three days for divine guidance, to God's greater glory. During this space of three days I reflected and talked with others about it, and experienced certain fears, or at least not that liberty of spirit to speak against and prevent the project, saying to myself, "How do I know what God our Lord wishes to effect?" Consequently I did not feel entirely safe in speaking against it. At other times, in my customary prayers, I felt that these fears had taken themselves off. I repeated this prayer at intervals, now with the fears now without them, until finally, on the third day, I made my usual prayer with a determination so final, so peaceful and free, to do all I could with the pope and the cardinals to prevent it. I felt sure at the time, and still feel so, that, if I did not act thus, I should not be able to give a good account of myself to God our Lord—indeed, that I should give quite a bad one.

Therefore I have felt, and now feel, that it is God's will that I oppose this move. Even though others might think otherwise, and bestow this dignity on you, I do not see that there would be any contradiction, since the same Divine Spirit could move me to this action for certain reasons and others to the contrary for other reasons, and thus bring about the result desired by the emperor. May God our Lord always do what will be to His greater praise and glory. I believe it would be quite in order for you to answer the letter on this subject which Master Polanco is writing in my name, and declare the intention and purpose with which God our Lord has inspired you and may now inspire you. Your opinion would thus appear in writing and could then be produced whenever it may be called for, leaving the whole matter in the hands of God our Lord, so that His holy will may be done in all our affairs.

Your letter of March 13 will be answered in another letter. May it please God our Lord that your journey and all things else have met with the success we have hoped for in His Divine Majesty, and that you are now in perfect health of body and mind, as I desire and constantly ask God our Lord in my poor unworthy prayers, to the greater glory of His Divine Majesty. May He in His infinite mercy be our constant help and support.

¶ TO FATHER CLAUDE LE JAY
IV, 348-50, Letter 2769

Ignatius recommends the German College to Le Jay and asks him to try to send a high quality of students to it.

Rome, July 30, 1552

JESUS

My dear Brother in Christ.

May the grace and peace of our Lord Jesus Christ be ever preserved and increased in us. Amen.

I think that you have heard more than once of the German College which is to be built here in the city of Rome. It will undertake the education and moral training of selected young men of good character who give promise of fruits of Christian piety and virtue. It will be under the protection of the supreme pontiff and a board of five cardinals, and the young men will live in the college and be in the care of the Society. Measures will be taken to see that they lack nothing in the way of necessities as to their dwelling, board, clothing, books, and furnishings—in a word, anything that makes for student comfort. When they have made creditable progress in learning and virtue, they will be sent back to Germany and given ecclesiastical benefices. Indeed, those who have been conspicuous for special attainments in virtue will be promoted to bishoprics and the highest dignities. Those who are intensely interested in the saving of Germany see in this college the surest and almost only means to support the tottering and—alas that we should have to say so, of many places at least—the collapsed Church in Germany. It is hoped that very many faithful and energetic young men of that nation and tongue can be sent here, who by the example of a life of study and the influence of their solid learning will preach the word of God, and by their lectures, or at least by their personal influence, will be able to open the eyes of their fellow countrymen to the light of the true faith and tear down the veil of ignorance and vice.

Those therefore who come to Rome to this college which has been erected for the benefit of Germany (as you can see from the transcript or copy of the apostolic letter enclosed), will have professors to train them carefully in Latin, Greek, and Hebrew. Those, however, who have finished their humanities will follow courses in logic, physics, and other subjects. They will finally get a good training in theology, both by means of lectures and constant practice. They will also have competent guides in the spiritual life and watchful regents in domestic affairs. These will all be members of our Society, men at once learned and pious, most of them from Germany or neighboring countries. We should like to begin this important work this year, and their most reverend eminences, the cardinals who have undertaken the protection of this venture, and especially the cardinal of Augsburg, whose warmhearted charity is very active in it, thought that we should write to you and Master Canisius and others of our dear brothers of the Society in Vienna, to have you send to Rome as soon as possible a number of young men of German birth and language, so that, if at all possible, they get here sometime in the month of October, or at least by November. We should, of course, gladly undertake this burden with all proper zeal, and I lay on you the serious obligation of using all the energy and zeal in seeking out and sending these young men that you would use in a matter of the greatest importance for God's glory and the salvation of souls.

¶ TO FATHER JEROME NADAL
IV, 353-54, Letter 2774

This and the following letter complement each other. Both treat of the same matter, a grandly conceived plan of sweeping the Turk from the Mediterranean. Ignatius wishes Nadal to explain it to Emperor Charles V. By means of it he thinks that a great undertaking for the crown and the Church could be realized at small cost. The plan reveals a broad political vision and no common gifts of organization. But no less interesting are the general principles which rule the project, and especially the supernatural motives so familiar in the saint's spiritual outlook which are at the base of the plan.

This first letter, written by Polanco under instructions from Ignatius, reveals only the impression which the frequent inroads of the Turks produced upon the soul of Ignatius and his conviction of the need of assembling a fleet against them. So interested was he in the enterprise that he would not have hesitated to employ the rest of his life in it.

Rome, August 6, 1552

JHS

My dear Father in Christ.

Pax Christi.

I must not fail to share with your reverence, being commissioned to do so by our father master Ignatius, an impression that is much with him these days and about which he would like to have your opinion. If God gave his paternity some interior sign more effective than hitherto, or if he were persuaded that he stands well with his majesty, he would not wait for counsel from anyone. He is thinking of the Turk, falling with his ships year after year on Christian lands and inflicting such great losses, carrying off so many souls who are going to perdition for denying their faith in Christ who died for them. Besides, they are making themselves familiar with these waters, where they are practically masters, burning one place after another. Seeing all this and the losses which the pirates are wont to inflict on the coast lands, on the souls and bodies and belongings of Christian men, he has come to understand in our Lord and to hold the firm conviction that the emperor ought to muster a great fleet and regain control of the sea. He could thus do away with all these troubles, and achieve gains that will promote the universal good. Our father is not only moved by his zeal for souls, but he is drawn by the light of reason as to something that is very necessary, and that can be brought about by the emperor at a smaller expenditure than he now makes. Our father has his heart so set on this matter, as though, as I said, he thought his majesty would agree with him, or as though he had a special inspiration from God. He would be glad to devote the rest of his old age to this plan, with no thought of the labor involved in journeying to the emperor and to the prince, or of the dangers along the way, or of his bodily ailments, or any other discomfort whatever. Let your reverence recommend this matter to God. Give it some thought, and let us know at once what you think of it in the sight of God.

¶ TO FATHER JEROME NADAL
IV, 354-58, Letter 2775

St. Ignatius was brokenhearted at seeing the havoc caused by the raids of the Mediterranean pirates "in the souls, bodies, and possessions of Christian men," and in an effort to find some means of putting an end to these evils he wrote on August 6, 1552 two letters to Father Nadal, who at the time was in Sicily promulgating the Constitutions of the Society. In the first (Letter 2774) he indicates the idea to be presented to Emperor Charles V to equip a fleet to patrol and defend the Mediterranean. In the second, which we are here translating, he submits in the first place a large number of reasons to prove that the fleet ought to be prepared and shows that the project can be realized at no greater expense than is now incurred by his majesty in his maritime affairs. If the plan of St. Ignatius, which does not differ much from the one later adopted, had been carried out in the lifetime of Charles V, the victory of Lepanto would have been less costly and most lasting in its results.

Rome, August 6, 1552

JESUS

In my former letter, which was more general in scope, I spoke briefly of how the zeal and charity of our father were stirred, and how he also brought the light of reason to bear on the conviction that a large fleet should and could be prepared. In this letter I will carry the argument further and show, first, that it ought to be prepared and that it is high time it was; second, that it can be done at little expense, even less in fact, than what is now spent by his majesty on maritime affairs.

The reasons I have for thinking it should be done are:

1. God's honor and glory suffer not a little when from nearly all parts Christians, great and small, are seized and carried off to live among the infidels, where every day we see many of them denying their faith in Christ to the great pity of those who retain some zeal for the preservation and advancement of our holy Catholic faith.

2. The conscience of those who fail in their duty to make suitable provision is burdened with the loss of so many who from childhood and in every age become Moors and Turks merely from the weariness of their toilsome slavery and the countless evils they are made to suffer at the hands of the infidels. On the day of judgment our rulers will see whether they should have held in so little esteem the bodies and souls of so many thousands who are worth more than all their incomes and honors and patents of nobility, since for each and every one of them Christ our Lord paid the price of His life's blood.

3. Christendom will thus be rid of a great danger from these comings and goings of the Turks, who up to the present have shown no warlike activity at sea. But now they are beginning to learn their lesson and to take matters into their own hands. Beginning with what little is left of Christendom, they are employing the tactics which enabled them to take Constantinople; that is, playing one prince against another, and then taking what they please from both vanquished and survivor. They are now using this strategy with France, and there is danger that later they will not only come when called, but will be able to apply pressure on Christian forces both by land and by sea. This difficulty and those men-

tioned above will be obviated if his majesty succeeds with the help of a strong fleet in getting mastery of the sea.

4. This fleet will be able to free the kingdom of Naples in great measure of the disturbances and uprisings which, if they had no help from the Turks, these revolutionaries would have no reasonable hope of carrying through to success. Not even France could offer them hope of help by sea, and these rebels would then fear that the fleet would soon be upon them. And not only would Naples be at peace, but all the rest of Italy and Sicily, and all the other neighboring islands.

5. When the fleet is strong enough to deprive the king of France of any hope of Turkish help in creating a costly diversion of your majesty's forces, he would understand that it would be better to keep the peace. Even if he were unwilling to remain within his own frontiers, he would have no opportunity of returning to Italy. Being always inferior in sea power, and without any help coming by sea, he would be weaker, and consequently much more disposed for peace.

6. We should be freed from the losses which the Turks and the pirates are continually inflicting on all the coasts of Spain and Italy, and elsewhere, to say nothing of the costs of the garrisons which must be maintained in all ports, since we never know just where the Turkish fleet will strike. How costly this is can easily be seen in the past two years in the kingdom of Naples and Sicily and elsewhere. A fleet, being a worldwide wall, would make these costs unnecessary.

7. The passage from Spain to Italy will be made safe, and it is known how important this is for the good of these kingdoms in general and for the individual good of many who have so much to suffer if this path of communication is broken.

8. If we have a powerful fleet and mastery of the sea, it will be very easy to recover what we have lost, and much more, on all the coasts of Africa and even Greece and the islands of the Mediterranean. We can even get a foothold on lands belonging to the Moors and other infidels, and open a way to their conquest and ultimate conversion. But without a fleet even other places of importance to Christendom, such as Tripoli, will also fall.

9. The reputation and honor of his majesty are involved, a reputation which must be sustained among the faithful and even the infidel. This will be vastly improved by a fleet which could seek honor and reputation in foreign parts and defend them at home without effort. As it is now, much credit and authority is lost. Even this authority can be a defense in many places to one's nationals even without the backing of arms.

These are the arguments from reason that convince our father that a fleet should be raised.

And now for the second part. The following occurs to him as a possible method of procedure. It is taken for granted that his majesty has no shortage of man power, for by God's grace he is better supplied with men than any known sovereign in the world. Funds can be raised from various sources:

1. An order could be issued that many of the rich religious orders in the estates of his majesty, which could get along with much less than they have, should provide a good number of galleys; for example, the Hieronymites so many; the Benedictines, so many; the Carthusians, so many, and so forth. Among them could be included the abbeys of Sicily and Naples which are without religious.

2. A second source would be the bishoprics and their chapters and beneficiaries, which taken all together could contribute a large sum of money with which to equip a good number of ships for the benefit of Christendom.

3. The four orders of knights which, like that of St. John, are bound by their institutes to contribute men and money to the fleet against the infidel. And that all be done in due form, the pope could give permission to make this levy, or to deal with superiors there in Spain and their other dominions, seeing that the universal good of Christendom is at stake.

4. A portion of the money which some of the grandees and nobles of their kingdoms spend in hunting and feasting and extravagant entertainment would be most justly used in equipping ships against the infidel and for God's glory. If they do not render personal service, they can render the service of their wealth and possessions. There are resources here for a large number of galleys.

5. Merchants surely among themselves could contribute a sum sufficient for a good number of galleys or ships, since over and above the good of Christendom, they stand to reap a benefit for their own interests.

6. The cities and towns of your kingdom and realms, especially those on the coast which suffer so many losses at the hands of the Turks and Moors and other pirates, have been robbed of much more than they would lay out in ships for the fleet to wipe out the robbers. Let them spend on the fleet what they have been accustomed to spend on defense. This would put an end to their expenditures and allow them to devote themselves entirely to their commerce without being worried by thought of defense. A heavier contribution could be expected from the regions that draw greater profit, such as Naples and Sicily.

7. Some help could be expected from the king of Portugal, who could apply to his kingdom this or a similar method for raising a certain number of galleys and other sailing vessels.

8. There are the dukedoms. Genoa could provide a few galleys; Lucca and Siena will always help, now that Venice cannot.

9. The duke of Florence, who will reap some advantage over and above the general good to Christendom, might be able to help in some such way as was suggested for the king of Portugal, and from ecclesiastical and secular sources, as was pointed out above.

10. Some help could and should come from the pope and the states of the Church, if God will inspire them. If not, they will at least allow what has been outlined above, and this will be no small contribution.

From this you will see, dear father, what suggests itself to our father as he examines the situation in the light of reason. Apart from what the emperor himself could contribute from his own income, which is large, it seems that from these ten sources enough could be collected to maintain a large fleet. And with the help also of the royal exchequer it seems that without much strain more than two hundred ships could be provided and maintained, and even three hundred, if necessary. The larger number of them, or nearly all of them, could be galleys. A great benefit would accrue to what is left of Christendom. It is hoped she could in this way even extend her boundaries, whereas now we see them dwindling and suffering considerable loss.

Give some thought to this and tell me what you think. If others who could do so more properly do not speak out, it might be that one of the poor members of the Society of Jesus should undertake to do so.

May God, who is eternal wisdom, grant to his majesty and to all of us the light to know His most holy will in all things and grace perfectly to fulfill it.

¶ TO JOHN STEPHEN MANRIQUE DE LARA

IV, 385-86, Letter 2816

John Stephen Manrique de Lara, to whom this letter was addressed, was the duke of Najera. Relations between the house of Najera and St. Ignatius had been very close. As a youth Ignatius served under Anthony Manrique de Lara, duke of Najera and viceroy of Navarre. After his conversion one of the few visits he made was to him. Later, when he was given entirely to the service of the Spirit, he had no further relations with this family. But now an opportunity was presenting itself. He was asked to intercede in favor of a proposed marriage between a niece of his, Laurentia de Onaz, and a relative of the duke of Najera.

In this letter St. Ignatius first draws attention to his reasons for not having written in the years that had elapsed to a house to which he owed so much. He then speaks of the matrimonial affair. The business of arranging marriages is foreign to his profession and he prefers not to be involved in it. He merely suggests the propriety of their writing to his nephews about the matter.

The projected marriage never took place. Laurentia was finally married to John Borgia, a son of St. Francis Borgia.

Rome, August 26, 1552

My Lord in our Lord.

May the sovereign grace and everlasting love of Jesus Christ our Lord greet and visit your lordship with His supreme gifts and spiritual graces.

Yesterday Don John de Guevara[1] gave me a letter of yours dated January 22. I will not delay to excuse the want of care on my part in answering. It has been my practice, as it is with all those who have left the world for Christ our Lord, to forget as much as possible the things of the world in order to be more mindful of those of heaven, and to make all the less account of merely human courtesies as we make more of those things which pertain to God's service. But if an opportunity had offered itself of serving your lordship to God's glory, I would not have failed you, insofar as my poverty and my profession would allow, and would have shown you the affection which I owe to you personally and to the family of your lordship in return for the favors and affection by which your predecessors have laid me under obligation. So in my poor prayers, my only opportunity of serving you, I have commended you, and with God's grace will continue to commend, your lordship personally and all your affairs to God our Creator and Lord. May your lordship and all your house always experience His very special protection and grace, to the glory of His Divine Majesty.

Regarding the matter of the marriage of which your lordship writes, it is of such a nature and so alien to my least profession that I feel that any interference on my part would be out of place. It is in fact ten or eleven years since I have written to anyone in the house of Loyola. I felt that,

---

[1] John de Guevara was a nephew of the duke of Najera.

once I had left home and the world for Christ, I should not in any way look upon it again as belonging to me. And yet, if your lordship thinks that it would be to God's greater glory that this union between the two houses take place and that it will be for their good in view of the end we ought to desire, I think it would be proper to write to the lord of Ozaeta[2] and to Martin Garcia Loyola, my nephews, to have a conference with your lordship, and that you personally deal with them about the marriage. I believe that these two can speak for the family, as I have spoken to Don John at length about it.

I have nothing further to suggest in the matter, except to submit to the judgment of your lordship in our Lord. I beg of Him by His infinite and sovereign goodness to give us all His abundant grace always to know His most holy will and perfectly to fulfill it.

¶ TO THOSE SENT TO THE MISSIONS
XII, 251-53, Appendix I, Letter 24

By October 1552 the Constitutions were drawn up, and Nadal a few months earlier had already begun to promulgate them in Sicily. But nothing was printed, and copies were made everywhere as Nadal continued his journey across the rest of Europe. In the controversies with the Protestants the idea of a mission is outstanding. It takes for granted the hierarchical constitution of the Church. As St. Paul said, "How shall they preach unless they be sent?" (Romans 10:15). In the Seventh Part of the Constitutions St. Ignatius adopts this formula, and he calls it a mission whether the ministries be those imposed by the pope or those designated for each one of the superiors of the Society. Several principles are there set forth for the proper regulation of zeal. In October 1552 Ignatius dictated the following instructions, which have the same meaning and purpose. His letter is divided into three sections: the first offers the missionary principles for governing himself; the second concerns his relations with his neighbor; the final section his regard for the Society.

October 8, 1552

IHS

He who is sent on a mission in this Society, to labor in the vineyard of the Lord, should keep three things in mind: the first concerns himself,

---

[2] Bertram Lopez de Gallaiztegui, son of Magdalene Loyola, sister of St. Ignatius, was the lord of Ozaeta and guardian of Laurentia de Onaz.

the second, the neighbor with whom he deals, and the third, the head and the whole body of the Society of which he is a member.

Principles concerning self

1. With respect to himself, he should not be unmindful of himself because of his interest in the neighbor. He should refuse to commit even the slightest sin to further the greatest gain in the world, and not even place himself in danger of committing one.

2. They will find it a help if they avoid dealing with persons from whom they have reason to fear danger; and if they do, it should be rarely and in public. They should make little account of external appearances, and look upon the creature, not as fair or attractive but as bathed in the blood of Christ, as the image of God, as the temple of the Holy Spirit, and so forth.

3. They should defend themselves from all evil and acquire every virtue; and the more perfectly they possess them, the more successfully will they be able to draw others to them. To this end, it will be helpful to assign some time daily for the examen of conscience, prayer and the reception of the sacraments, and so forth.

4. They should take into account their health and strength of body.

Principles concerning the neighbor

1. With regard to the neighbor, we must be careful with whom we deal. They should be persons from whom we can expect greater fruit, since they cannot deal with all. They should be such as are in greater need, and those in high position who exert an influence because of their learning or their possessions; those who are suited to be apostolic workers, and, generally speaking, all those who if helped will be better able to help others for God's glory.

2. With regard to the work he undertakes, he should prefer to all others that for which he is especially sent. Among other works, he should prefer the better; that is, the spiritual to the corporal, the more urgent to the less urgent, the universal to the particular, those that have some permanence to those that are ephemeral, since he cannot do both. We should remember that it is not enough to begin, but that we must as far as possible finish and insure the endurance of good and pious works.

3. As to the instruments we must use, besides good example and prayer that is full of desires, we must consider whether to make use of confession or spiritual exercises and conversations, or teaching catechism, or lectures, sermons, and so forth. We should select those weapons (since we

cannot make use of all) which will be judged to be more effective and with which we are better acquainted.

4. As to our method of procedure, we should try to be humble by beginning at the bottom and not venturing into lofty subjects unless we are invited or asked, or discretion should dictate otherwise, taking into consideration time, place, and persons. This discretion cannot be confined within any hard-and-fast rule. Our method should include an effort to secure the good will of the person with whom we are dealing by a manifestation based on truth, on virtue and affection, and which will command some authority with them. We should make use of a holy prudence in adapting ourselves to all. This prudence will indeed be taught by the unction of the Holy Spirit, but we ourselves can assist it by reflection and careful observation. The above-mentioned examen of conscience could be extended to include this consideration, and it should be made at a fixed hour of the day. Special attention should be given to cases of conscience; and when the solution of these difficulties is not clear in the mind, we should not hazard an answer or solution, but first give it the study and consideration it requires.

Principles concerning the Society

1. The regard we should have for the head and body of the Society is shown principally by allowing oneself to be directed by the superior and by keeping him informed of what he should know and by obediently obeying the orders he shall give.

2. You can serve the good name and reputation of the Society by helping wherever you can for the glory of God, and this will be done especially by encouraging foundations of colleges, particularly when you see the opportunity, by recruiting acceptable candidates for the Society. These should be persons of some education, alert, youthful, especially when they have personality, health, intelligence, are disposed to good and free of other impediments, and so on.

¶ TO **FATHER JAMES LAINEZ**
    IV, 498-500, Letter 3002

This letter, written to Father Lainez, is one of reproval. Ignatius had recalled Frusius to Rome. Lainez disagreed openly with this decision. He sent Gaspar to Rome without first informing Ignatius that he was coming or the condition he was in. Lainez also encouraged the prior of La Trinita to request a man whom it was not possible for Ignatius to send. In these ways he drew upon himself the following reprehension. This letter, which was written by Polanco, was marked "confidential."

Rome, November 2, 1552

My dear Father.

Let this letter be understood not as coming from a son of your reverence, as I, Polanco, really am, who owe you all respect and reverence, but from the pen of our father, who has bidden me write what is here contained. I have wanted to write for some days, but as you have had a quartan fever, I have waited to give you a chance to improve.

Our father is not a little displeased with your reverence, and the more so, that the faults of those who are loved are always more serious to those who love them. How much more reason we have to bewail these faults when they are committed by one we least thought would be guilty! He has charged me to write you concerning a few of these faults, so that, once they are called to your attention, you will avoid repeating them in the future. This will be easy for one to whom God has given so much good will as He has to your reverence.

First of all, then, the prior of La Trinita[1] wrote about Master Andrew, urging that he [Ignatius] send Master Jerome Otello in his place. To quote his own words, "For many reasons, my dear son in Christ, Master Jerome Otello would be quite acceptable, according to what Father Lainez has told me." This was no slight mistake, even though it was done with a good intention; for there is no reason why you should have encouraged or counseled the prior to ask our father for what he did not have to give. At least, you might have learned the mind of our father before giving such advice to the prior. I wanted to give the reasons for this, and for what follows, but our father thought otherwise; that is, that none should be given, since the submission of your own judgment, which you owe to your superior in all that pertains to his office, should be reason enough for you. Besides, it is expressly forbidden to suggest to persons of position to write to our father and ask for certain individuals without first consulting him. Otherwise many inconveniences may follow, especially when the request has to be refused.

The second mistake was the cause of the first; more than a merely personal fault, it was your disagreeing with your superior over the removal

---

[1] Andrew Lippomani. See Letter 117. This incident is treated very sympathetically by Father J. Brodrick, S.J., in his *Origin of the Jesuits,* pp. 233-34.

of Father Frusius from Venice. You not only disagreed, but you showed Frusius himself and Father Salmeron and Father Olave that you disagreed, or that you did not approve our father's order. Of course, your reverence sees how becoming it is to let newcomers, who should find in him a mirror of perfection, see that he thinks bad what the superior thinks good. Later Master Andrew wrote a few reasons which to himself and Fathers Salmeron and Olave seemed sufficient to warrant his removal from Venice to Rome. Neither did he like some of the observations made by your reverence in your answer, such as the remark about the bad feeling that spread through the towns, and so forth, as indicating a disagreeing of your own judgment with the judgment of the superior. Advice or representation is good if it is seasonable, but a difference of opinion is not.

The third mistake which has caused our father no little pain is that you sent Gaspar here, without first giving some notice of his condition, merely contenting yourself with saying, "because they were from Padua," and so forth. It is not right for your reverence to act so secretly when sending a person like him to our house here. Every kind of dissembling and pretense like this with the superior, who ought to be helped with one's knowledge and not impeded, is looked upon as quite out of place in this Society, or in any other order. Our father has also been displeased because, after having sent him to you to be dismissed by you, you approved of his wish to return here, saying that you thought he was worthy of mercy, among other things, which our father calls "decrees." It does not at all please him to see you act in this way, as though you were issuing decrees, seeing that it is so unbecoming in writing to a superior. What is more, he has told me to write to you and tell you to attend to your own office, which if you do well, you will be doing more than a little. You are not to trouble yourself in giving your view of his affairs, as he does not want anything of the kind from you unless he asks for it; and much less now than before you took office, since your administration of your own province has not done much to increase your credit in his eyes. Examine these mistakes in the presence of God our Lord, and for three days take some time for prayer to this end. Then write, if you admit that they are mistakes and faults. Choose also the penance you think you deserve; write it out and send it to him. But do no penance in this matter before you receive the answer of our father.

This is all for the present, except that I pray God our Lord to grant all, and especially to this scribe as the most needy, much light to know ourselves and abase ourselves, and grace to know and do His holy will in all things.

¶ TO IGNATIUS, FROM LAINEZ
I, 216-19, Lainii Monumenta

Readers of the foregoing letter will be curious to know how it was received by Father Lainez. Their curiosity will be satisfied and their admiration aroused by the following letter from a loving and contrite son to a loving and offended father.

Florence, November 15, 1552

IHS

To all, the grace and peace of Christ our Lord. Amen.

I received your confidential letter and have read it many times. By our Lord's grace I have seen nothing in it but reason to praise His mercy, to my own confusion. It will cause me to grow in many ways in the love and respect I owe you. I beg of you to correct me whenever it should be necessary—may it never be so—without any thought of my quartan, or anything else. By God's grace I am sorry that there is matter, and that I fail to amend. I really accept in love what is said in love, and my heart seems to expand, so that I might even consider it an excess of kindness that is done me without any merit of my own.

But to answer you, as you bid me. After having looked into the matter and commended myself to God, as you directed, I answer the first of your reverence's questions by saying that I recognize my faults and mistakes as conspicuous, and this not only because you think they are (which I am sure would be enough to persuade me, for it is easy to believe that he sees more whose vision is sharper), but because, even with the little light and mortification that are mine, I see that such things have been a bad example to my neighbor, and have stood in the way of the greater service of our Lord, and have of themselves given pain and annoyance to you who are my superior, deflecting your government from the direction your better vision had given it to one that was less expedient, and so forth, while I am obliged more particularly because of my office not to deflect it, but rather to keep it turned in the same direction as he who guides the whole ship, and so forth.

As to choosing the penance, Father, seeing that it is within a few days of being almost twenty years since I began to serve our Lord in the evangelical counsels, and considering the great help I have had and the little fruit I have gathered and the nearness of the end of this short life, I have had a special desire of dying to myself and all I have, to live only to our Lord, with the wish to fulfill His holy will and please Him alone. I have imagined to myself that, if I had been treated according to my deserts, as refuse and mere sweepings, it would help me to live more within my own soul and with my God, as I could devote all my reverence and affection to His praise as though dead to the world and the world to me.

When therefore your letter arrived commending me to God, I chose with many tears (which is unusual with me), and I now choose with tears, in reparation for those faults and for the root of them all, that you—and with this I unburden my conscience with peace and repose in what you have commanded me—that for the love of our Lord you relieve me of the care of others, take away my preaching and my study, leaving me only my Breviary, and bid me come to Rome, begging my way, and there put me to work in the kitchen, or serving table, or in the garden, or at anything else. And when I am no longer good for any of this, put me in the lowest class of grammar and that until death, without any more care for me (in external things), as I have said, than you have for an old broom. This penance is my first choice.

For the second, I choose the same, but with a time limit, say, for one, two, or three years, or more, if you so order.

For the third, I choose to abstain from the evening repast during Advent, and every Friday to take a discipline in my room; to be removed from office, and that from now on I write to you, commending myself first to God and thinking of what I am going to write, and having written it, read it with care, to avoid mistakes or anything that could in any way give pain to you instead of relief and comfort. I recognize my great obligation, if for no other reason, at least because you act thus toward me, and still I recognize infinitely more reasons. I will observe this same care of avoiding any word or act that could offend you, whether absent or present. I have the same mind of not offending you even in my heart, although here, thanks to our Lord, I have had little trouble all my life, except for those temptations I had in Rome and of which I have already told you. And because others, as you say, may have been disedified by me, I think that they might be shown this letter in which I admit in all truth that I have been at fault, and declare my sorrow and my resolve to amend, for which I ask them for the love of our Lord to forgive me and help me with their prayers.

One of these three in the order given is the penance I ask and desire. But that one will finally please me most which your reverence shall deign to impose upon me, whether it be one of these or another; because, as I have said, I do not wish to do my will, but God's, and in His place yours. I earnestly beseech you before God not to cast me out of your heart or spew forth my soul in disgust, but rather take me in your arms and help me as you have begun and continue doing these many years now. I do not mind if in outward things you take no account of me; only make me walk straight and carry our Lord's cross in all lowliness and simplicity, desiring only our Lord's glory. May He protect and increase in you His gifts and mercies, as we all desire and need.[1]

¶ TO JOAN OF ARAGON
IV, 506-11, Letter 3014

Polanco tells us (Chronicon, II, 427-28) that Ignatius went to Alvito in the kingdom of Naples on November 2 in an effort to reconcile Joan of Aragon with her husband, Asconius Colonna, duke of Pallianio and Tagliacozzo, from whom she had been estranged. In the two and a half days he remained there he almost accomplished the purpose of his visit. But when the duchess later came to Rome and others undertook to meddle on other grounds than those chosen by Ignatius, they brought to naught what he had all but succeeded in accomplishing. His letter was evidently written to the duchess after her arrival in Rome, some ten or eleven days after his own return.

Late in November, 1552

JESUS

My Lady in our Lord.

Although I have already discussed with your excellency the means of reconciliation with Señor Asconius, which I think in our Lord will be most conformable with His holy will and which will be most becoming for your excellency, the affection which His infinite goodness has given me for the service and spiritual perfection of your excellency impels me to put into writing (against my custom) the reasons which move me, so that, reflecting on them and weighing them from time to time together with the good and holy purpose which God our Lord has given you, and especially with the help of His grace, you might be able to change the view and purpose which your excellency now holds. I say then, dear Lady, that the best step I can think of, all things considered, is that your excellency resolve with greatness of mind and trust in our Lord to go to the home of Señor Asconius and place yourself completely under his

---

[1] St. Ignatius was satisfied—how could he help it?—with the heroic submission of Lainez and did not accept any of his proposals. He kept him in office as though nothing had happened and showed him the same affection and confidence as ever.

care, without asking for guarantees or agreements, but freely, just as a wife is wont to be, and ought to be, under the authority of her husband. My reasons are as follows:

1. If the reconciliation is to be perfect and complete, there is no other way of winning the wholehearted affection of Señor Asconius. This will be done, not by means of agreements and guarantees, as though you were enemies, but by a manifestation of love, humility, and confidence in him as your husband. This can be done as I have indicated.

2. This way more than any other will show a more perfect humility in your excellency. In fact, if one of the parties does not yield humbly, no agreement can be reached as long as hearts remain embittered. Therefore, if one of you must humbly yield, how much more reasonable is it for the wife than the husband to signalize herself in this virtue, and how many fewer excuses will she have before God and men if, because of her unwillingness to be humbled, the proper union between her and her husband comes to naught.

3. Moreover, this would be an act of courage and greatheartedness which becomes the race and noble soul of your excellency, since by it you will show that you have no fear, not even of the danger of death, which some would fear. It is in this that great hearts are recognized, while, on the contrary, reserves and guarantees are not resorted to by noble souls.

4. The more difficult this way is, the more heroic it will be in your excellency to conquer self and subdue whatever anger you may have had or now have toward Señor Asconius. You will consequently acquire much greater merit before God our Lord if you do it for love of Him. And so you should prefer this way as more perfect, even if something easier should occur to you.

5. It would be a work of greater perfection, and consequently more pleasing to Christ our Lord and more in keeping with His counsels, for He is so great a lover of peace between all, even strangers, that He wishes us to defer our offerings and sacrifices until we are reconciled. How much more will He look for this peace between those whom He has united in matrimony? It is of this union He speaks in the Gospel, "What therefore God hath joined together, let no man put asunder," for they shall be two in one flesh, and one to live with the other must leave father and mother, and so forth.[1]

6. It will be more in keeping with the laws on which His Divine Majesty founded holy matrimony, as the Scriptures declare for us in many

---

[1] Matthew 19:5-6.

passages when they affirm that the husband is the head of the wife, that wives must be subject to their husbands, and hold up Sarah, who called her husband lord, as an example.[2]

7. Because this would be an act of greater confidence in our Lord, who is pleased by the confidence we place in His providence over us. It would not be to tempt His Divine Majesty, since it is the opinion of prudent and learned men that this confidence is very praiseworthy, and in other respects accompanied by little or no danger.

8. That it would be all the more pleasing to God, as it deprives the devil of many weapons to offend His Divine Majesty, not only as regards your excellency but others also, as you are now situated, which, would to God, were not so plainly recognized.

9. It would be an act of charity toward Señor Asconius, as it is your intention to win him in this way (as I am sure in our Lord you will) and bring him to a condition that will insure his salvation, where he can live more in God's grace and service. By this act of virtue you lay upon him the obligation of trying in turn to signalize himself in all the Christian virtues.

10. It would be a great act of charity toward him, not only by relieving him of domestic worries, as your excellency would by assuming direction of his household, as he wants you to, but you would also contribute to his peace and contentment of soul and a good old age, from which, being now past sixty, he is not far distant. He could thus end his life in a loving union with wife and children.

11. Again, this manner of reconciliation will contribute more quickly and effectively to better the situation of your daughters, when they come to win the heart of Señor Asconius.

12. Even Señor Mark Anthony will be more completely reconciled with Señor Asconius, since his adherence to his father is dependent on that of your excellency, and thus an end will come to some of his present trials.[3]

13. Your excellency will free your own servants and those of Señor Asconius from many passions and sins and annoyances, to say nothing of the friends and following of each side, and give them a good opportunity of being comforted in our Lord.

14. All women will be given an example of humble submission and charity which they should have with regard to their husbands.

---

[2] Ephesians 5:22-23; 1 Peter 3:6.
[3] Mark Anthony Colonna took sides with his mother in this estrangement

15. By such an act of virtue and nobility of soul your excellency will give all the world, both great and small, for whom this quarrel has been such an occasion for talk and gossip, great edification and provide them with reasons for praising God our Lord.

16. If account must be taken of the honor and reputation of your excellency, as is no more than right, I am certain that this way will lead to something very outstanding. For honor is, properly speaking, a reward due to virtue. Consequently, the more generous and perfect the act by which this reconciliation is effected, the greater the honor that will be attached to it by all the good. And the more public and widely known the incident becomes, the wider will extend the fame of your excellency's magnanimity, with all the greater glory to you both in heaven and on earth.

17. The good and noble heart of your excellency should be touched by the fact that the honor of Señor Asconius will be repaired and advanced, which you and your children should look upon as your own.

18. Therefore, if your excellency takes account of your temporal advantage, be assured that this is the way you should follow, for thus Señor Asconius becomes your captive and remains your slave. It follows that, besides providing a dowry for your daughters, he will pay all debts and enable your excellency to meet future expenses, as you will be mistress of all he possesses with authority to rule all, as I understand from Señor Asconius himself. I am sure that this will be a great relief to your excellency, as it will free you from the necessity of being a burden to your friends.

19. Your excellency would also be relieved of certain expenses, since a part of the household which you have to maintain could be dismissed.

20. This is also the best way of all to maintain your own personal security, as far as I can make out, for in this way a sovereign remedy is applied to the wound in the heart, you win the good will of Señor Asconius, and you are rid of the occasion of being offended with him and consequently of all fear, since no one fears where he loves, and he cannot fail to love, seeing that your excellency trusts and honors him in such a way. Thus all his efforts will be directed toward the defense of your excellency rather than otherwise.

21. Even though he should retain some ill will (which, however, I consider impossible in the event of your excellency's taking this step), it is not at all likely that he would be personally offensive. If he did not fear God, he would the pope, the emperor, his son, and the whole Spanish nation. He would see that such conduct would ruin his reputation, his station in life, everything. And then how much less likely is he to ven-

ture on such a course when he sees you humbling yourself, as I suggest, and obeying him in all that is proper.

22. If you consider the satisfaction or relief to your excellency, the way to obtain it is to set aside your fear and distrust, your suspicion and dread, which will be inevitable if you have to be on your guard against your husband because you do not make a complete surrender of yourself into his hands.

23. Another means of attaining quiet and peace of mind is to get rid of the many occasions of uneasiness you now have. You will thus live in spiritual and temporal comfort in your own home.

24. Moreover, if you consider the ease with which this reconciliation can be brought about, it is certain that the way I proposed is easier than any other, for it avoids their exceedingly troublesome roundabout methods.

25. If you are looking for a speedy settlement, the matter can be arranged even today, or whenever your excellency wishes to do so, in the way I propose. If you take any other way, I have no idea when it could be concluded.

26. Finally, let your excellency reflect that this is the opinion of those who are most devoted to your service in Christ our Lord, and that in one's own cause it is quite safe to trust others even more than oneself.

¶ TO FATHER JAMES MIRON
IV, 558-59, Letter 3104

The provincial or the general should not busy himself with particular details or interfere too much in the management of affairs. It is much better for him to act through immediate helpers. Ignatius explains his own method in these matters.

Rome, December 17, 1552

It is not the duty of the provincial, nor of the general, to take into account the minute details of affairs. Even if he had the greatest possible ability to do so, it would be better to entrust such details to others, who can later report to the provincial on what they have done, and he will determine, after hearing what they have to say, whatever it is his business to determine. If it is something the handling and decision of which he can leave to others, it would be better for him to do so, especially in temporal matters and even in many that are spiritual. This is my own practice, and I find, not only help and relief but even greater peace and quiet of soul. Thus as your office demands be actuated by love, and give your thought to the general good of your province. In giving an order, give ear in various instances to those who in your judgment are in close touch with the matter you are dealing with.

Do not let yourself be involved in the carrying out of orders, and avoid personal embarrassment. But, like the universal mover, operate and set into motion subordinate movers, and you will get more done and get it better done, and more in conformity with your office than you would have achieved otherwise. Should they fail in any point, it will be less embarrassing than if you failed, and you will be in a better position to rectify the mistakes of your subordinates than they are themselves. And they will not have to correct the mistakes you make, which would happen if you meddled more than was right.

May Jesus Christ our Lord give us always the grace to know His most holy will and perfectly to fulfill it.

¶ TO FATHER JAMES MIRON
IV, 559-63, Letter 3105

Ignatius bids him dismiss from the Society those who are unwilling to obey their superiors, or to send them to Rome if there is any reason to hope for their amendment.

Rome, December 17, 1552

IHS

May the sovereign grace and everlasting love of Christ our Lord be ever our protection and support.

According to information coming to us from Dr. Torres,[1] whom I sent to the Province of Portugal as my representative and visitor in the Lord, I understand that there is a notable failing among not a few of Ours in that virtue which is more necessary and essential in the Society than anywhere else, and in which the vicar of Christ, in the bulls of our Institute, most carefully recommends that we distinguish ourselves. I mean the respect, reverence, and perfect obedience to our superiors who hold the place of Christ our Lord, even of His Divine Majesty, in their regard. You can realize from what you have heard of how I should and do desire

---

[1] Father Michael de Torres. Polanco gives an account of his activities (*Chronicon*, II, 694 ff.).

this virtue in my brothers, what satisfaction must be mine to hear that there is among you one who says to his superior without any respect, "You should not bid me do this," or "It is not well that I do this," who is unwilling to do what he is told, or who by act or gesture shows so little interior reverence and submission, so I hear, to the one whom he ought to reverence as the representative of Christ our Lord, and as such, humble himself in all things before His Divine Majesty. This matter seems to have gone so far because of the fault of one whose duty it was to correct it, but who failed to do so. May God our Lord forgive him! How much better it would have been to remove from the Society a diseased member and protect the healthy, than to allow it to remain and infect with so serious a disease many others by example and association. On another occasion I have written how gratified I was that Master Leonard[2] in Cologne had dismissed nine or ten together who had gone wrong. Later he did the same again, which I approved, although, if measures had been taken at the start of the trouble, it might possibly have been enough to dismiss one or two. Now, although late, the remedy is being applied in Portugal. Better late than never. I command you in virtue of holy obedience to take the following step with regard to the safeguarding of that virtue. If there is anyone who is unwilling to obey you—and I say this, not to you alone but to any of the superiors or local rectors in Portugal—do one of two things: either dismiss him from the Society, or send him here to Rome if you think that a particular individual can be helped by such a change to become a true servant of Christ our Lord. If necessary, keep their highnesses informed, who I doubt not will make no objections, in keeping with the spirit and holy good will which God our Lord has bestowed upon them. To keep with you one who is not a true son of obedience does no good for the kingdom. Nor is there any reason for thinking that such a person, his own soul being so destitute, can help other souls or that God our Lord would wish to accept him as an instrument for His service and glory. We see from experience that, not only with average talents but even less than average, men can often be the instruments of very notable supernatural fruit because they are completely obedient and through this virtue allow themselves to be moved and possessed by the mighty hand of the author of all good. On the other hand, great talent may be seen to perform greater labor with less than ordinary fruit because being themselves—that is, their own self-love—the source of their movement, or at least not allowing themselves to be moved by God

---

[2] Father Leonard Kessel. See *Chronicon*, II, 584.

our Lord through obedience to their superiors, they do not produce results proportionate to the almighty hand of God our Lord, who does not accept them as His instruments. They achieve results proportioned to their own weak and feeble hands. Their highnesses understand this, and I am sure that they will make no difficulty. And while we have enough to do here without burdening ourselves with this additional task from Portugal, we will not decline the added burden because of the special charity which God our Lord causes us to feel toward Portugal.

This is all for the present, except to beg the divine and supreme Goodness to give us all His abundant grace to know His most holy will and perfectly to fulfill it.

The precept of obedience which I am sending you requiring you to dismiss those who are disobedient, or send them here to Rome, is to be published in all the colleges and houses throughout the province. And see that the king is informed of it, so that those who are sent beyond the limits of the kingdom because they have need of help may not seem to be withdrawn from Portugal because we are here looking for workers who would be useful within the territory of his highness. Rather, let it appear that they are being sent elsewhere to prepare them to be such, when they return, as his highness desires, as are all the others in the service of God and of souls in his kingdom.

¶ TO MEMBERS OF THE SOCIETY IN EUROPE

IV, 564-65, Letter 3107

Ignatius exhorts the members of the Society scattered throughout Europe to a ready and cheerful practice of poverty.

Rome, December 24, 1552

The peace of Christ.

From various letters we learn that God our Lord is visiting your reverences with the effects of holy poverty; that is, the annoyances that come from the privation of certain temporal conveniences which are necessary for health and the well-being of the body. It is no slight grace that the Divine Goodness deigns to bestow on us in allowing us actually to taste that which we should always desire if we are to walk in the footsteps of our guide Jesus Christ, conformably to the vow taken according to the Institute of our holy order. In truth, I do not know that there is any place in the Society where they do not have a share in this grace, although one place might feel it more than another. Suppose we compare ourselves with our brothers in India, who in such corporal and spiritual toil are so ill provided with food, in some places not even having bread, to say nothing of wine for their drink. They must get along with a bit of rice and water, or something as little nourishing. They are ill clothed and have a minimum of bodily comfort. If we compare ourselves with them, I cannot think that our suffering is excessively hard. We can also imagine that we are having our own India, which is to be found everywhere. In fine, if he who ordinarily should provide for our necessities fails, we can have recourse to a holy mendicancy, by means of which our needs may be supplied. If in spite of all, God our Lord should wish us to have something to suffer, see that nothing is lacking the sick; those in better health will have a chance to exercise patience. May He give it to us all who has made it so lovable by His teaching and example and grant us His love and a relish for His service in preference to everything else.

¶ TO FATHER JAMES MIRON
IV, 625-28, Letter 3220

King John III of Portugal was an outstanding benefactor of the Society of Jesus, as the fifteenth letter of this collection would give us to understand. When, therefore, Simon Rodrigues laid down the government of the Province of Portugal and left the kingdom, the king urged Father James Miron and afterwards Father Louis Gonzales de la Camara to undertake the office of confessor to the king and to his son and heir, Prince John. Both fathers were firm in declining the honor, alleging all the reasons which their humility must have suggested. Ignatius praised this spirit, but convinced them by very weighty reasons, given in the following letter, that they were not doing well in refusing the office. He bids them, therefore, to obey the king in this matter and to acquaint him with the decisive order they have just received.

Rome, February 1, 1553

The grace and love of Christ our Lord be ever our help and favor.

From various letters which we received from Portugal we learn that his highness[1] has asked with pressing devotion that you and Father Louis

---

[1] John III of Portugal.

Gonzales act as his confessors, but that you have both excused yourselves, not on the grounds of conscience or because of scruples in directing his highness, whom you consider a saint, as you say, but because you think that this is an honor which should be refused no less than a bishopric or a royal chaplaincy. For the same reason Father Louis Gonzales has resigned his post with the prince,[2] I understand. I can see, of course, your reasons, based on humility and the security which is more easily found in lowly than in prominent occupations, and I cannot but approve and be edified by your motives. But, all things considered, I am convinced that you are ill advised in this determination, if you consider the greater service and glory of God our Lord. In the first place, it is your vocation and in keeping with your Institute to administer the sacraments of confession and Communion to men of all conditions and ages. And the same duty of giving consolation and spiritual help to your neighbor obliges you to the care of those in high position as well as those in low. Secondly, the whole Society from its very beginning is under special obligation to their highnesses, more indeed than to any other Christian princes, whether we consider their good works or the special love and charity which more than anything else ought to win over your hearts. I cannot think of any excuse that would justify our failure to serve their highnesses in a matter that is so much in keeping with our vocation, and in which they show that they will receive consolation and satisfaction of soul.

Now, if we consider the universal good and God's greater service, even greater good will follow from this, as far as I can see in the Lord, because all the members of the body share in the good of the head and all his subjects in the good of their sovereign, so that the spiritual good which is done to the sovereign should be more highly esteemed than if it were done to others. Since you can judge of one instance by another, consider whether there could have been a more important reminder by a confessor than to bring to a conclusion the appointment of the patriarch of Ethiopia,[3] which involves the salvation, not of many souls but of many cities

---

[2] Don John.
[3] This same year, 1553, negotiations were opened regarding the patriarchate of Ethiopia. The king of Portugal charged St. Ignatius with the appointing of a competent candidate among the fathers of the Society of Jesus. The saint organized a mission band of twelve Jesuits, at the head of whom were the patriarch and two auxiliary bishops who, armed with a precious letter from Ignatius addressed to the king of Abyssinia on the primacy of Rome, began their journey on March 30, 1556. They were doomed to early disappointment. The king had no intention of renouncing the schism of his ancestors. The sequel proved that God in this instance had not given Ignatius any prophetic vision. But it also proves the greatness of heart and the ardent spirit of faith which made him ever ready to promote the kingdom of God wherever a determined effort had any hope of success.

and provinces. Whichever of you acts as confessor to his highness, be sure that you do not fail to come to some understanding on this appointment, and every time you write to Rome be sure to mention this matter and let me know what you have done.

To return to the reasons why you should not refuse this task, I do not think your security of soul is relevant, because if all we looked for in our vocation was to walk safely, and if to get away from danger we had to sacrifice the good of souls, we should not be living and associating with our neighbor. But according to our vocation, we associate with all; rather, as St. Paul says of himself, we should make ourselves all things to all men to gain all to Christ;[4] and if we advance with a pure and upright intention, seeking not our own interests but those of Jesus Christ, He Himself in His infinite goodness will be our protection. If our vocation did not take hold of His powerful hand, it would not be enough merely to withdraw from such perils to keep from falling into others perhaps greater.

Whatever people may say about your seeking honor and position will fall to the ground of itself under the weight of the truth and the evidence of the work when they see that you preserve the lowliness that you have chosen for Christ our Lord. And so, for whatever the crowd might think or say, you should not neglect anything that can be turned to the service of God or of their highnesses and the common good.

Finally, to satisfy my conscience once for all in this matter, I command you in virtue of holy obedience, you and Father Louis Gonzales, to do what their highnesses bid you in this matter; that is, one or other of you, unless some one else in the Society appears better qualified to you and at the same time is acceptable to his highness. And have confidence in the Divine Goodness that all will be for the best, whatever is done this way through obedience. You must make this command known to his highness, and show him this letter should he wish to see it or at least give him a summary of it.

As Master Polanco is going to write at length on other matters, I will say no more here except to commend myself to your prayers and sacrifices. I beg God our Lord to give us all His bountiful grace always to know His most holy will and entirely to fulfill it. Yours in our Lord . . .

---

[4] 1 Corinthians 9:22.

PART V

1553-1556

¶ TO THE MEMBERS OF THE SOCIETY IN PORTUGAL

IV, 669-81, Letter 3304

"This letter," says Father de la Torres in the Madrid edition of the letters (III, 186), "is the most celebrated, the best known, and most widely read of all the letters of St. Ignatius. The letter was occasioned by those members of the Province of Portugal who were very attached to Father Simon Rodrigues, excessively so, with an affection that was too natural and unspiritual. Rodrigues' method of government had erred on the side of mildness and softness, with the result that, when he was removed, these subjects refused obedience to any other superior than himself or one appointed by him. In this letter all that there is to say on the virtue of obedience is explained clearly, eloquently, and persuasively. There is scarcely a writer on asceticism who does not refer to this letter as the most finished treatise on the subject."

Printed copies of the Letter on Obedience soon began to appear, and became part of the prescribed reading of all members of the Society. The original of the letter, one of the most precious of relics, came into the possession of the Province of Toledo on the death of Father Ribadeneira. It had a varied history, due to the changes caused by the persecutions of the eighteenth century, but was returned to the Province of Toledo and was preserved in the professed house of Madrid until the tragedy of May 11, 1931, when a communist mob set fire to both the professed house and the church of the Jesuits in that city. The conflagration that ensued consumed not only the Letter on Obedience but many other precious relics, principal among which was the body of St. Francis Borgia.

Rome, March 26, 1553

JHUS

May the perfect grace and everlasting love of Christ our Lord greet and visit you with His most holy gifts and spiritual graces.

It gives me great consolation, my dear brothers in our Lord Jesus Christ, when I learn of the lively and earnest desires for perfection in His divine service and glory which He gives you, who by His mercy has called you to this Society and preserves you in it and directs you to the blessed end at which His chosen ones arrive.

And although I wish you all perfection in every virtue and spiritual gift, it is true (as you have heard from me on other occasions), that it is in obedience more than in any other virtue that God our Lord gives me the desire to see you signalize yourselves. And that, not only because of the singular good there is in it, so much emphasized by word and example in Holy Scripture in both Old and New Testaments, but because, as St. Gregory says,[1] obedience is the only virtue which plants all the other virtues in the mind, and preserves them once they are planted. And insofar as this virtue flourishes, all the other virtues will flourish and bring forth the fruit which I desire in your souls, and which He claims who by His obedience redeemed the world after it had been destroyed by the lack of it, becoming obedient unto death, even to the death of the cross.[2]

We may allow ourselves to be surpassed by other religious orders in fasts, watchings, and other austerities, which each one following its institute holily observes. But in the purity and perfection of obedience together with the true resignation of our wills and the abnegation of our judgment, I am very desirous, my dear brothers, that they who serve God in this Society should be conspicuous, so that by this virtue its true sons may be recognized as men who regard not the person whom they obey, but in him Christ our Lord, for whose sake they obey. For the superior is to be obeyed not because he is prudent, or good, or qualified by any other gift of God, but because he holds the place and the authority of God, as Eternal Truth has said: "He that heareth you, heareth me; and he that despiseth you, despiseth me."[3] Nor on the contrary, should he lack prudence, is he to be the less obeyed in that in which he is superior, since he represents Him who is infallible wisdom, and who will supply what is wanting in His minister; nor, should he lack goodness or other desirable qualities, since Christ our Lord, having said, "The scribes and the Pharisees have sitten on the chair of Moses," adds, "All things, therefore, whatsoever they shall say to you, observe and do; but according to their works do ye not."[4]

Therefore I should wish that all of you would train yourselves to recognize Christ our Lord in any superior, and with all devotion reverence and obey His Divine Majesty in him. This will appear less strange to you if you keep in mind that St. Paul, writing to the Ephesians, bids us obey even temporal and pagan superiors as Christ, from whom all well-ordered authority descends: "Servants, be obedient to them that are your lords according to the flesh, with fear and trembling, in the simplicity of your heart, as to Christ, not serving to the eye, as it were pleasing men, but as the servants of Christ doing the will of God from the heart, with a

---

[1] *Moralium*, lib. XXXV, c. 10 (PL 76, col. 765).
[2] Philippians 2:8.   [3] Luke 10:16.   [4] Matthew 23:2-3.

good will serving, as to the Lord and not to men."⁵ From this you can judge, when a religious is taken not only as superior, but expressly in the place of Christ our Lord, to serve as director and guide in the divine service, what rank he ought to hold in the mind of the inferior, and whether he ought to be looked upon as man or rather as the vicar of Christ our Lord.

I also desire that this be firmly fixed in your minds, that the first degree of obedience is very low, which consists in the execution of what is commanded, and that it does not deserve the name of obedience, since it does not attain to the worth of this virtue unless it rises to the second degree, which is to make the superior's will one's own in such a way that there is not merely the effectual execution of the command, but an interior conformity, whether to wish or not wish a thing done. Hence it is said in Scripture, "Obedience is better than sacrifices,"⁶ for, according to St. Gregory, "In victims the flesh of another is slain, but in obedience our own will is sacrificed."⁷

Now, because this disposition of will in man is of so great worth, so also is the offering of it, when by obedience it is offered to his Creator and Lord. How great a deception it is, and how dangerous for those who think it lawful to withdraw from the will of their superior, I do not say only in those things pertaining to flesh and blood, but even in those which of their nature are spiritual and holy, such as fasts, prayers, and other pious works! Let them hear Cassian's comment in the Conference of Daniel the Abbot: "It is one and the selfsame kind of disobedience, whether in earnestness of labor or the desire of ease one breaks the command of the Superior, and as mischievous to go against the statutes of the monastery out of sloth as out of watchfulness; and finally, it is as bad to neglect the command of your abbot and spend the time reading as it would be to sleep."⁸ The activity of Martha was holy, and holy the contemplation of Magdalene, and holy the penitence and tears with which she bathed the feet of Christ our Lord. But all this was to be done in Bethania, which is interpreted to mean, the house of obedience. It would seem, therefore, that Christ our Lord would give us to understand, as St. Bernard remarks, "that neither the activity of good works, nor the leisure of contemplation, nor the tears of the penitent would have pleased Him out of Bethania."⁹

---

⁵ Ephesians 6:5-7. ⁶ 1 Kings 15:22.
⁷ *Moralium*, lib. XXXV, c. 14, n. 28 (PL 76, col. 765).
⁸ *Collationes*, lib. IV, c. 20 (PL 49, col. 608-09).
⁹ *Sermo ad milites templi*, c. 13 (PL 182, col. 939).

Therefore, my dear brothers, try to make the surrender of your wills entire. Offer freely[10] to God through His ministers the liberty He has bestowed on you. Do not think it a slight advantage of your free will the ability of restoring it wholly in obedience to Him who gave it to you. In this you do not lose it, but rather perfect it in conforming your will wholly with the most certain rule of all rectitude, which is the divine will, the interpreter of which is the superior who governs you in place of God.

For this reason you must never try to draw the will of the superior (which you should consider the will of God) to your own will. This would not be making the divine will the rule of your own, but your own the rule of the divine, and so perverting the order of his wisdom. It is a great delusion in those whose understanding has been darkened by self-love to think that there is any obedience in the subject who tries to draw the superior to what he wishes. Listen to St. Bernard, who had much experience in this matter: "Whoever endeavors either openly or covertly to have his spiritual father enjoin him what he himself desires, deceives himself if he flatters himself as a true follower of obedience. For in that instance he does not obey his superior, but rather the superior obeys him."[11] And so he concludes that he who wishes to rise to the virtue of obedience must rise to this second degree, which, over and above the execution, consists in making the superior's will one's own, or rather putting off his own will to clothe himself with the divine will interpreted by the superior.

But he who aims at making an entire and perfect oblation of himself, in addition to his will, must offer his understanding, which is a further and the highest degree of obedience. He must not only will, but think the same as the superior, submitting his own judgment to the superior, so far as a devout will can bend the understanding. For while this faculty has not the freedom of the will, and naturally gives its assent to what is presented to it as true, there are, however, many instances where the evidence of the known truth is not coercive, and it can with the help of the will favor one side or the other. When this happens every truly obedient man should conform his thought to the thought of the superior.

And this is certain, since obedience is a holocaust in which the whole man without the slightest reserve is offered in the fire of charity to his Creator and Lord through the hands of His ministers. And since it is a complete surrender of himself by which a man dispossesses himself to be possessed and governed by Divine Providence through his superiors, it

---

[10] The copy destroyed in Madrid began here.
[11] *Sermo de tribus ordinibus ecclesiae*, n. 4 (PL 183, col. 636).

cannot be held that obedience consists merely in the execution, by carrying the command into effect, and in the will's acquiescence, but even in the judgment, which must approve the superior's command, insofar, as has been said, as it can with the will's energy bend itself to it.

Would to God that this obedience of the understanding were as much understood and practiced as it is necessary to anyone living in religion and acceptable to God our Lord. I say necessary, for, just as in the celestial bodies, if the lower is to receive movement and influence from the higher it must be subject and subordinate, the one body being ordered and adjusted to the other; so, when one rational creature is moved by another, as takes place in obedience, the one that is moved must be subject and subordinated to the one by whom he is moved, if he is to receive influence and virtue from him. Now, this subjection and subordination cannot be had unless the understanding and the will of the inferior is in conformity with the superior.

Now, if we regard the end of obedience, as our will so our understanding may be mistaken as to what is good for us. And therefore we think it expedient to conform our will with that of the superior to keep it from going astray, so the understanding ought to be conformed with his to keep it from straying likewise. "Lean not upon thy own prudence," says Scripture.[12] Thus, they who are wise judge it to be true prudence not to rely on their own judgment even in other affairs of life, and especially when personal interests are at stake, in which men as a rule, because of their lack of self-control, are not good judges. This being so, we ought to follow the judgment of another (even when he is not our superior) rather than our own in matters concerning ourselves. How much more, then, the judgment of the superior whom we have taken as a guide to stand in the place of God and to interpret the divine will for us? And it is certain that this guidance is all the more necessary in men and matters spiritual, as the danger in the spiritual life is great when one advances rapidly in it without the bridle of discretion. Hence Cassian says in the Conference of the Abbot Moses: "By no other vice does the devil draw a monk headlong and bring him to death sooner than by persuading him to neglect the counsel of the elders and trust to his own judgment and determination."[13]

On the other hand, without this obedience of the judgment it is impossible for the obedience of will and execution to be what they should. For the appetitive powers of the soul naturally follow the apprehensive,

---

[12] Proverbs 3:5. [13] *Collationes*, lib. II, c. 11 (PL 49, col. 541).

and in the long run the will cannot without violence obey against one's judgment. When it does obey for some time, misled by the common apprehension that it must obey when commanded amiss, it cannot do so for any length of time. And so perseverance fails, or at least the perfection of obedience, which consists in obeying with love and cheerfulness. But when one acts in opposition to one's judgment, one cannot obey lovingly and cheerfully as long as such repugnance exists. Promptitude fails, and readiness, which are impossible without agreement of judgment, such as when one doubts whether it is good or not to do what is commanded. That renowned simplicity of blind obedience fails, when we call into question the justice of the command, or even condemn the superior because he bids us do something that is not pleasing. Humility fails, for although on the one hand we submit, on the other we prefer ourselves to the superior. Fortitude in difficult tasks fails, and in a word all the perfections of this virtue.

On the contrary, when one obeys without submitting one's judgment, there arise dissatisfaction, pain, reluctance, slackness, murmurings, excuses, and other imperfections and obstacles of no small moment which strip obedience of its value and merit. Hence St. Bernard, speaking of those who take it ill when commanded to do things that are unpleasant, says with reason: "If you begin to grieve at this, to judge your superior, to murmur in your heart, although outwardly you fulfill what is commanded, this is not the true virtue of patience, but a cloak for your malice."[14]

Indeed, if we look to the peace and quiet of mind of him who obeys, it is certain that he will never find it who has within himself the cause of his disquiet and unrest, that is, a judgment of his own opposed to what obedience lays upon him.

Therefore to maintain that union which is the bond of every society, St. Paul earnestly exhorts all "to think and say the same thing,"[15] because it is by the union of judgment and will that they shall be preserved. Now, if head and members must think the selfsame, it is easy to see whether the head should agree with the members, or the members with the head. Thus, from what has been said, we can see how necessary is obedience of the understanding.

But how perfect it is in itself and how pleasing to God can be seen from the value of this most noble offering which is made of the most worthy part of man, the obedient man in this way becoming a living

---

[14] *Sermo III de circumcisione*, n. 8 (PL 183, col. 140).
[15] Romans 15:5; I Corinthians 1:10; Philippians 2:2.

holocaust most pleasing to His Divine Majesty, keeping nothing whatever to himself; and also because of the difficulty overcome for love of Him in going against the natural inclination which all men have of following their own judgment. It follows that obedience though it is a perfection proper to the will (which it makes ready to fulfill the will of the superior), yet it must also, as has been said, extend to the understanding, inclining it to agree with the thought of the superior, for it is thus that we proceed with the full strength of the soul—of will and understanding—to a prompt and perfect execution.

I seem to hear some of you say, most dear brothers, that you see the importance of this virtue, but that you would like to see how you can attain to its perfection. To this I answer with Pope St. Leo, "Nothing is difficult unto the humble, and nothing hard unto the meek."[16] Be humble and meek, therefore, and God our Lord will bestow His grace which will enable you to maintain sweetly and lovingly the offering that you have made to Him.

In addition to these means, I will place before you three especially which will give you great assistance in attaining this perfection of obedience.

The first is that, as I said at the beginning, you do not behold in the person of your superior a man subject to errors and miseries, but rather Him whom you obey in man, Christ the highest wisdom, immeasurable goodness, and infinite charity, who, you know, cannot be deceived and does not wish to deceive you. And because you are certain that you have set upon your own shoulders this yoke of obedience for the love of God, submitting yourself to the will of the superior in order to be more conformable to the divine will, be assured that His most faithful charity will ever direct you by the means which you yourselves have chosen. Therefore, do not look upon the voice of the superior, as far as he commands you, otherwise than as the voice of Christ, in keeping with St. Paul's advice to the Colossians, where he exhorts subjects to obey their superiors: "Whatsoever you do, do it from the heart, as to the Lord, and not to men, knowing that you shall receive of the Lord the reward of inheritance. Serve ye the Lord Christ."[17] And St. Bernard: "Whether God or man, His substitute, commands anything, we must obey with equal diligence, and perform it with like reverence, when, however, man commands nothing that is contrary to God."[18] Thus, if you do not look upon

---

[16] *Sermo V de epiphaniae*, c. 3 (PL 54, col. 252).
[17] Colossians 3:23-24.
[18] *De praecepto et dispensatione*, c. 9 (PL 182, col. 871).

man with the eyes of the body, but upon God with those of the soul, you will find no difficulty in conforming your will and judgment with the rule of action which you yourselves have chosen.

The second means is that you be quick to look for reasons to defend what the superior commands, or to what he is inclined, rather than to disapprove of it. A help toward this will be to love whatever obedience shall enjoin. From this will come a cheerful obedience without any trouble, for as St. Leo says, "It is not hard to serve when we love that which is commanded."[19]

The third means to subject the understanding which is even easier and surer, and in use among the holy fathers, is to presuppose and believe, very much as we are accustomed to do in matters of faith, that what the superior enjoins is the command of God our Lord and His holy will. Then to proceed blindly, without inquiry of any kind, to the carrying out of the command, with a kind of passion to obey. So we are to think Abraham did when commanded to sacrifice his son Isaac.[20] Likewise in the New Testament, some of those holy fathers to whom Cassian refers, as the Abbot John, who did not question whether what he was commanded was profitable or not, as when with such great labor he watered a dry stick throughout a year.[21] Or whether it was possible or not, when he tried so earnestly at the command of his superior to move a rock which a large number of men would not have been able to move.[22]

We see that God our Lord sometimes confirmed this kind of obedience with miracles, as when Maurus, St. Benedict's disciple, going into a lake at the command of his superior, did not sink.[23] Or in the instance of another, who being told to bring back a lioness, took hold of her and brought her to his superior.[24] And you are acquainted with others. What I mean is that this manner of subjecting one's own judgment, without further inquiry, supposing that the command is holy and in conformity with God's will, is in use among the saints and ought to be imitated by any one who wishes to obey perfectly in all things, where manifestly there appears no sin.

But this does not mean that you should not feel free to propose a difficulty, should something occur to you different from his opinion, provided you pray over it, and it seems to you in God's presence that you

---

[19] *Sermo IV de jejunio septimi mensis* (PL 54, col. 444).
[20] Genesis 22:2, 3.
[21] *De institutis renuntiantium* (alias, coenobiorum), lib. IV, c. 24 (PL 49, col. 183).
[22] Cassianus, *Collationes,* lib. IV, c. 26 (PL 49, col. 185).
[23] S. Gregorius, "Vita Sancti Benedicti" (PL 66, col. 146).
[24] *De vitis patrum,* lib. III, n. 27 (PL 73, col. 756).

ought to make the representation to the superior. If you wish to proceed in this matter without suspicion of attachment to your own judgment, you must maintain indifference both before and after making this representation, not only as to undertaking or relinquishing the matter in question, but you must even go so far as to be better satisfied with, and to consider as better, whatever the superior shall ordain.

Now, what I have said of obedience is not only to be understood of individuals with reference to their immediate superiors, but also of rectors and local superiors with reference to provincials, and of provincials with reference to the general, and of the general toward him whom God our Lord has given as superior, His vicar on earth. For in this way there will be complete subordination, and as a result, union and charity, without which the welfare and government of the Society, or of any other congregation, would be impossible.

It is by this means that Divine Providence gently disposes all things, bringing to their appointed ends the lowest by the middlemost, and the middlemost by the highest. Even in the angels there is the subordination of one hierarchy to another, and in the heavens and all the bodies that are moved, the lowest by the highest, and the highest in their turn, unto the Supreme Mover of all.

We see the same on earth in well-governed states, and in the hierarchy of the Church, the members of which render their obedience to the one universal vicar of Christ our Lord. And the better this subordination is kept, the better the government. But when it is lacking everyone can see what outstanding faults ensue. Therefore in this congregation, in which our Lord has given me some charge, I desire that this virtue be as perfect as if the whole welfare of the Society depended on it.

Not wishing to go beyond the limits I set at the beginning of this letter, I will end by begging you for the love of Christ our Lord, who not only gave us the precept of obedience, but added His example, to make every effort to attain it by a glorious victory over yourselves, vanquishing the loftiest and most difficult part of yourselves, your will and understanding, because in this way the true knowledge and love of God our Lord will possess you wholly and direct your souls throughout the course of this pilgrimage, until at length He leads you and many others through you to the last and most happy end of bliss everlasting.

I commend myself most earnestly to your prayers.[25]

---

[25] A masterful and complete commentary on the *Letter of Obedience* was written by Father Manuel Maria Espinosa Pólit, S.J., an English translation of which was published by the Newman Bookshop in 1947.

¶ TO THOMAS OF VILLANOVA
v, 24-25, Letter 3335

St. Ignatius highly esteemed the archbishop of Valencia. In this letter he praises the archbishop's zeal and promises to send him either Father Domenech or Father Miron.

Rome, April 16, 1553

JHS

My most reverend Lord in our Lord.

May the sovereign grace and everlasting love of Christ our Lord greet and visit your most reverend lordship with His most holy gifts and spiritual graces.

Your lordship's letter of October 9 was very late in arriving at Rome, as was its bearer. From it I understand the great care and vigilance which God our Lord gives to your most reverend lordship in seeking every spiritual assistance for the flock which His Divine Wisdom has entrusted to you, showing, as you do, such special interest in the little members of that flock in our college. I am aware of the great obligation which not only this college, helped and supported as it is, but even the whole of our least Society, on which your favor overflows, is under to serve your most reverend lordship in our Lord. I have indeed a great desire not to fail in this obligation, as far as in me lies. At the first opportunity, therefore, which God our Lord gives us, I will try (if Master Jerome Domenech cannot go), to send you Father Master Miron if I can withdraw him from Portugal, or someone else. I will make this recommendation to Father Araoz, provincial of our Society in those kingdoms.

I humbly commend myself and all our Society to the holy prayers of your most reverend lordship, and in keeping with our lowly profession offer myself to the service of your lordship in our Lord, only asking His divine and sovereign goodness to give us all abundant grace always to know His most holy will and perfectly to fulfill it. Your most reverend lordship's most humble servant in our Lord . . .

¶ TO SIMON RODRIGUES
v, 73-74, Letter 3417

At this time Simon Rodrigues occupied a unique position at the court of Lisbon. Although the religious of his province considered him fully faithful to his appointment, reports received in Rome said that he could not be retained in office without detriment to the religious life both of himself and of those around him. After preliminary steps to which Simon responded with ill grace, St. Ignatius summoned him to Rome. There are two letters on this matter, the first from the superior who commands, and the second from the father who pleads. In this letter, the second, Ignatius pleads with Rodrigues to come to Rome. He says God will help him to bear the weariness of the journey and that they should meet once again here below. He tells Rodrigues that Gonzales is coming, and he should come also. The whole episode is treated at greater length by Dudon, Loyola, *page 343 and following pages.*

Rome, May 20, 1553

I received your letters of March 23 and 26 and April 12. Considering what you there write, and many other matters which concern you, I do not see, my dear brother, any other way out of the difficulty than to have you come here to Rome. Once you are here, I have every hope in Christ our Lord that He will permit us to come upon some way of giving you consolation, to God's glory.

As to your reputation, I will only say that I shall have as much care for it as you yourself could have. I see very clearly why it should be so. And I have means, which you yourself could never think of, for giving you complete satisfaction of mind. Trust me in this, for the love of Christ our Lord, and come to Rome.

Indeed, if it please His Divine Majesty, it will be a great consolation to me to be able to see you and leave your affairs in better condition before I depart from this world. If I should feel a desire like this toward all my brethren, how much more so toward the first companions whom God was good enough to associate with me in this Society, and toward you especially. You know that I have always had a very special affection for you in our Lord. Don't be afraid of your health. He who is eternal health will, because of the virtue of obedience, give you all the health you need. Once before you made this journey, with less obligation than now, suffering from a quartan fever, and God, who is the author of health, gave you what you needed. You have a good pretext for wishing to come in Louis Gonzales, who is coming, and has not yet arrived.

Again I say, trust me. No matter what may be said, I will have a care, as is only right, for your consolation and reputation, for God's glory.

May His divine and supreme Goodness be pleased to give us all His grace always to know and perfectly to fulfill His most holy will.

¶ TO FATHER FRANCIS XAVIER
v, 148-51, Letter 3505

Ignatius recalls Xavier to Europe, and gives his reasons. The informed reader may be excused for seeing here a play of divine irony, as Francis had been dead many months by the time Ignatius' letter reached its destination. He passed to heaven December 2, 1552.

Rome, June 28, 1553

IHS

My dear Brother in our Lord.

The grace and love of Christ our Lord be ever our help and support.

We received your letters of January 28, 1552 later than we should have, because of the difficulty of getting them from Portugal to Rome, and for this reason you will not have an answer as early as I could have wished. We have heard of the door which our Lord has opened to the preaching of the gospel and the conversion of the people of Japan and China by means of your ministry, and we are greatly consoled in His Divine Majesty with the hope that His glory and the knowledge of Him will spread daily among those nations, and that with God's favor they will be able to preserve and develop what they have already got.

It also seems quite proper for you to have sent Master Gaspar[1] and others to Japan and China. And even if you yourself had gone to China, as you said you intended to go if not held back by business in India, I quite approve, as I am satisfied that you are acting under the guidance of Divine Wisdom. And yet, as far as I can understand the situation at this distance, I believe that God our Lord would be better served by you had you remained in India, and sent others under your directions to do whatever you had planned on doing. In this way you can accomplish in many places what you accomplish by your actual presence in only one. I will go even further and say, considering God's greater service and the help of souls in those countries which are dependent on Portugal for help, that I have made up my mind to give you a command in virtue of holy obedience to choose among all those highways the one that leads to Portugal and take passage at the first favorable opportunity. I command you in the name of Christ our Lord, even though you return at once to India. In order that you may inform those who might wish to detain you for the good of India, I will give you my reasons for recalling you, among which you will see is the good of India itself.

---

[1] Gaspar Berse.

First, you know how important for the preservation and increase of the faith in those lands, and in Guinea and Brazil, are the rules and regulations which the king of Portugal can give from Portugal. Now, if a king of such Christian desires and holy purposes as the present king is informed of conditions by one who knows them as well as you do from personal contact, you can see that he would be moved to do many things for the service of God and the good of those lands from the suggestions you could make.

Besides, it is very important for the Apostolic See to have certain and complete information about India from someone who is trustworthy. This will help it in making necessary or important provision in spiritual matters for the good of recent converts and of the old Christians who are living there. You would be much more acceptable for this service than any other because of the knowledge you have and because you are better known.[2]

You also know that much depends for the good of India on the kind of men that are sent there. They should be fitted for the work. Your coming to Portugal and to Rome will have a good effect in this respect. For not only will many be encouraged to go to the Indies, but of those who so wish, you could see who are suitable and who are not, who for one place and who for another. You yourself know how important is the right choice in such matters. All that you write of India is not enough to give us a proper understanding. You, or one who has your knowledge, must meet and make the acquaintance of those who are to be sent.

Over and above these reasons, all of which look to the good of India, I feel that you would stir the king's interest in Ethiopia. For so many years now he has been on the point of doing something, but nothing is ever done. From Portugal you would also be of no little help in the affairs of the Congo and of Brazil, something you cannot do from India, as you have no connections there with them. If you think that your presence in India is important in the interests of good government, you can govern no less well from Portugal than you can from Japan or China—in fact, even better. Consequently, as your former absences have been longer, absent yourself for this time, and leave in your place whatever rectors you wish, with one who will have over-all responsibility, together with those consultors you may judge to be suitable, and God our Lord will be with them.

---

[2] One thinks of what might have happened to the Chinese and Malabar rites disputes, which arose later, if Xavier's information had been such as to forestall the debates.

For other news I refer you to Master Polanco. I recommend myself very earnestly to your prayers, and ask the divine and sovereign Goodness to give us all His perfect grace always to know His most holy will and perfectly to fulfill it.

On your arrival in Portugal you shall be under obedience to the king. Place yourself entirely at his disposal. Entirely yours in our Lord . . .

¶ TO FATHER SIMON RODRIGUES
v, 189, Letter 3547

With signs of great affection and good will Ignatius asks Rodrigues to come to Rome, and commands him in virtue of holy obedience to do so.

Rome, July 12, 1553

Master Simon Rodrigues, beloved Son in our Lord.

After reading and reflecting on your letters of February 10, March 23 and 26, and April 12, and many others which we have received, I have judged it best in our Lord to put you to a little inconvenience by having you come to Rome. I am sure in our Lord that this will contribute to the greater peace and consolation of those who are still persevering in our Society in the kingdom of Portugal. I wish also to confer with you on other matters of universal import which concern the whole Society, and which cannot be satisfactorily dealt with unless you are actually present. As it is a matter therefore of great importance, I bid you in virtue of holy obedience and in the name of Christ our Lord to come, taking a land or sea route as you shall judge best. And this must be with the least possible delay. You must begin your journey, which is not to be interrupted, not later than eight days after you have received this letter.

I beg God our Lord to be your guide and companion, and that He will give us all the grace ever to know and fulfill His most holy will.

¶ TO THE WHOLE SOCIETY
v, 220-22, Letter 3578

It was St. Peter Canisius who obtained the circular letter given below. Of all the Jesuits sent to Germany he was the greatest, the most active, and the most persevering in labor. For him, as for St. Paul, the work done was nothing in comparison with what remained to be done. As a support for his zealous efforts, he asked Ignatius to order prayers throughout the Society. Ignatius did so at once. On the same day that he ordered the prayers, he notified Canisius through Polanco that his request had been heard.

*Following is the letter in which the saint asks monthly prayers and Masses for the conversion of the German lands, England, and the northern lands that had been won over to Protestantism. He asks the Jesuits working in the Indies to unite themselves with their brethren in Europe in this intention. In his correspondence with Cardinal Pole, and notably in his offer to the English students at the German College (*Epistolae et instructiones, V, 305; VIII, 309*), it is apparent with what great zeal Ignatius looked upon this apostolate.*

Rome, July 23 and August 7, 1553
JESUS

Ignatius of Loyola, general of the Society of Jesus, to my dear brothers in Christ, superiors and subjects of the Society of Jesus, everlasting health in our Lord.

The order of charity by which we should love the whole body of the Church in her head, Jesus Christ, requires a remedy to be applied, especially to that part which is more seriously and dangerously affected. Therefore it seems to us that we should, as far as our slender resources allow, bestow with especial affection the help the Society is able to give to England, Germany, and the northern nations which are so grievously afflicted with the disease of heresy.

Although many of us have already carefully attended to this by other means,[2] applying Masses and prayers for many years now, still, in order to give this duty of charity a wider field and a longer life, we enjoin on all rectors and superiors who are placed over others to offer themselves, if they are priests, and to have those under their authority offer, one Mass monthly to God; and those who are not priests, their prayers for the spiritual needs of England and Germany, so that at length the God of these nations and of all others that are infected with heresy may have pity on them and deign to lead them back to the purity of the Christian faith and religion.

---

[2] This is a clear allusion not only to the apostles sent to Germany beginning with 1543, but also to the German College. It was on March 12, 1552 that St. Ignatius showed his plans for this college to St. Francis Borgia (*Epistolae et instructiones*, IV, 186). On February 25, 1553 he was able to tell Cardinal Morone of its happy beginning (*ibid.*, IV, 652, 654).

It is our desire that these prayers continue as long as these nations need our help, and that no provinces, even those in the farthest Indies, be exempt from this duty of charity.[3]

¶ TO FATHER JAMES MIRON
v, 233, Letter 3584

If N— does not obey, he is to be given three warnings and then dismissed from the Society.

Rome, July 26, 1553

May the grace and love of Christ ever be our help and support.

In view of the obligation which God our Lord has laid upon me of safeguarding the universal good of the whole body of this Society, I feel that it is my duty, when a member has become so diseased as to be not only incurable but a source of harm to others, to sever it and remove it, no matter how great the pain involved. Now, seeing that . . .[1] is not only incorrigible in the great obstinacy of his disobedience, but is also a source of harm to others, as experience has proved to my sorrow, I have decided to command you, and I do now command you in virtue of holy obedience, to give him three warnings, as I have already directed you; and if he is still disobedient, to dismiss him and cut him off in my name from the whole body of the Society, and declare him dismissed because of the faults of inconstancy in his vocation and obstinacy in disobedience, and that I judge him, not only to be incorrigible but a source of great scandal to others in the Society with whom he associates.

May it please the Divine Goodness to give him grace to find a way by which he can be saved, although he has withdrawn many others from the way of their salvation.

¶ TO FATHER JAMES MIRON
v, 270-71, Letter 3605

In this letter St. Ignatius gives Father Miron specific and detailed instructions concerning Rodrigues. He is to give Rodrigues three times

---

[3] These prayers are said and Masses offered to this very day in all Jesuit communities.
[1] One or two words are here erased, which the editors of the *Monumenta* are certain were "M°. Simon."

the saint's order to come to Rome, each time showing him the letter and writ from his superior. If Rodrigues refuses to obey, Father Miron is to dismiss him from the Society, but only after having secured the king's consent and the approval of his consultors.

Rome, July 24 and August 3, 1553

Owing to the infrequent mails between Portugal and Rome, and Rome and Portugal, I have judged it good in our Lord this time to see that sufficient precautions are taken in the business of Master Simon. Therefore the first thing you are to do is to give him the dispatch I am sending you, both the letter and the writ, and show a copy of it to his highness. If this is not enough, give him the copy a second time, which will be his second warning. If he alleges some indisposition, consult some men of learning who you think are competent, especially of the order of St. Dominic, and if they judge that he ought to come, show their opinion to the king. Tell his highness that you have the instrument, which I am sending herewith, for the dismissal of Master Simon if he does not obey after the third warning you have given him, and that, if his highness does not object, you are to command Simon to obey and to come to Rome. In this procedure make it known to Master Simon for the last time, pointing out to him the authority you have, if he persists in disobeying, to dismiss him from the Society as one who is obstinately and incorrigibly disobedient and a source of harm to the whole body of the Society. If these warnings are not enough, let an interval elapse between them, and after referring the matter to his highness and begging him to agree with you, you will dismiss him with the consent of his highness, on the authority of this my letter. And so that he may not be able to say that you have not followed my instructions, I declare that I am leaving it to your judgment, together with the other three or four of your ordinary consultors, or any that you may choose, to do what you judge best. I approve now whatever you shall do. But when you have dismissed him, do not fail to beg his highness to command him and compel him to come here. I hope, however, that, before you have to resort to these measures, he will see fit to do your bidding and put an end to the deep wrong he has done his own soul and the souls of many others whom he is harming by his example.

May the Eternal Wisdom give us all the light to bring to a happy end all things that are needful to us in His service. Do not carry out my instructions about dismissing Master Simon unless his highness consents. Keep the letter which I have written so secret that only Dr. Nadal and Dr. Torres will know that you have such a message from me.

Sealed on the third day of August 1553.

If the two whom I have named are there with you, let them know all, and carry out your instructions with their approval.

¶ TO REGINALD POLE, CARDINAL OF ENGLAND
v, 304-05, Letter 3627

In 1553 Edward VI of England was succeeded on the throne by Mary Tudor, half sister of Edward and daughter of Henry VIII by Catherine of Aragon. With the coming of Queen Mary to the throne the end of the persecution begun under Henry and the restoration of England to the Church were looked upon in Rome as almost accomplished. Julius III had determined to send Cardinal Pole to England as his legate, hoping thus during the reign of Queen Mary to restore the Church in the island. Many were opposed to Pole's going, but he went the year following the marriage of Mary with Philip II of Spain. Ignatius, sharing the optimism felt by so many, writes to tell Pole of the blessings which he expects to result from Pole's mission to England. He tells of the Masses and prayers which he had ordered Jesuits throughout the world to offer for the conversion of the northern nations.

Rome, August 7, 1553

IHS

Most reverend and respected Monsignor in Christ.

May the sovereign grace and everlasting love of Christ our Lord greet and visit your most reverend lordship with His most holy gifts and spiritual graces.

I have lately been visited in the name of your most reverend lordship by one of your gentlemen, with all those signs of great charity and kindliness which we have always known to be characteristic of your most reverend lordship. Christ our Lord, the author of this and of every other blessing, will Himself be the reward of His gifts in your most reverend lordship. For this reason I cannot but congratulate myself and give thanks to God our Lord from the depths of my heart for the door which He has deigned to open for the restoration of the kingdom of England to the bosom of our holy Church and the purity of our Catholic faith. As our hopes of this consummation are all the higher, we are certain that it was not the bad will of the people but of their leaders and princes which has been the cause of their errors, and that from now on it will be the prudence of more level heads that gives ground for the reasonable hope that the people will return to themselves, who in other times so exalted and glorified the name of Christ.

Your going to England by order of the Holy See gives us the certainty that this will be an efficacious means of divine grace and that the holy and long-standing desires of your most reverend lordship will by the mercy of God be gratified, together with those whom we do not doubt God has kept in reserve, and who have not bent the knee to Baal.[1]

As to ourselves, I offer your most reverend lordship the continual supplication of our sacrifices and prayers in the presence of God's supreme goodness. It is now some time since I gave orders that, wherever there are any of our Society, even including India, all the priests should offer Mass and the others say special prayers for the spiritual help and the return of the northern nations. These prayers and Masses are to be said as long as the need lasts.[2] I now renew these orders, as it seems that this beginning which the Divine Wisdom gives us lays a fresh obligation upon us, and the occasion likewise of reviving our desires with fresh hope.

This is all, except to commend myself and this house and the whole Society to your most reverend lordship's holy prayers. May God our Lord grant you a happy voyage in His holy service, and to us all abundant grace always to know His most holy will and perfectly to fulfill it.

¶ TO THE COUNT OF RIBAGORZA
v, 367-68, Letter 3668

Martin de Aragon y Gurrea, count of Ribagorza, was the husband of Louise Borgia, the sister of Francis. In this letter Ignatius graciously approves his request to have Francis Borgia come to Saragossa and stop at Valencia, in the hope of bringing about an understanding between opposing factions.

Rome, August 20, 1553

My Lord in our Lord.

It is a few days since I received a letter from your lordship, in which for reasons very worthy of your Christian heart and zeal for the service of God in Saragossa your lordship bids me order Father Francis Borgia to go

---

[1] Romans 11:4.   [2] They are still being said.

to Saragossa and stop there. I shall be very glad to do what you ask, as I have the same hope as your lordship with regard to the spiritual help of many souls. Besides, your lordship is one to whom I am bound to render every service in our Lord. There will be no need to give Father Francis a command under obedience, because God our Lord has given him so much of it that it is enough for him to know the will of him who holds the place of our Lord for him to do everything possible to carry it out. It is quite possible that he has already left for Portugal, as I know that the king has written him. But I will let him know that on his return I think it will be good for God's greater glory for him to spend some time in Saragossa, and from there pay a visit to Valencia. It is quite possible that God our Lord will make use of him to settle the serious misunderstandings which I hear exist there.

May it please the divine and supreme Goodness to direct all his steps in His holy service, and give us all bountiful grace always to know His most holy will and perfectly to fulfill it.

¶ TO THE COUNTESS OF RIBAGORZA
v, 368-69, Letter 3669

Ignatius here repeats his promise to the count of Ribagorza, and very politely promises to write to Borgia to stop at Saragossa on his return from Portugal.

Rome, August 20, 1553

IHS

My Lady in our Lord.

May the sovereign grace and everlasting love of Christ our Lord greet and visit your ladyship with His most holy gifts and spiritual graces.

The Most Reverend Cardinal de la Cueva gave me a letter from your ladyship and another from my lord the count, fulfilling at the one time the task your ladyship had entrusted to him of having Father Francis Borgia sent to Saragossa. I have no doubt that it is spiritual rather than natural affection that makes his presence so desired at Saragossa, although your ladyship, fearing that I might have my suspicions, seems to anticipate me at the beginning of your letter. I am convinced that, although your ladyship is a sister in the flesh to Father Francis, you are much more so in the spirit and in your desire for God's glory, which has no thought for your own consolation and satisfaction but for that which will most contribute to the help of souls, and in them, serving and glorifying God our Creator and Lord.

I will write to Father Francis to do your ladyship's bidding, but without giving him an order of obedience. Your ladyship need have no doubt about his complying, although I think he will first go to Portugal, if he has not gone already at the request of the king. But he will not be there long. I am writing him by this same post, and the letters shall have gone several months in advance if there is anyone to bear them. What your ladyship says, moreover, about devotion in Saragossa and the frequentation of the sacraments is reason for giving many thanks to God our Lord as the author of this and of all good.

In the prayer which your ladyship bids me say, and in every other command which your ladyship may lay upon me to the glory of God our Lord, I will be very glad to obey, as I have every reason to do.

I close with the prayer that God's goodness will be pleased to give us all His bountiful grace, so that we may know His will and perfectly fulfill it. Your most illustrious ladyship's humble servant in our Lord . . .

¶ TO FATHER FRANCIS BORGIA
v, 370, Letter 3670

Ignatius writes that he should accede to the request of the count and countess of Ribagorza and go to Valencia as well.

Rome, August 20, 1553

From the letters which I am enclosing from the count and countess of Ribagorza you will see, my dear brother in our Lord, the eagerness with which they ask me to have you go to Saragossa. I have answered that there is no need of a command under obedience, but that I would let you understand my mind in the matter. It is that on your return from Portugal it will be quite for the service of Christ our Lord for you to go by way of Saragossa, and also Valencia. For not only in the matters pointed out by the count, but also in others of greater importance, I have hopes that God will make use of your services. Therefore, instead of commanding you under holy obedience, I will content myself with having made this representation to you, that apart from what their lordships write and Cardinal de la Cueva says, I am of the same opinion. And yet I will consider as best whatever is to your greater spiritual consolation and meets with your approval.

As this is all I have to say, I will only commend myself to your sacrifices and prayers, begging God our Lord to grant us all His bountiful grace always to know His most holy will and perfectly to fulfill it.

¶ TO NICHOLAS PETER CESARI
v, 418-20, Letter 3706

St. Ignatius gives his reasons for not allowing Octavius, Nicholas' son, to visit his mother in Naples.

Rome, August 27, 1553

JESUS

Very honorable Sir in our Lord.

Although I have nothing else substantially to write except what I wrote your lordship two weeks ago, I will nevertheless give an answer to your letter and say that I am convinced that your lordship speaks his mind quite frankly. I cannot in good conscious bid Octavius go, fearing as he reasonably does the disturbing effect his visit would have on his spiritual life. Even if he had no such fear, every day furnishes us with reason for it, seeing that his lady mother would not leave him in peace at Naples any more than she did earlier in Sicily. Your lordship will not be surprised that I think it improper to allow this consolation to the mother at such cost to the son. This is the common teaching and practice of the saints and all the servants of God. If his mother were reasonable, she would be satisfied with knowing that he is well, advancing in studies and virtue, and that in two or three days from where he is one could make the journey to Naples and back. She is not the first mother to have a son in religion, and should not look upon him as lost to her, but rather consider him as saved for her. Had she given him to the service of a worldly prince, she would have to put up with his absence. Let her be patient for a few years, and leave him in the service of God until he has matured. There will not then be the same fear from the contrast in the two ways of life, and it would be easier for him to return to Naples. Meanwhile, if Octavius hears that his parents are uneasy, he will ask to be removed to Spain or Portugual, where perhaps she would not see him again. Therefore let your lordship encourage her to bear bravely this trial with her son, in which Christ our Lord really has the greater part. Finally, she should not be surprised that the son prefers the service and good pleasure of Christ to that of herself or any other creature. Let your lordship assure her that, if she will remain quiet, I will give orders for her to have frequent letters from her son. But if she does not, she may not have any for a long time. Finally, I will do what I can to obtain some consolation for her provided it be without detriment to the spiritual interests of her son.

I close here, asking God our Lord to give us all the grace always to know and fulfill His holy will.

¶ TO JOHN LOUIS GONZALEZ DE VILLASIMPLEZ
v, 488-89, Letter 3756

De Villasimplez was royal treasurer in the kingdom of Aragon. Ignatius encourages him to the pursuit of virtue and tells him of Michael Spes, a former servant, who was thinking of entering the Society.

Rome, September 16, 1553

My Lord in our Lord.

May the sovereign grace and everlasting love of Christ our Lord ever be our help and support.

I received your letter of the ninth of this month. If one were looking for a proof of the great love that God our Lord has given you for us, one would find convincing testimony in this letter. May God our Lord, in whose love every other love ought to be rooted and ruled, repay you by increasing His love in your soul to such an extent that the absence of no one would ever cause you pain, except the absence of Him who is the supreme and perfect good and without whom, as there is nothing apart from Him howsoever good it be, so where He is present, no good is absent, since all the good which is sought in His creatures is present in greater perfection in Him who created them. I beg of Him to give you the grace to know Him better every day, and I ask Him to place in the very interior of your soul the teaching and example which Christ our Lord placed before the eyes of the whole world. If you continue in your excellent and Christian practice of frequent confession and Communion and in prayer and almsgiving, Christ our Lord will keep you from stumbling, let alone falling. It is of one who acts thus that it can be said, "He hath given his angels charge over thee, and in their hands shall they bear thee up, lest perhaps thou dash thy foot against a stone."[1] Do not

---

[1] Psalm 90:11-12; Matthew 4:6; Luke 4:10-11.

fear, therefore, the stumbling of which you write, but rather fear that which every Christian must if he is to avoid the occasions of a fall. There is no reason on our part why we should fail to remember you. The love which God our Lord has given us will not permit it.

Concerning Spes,[2] your servant, I suppose that his letter shall have informed you of his decision. He is now in our house, I think, with a vocation from God our Lord. Your interest in him is a circumstance which increases the happiness of us all in his vocation.

Señor Peter Garate is much beholden to you for the special memory you have of him, and I do not think he will allow himself to be surpassed in this respect, and in his great desire of being of service to you.

Señor Thomas Spinola and Señor Francis Cottaneo will deliver this letter to you. In them you will recognize men of Christian zeal and great virtue, so far as we know anything of them here.

In your last letter there was nothing about your going to Spain. May it please the Divine Goodness to bring it about when it will be best for you.

This will be all, except to ask God our Lord to give you, and all of us, His bountiful grace always to know His most holy will and perfectly to fulfill it.

¶ TO MARGARET OF AUSTRIA[1]
v, 699-700, Letter 3913

Ignatius wrote this letter to Margaret, the duchess of Parma, thanking her for the messages she had sent to him through Master Adrian. Ignatius looks upon her special charity toward the Society as a gift from God. He reminds her of the frequent prayers that he offers to God for her intention. He points out the graces gained from adversity and wishes her all possible happiness in the service of God.

Rome, November 17, 1553

IHS

My Lady in our Lord.

May the supreme grace and everlasting love of Christ our Lord greet and visit your excellency with His most holy gifts and spiritual graces.

---

[2] Michael Spes. He left the Society, however, in 1556.
[1] Daughter of Charles V.

I was greatly consoled in our Lord by the visit of Master Adrian, who came in the name of your excellency. I look upon it as a very special favor, this mark of the customary remembrance and special charity which He who is infinite and supreme charity has given to your excellency toward our Society. He likewise is the author of what we all feel in the depths of our hearts for the service of your excellency and the glory of His Divine Majesty, whose infinite wisdom knows how often I offer the remembrance of your excellency in His holy presence, praying that He preserve His gifts in you and increase them for His greater service and praise, and that from all these trials, which He has permitted, He will draw the fruit which His divine goodness can and usually does draw for the greater perfection of your excellency's soul in this life and the merit of a special and lasting crown in the next, where He is keeping for us our supreme and most happy bliss unmixed with any toil or sorrow, He who won them for us at the price of His life's blood. May it please Him to give us meanwhile a great knowledge of the sweet dispositions of His providence, if only He thus bless us in adversity and prosperity with occasions of attaining our everlasting happiness.

In this house and college we are all well, and here and elsewhere God our Lord bears us onward and makes use of this least Society, which is entirely your excellency's and always will be, to the glory of His Divine Majesty. May He be pleased to give us all His perfect grace ever to know His most holy will and perfectly to fulfill it.

¶ TO FATHER NICHOLAS GAUDANO
v, 713-15, Letter 3924

Ignatius praises Father Gaudano for his eagerness to be of help in Germany. Next he goes on to speak of the gift of tears. Ignatius says that feeling compassion in the will and the superior part of the soul is just as meritorious as the gift of tears. He encourages Father Gaudano to keep his will strong and energetic and reminds him that this will be sufficient for his own personal perfection.

Rome, November 22, 1553

My dear Father in Christ Jesus.

The peace of Christ.

I received your letter of October 12. It gives me great edification to see the desire you have of being of help to souls in Germany, not only by preaching and the use of other external means but also with your tears, the gift of which you desire from the giver of all good.

As to the first of your desires, to be of practical help to the neighbor by the external means of preaching and so forth, we will beg of Christ unconditionally to deign to "give to his voice the voice of power,"[1] and to the administration of the sacraments the desired efficacy. But the gift of tears may not be asked unconditionally, nor is it, absolutely speaking, good and proper for all without discrimination. However, I have taken the matter up with our Father Ignatius, and I myself have asked of God, and will continue to ask, that our Lord will grant it to you in the measure that will be good for the end itself that your reverence has in seeking it, the help of your own soul and the souls of your neighbor. "A hard heart shall fear evil at the last,"[2] but the heart, my dear father, that is full of the desire of helping souls, as is that of your reverence, cannot call itself hard in God's service. If in the will and the superior part of the soul, this heart feels compassion for the miseries of the neighbor, and seeks to do what it can to relieve them and performs those services which a man of determined will undertakes, tears are not necessary for such a heart, nor other tenderness of heart. Some indeed have them naturally, when the higher emotion of the soul makes itself felt in the lower, or because God our Lord, seeing that it would be good for them, allows them to melt into tears. But this does not mean that they have greater charity or that they are more effective than others who enjoy no tears. They are no less moved in the higher part of the soul—that is, in a strong and energetic will, which is the proper act of charity in God's service and the good of souls—than they who abound in tears. I will tell you, reverend father, what I really think. And that is that, even if it were in my power to allow this gift of tears to some, I would not give it, because it would be no help to their charity, and would harm their heads and their health and consequently stand in the way of every act of charity. Do not lose heart, then, because of this absence of external tears, but keep your will strong and energetic, and show it in your actions. This will be sufficient for your own personal perfection, the help of others, and the service of God. Remember that the good angels do what they can to preserve men from sin and obtain God's honor. But they do not lose courage when they fail. Our father has much praise for those of Ours who in this sense imitate the example of the angels. No more for the present, except to commend myself to your reverence's prayers.

---

[1] Psalm 67:34.   [2] Ecclesiasticus 3:27.

¶ TO HECTOR PIGNATELLI
VI, 49-51, Letter 3983

In August (see Letter 3706) Ignatius had refused the request of Nicholas Cesari that his son Octavius be sent to Naples to visit his mother. He is now answering a letter on the same subject received from Hector Pignatelli, duke of Monteleone. Ignatius politely refuses to recall Octavius to Naples, both because a sense of religious duty forbids it and because he thinks that he has already been sent to Spain or Portugal.

Rome, December 10, 1553

JHUS

Most illustrious and honorable Sir in our Lord.

May the sovereign grace and everlasting love of Christ our Lord greet and visit your most illustrious lordship with His holy gifts and spiritual graces.

I received your letter of the sixth from the hands of your messenger. I am very glad that your lordship knows so well my desire to serve you, which to the glory of God our Lord I promise to make good, as far as it rests with me. In fact, I do not think that in this matter good reason and the sense of obligation which we all feel toward your lordship will permit me to fall short. On the other hand, I am very sorry that I am unable to satisfy the desire of your lordship and have Octavius Cesari transferred to Naples. I do not think that I am failing in my promise, as it is not to be believed that I could promise what I should find to be impossible to fulfill. Among those who fear and love God that is felt to be impossible which cannot be done with a good conscience. In this matter I am convinced beyond the possibility of doubt that I would offend God our Lord were I to give an absolute command, as Octavius' mother seems to wish to have me do. I have the greatest sympathy with her in her suffering of soul and body, and I sincerely desire a true remedy for her. This will be to conform her will with God's will. But to please her with a bad conscience—this I would not know how to do, nor could I do it for anything in the world. We must not think Divine Providence so short of resources that it cannot console the mother except with a sight of her son. I don't see how I can send him to Naples without being guilty of sin. And what is more, I want your lordship to understand that, when Ours from Sicily saw that the boy was so disturbed, they feared that his mother would be a constant source of disquiet if he were near her, and resolved to send him to Spain or Portugal as soon as a favorable opportunity of sailing presented itself. They may even be at this moment on the way there. I offered no objection, as I thought that, besides removing the young man from danger, the mother would be consoled and would receive some spiritual help when she realized that there was no hope of seeing him for some time. This is the second reason why I cannot yield to the mother and give the son a direct order to visit her.

Your illustrious lordship, in that light which our Lord has given you, will understand that I can give no other answer, and you will know how much of what I say should be communicated to the mother.

I pray the divine and supreme Goodness to deign to grant us to know and love as we should, and to take possession of that lady's heart, so that she will love all creatures in Him and for Him. May He grant us all the grace to know and fulfill perfectly His most holy will.

¶ TO LOUIS, PRINCE OF PORTUGAL
VI, 85-86, Letter 4008

A letter of thanks. The prince's devotion to the Society has been extolled by several of its writers.

Rome, December 24, 1553

IHS

My Lord in our Lord.

May the sovereign grace and everlasting love of Christ our Lord greet and visit your highness with His most holy gifts and spiritual graces.

I should like to be able to answer your highness' letter of September 27 not so much in words as with a feeling of gratitude in recognition of God's mercy and giving Him infinite thanks for the favor He confers on this least Society by inspiring your highness with the desire to help and support it in His divine service.[1] Although the value of the works makes clear the earnestness of your highness' purpose in supporting us, one can still see that there is even yet much more hidden in the treasury of your highness' heart which no outward effects have succeeded in revealing. It is this eagerness which impels your highness to command us to consider in what way you can favor us, and we should only have to ask your highness to have it done. This makes us conscious of the infinite and supreme goodness of God our Lord, who has left this trace of Himself in the soul

---

[1] For instances of the prince's devotion see *Chronicon*, III, 400, 470; *Epistolae mixtae*, III, 321, 396.

of your highness. It is characteristic of Him to wish to give us greater graces than we are ready to receive, and to dispose us to desire and hope from His divine liberality that He will fulfill and even surpass our hopes and desires. May He be blessed and praised in all His creatures and all the good He has imparted to them. Amen.

I am very glad that your highness has been so pleased with the coming of Father Francis Borgia and Master Nadal. I have observed that their letters sound the same note as your highness.'

Your highness shall have heard other news of Ours from them, and I refer you to them. I humbly commend to your highness this whole Society, which is more your highness' than ours.

May God our Creator and Lord give us all His bountiful grace, so that we may always know His most holy will and perfectly fulfill it.

¶ TO FATHER GASPAR BERSE
VI, 87-88, Letter 4010

Ignatius answers a letter received. He approves of Berse as rector of the College of Goa and superior of the Jesuits in India, in the absence of Xavier who had given him the appointment. He praises his desire of cultivating the Chinese and Japanese, but wishes him to follow obedience, which is the interpreter of God's will. He informs him of preparations for the mission to Ethiopia, and bids him to wait for this unless circumstances demand otherwise. After hearing the opinion of the brethren, he should give this mission precedence and set out for Ethiopia.

Rome, December 24, 1553

IHUS

May the sovereign grace and everlasting love of Christ our Lord ever be our help and support. Amen.

We received your letters of January 12 of this year, together with others which our dear brother, Master Francis, had written and left. From both sources we understand that you have assumed office in that college and for the rest of India during the absence of Master Francis. I am quite satisfied with his choice, and I hope that the divine and supreme Goodness will make up for the faults and shortcomings of His instruments, and thus give you the grace of rendering Him great service in your office.

I do not think that your desires to go to China and Japan have been without result in the service of His Majesty, for the offering of your will shall have been accepted. In all other things as well, you should look upon what you are ordered to do by obedience to Master Francis as a positive interpretation of God's will.

With regard to going to the land of Prester John, if you have not done so by the time this reaches you, I think you should put off your journey until you get word from the patriarch, who with ten or twelve others are being sent to Ethiopia. If this does not take place this year, you may be sure that it will by the time of the first subsequent sailing. However, if the situation is such that you judge it better in our Lord to go rather than to await the arrival of those whom we are sending, I defer to your judgment. But you should first get the view of your consultors, as I have written you and as you will see in the Constitutions if they have sent you copies from Portugal.

For other matters I refer you to Master Polanco, who will deal with the details as I have instructed him.

May it please the Divine Wisdom to communicate itself to you in all your activities, and give us all bountiful grace always to know His most holy will and perfectly to fulfill it.

¶ TO FATHER PHILIP LEERNO
VI, 109-10, Letter 4020

A letter with solid spiritual instruction for Father Leerno.

Rome, December 30, 1553

My dear Father Master Philip.

The peace of Christ.

The office of rector which your reverence holds is in good hands. You ought to be on your guard against allowing your desire for humiliation to give place to the spirit of pusillanimity. We should not have a slight regard for God's gifts, although we may and should despise our own imperfections. Let your reverence be of good heart and let your companion, Master John Lorenzo, help you when he can. Do not lose heart or hold yourself cheaply. Be assured that we have a higher esteem of God's gifts in your reverence than you yourself have.

As to that blindness or dryness of soul which you think you find in yourself, it may easily come from a lack of confidence, or pusillanimity, and consequently can be cured by its contrary. Above all remember that God wishes to find solid virtues in us, such as patience, humility, obedience, abnegation of our own will—that is, the good will to serve Him and our neighbor for Him. His providence allows us other devotions only so far as He sees that they are expedient for us. But as they are not substantial, they do not make a man perfect when they abound, nor imperfect when they are absent.

I will say no more, except to pray that Jesus Christ our Lord may be the strength and stay of us all.

¶ TO THEOTONIUS BRAGANZA
VI, 130-31, Letter 4031

Ignatius gently exhorts him to reap some spiritual fruit from his illness, and suggests that, rather than come to Rome, he go to Cordova to finish his studies.

Rome, January 1, 1554

May the sovereign grace and everlasting love of Christ our Lord be always our stay and support.

Letters from Master Nadal, our commissary, inform me, my dear brother, that God our Lord has afflicted you with no slight illness.[1] I am quite convinced in His Divine Goodness that this illness has been sent you in the interest of a more important health, as an occasion for merit and the exercise of virtue. I am sure that you have tried to draw the fruit which God our Lord wishes you to draw from such visitations. In his infinite mercy and love He seeks our greater good and perfection no less with bitter medicines than with consolations that are sweet to the taste. Nevertheless, I hope with His divine favor soon to have news of your improvement, and I am sure that you will make much use of your better health in His service.

As to your coming to Rome, although it would give us the greatest consolation to see you, yet considering that in all this time there has been no opportunity to satisfy a desire which we both have, and taking your illness into account, I suppose that we had better for the present give up the thought, and that it would be more for your progress in studies and your spiritual consolation if you were to go to Cordova, where you will

---

[1] Much is said about Theotonius Braganza in the letters of Nadal (I, 205-11). See also *Chronicon*, III, 436-37. His days in the Society were not many. After taking leave of it he attained to high honors in the Church and gave encouragement and help to St. Teresa in her work of reform.

be able to continue your education. Put aside whatever other care you may have, and rest assured that we will look after you, and that all will in the end redound to the greater service and glory of our Lord. May His infinite and supreme Goodness grant us all the bountiful grace to know and do His most holy will.

¶ TO MAGDALENE ANGELICA DOMENECH
vi, 160-62, Letter 4054

This lady, a sister of Father Jerome Domenech, suffered from great infirmities and no less trials of soul. The saint consoles her in the following letter.

Rome, January 12, 1554

My Lady in our Lord.

May the perfect grace and eternal love of Christ our Lord be always in our aid and favor. Amen.

Letters from Valencia inform me that God our Lord has been visiting you with trials of body and soul, thus showing, in giving you so many occasions for merit, the very special love He has for you. You may be sure that, the less He seems to reward you in this world and life that passes, the more bounteous is the reward He is keeping in His eternal happiness for your good desires and works. Indeed, madam, I desire for you all the contentment and consolation that I could desire for myself, and I sympathize with you in your trials, as reason and the law of charity would expect me to. And yet I cannot but think it a very special gift of God our Lord when He provides you with the material on which you can exercise the virtues of patience, faith, and hope in Him. Be persuaded that the divine and supreme goodness and love of our most wise Father in heaven is favoring you with that which will perfect you more, since in adversity no less than in prosperity, and in afflictions as well as in consolations, does He manifest the everlasting love with which He guides His chosen ones to eternal happiness.

So great is His loving kindness that, if it were good for us, He would on His part be more inclined to keep us always consoled rather than afflicted, even in this life. But as the condition of our misery in this present state requires that at times He visit us with trials instead of delights, we can see in this His fatherly and supreme mercy that He confines our trials to the brief course of this life and not without an occasional mingling of many consolations. In the life which is eternal and without end He will reward our patience with indescribable satisfaction and glory, and without any mingling of trial or sadness or dissatisfaction at all, since there is none in heaven, but only the fulfillment of every joy and happiness. If you try to put yourself into the hands of Christ our Lord by conforming your own will entirely with His, including a readiness to follow Him in the trials He underwent in this world when He wishes to share them with you, so that you can follow Him later in the glory of the other world, I have no doubt that your trials will cease in great measure, and so great will be your fortitude in bearing them that you will hardly notice them.

On my part, I shall not cease together with those with me here earnestly to recommend your interests to God our Lord. If there is any way in which I can comfort you, I will do so most gladly, as one who holds you in great affection in our Lord. May it please Him to give us His bountiful grace that we may always know His most holy will and perfectly fulfill it.

¶ TO FATHER JEROME DOMENECH
VI, 178-80, Letter 4066

A letter of reproof. Ignatius reprehends Domenech for having complained too freely about the lack of personnel and for laying the blame on him, when in fact the Province of Sicily is much better off than the other colleges of Italy. He invites Domenech to make known his needs but to do it circumspectly, and to keep his own judgment in submission.

Rome, January 13, 1554

My dear Father in Christ.

Pax Christi.

I would much prefer to write in a way that would console you rather than wound you, but your reverence must leave off giving me such occasion. Indeed, if our father were not restrained by certain considerations, he would show in a much more effective way his dislike of your reverence's complaints, which reflect discredit on him, not only because you do not submit your own judgment to his in his appointments but because you also condemn them as bad in the presence of others. This is plainly seen in the instance of the three who have lately come from Spain. You wanted to keep Master Peter Canal, and you complained to them that, while our father at first sent you important men in the Society, he later withdrew them all, and so forth. Your reverence overlooks the fact that some recompense was made for those who were taken away, and you fail to see (something still more surprising) that our father is obliged to keep the universal good in mind. Thus, besides providing you with sufficient man power to carry on the works you have undertaken, he must remember others in which our Lord wishes to make use of the Society and its members. The college at Venice has only one priest,[1] who has no knowledge of philosophy or theology; that of Padua has two[2] who are weak in literature and without higher learning; that of Modena has two[3] who are only average in Latin and still mere youths. At Ferrara, Pelletier was alone until another was sent to help him, who does not know a great deal of literature or higher studies.[4] Father Francis Palmio is at Bologna, but no other priest can be sent as companion to him, as there is no other. Master Louis is at Florence,[5] and another who has scarcely made his literary studies.[6] There are two at Gubbio, but neither of them is a theologian.[7] There is a single theologian at Perugia[8] and another who is no theologian.[9] And I think that there is an equal or even greater lack of schoolmasters in these places. But this does not prevent them from producing fruit, God making up for what our poor efforts cannot accomplish. If we compare conditions in Sicily with conditions in all of Italy, there is no doubt that it is better provided than any other place, even after making all necessary allowances.

Now, despite all this, our father does not wish that your reverence fail to declare your mind. Rather it is his wish that you do so. But he does not wish that your reverence allow any word to escape that would seem to indicate that you are complaining of what he does. Do not broadcast your needs. He will be satisfied if you make them known to him, and then leave everything to him. You should prefer the general good to the particular, and convince yourself that our father, once he has been informed simply and without any attempt to use pressure, will decide what will be to the greater service of God our Lord and the general good. Indeed, this should be the aim of all, even when local angels have a special

---

[1] Father Cesar Helmi.
[2] Fathers John Baptist Tavono and Aloysius Napi.
[3] Fathers Philip Leerno and John Laurence de Patarinis.
[4] Possibly referring to Father Louis Harmeville, recently ordained.
[5] Louis Coudret. [6] Father Desiderius.
[7] Fathers Albert Ferrarese and Augustine de la Riva.
[8] Father Everard Mercurian. [9] Father John Black.

leaning toward their own provinces or localities. To help your reverence not to forget this way of keeping confidential what you think you need in Sicily, and to write by way of representation and so forth, send in your own writing what you are thinking of doing. This our father expressly commands. Try also to console him occasionally, seeing that he has so much trouble keeping so many places here in Europe and Ethiopia supplied with men, besides keeping up this university here in Rome, where there is so much sickness among professors and students. Dr. Olave, who had two lecture courses a day in theology, is worn out, and it has become necessary to relieve him of one course to save his health. This course will be taken by Master John Cuvillon, who has come from Sicily. However, God is our help, whose glory we are seeking in Sicily, Rome, and everywhere. May He fill us with knowledge of Him and hope in Him, and dwell in our souls with perfect love. Amen.

¶ TO MARY FRASSONA DEL GESSO
VI, 223-24, Letter 4094

Mary Frassona del Gesso belonged to a noble family of Ferrara which was very devoted to the Society. She founded a college of the Society in Ferrara, and alleviated with a mother's solicitude the poverty of its beginnings. Ill health and difficulties with some of her relatives inclined her to sadness. She was in especial need of some spiritual consolation, and Father Pelletier, the rector of the college, did what he could. Ignatius, always attentive to the duty of gratitude, had made her a sharer in all the spiritual benefits of the Society. He here counsels her to fix her gaze on the reward for trials borne with Christian fortitude.

Rome, January 20, 1554

JHUS

Esteemed Lady in our Lord.

May the perfect grace and eternal love of Christ our Lord greet and visit your ladyship with His holy gifts and spiritual graces.

I have heard in letters from Ours that your ladyship has been visited by God our Lord with a bodily infirmity as well as trials of soul, and I thought I should visit you by letter—no other way being possible—and remind you that the providence of our most holy Father and wise physician usually proceeds in this way with those whom He loves much. And the sooner He wishes them to participate in His own eternal happiness, once this present life has passed away, the more does He purify them with such trials in this life, where He is unwilling that our love find any place of rest or repose. For this reason it is His wont to stimulate His chosen ones, not only with a desire for heaven but also with a weariness and a distaste for earth. And yet these experiences are useful to increase our glory if they are received with the patience and thanks with which it is becoming to accept the gifts of a fatherly charity, whose hand is raised to strike as well as to caress. If there is any sure way in this world to escape trials and affliction of spirit, it is to force our own will into a perfect conformity with God's. For if He has complete possession of our heart, we will not be able to lose it against our will, and nothing that can greatly afflict us can happen to us, since all affliction is born of having lost, or of fear of losing, what we love.

I am writing to our brother Master John [Pelletier] not to fail to visit your ladyship as before because of the new occupation which has been added to those he already has.[1] In reality, he is in Ferrara just because of your ladyship, and for the satisfaction and comfort of your ladyship I propose to keep him there continually, as far as it depends on me and God our Lord spares his life.

No more for the present, except to commend myself earnestly to your ladyship's prayers. I beg God our Lord to grant us all the grace always to know His most holy will and perfectly to fulfill it. Entirely your ladyship's in our Lord . . .

¶ TO DOIMO NASCIO

VI, 343, Letter 4181

Doimo Nascio came from Ameria, and had a great affection for Ignatius. Although advanced in years, he wished to enter the Society. He was given a few months trial with the result that it was thought better for him to work out his salvation free from any obedience to the Society.

Rome, February 22, 1554

Reverend and dear Master Doimo in Christ.

I received your letter and quite understand the hesitation you feel about going to Venice. I have prayed over the matter as you asked me,

---

[1] That of introducing to the duties of his new state Prince Louis, son of Duke Ercole d'Este. Louis had just been named bishop of Ferrara.

and I will tell you what I think with all the affectionate frankness which our friendship in our Lord demands.

If I had made up my mind to serve a master, especially one in whom I found as much satisfaction as you say you have found in yours, I should wish, if I had to make a change, to know his will and to accommodate myself entirely to it in the service of God our Lord. If I wanted to know whether I should go to Venice or not, I should want to know just what was Señor Asconius Colonna's wish in the matter, and make my decision in conformity with it, supposing I had no other means of seeing clearly what would be to the greater service of God our Lord. Once I knew this, there would be no further need of deliberating, but I would simply follow the line I knew would be more pleasing to God. This, therefore, is what I think.

Although there is little hope of that agreement which we all desired so much, you could leave this matter in the hands of God and employ your charity in other things to God's glory. I ask you to commend me earnestly to Him, and beg the divine and sovereign Goodness to give us all the grace ever to know and fulfill His most holy will.

¶ TO FATHER JAMES LAINEZ
VI, 344-45, Letter 4182

Ignatius gives him some advice on preaching, and urges him to regulate his labors with a view to preserving his health.

Rome, February 22, 1554

IHUS

Pax Christi.

I received your reverence's letter of the fifteenth of this month and understand from it that you are preparing to preach every day, beginning with the second Sunday of Lent. Those gentlemen who are not satisfied with less than a sermon every day must be actuated by great zeal and charity for their Church. But as our father is bound to exercise zeal and charity in your regard especially, and in that of others too who are under his care, he does not want you to undergo fatigues that your strength of body is not able to bear. In this matter you should follow the doctor's advice. If you do not, it can easily happen that, because of your excessive desire for labor this Lent, you may be prevented from preaching for a number of years and from attending to other business in the service of

God. This is a point that escapes those perhaps who want you to preach every day, having their eyes merely on the present.

You have more than a few companions in your desire to die among the infidel.[1] But you will finally have to be satisfied with what Providence arranges by means of your superiors.

Your reverence will have news of India from Florence, as Father Louis[2] has directions to send you the news.

No more for the present, except to commend ourselves earnestly to the prayers of your reverence.

I forgot to say that the king of the Romans[3] has written rather eagerly about the compendium.[4] But we will talk about that after you have recovered from the fatigues of your lenten preaching. I am sending you a copy of the letter. May Christ Jesus be with you all.

POSTSCRIPT. Although the other letter is written absolutely, so that you can use it if necessary, it leaves it entirely to your own judgment to preach or not, just as before. But for the love of God, don't kill yourself, and be satisfied with your limitations, and so forth.

¶ TO FATHER GASPAR BERSE
VI, 357-59, Letter 4193

Ignatius seriously warns him against excess in penances and labors, and appoints a companion whom he is to obey in the care of his person. He adds some instructions on letter writing.

Rome, February 24, 1554

My dear Father in Jesus Christ.

May the grace and peace of Christ our Lord be present in ever-growing measure in our souls.

I did not think that we would be writing more than we have already for this sailing, but we received a letter from Portugal later, written in

---

[1] The golden words of Lainez are as follows: "Concerning the news from . . . the heathens, God knows how greatly pleased I am. . . . From time to time I feel the desire, though not overwarm, of going to Jerusalem. Although I know that the best way to die well is to live well, seeing that my living is so faulty, I desire that our Lord by way of mercy will allow me to die well. And this would be by confessing His faith, or by disposing oneself to do so, to die."
[2] Louis Coudret, rector of the college in Florence.
[3] Ferdinand I.
[4] The *Summa Theologica* which Lainez had undertaken to write.

Goa, concerning your reverence's illness and the work you continue to do in spite of it, preaching and so forth. Our father has thought it best, therefore, to write this letter to your reverence, to inform you from him that such action on your part does not seem wise or something that can last. Although he is much edified by your holy zeal and love of mortification, he does not think that it is seasoned with that salt which God our Lord looks for in every sacrifice, namely, a "reasonable service," such as St. Paul wishes to see in those who offer themselves to God our Lord.[1]

There are two drawbacks in dealing with yourself so severely. The first is that without a miracle your reverence will not last long in the holy ministries you undertake; rather, death would tie your hands.[2] Or you would become so ill that you could no longer continue with them, which would be to put quite an obstacle in the way of God's greater service and the help of souls, in which works you could with better health employ yourself for many years. The second is that, being so harsh with yourself, you could easily come to be excessively so with those under your charge. And even though you gave them no more than your example, it must result in making some run too fast, and that the more so among the better of your subjects.

In a word, our father recommends moderation to your reverence. He would not have you preach when you are ill unless the doctor says that such exercise will do you no harm. Since in your own cause your reverence might doubt just where moderation began, it would be good to choose someone who is living with you in Goa, or who accompanies you, who should have authority over you in the matter of food and sleep and the amount of work to be undertaken. You should obey him in the Lord on these points. Here we have made use of such means to control the activity of some of the leading men in the Society and who hold important offices in it. This should suffice for the care of your person.

Persons of importance in the city who read with great profit to themselves the letters from the Indies usually wish, and on various occasions have asked, for something to be written about the geography and the flora and fauna of the countries to which Ours are sent. They would like to know, for instance, the length of the days in summer and winter, when

---

[1] Romans 12:1.
[2] Ignatius did not know that Father Gaspar had died on October 18, 1553, four months before this letter was written. He was preaching on the parable of the king who wished to take an account of his servants, and without finishing his sermon had to be carried from the pulpit. He lingered for twelve days, and died on October 18, the Feast of St. Luke. He was a man who sorely needed such advice as is here given, for his desires were as wide as the world, and he literally worked himself to death (*Chronicon*, III, 485, 486).

the summer begins, whether the shadow falls to the left or to the right. In a word, they would like information about anything that appears extraordinary, such as unknown animals and plants, their size, and so forth. And this condiment for the taste of a certain innocent curiosity in men can be sent in the letters themselves, or on separate sheets.

And since we have observed in persons of quality and understanding that this exerts a very good influence on them, it will be good if in the letters which can be shown to people outside the Society less time is spent on those things which concern members of the Society and more given to matters of general interest. Otherwise the letters cannot be printed here without considerable editing. True it is that what concerns members of the Society will have more edification for our own members here; but this can come by itself. If in the latter case they miss the mark, some remedy can be applied here, although it will take some trouble. But the former cannot be supplied by us here. Your reverence can see to it that the members of the province write according to directions.

For other matters I refer you to other letters, and I will say no more here than that in this house, the Roman College, and the Germanico we are all well by God's grace. May Jesus Christ our God and Lord, who is the health and true life of the world, give us the health and life that is interior. Amen.

¶ TO THE COLLEGE OF COIMBRA
VI, 378, Letter 4206

With great charity Ignatius shields the reputation of Rodrigues.

Rome, February 26, 1554

Enclosed is a letter from our dear brother, Master Simon,[1] and although he is hard on a number of things, I want you to know that here at Rome we think that his intention was good, and that where he has failed in anything, both when he was superior and afterwards, it was without malice and even with the persuasion that what he was doing was correct. I am daily more satisfied with his society and his manner of acting. And yet, as the Constitutions limit the provincials to three years, and because he himself was anxious to be freed of his responsibility, and because of the striving for perfection which the Society and its govern-

---

[1] This letter has never been found and must be presumed to have perished.

ment demands, it has seemed best to us to make a change in the provincial of Portugal. We have called him, therefore, to Rome, where he will find abundant opportunity of employing himself in God's service.

If you show his letter to anyone, you are ordered by obedience to show this along with it. In this way no one will take away a wrong impression.

May Christ our Lord give us His grace always to know His most holy will and perfectly to fulfill it.

¶ TO EMPEROR CHARLES V
VI, 421-22, Letter 4231

This letter deals with the introduction of the Society of Jesus into Flanders and the endowing of a college at Louvain. St. Ignatius addresses this letter to Emperor Charles to ask his support for the undertaking and to solicit the interest of his sister Mary, then regent of the Low Countries. Although this letter was written, it was never mailed. The reason why it was not sent is unknown.

Rome, March 3, 1554

IHS

May the sovereign grace and everlasting love of Christ our Lord greet and visit your majesty with His most holy gifts and spiritual graces.

When I consider that the providence of God our Creator and Lord has placed your majesty in a position of such lofty responsibility and has added the spirit which takes a personal interest in what concerns the universal good and God's glory, and when I reflect that the same providence has raised up, in the days of your majesty, our least Society, whose services your majesty is using, and I hope will continue to use, with great effect daily in your kingdoms and elsewhere within and beyond the limits of Christendom, it occurred to me that in the face of a great obstacle to this work in the service of God, I ought to have recourse to your majesty. I am sure that your thoughts are centered on that service, and I humbly beg your majesty to give ear to certain information which we may give you, and to make that provision which you will see to be for God's greater glory. We look upon ourselves as belonging, as we actually do, to your majesty and to the king of England,[1] and the most serene princess,[2] your

---

[1] Philip, the future Philip II, king of England as a result of the marriage arranged a short time before with Mary Tudor, and which took place June 25, 1554.
[2] Joan of Austria, daughter of Charles V and regent of Spain.

children; and also to the king of the Romans,³ the queen of Portugal,⁴ your brother and sister, not merely as vassals, as most of us are (some of us being of families known to your majesty), but as under great obligations to the benevolent affection which God our Lord, the author of all good, has given them to assist this Society in its beginnings.

May He be pleased to give us all His abundant grace always to know His most holy will and perfectly to fulfill it.

¶ TO FATHER JOHN BAPTIST VIOLA
VI, 447-50, Letter 4251

Ignatius bids him to take care of his health and never to think that in doing so he will cause any annoyance to the Society. He may visit Garfagnana when he pleases. He advises him about taking a companion, and sends him a letter appointing him procurator, telling him to have no fear of incurring necessary expenses. He should choose a place and house where he thinks that he will be more likely to recover his health. He bids him write, gives him news of John Anthony and Thaddeus, and dispenses him from fast and abstinence and the Breviary.

Rome, March 10, 1554

My dear Father in Christ.

The peace of Christ.

We received your letter of the third of this month, and this will serve as an answer.

In the first place, your reverence should put aside the thought of any annoyance or vexation you might be causing the Society. And be certain of this, that the Society will never begrudge you any expense or trouble. It would show little faith on your part, or indeed little confidence in her, to have had any such doubts.

As to going to Lunediana or Sarzana and visiting some of the fathers at Garfagnana, you should feel at perfect liberty to go whenever it suits your convenience and will give you greater satisfaction, on condition, however, that the doctors have no objection, as it is only reasonable to trust them in matters of their craft and obey them *aliquatenus*. In a word, be persuaded that you are acting under obedience in whatever you do to recreate yourself in the Lord, as a means to recover your health. This is

---

³ Ferdinand I.   ⁴ Catherine of Austria, wife of John III.

the mind of our father, and you should entertain no scruples whatever on this score.

As to taking a companion, have more regard for your convenience than for expense. If the money from the sale of the house cannot supply you with what you need, we shall be very glad to make up what is lacking. It is true that the reason which you offer, with regard to which we will write later, rather persuades us to let you go without a companion from the Society, because he would be of less help than another in looking after your own health and comfort. But do as you think best, and do not think that because we have many debts we can fail to provide you with all the funds you need. When it comes to these things God never fails us.

We are sending you herewith your appointment as procurator, which will authorize you to collect money and give receipts, together with the authorization to appoint a substitute, so that you could make the collection at Parma through someone else. I am also sending two testimonial letters, the one concerning your expenses, the other to signify that wherever you are, you are there under obedience, for reasons of health.

If Master John Francis does not bring the money with him from Parma from the sale of the house, and does bring it in some other way, take the sum you mention, or more if you think best. If no one brings the money, and the doctor says that you ought to get away at once, tell Father Don Francis Palmio to borrow on my account all the money that you may want to take with you, and I will pay it back in eight days, or as is customary, on the presentation of letters to me; or let those who do the borrowing pay it back in Bologna in fifteen or twenty days, and we shall send the money through some bank as soon as we are notified. Not that it makes any difference which house supplies the sum needed, because they are all of the Society, and wherever you wish some house will supply your expenses, whether they exceed or fall short of the sum realized on the house. And because there is talk of the said sum, your reverence should not think that there is question of being assigned to any particular house, whether you are in Parma or some place nearby.

If you do not improve in your native air within the limits of Lombardy, and you doubt whether you should remain there in some other place or return to Bologna, our father says that you should feel perfectly free to stay wherever you wish. You may return to Bologna or go on to Genoa or come to one of the colleges nearer Rome—Tivoli, for instance, which is about fifteen miles from Rome and enjoys a pleasant climate. Our father would be quite satisfied were you to come to Rome, or remain at a distance, or go to Tivoli when you choose, where we have a nice house and a few brothers. He supposes that the doctors will have no objection. But first, try your native air, and then you will be free to move wherever you wish and where you think you will feel most at home. There is only one obligation he would put upon you, and that is, to keep him advised of the state of your health. If it will console you to have news of the Society, it will always be sent you from here or from some nearer point. As to your insisting that you are not separating from the Society, not at least in soul but only in body and for a time, our father says that this is perfectly clear. Because, even if you wished to separate yourself, we would hold you back with a rope. But you should not look upon yourself as separated even in body. In fact, one who is sent from one place to another by obedience, even if he is all by himself, as long as the bond of obedience is kept intact, is not separated either in body or in soul from his community. As time goes on, if you wish a companion for fear of appearing a solitary, write and ask for anyone you wish from any college whatsoever.

They have need of a priest at Bologna, it seems, and one will be provided, with God's help, after Easter.

We have heard that John Anthony and Thaddeus have reached Ancona, and from there have gone on to Perugia, one of them to see whether he can go on to Florence and the other to Siena. But we have heard nothing further of them.

We commend ourselves very earnestly to your prayers, even though they be short. May Christ Jesus be with us all.

I forgot to tell you that you should consider yourself dispensed from fasting and abstinence, and the Office, and so on, in the interest of your health. You may avail yourself as much as you please of all the other privileges of the Society for your own consolation and God's glory.

¶ TO MARY FRASSONA DEL GESSO
VI, 460-61, Letter 4260

A letter of thanks for help sent to the community at Rome. He gives her some good advice, and speaks about Father Pelletier.

Rome, March 13, 1554

My illustrious Lady in our Lord.

A few days ago I answered your ladyship's letter of February 15. Later I received another dated December 18, together with some articles you sent as a gift and alms, which were most welcome in our Lord, as we see in them the great charity and devotion which urged you to send them. God, for whose love every good gift is made and accepted, will be your ladyship's most liberal recompense, for us and for all His poor.

As to the dispositions which your ladyship desires as a preparation for the cross, God will arrange it in His own time—I mean at the moment when patience will be necessary for you. There can be no doubt of this, for we have the promise of the Eternal Truth that He will never permit us to be tempted or tried beyond our strength. Rather, one who reflects on His sweet providence ought confidently to hope that all will cooperate to his good, and hold it for certain that the divine and sovereign Goodness, now by chastising, now by caressing, His children, always acts with equal charity as He seeks their greater good. We can, therefore, with full confidence conform our will with God's, and make up our minds to be satisfied with whatever disposition He may make of us. If we do this, when the time of temptation comes we shall not fail in the patience necessary to bear our trials, not only without complaint but even thankfully, as we convince ourselves that not only prosperity but adversity too is a favor from God, as it really is, for those especially who sincerely dedicate themselves to His divine service.

As to the fatiguing labors of our dear brother, Master John,[1] my intention is that they should be moderate, and I have written him to this purpose. If he acts otherwise, it will be contrary to my intentions and my directions, which I hope he will not do, although a man's very good will sometimes causes even a servant of God to exceed the limits laid down. Against this they sometimes need a reminder, and your ladyship does well to call his attention to it from time to time.

Nothing else occurs to me except to commend ourselves most earnestly to your ladyship's prayers.

May God our Lord deign to grant us all His grace always to know His most holy will and perfectly to fulfill it.

¶ TO ANTHONY ENRIQUEZ
VI, 522-25, Letter 4306

This letter to Anthony Enriquez is an affectionate answer from Ignatius. He encourages Anthony to lay up treasures in heaven. He re-

---

[1] Father John Pelletier, who was in charge of the College of Ferrara.

minds him that men are only pilgrims on earth and that earthly treasures are temporary. Ignatius advises Anthony to frequent the sacraments and to read spiritual books and pray each day. In the postscript he sends some items of news.

Rome, March 26, 1554

Honorable Sir in our Lord Jesus Christ.

I have been waiting to answer a letter I received from you from Florence, and I have asked a friend who is attending the court to let me know whether you are with it. But now I have another letter from Brussels, dated February 22, which answers the question, and gives to our father and the rest of us here who are so devoted to your service a great amount of consolation in our Lord. Although the letter which you say you wrote on your arrival and which contained a description of your journey has not arrived, the trouble you take to write so often is a favor which we should highly esteem, and one which shows the kindly affection which God our Lord has given you. May His supreme and divine Goodness, with the gifts of His grace, bring to perfection those of nature which He has given you in such abundance, so that they may both be employed in His greater service and praise, and merit for you the crown of a happy eternity.

Our father is enjoying only moderate health, and sends you many cordial greetings. We shall not fail to commend your affairs to God our Lord, for longer than the way to Brussels there remains the way to our heavenly country. We must never lose sight of the fact that we are pilgrims until we reach it, and we must not let our affections tarry in the hostelries and the lands through which we pass, lest we forget our destination and lose our love of our last end. And the better to attain it, our eternal Father has given us the use and service of creatures. But He would not have us fix our affections on them to such an extent that, for the temporary and imperfect possessions of this fleeting life, we lose the perfect and lasting goods of the life that is without end. This is an imprudence which, while plainly manifest to any man whose understanding is illumined by our holy faith, sometimes is lost sight of by the prudent of this world. This is to walk in the way of dissipation without ever seriously entering into oneself. It is to misuse the light of the understanding to keep it busy with things of little account and never apply it to those which are of supreme importance for our happiness. One can thus spend an entire lifetime seeking to pass these few days of our pilgrimage in the midst of honors, wealth, and self-satisfactions, without a thought of that which must be the cause of inestimable and unending riches, honor, prosperity, and satisfaction in our heavenly fatherland. Truly, that saying of the prophet applies to such men: "And they set at nought the desirable land."[1] Or if they did have regard for it, they would do as much to live happily in it as they do to live contentedly in the pilgrimage in which God has placed us all on the way to that land.

I will not pursue this thought further, as I hope in God our Lord that you will not be in the number of such pilgrims. And yet, so great is the misery of the old man that, if the new man who has been refreshed with the grace of Christ our Lord does not make use of the proper means, he will easily stoop to every kind of imperfection. And therefore, since I am so truly a servant of yours, I cannot omit reminding you to frequent the sacraments, to read some good spiritual books, to pray with as much recollection as possible. Set aside some time each day so that the soul will not be without its nourishment, and you be led to complain like him who said, "My heart is withered because I forgot to eat my bread."[2] In the same sense you will be much helped if you associate with good and spiritual persons, and continue, and even increase, your good practice of giving alms, which is a universal means of obtaining every blessing from Him who is the never-failing source from which every blessing flows.

If I have spoken at too great length for a first letter, put the blame on the deep devotion I have to your service in Christ our Lord. May it please Him to multiply each day most abundantly in your heart, and in the hearts of all of us, His spiritual graces. Amen.

POSTSCRIPT. I recall that you once manifested a desire to have some news of our Society. Having heard it mentioned occasionally, you wished to be better informed about it. To answer this request, and to render the service which charity requires, and to satisfy the interest which God has given you, I am sending herewith some information about our house here in Rome, our college, and the Germanico, so that you will understand matters more in detail and afterwards make use of what you judge proper. Knowing something of this house and this college here in Rome, you will understand the ordinary activity of other houses of Ours, at least the more important ones, in every part of Christendom and even among the heathen in India and Africa, where God our Lord is making use of the ministry of these lowly instruments of His. If you wish for further particulars, I will send them, or Ours in Louvain will do so, whom you may look upon as your devoted servants, just as we are in our Lord Jesus Christ.

---

[1] Psalm 105:24.   [2] Psalm 101:5.

¶ TO FATHER JAMES MIRON
vi, 564-66, Letter 4336

Ignatius praises the decree of John III, and proposes a way which he wishes suggested to the king of abolishing the practice of dueling.

Rome, April 5, 1554

Referring to other letters that are being sent along with this, I will only say here that I have learned that two brothers, Portugese, here in Rome were challenged to duels, and that each killed his challenger. I detest this perverse and diabolical practice among Christian men—even the infidels avoid it—of risking both body and soul out of a vain sense of honor. It is, therefore, with great joy and edification that I hear that his highness has made a ruling throughout his kingdom forbidding the giving of such a challenge under pain of losing both lands and life.

This indeed appears to be a good and holy law, but if I were ever in the presence of his highness, I would not fail to submit two other points for his consideration, which I think when taken together with the first will be a great help in carrying out his highness' purpose.

The first is that anyone who accepts a challenge is to be considered a traitor and branded with infamy, together with loss of property and life. This disease will thus be cured by its contrary, and a man who would accept a challenge to preserve his honor unsullied will now refuse such a challenge in order to avoid losing his honor completely.

The second is that his highness appoint four prominent men, or as many as he likes, who will have authority to settle disputes which arise involving wrongs or any kind of dishonor that give occasion for such challenges. These officials could examine the alleged wrongs or dishonor and apply the proper remedy in the name of his highness, who could then take upon himself the reputed dishonor. In this way peace could be restored to the satisfaction of both parties.

If God our Lord be pleased to bring about this great service by doing away with so impious an abuse and one so opposed to all reason, human and divine, that it can have no other author than the devil, it is quite possible that other Christian sovereigns will follow the example of his highness. For all must indeed look upon this practice as an evil thing, a disorder to the point of perversion, without any foundation, except in the erroneous opinion of worldly men, the majority of whom admit the tyranny of this accursed practice, subjection to which weighs heavily upon them. Thus, if it is publicly declared to be wrong, and those who submit to it are branded with infamy, it is quite possible, and indeed it would be a matter of only slight difficulty, to drive this tyranny of the devil from all Christian lands. Of the many achievements of his highness which history will recognize, this certainly will be one of the most outstanding.

The removal of this fear might make it easier for one to do wrong to another. To prevent this, as pointed out above, the aggressor must be punished with disgrace in the first place, and then in his person and property, as shall seem proper. If Christian princes will take the matter seriously in hand, it will be easy to introduce this principle into the thinking of men, seeing that it is so much more conformable to reason, not only for the Christian but for any man, than the contrary practice which was introduced by the devil.

As I cannot do so in person, I earnestly recommend that you bring this to the notice of his highness. May the sovereign and eternal wisdom communicate the clearness of His holy light, so that his highness may in all things perceive what will be to God's service and the universal good of souls. May He grant us all to know and fulfill His holy will.

¶ TO KING JOHN III
vi, 570-71, Letter 4340

Ignatius consoles the king on the death of his only son and heir, and rejoices at the birth of the prince Sebastian.

Rome, April 6, 1554

My Lord in our Lord.

May the sovereign grace and everlasting love of Christ our Lord greet and visit your highness with His most holy gifts and spiritual graces.

The great sorrow that all of us have felt in this loss[1]—not his whom God our Lord has taken to Himself, for he is much the gainer in this exchange of a temporal for an eternal kingdom, but ours, whom His infinite wisdom has seen fit to deprive of such a prince and lord—helps us to understand what must be the sorrow in the fatherly heart of your highness. And this in turn is a fresh and more than ordinary sorrow for us.

And yet, considering the great and royal soul and the special gifts with which God our Lord has enriched your highness, it seems as though He wishes to test them in this extraordinary visitation, and in your highness

---

[1] Polanco relates the pious death of Prince John and the bitter grief of his parents, even of all Portugal (*Chronicon*, IV, 543-44).

to give to the world a very salutary lesson in fortitude and conformity with the will of God. The report of this, your conformity, has elicited expressions of great admiration from those who hear of it, and provides an occasion of great praise for Him who is the never-ceasing and unfailing source of every blessing. In these clear effects God shows the great love and confidence He has in your highness' virtue, when He provides you with such striking opportunities of practicing it to His glory.

On the other hand, His most gentle providence has seen fit to bestow this gift, and to console us all with the birth of this new prince,[2] thus showing Himself, as He really is, the father of mercies and the God of all consolations. May He be blessed for ever, and may He deign to preserve this gift of His for His greater service and the good of all men. In our prayers and sacrifices we will frequently be mindful of him who is living, as well as of him also who is now with God in His glory. Your highness will understand, without our insisting on it, that this remembrance will be in keeping with the obligations of this least Society, which belongs entirely to your highness.

May the divine and supreme Goodness give us all His bountiful grace, so that we may always know His most holy will and perfectly fulfill it.

¶ TO FATHER FRANCIS DE ATTINO
VI, 585-87, Letter 4351

A letter full of affection and kindly interest. Ignatius bids Father Francis take care of his health.

Rome, April 7, 1554

My dear brother in Christ Jesus, Master Francis.

The grace and peace of Christ abide and grow in our souls.

You will have understood the answer to your letter in the event of your remaining at Naples. Our father desires every spiritual consolation for you. Because you would find that consolation among your brethren at Naples, he gave you permission to remain there if your health could stand it. But since the doctors thought that you should by all means seek your native air for a restoration, this advantage should be preferred to consolation. Be certain of this, my dear brother, that, although you are separated

---

[2] "On the Feast of St. Sebastian, the day on which Prince John died, Princess Joan gave birth to a son who was called Sebastian" (*Chronicon*, IV, 544).

from us in body, we feel that we are intimately united in the bond of charity, and that you return the feeling. But you must be sure of being united, not only by this bond but also by that of holy obedience, which binds all the members of our Society into one spiritual body, to which you will belong no matter where you are. Remember that it is through obedience that you are making use of all these remedies and cures and every form of reputable recreation, even physical, that is suggested to you. Because all the sooner, then, with God's help you will be freed from your illness to give yourself entirely to the service of God. And do not think that trying to recover your health is a slight occupation. Your only purpose in desiring it is to serve God, and according to His holy will. Even though you employ every reasonable means to get well, great resignation is required if you are to be content with whatever disposition God makes of you. As long as He visits you with illness, accept it from His hand as a very precious gift from the wisest and most affectionate of fathers and physicians. Be resolved especially both in mind and body, in work and in suffering, to be content with whatever pleases His divine providence. And write once in a while at least, even though it be but briefly.

Master Pompilius tells me that you have asked for some spiritual books. It would be all right for you to read from time to time or have someone read to you, for your soul's refreshment and consolation. But do not go in for much reading or for many devotions, especially those that are mental, as this would be to close the door on your recovery, which is the very reason for your going home and for the obedience that sent you. Be very moderate, therefore, in every mental exercise. Remember that bodily exercise, when it is well ordered, as I said, is also prayer by means of which you can give pleasure to God our Lord.

May His grace be ever abundant in your soul. We all earnestly commend ourselves to your charity.

¶ TO THE MARQUISE DE PRIEGO
VI, 709-12, Letter 4454

Ignatius tells the marquise he will see that Borgia visits Cordova.

Rome, May 15, 1554

My Lady in our Lord.

I received recently two letters from your ladyship dated July 9 and December 18, respectively, and with them not only a large measure of satisfaction because of the interest your ladyship shows in the founding of the college at Cordova, but a very special consolation when I see the spirit of complete conformity with God's will that is so evident in your letter, when God takes for Himself two such excellent sons, the one to live with Him entirely in heaven,[1] the other, to die from now on to the love and designs of earth. By dedicating himself exclusively to the glory and service of his Creator he will have no other occupation than to guide himself and many others to heaven.

This is a very singular favor which God has conferred on Father Anthony,[2] and all the greater as he has had greater occasion to direct his affections to the interests of earth, at least in a limited extent.[3] All this he has reversed for the present, to occupy himself with the things of heaven. It is not every mother who will appreciate such a favor done her sons. And God's grace must have been very active and deeply impressed on the soul of your ladyship to make you feel such a love of eternal blessings as to be consoled by the thought that Don Anthony had given the blessings of time in exchange for them. May it please Him who is the source of light and of all well-ordered love to increase in your ladyship what He has begun to communicate with such infinite and supreme liberality, and give you this true and Christian consolation of seeing all your children, each one in the state to which God calls them, employing themselves generously in His praise and service, marching always by the most direct path to the last and happy end which He has prepared for them.

As to the business of the union,[4] since it is in the hands of such intelligent persons as Andrew Vela and the licentiate Cassarubios, I feel that there is little need of any effort on our part, unless it be to beg God our Lord to reward, according to His infinite riches and liberality, the charity which He Himself has bestowed on your ladyship and Father Don Anthony, and which urges you to make this donation and give other assistance to advance this work in His divine service. I have told them, therefore, that, if we can be of assistance in anything, we shall not fail, at least in good will, although we do not usually meddle in such affairs as being too far removed from our way of life.

With regard to what your ladyship writes about bidding Father Francis[5] to go to Cordova and visit your ladyship and the countess of

---

[1] Catherine Fernandez de Cordova, to whom this letter was addressed, had several sons. The eldest, Peter Fernandez de Cordova, count of Feria, died in the flower of his age.
[2] Anthony de Cordova, already in holy orders, entered the Society.
[3] Charles V had made up his mind that Anthony should be raised to the purple.
[4] The reference is to ecclesiastical revenues held by Anthony.
[5] Francis Borgia.

Feria,⁶ I should have been very glad in our Lord to have notice of this, because earlier, at the request of the count and countess of Ribagorza,⁷ I promised that Father Francis would go to Saragossa on his return from Portugal. And so I wrote him some months ago to go there and make a short stay there. I think he must be there now, or on the way thither. However, I will suggest that, when he has finished with them and the city, he turn his attention to the work in Cordova and the service and consolation of your ladyship and the countess.

We have had word of the house which Señor Don John de Cordova gave for the college. May the Divine Goodness be pleased to build it in heaven, and give him a share of all the good that will accrue to God's glory and the good of souls. Certainly, not merely in Cordova but everywhere, such devotion, charity, and liberality as his have put the Society under great obligations to him in our Lord.

My deepest respects to my lady the countess.⁸ I heartily commend myself and all the Society to her prayers. As her example has been and continues to be so edifying to the world, I hope that her prayers will be very efficacious before God's throne. I also promise often to present your ladyship to His presence, and beg the divine mercy to preserve and increase the gifts which He has bestowed and bring them to their glorious consummation in His kingdom. May He give us all the bountiful grace ever to know His most holy will and perfectly to fulfill it.

¶ TO HENRY DE LA CUEVA
VII, 43-45, Letter 4485

Henry de la Cueva was the son of the noble and celebrated Spaniard, Bartholomew de la Cueva y Toledo, who was viceroy of the kingdom of Naples. He was created cardinal by Paul III on May 5, 1546 at the suggestion of Charles V. Henry, a doctor in civil and canon law and professor of the University of Salamanca, had asked admission to the Society. In this letter St. Ignatius admits him despite his poor health.

Rome, May 22, 1554

May the sovereign grace and everlasting love of Christ our Lord ever be our help and support.

---

⁶ Anna Ponce de Leon, wife of the deceased Peter Fernandez de Cordova.
⁷ Martin de Aragon y Gurrea, and Louise Borgia, sister of St. Francis Borgia (V, 367-69, 670).
⁸ The countess of Feria, bereaved widow of Peter Fernandez de Cordova.

A few days ago, after answering your letter, I again consulted the most reverend cardinal, our common father and lord,[1] concerning the matter of your vocation. We came to the same conclusion as before. He warmly approved the sacrifice of yourself which you have made to His Divine Majesty, and thinks it is very acceptable to our Lord. He takes into full consideration, not only the talents and spiritual gifts with which God has favored you but also the condition of your health and everything else which should be kept in mind. We believe in our Lord that in our Institute we can make good use for His service and glory of all that His divine goodness has bestowed upon you. Even if you have less strength and health than is needed for certain labors and vexations which some have to undergo and whose health and strength are equal to their good desires, you will not lack the means of giving good service to God our Lord. You will not lack even that relief which will be considered opportune, just as one who is living at home and away from a house of his order. For besides the fact that our Institute itself provides for work and a regime which are suited to the constitution of each of its members, we could not fail to take a very lively concern in all that touches you personnally.[2] And this because of the respect and sense of duty which the whole Society feels toward the most reverend lord, Cardinal de la Cueva, whom we regard as our father and lord, as I have already said, with a very special affection and devotion to his service and all his interests. You can be certain that God will not fail to provide all that He deems necessary who by His most benign providence governs and gives daily growth to this new plant which He has been pleased to place among the others in the garden of His Church.

I have written regarding everything else, and will write again to Master Nadal, to take thought about the most suitable time and manner of taking leave of the engagements that have delayed you for some time. It may be that you have already done so. In this way we can be conformed to our Institute, not only interiorly but also in externals. For this reason I will accommodate myself in the manner of writing which prevails among us.[3]

In the meantime I earnestly commend myself to your prayers, and I ask God our Lord to grant us all abundant grace to know His most holy will and perfectly to fulfill it.

---

[1] Bartholomew de la Cueva, Henry's father.
[2] Henry was a member of the Inquisition at Cuenca.
[3] This remark may contain a delicately veiled admonition. The cardinal, Henry's father, had complained of the lack of due deference in Don Henry's letters to himself.

¶ TO FATHER BARTHOLOMEW HERNANDEZ

VII, 268-70, Letter 4619

A letter known to have been sent from Salamanca is still undelivered. Concerning a certain document and permission for lacticinia. *Scholastics of the Society not yet in holy orders may be allowed to preach when told to do so. On the ordination of Francis de Valencia. On scholastics conversing with students of the university. It is not strange if heavenly consolations are fewer during the years of study. The study of letters undertaken with a pure and upright intention is the best of devotions; but this devotion is not to be sought too anxiously, provided the solid virtues are practiced.*

Rome, July 21, 1554

The peace of Christ.

As far as I know we have no letters from Salamanca for the year 1554 other than that of January 15, which was accompanied by others dated December 1.

There was a copy of the faculty which the most reverend cardinal of Burgos[1] had asked for. It has been sent to him at the court of his majesty, where he now is.

By this time you have received the faculty for granting degrees, and also that for eggs [?][2] and such things. If anything else is needed, we think it can be easily obtained from the nuncio.

The scholastics of the Society may, with the permission of superiors, preach and teach catechism, and so forth, as you can see in the brief of Pope Paul III, even if they are not in holy orders. It is done here in Rome, and in Italy and Sicily, and even beyond. . . .

We had a letter from Father John Juarez, but as it bears no date, we do not know whether it is recent or old. What seems to stand out as pertinent is that Master Nadal has been in Salamanca, and that Fathers Gonzalez and Avila have been withdrawn from that college to begin another. And so of several other brothers, whose places have been taken by newcomers. May it please God our Lord to make use of them everywhere.

You are quite right that, since spiritual conversation cannot extend to all, it should be had especially with the students of the university, for the profit will be not only in them, but through them in many others, the

---

[1] Francis de Mendoza.
[2] Even the editors of the *Monumenta* put a question mark after this word. It seems that there was some question of a permission to use *lacticinia* (eggs and milk) in the diet.

similarity of their occupations making it possible to pass on to others what they receive to God's glory.

It is not surprising that all the scholastics do not experience that relish for devotion which is desirable, for He who dispenses this grace does so when and where He thinks fit. During the time of studies, which require no little spiritual effort, it is to be thought that the Divine Wisdom suspends such sensible visitations. For, although the mind can take great delight in them, they sometimes have a weakening effect beyond measure on the body. Besides, the occupation of the understanding with scholastic pursuits usually brings on a certain interior dryness. But when the study is directed purely to God's service, there is very much devotion. Finally, if one does nothing to endanger the solid virtues and gives the time to prayer required by the Constitutions, with few or many consolations, he should in no way be disturbed, but accept from God's hand what He disposes in the matter, always making more account of what is really important; that is, patience, humility, obedience, charity, and other virtues.

I will add no more, except earnestly to commend ourselves to the prayers of your reverence and all with you in that college.

May Jesus Christ be present in our souls with an abundance of His spiritual gifts. Amen.

¶ TO FATHER JOHN NUNEZ BARRETO
VII, 313-14, Letter 4645

Ignatius encourages Father Barreto to undertake the Ethiopian mission and to bear the burden of obedience which the sovereign pontiff lays on him. Ignatius reminds him that he should not depend upon his own resources since his sufficiency will come from God. God will not neglect him in so important a task. He adds a word about the companions of the mission and certain documents which are necessary for the due discharge of his office. He hopes that the Holy Spirit will help him to make progress in this mission.

Rome, July 26, 1554

I received your letter of April 6 written in duplicate.[1] In what concerns affairs in Africa, where for some years you have been active in the interests of the captives, we have all much reason to give thanks to God

---

[1] *Epistolae mixtae*, IV, 134.

our Lord for having in so many ways deigned to make use of your person and services, thus preparing you to be deserving of greater labors still, and to be of more extended help to souls. Do not be afraid of the magnitude of the undertaking as compared with your slender resources, since all of our sufficiency must come from Him who calls us to this work. It is He who must give you all that is required for His service. It was because of no desire of yours that He gave you this burden, for which no shoulders without the help of God's hand are sufficiently strong or able to bear the weight or find the way to the goal. Therefore the greater your distrust of self, the greater should be your confidence in Him who through His vicar bids you assume this undertaking. I hope that in the divine and supreme Goodness it will result in a very notable spiritual gain for all those regions by bringing them back to the true and genuine worship of God our Lord. If any scruple should assail you, get rid of it, whether it concerns me, whose judgment you follow, or even the supreme pontiff, at whose command, speaking in the place of Christ our Lord, you accept the responsibility which has been given you.

Regarding the persons in Portugal whom you designate, no action can easily be taken here. Hence, when the eight arrive in Portugal who are being sent from here and Castile, as many as twelve can be chosen in Portugal, as they shall think best there, and God our Lord in all details will direct this His work.

I hope that the Holy Spirit will give you the instruction you ask for making progress in God's service on this mission, and give it in full measure together with His holy unction and the gift of prudence as circumstances require. If there are any memoranda or information on those provinces to be had here, they will be sent to you, and we shall try to settle any doubts you have if you will let us know about them.[2]

I commend myself to your prayers and sacrifices, and I beg our Lord to grant us all the grace to know and perfectly fulfill His most holy will.

¶ TO FERDINAND VASCONCELHOS
VII, 327-28, Letter 4654

Ignatius reminds Vasconcelhos, then the archbishop of Lisbon, that the Jesuits everywhere have been instructed to consider their bishop

---

[2] Nunez wrote Ignatius on September 11, 1554, accepting the burden placed on his shoulders, relying on God's goodness and the strength he found in obedience.

as their father and lord. Not satisfied, therefore, with the fathers of Lisbon fulfilling their duty, the saint wishes personally to offer the archbishop the cooperation of the Society in whatever work he may be pleased to employ it.

Rome, July 26, 1554

My most reverend Lord in our Lord.

It is not only conformable to our Institute, but highly recommended in the Constitutions,[1] that the members of this least Society, wherever they may be living, should have recourse to their bishop, recognize him as their father and lord, and, as far as their weakness and profession allow, offer their services to help in the care of souls with which he is charged. In view of this it has seemed quite proper to me not only to recommend that those of Ours who have charge of the house and college in your city do their duty in this respect, but even to do so myself from Rome here in the name of the whole Society. I accordingly beg your most reverend lordship to accept us all both in Lisbon and in Rome. Look upon us as your sons and servants in our Lord and remember that you have in the members of our Society in your archbishopric of Lisbon so many other faithful and obedient ministers who will, conformably to their profession and their ability, carry a small part of the burden which God our Lord has placed on the shoulders of your most reverend lordship and which must be shared with others to enable you to carry it. It will be a very deep consolation to me, both because of the quality of the burden and of the great personal worth of your most reverend lordship, if you will look upon us all as belonging to you, and take under your special protection Ours of Lisbon, and give them the faculties which you perceive them to need for the help of souls under your care.

This will be all, except humbly to ask your most reverend lordship's blessing and prayers. May God our Lord deign to give us all His abundant grace ever to know and fulfill His most holy will.

¶ TO FATHER PETER CANISIUS

XII, 259-62, Appendix I, Letter 27

In this letter Ignatius shows Father Canisius the steps that should be taken by the Society in the interests of the Catholic faith in order to

---

[1] *Constitutiones,* Pars X, n. 11, B.

overcome the effects of heresy, especially in upper and lower Germany, and in France. A summary of theology or short catechism should be prepared and taught to all the children, university students, and adults. Pamphlets should also be written and circulated among the people.

Rome, August 13, 1554

JHS

Seeing the progress which the heretics have made in a short time, spreading the poison of their evil teaching throughout so many countries and peoples, and making use of the verse of the Apostle to describe their progress, "And their speech spreadeth like a canker,"[1] it would seem that our Society, having been accepted by Divine Providence among the efficacious means to repair such great damage, should be solicitous to prepare the proper steps, such as are quickly applied and can be widely adopted, thus exerting itself to the utmost of its powers to preserve what is still sound and to restore what has fallen sick of the plague of heresy, especially in the northern nations.

The heretics have made their false theology popular and presented it in a way that is within the capacity of the common people. They preach it to the people and teach it in the schools, and scatter booklets which can be bought and understood by many, and make their influence felt by means of their writings when they cannot do so by their preaching. Their success is largely due to the negligence of those who should have shown some interest; and the bad example and the ignorance of Catholics, especially the clergy, have made such ravages in the vineyard of the Lord. Hence it would seem that our Society should make use of the following means to put a stop and apply a remedy to the evils which have come upon the Church through these heretics.

In the first place, the sound theology which is taught in the universities and seeks its foundation in philosophy, and therefore requires a long time to acquire is adapted only to good and alert minds; and because the weaker ones can be confused and, if they lack foundations, collapse, it would be good to make a summary of theology to deal with topics that are important but not controversial, with great brevity. There could be more detail in matters controversial, but it should be accommodated to the present needs of the people. It should solidly prove dogmas with good arguments from Scripture, tradition, the councils, and the doctors, and refute the contrary teaching. It would not require much time to teach such a theology, since it would not go very deeply into other matters. In

[1] 2 Timothy 2:17.

this way theologians could be produced in a short time who could take care of the preaching and teaching in many places. The abler students could be given higher courses which include greater detail. Those who do not succeed in these higher courses should be removed from them and put in this shorter course of theology.

The principal conclusion of this theology, in the form of a short catechism, could be taught to children, as the Christian doctrine is now taught, and likewise to the common people who are not too infected or too capable of subtleties. This could also be done with the younger students in the lower classes, where they could learn it by heart.

For those in the higher classes, such as the first and perhaps the second, and those in philosophy and theology, at an hour of the day when they are not at lectures it would be good to teach them the summary of theology, as mentioned above, so that all of those who have some aptitude will learn the *loci communes,* and will be able to preach and teach Catholic doctrine and refute the contrary, at least enough to satisfy the needs of the people. This would seem to be especially the case in the colleges of upper and lower Germany and in France, and even elsewhere, where there is the same need. As to those who have no talents for serious study, or whose age will not permit it, it will be enough if, besides the study of languages, they attend the classes of this summarized theology and the cases of conscience. They will thus become good and useful workers for the common good.

The native priests and the foreign students of the higher division and any others so wishing could be admitted to these theological classes. By means of them it would not be long before an antidote had been provided in many places against the poison of heresy. Hearing the lectures with the book in their hands, they will be able to preach to the people and teach in the schools what the Catholic doctrine demands.

Another excellent means for helping the Church in this trial would be to multiply the colleges and schools of the Society in many lands, especially where a good attendance could be expected. There might possibly be need of a dispensation to accept colleges with a smaller number of students than our Institute demands, or else that classes be accepted without undertaking perpetual charge of a college, if there is among Ours, or elsewhere, someone to teach the said theology to the students and preach sound doctrine to the people, which with the administration of the sacraments will promote their spiritual welfare.

Not only in the places where we have a residence, but even in the neighborhood, the better among our students could be sent to teach the

Christian doctrine on Sundays and feast days. Even the extern students, should there be suitable material among them, could be sent by the rector for the same service. Thus, besides the correct doctrine, they would be giving the example of a good life, and by removing every appearance of greed they will be able to refute the strongest argument of the heretics—a bad life, namely, and the ignorance of the Catholic clergy.

The heretics write a large number of booklets and pamphlets, by means of which they aim at taking away all authority from the Catholics, and especially from the Society, and set up their false dogmas. It would seem expedient, therefore, that Ours here also write answers in pamphlet form, short and well written, so that they can be produced without delay and bought by many. In this way the harm that is being done by the pamphlets of the heretics can be remedied and sound teaching spread. These works should be modest, but lively; they should point out the evil that is abroad and uncover the evil machinations and deceits of the adversaries. A large number of these pamphlets could be gathered into one volume. Care should be taken, however, that this be done by learned men well grounded in theology, who will adapt it to the capacity of the multitude.

With these measures it would seem that we could bring great relief to the Church, and in many places quickly apply a remedy to the beginnings of the evil before the poison has gone so deep that it will be very difficult to remove it from the heart. But we should use the same diligence in healing that the heretics are using in infecting the people. We will have the advantage over them in that we possess a solidly founded, and therefore an enduring, doctrine. The most gifted will be able to take up a course of study in the Roman College and in other colleges of upper and lower Germany, as also in France. Later, when they are sent to different places where Ours are in residence, they will be the directors and instructors of others.

¶ TO THE WIDOW OF JOHN BOQUET
VII, 409-11, Letter 4713

Ignatius consoles her on the death of her husband.

Rome, August 16, 1554

IHS

May the grace and everlasting love of Christ our Lord ever be our help and support. Amen.

Among the many proofs of the lively faith and hope which we have in life everlasting, one of the surest is not to be saddened overmuch at the death of those whom we dearly love in our Lord. They who think that death ends everything may be allowed to indulge this sadness, for according to their erroneous thinking death is the greatest of miseries. But it can never be allowed to those who say with Ecclesiasticus that death is better than life.[1] For they know that it is a brief passage from present toils and miseries to the repose and glory of life eternal, especially for those who live and die like Christians. It was of such that God bade St. John write, "Blessed are the dead who die in the Lord."[2] Thus we see that, if we should not bewail the happiness of those we love, we should not mourn their dying, which is the beginning of, or at least the certain way to, that bliss.

I say this, my dear lady, because if the death of our dearest friend in Christ Jesus, John Boquet,[3] were a misfortune, I could not help feeling a deep sorrow over it, as over one whom I dearly loved in Christ our Lord. But hoping in the mercy of Him who created and redeemed him with His precious blood and allowed him to be helped in his dying moments with His holy sacraments, which are so necessary for eternal life, hoping, I say, that he will have a place among His elect, I feel no pain, but rather joy in our Lord, who by His dying has taken away the fear of death, and by rising and ascending into heaven has shown us what and where the true life is, to which one passes through death, in the sharing of His glorious kingdom. For this reason I can find no cause for grief if I think only of him.

Nor could we find such cause for grief with regard to yourself if we were able to recognize God's providence and love for us, and to trust the arrangements concerning us which are made by the providence of so loving and so kindly a Father and lover of our higher good. We should be strengthened by the belief that in prosperity and in adversity, in life and death, He seeks and provides what is for our greater perfection.

Hence it will be a help frequently to raise on high the love which is inclined to the things of earth, and clear the path of our earthly loves, so that with greater liberty we may return all our love to His infinite goodness and His heavenly gifts. For the fewer occasions that we have of dis-

---

[1] "Better is death than a bitter life" (Ecclesiasticus 30:17).
[2] Apocalypse 14:13.
[3] "One of these first friends and benefactors was Master John Boquet, a member of his majesty's council in that province, in whose house many spiritual conferences and exhortations were given by Ours" (Alvarez, *Historia ms. de la Provincia de Aragon de la Compania de Jesus*, lib. II, c. 2).

sipating our love on creatures, the more completely we can center it on our Creator and Lord.

Not to draw this letter out unduly, I will only say that for our part we beseech the Divine Goodness to grant a peaceful repose in His glory to Señor John Boquet, and at the same time console you by taking his place in your heart and the place of all things, and multiply in you and your family His very special gifts and graces. May it please His Majesty to make us daily grow in these graces and gifts in the way of His greater service, praise, and glory. Amen.

The bearer[4] of this letter, who is a father and a very dear friend in our Lord, will give you two Agnus Deis which I am sending you with him. He will be able to tell you about the graces attached to them.

¶ TO FATHER FRANCIS BORGIA
VII, 422-23, Letter 4721

A destructive fire had laid waste the famous sanctuary of Our Lady of Aranzazu, which was held in great veneration throughout Guipuzcoa. It was here that St. Ignatius himself had spent a night in prayer shortly after his conversion. A number of persons had written to him to obtain a jubilee of several years from the sovereign pontiff in order to help defray the expenses of the restoration.

In his answer St. Ignatius recalls his great debt to that venerated image, and goes on to allege the impossibility of obtaining this jubilee directly because of his poor health and of the difficulty in obtaining such a favor from the reigning pontiff, Julius III.

Rome, August 20, 1554

I received your letter of June 25 together with several others. The father minister provincial of Cantabria,[1] the Council of Oñate and Azpeitia,[2] Don John, and our brother Dr. Araoz also wrote.[3] The sum and substance of all the letters was that I try to obtain a jubilee of several years for the bishoprics of Pamplona and Calahorra to help in the rebuilding of Our Lady of Aranzazu. Indeed, the fire was a great pity and misfortune, especially for those of us who are acquainted with the devotion

---

[4] Very likely Dimas Camps, archdeacon of Barcelona.
[1] Father Francis de Castillo, O.F.M.
[2] The letters appear in *Epistolae mixtae*, IV, 30.
[3] John Borgia and Father Anthony Araoz. See *Epistolae mixtae*, IV, 239.

which flourished there and the great service rendered to God our Lord. Whatever measures are necessary for the restoration of the monastery should be undertaken with much devotion. I may say that I have a particular and personal reason for desiring it. When God our Lord granted me the grace to make some change in my life, I remember having received some benefit for my soul while watching one night in that church.

But you must know, my dear brother, that for the past two months I have scarcely spent four of the twenty-four hours in the day out of my bed, because of illness, God be praised. Besides, this matter of a jubilee is obtained from the present pontiff only with much difficulty. I think the best way of getting this jubilee would be to have the princess[4] write to his holiness and to the cardinal protector of the Franciscans, Cardinal Carpi, and to me also, if you think it well. Then, together with the cardinal protector, or with his holiness if I can muster sufficient strength, I might be able to do something in the matter. I think it will be easy to get these letters written in Spain through yourself or Dr. Araoz, or whomsoever you might suggest. Since the delay will be brief and there is no hurry, I would be of the opinion that the matter could be conducted in this way. A summary of what I have said, or this letter if that seems good to you, might be shown to those who have written to me on the matter, to whom I should like to reply with works rather than a mere letter.

As this is all I wished to say, I will close, commending myself earnestly to your prayers and asking our Lord to deign to give us His abundant grace always to know His most holy will and entirely to fulfill it. Entirely yours in our Lord . . .

¶ TO MICHAEL DE NOBREGA
vii, 446-48, Letter 4735

Nobrega was taken captive by the pirates, and Ignatius here attempts to console him. It is cold comfort, as he offers him only a slim hope of being redeemed. He is too poor to pay the price demanded.

Rome, August 25, 1554

IHUS

May the peace of Christ and His grace be ever present and grow in our souls.

---

[4] Joan of Austria, daughter of Charles V and regent of Spain.

Our father has received three letters from you, sent from Cairo, and learns from them the fact of your capture, and the capture of the Portuguese and other Christians who were taken prisoner with you. May God our Creator and Lord be blessed; and as He deigns to give you the grace to suffer in His service, may He likewise deign to give you all the patience and fortitude He sees to be necessary to enable you to bear so heavy a cross with gratitude. Recognize that the Divine Goodness sends with equal charity and love fatigues, trials, tribulations, and adversities, with which He is also wont to send repose, contentment, joy, and a sense of all prosperity. As a most wise physician He knows, and as a most devoted father desires, all that is best for the healing of the diseases of our souls, hidden and manifest. He provides what is best for them, although it may not be the most pleasing to us. While we make use of that diligence which, according to right reason, we should use for the alleviation or cure of the temporal evils which the hand of God sends or permits, once we have taken such steps, we ought surely to be glad of the participation in His cross which Christ our Lord shares with us. We should remember that it is not only better to be cleansed of our sins in this life than in the next, but that we can even merit an eternal reward by the short trials of this life. And not any common reward, but one of great excellence, according to the words of the Apostle: "Which is at present momentary and light of our tribulation . . ."[1] We know from many of the saints that God our Lord has brought them by this way of captivity to the liberty and bliss of His kingdom. Therefore, dearest brother, find your strength in Him who has created and redeemed you by His bloody death, and put your trust in His most kind providence, which in some way will either draw you out of this captivity, or at least make it very fruitful, no less so than liberty, for the end we have in view, which is the divine glory and service and with it our salvation and everlasting happiness.

Speaking of human means, you know that the houses of the Society are so poor that they neither have nor may have revenues or any possessions at all. We can help you with our prayers, and whenever anyone offers to give something for the redemption of captives, we could try to get some alms to redeem your reverence and the other Portuguese who share your captivity.

In fact, one of our brothers who was summoned from Spain to Rome fell into the hands of the Turks, and was put to rowing in the galleys, although he was a priest and theologian, and a very good servant of God.

---

[1] 2 Corinthians 4:17.

Because of the difficulty in finding funds we have not been able to effect his release. But God is great, and in one way or another will come to the aid of His own.

May it please Him to preserve you in the purity and firmness of your Catholic faith, and give you all the courage you need to be able to profit from these trials.

¶ TO FATHER JOHN FRANCIS ARALDO
VII, 528, Letter 4788

Araldo is called to time for having overstepped the limits of obedience in a burst of fervor. If Salmeron has forbidden certain ladies[1] to approach the sacraments in our church, he must have had a very serious reason for doing so. There must be no grounds for suspicion.

Rome, September 16, 1554

My dear Father in Christ, Master John Francis.

I have read your letter to Master Andrew,[2] and feel convinced that your good will and fervent desire to serve God have prompted you to write as you have. It is clear, however, that you have gone beyond the limits of holy obedience and her mother, humility, in thus manifesting an opinion that differs from and is even opposed to that of Father Master Salmeron, whose mind you wish to change as though he had made a mistake. And yet, if you remember that he is superior with the light of learning and prudence and experience that are his, to say nothing of the special help and light he receives from God our Lord to direct him in his duty as head of the college, you would see that it is easier for your judgment to be wrong than his, and that you ought to be more willing to submit your judgment to his than to set aside his for yours. For myself, I believe that Father Salmeron would not have forbidden these ladies to receive the sacraments in your church except for grave reasons. While he

---

[1] In 1554 some pious women of Naples organized a kind of lay convent, some supervision of which was committed to Father John Francis Araldo, a good man, who had, however, more zeal than prudence. Against the wishes of Salmeron these good ladies took possession of a house opposite the college of the Jesuits and in full view of their windows. The superior, Father Salmeron, then gave orders that they were not to be admitted to the sacraments in our church. He wished to forestall gossip and other difficulties which he had reason to fear, since the neighborhood was not friendly. It was this incident which gave rise to the complaints and intervention of good Father Araldo, to whom St. Ignatius through his secretary sent this answer.

[2] The Master Andrew mentioned is Father Andrew Frusius.

does not write me so, I fancy that the proximity of their house to the college could give rise to some suspicion. There might, of course, be a different reason known to him who has a more general view of the situation than has he who looks at it from a single point of view. It is because of the special love I bear your reverence that I wish to bring this to your attention.

I commend myself to the prayers and sacrifices of your charity.

¶ TO FATHER PHILIP LEERNO
VII, 558-59, Letter 4809

This letter answers a question proposed by Father Leerno concerning the best way to serve God through giving up one's possessions.

Rome, September 22, 1554

IHUS

The peace of Christ.

Concerning the two persons, husband and wife, who are rich but childless and desire to serve God in quiet of soul, the husband wishing to dispose of his property, while the wife wishes to keep it and leave it after her death for the repose of her soul, I will suggest two things. The first is that each could without sin follow his or her purpose, as they think best. The second is that the husband's plan seems the more spiritual, especially if he is a man who can and does find better use for his time than piling up possessions, and proposes after his death, or even before, to give away his possessions for his soul's benefit and God's service. I will add still a third suggestion. You could profitably advise both of them, whether they sell their property and buy bank stocks, or keep it, to make Him their heir who has given them all they have. This they could do in any pious work, which they could adopt as though it were a son, or make it their heir, as in the time of Pope Liberius did John the Roman patrician and his wife. Since both husband and wife are good and spiritual persons, they ought to realize that God has taken their son to give him the eternal possession of His kingdom thus opportunely, so that they, his parents, could, without any solicitude for him, employ the good inspirations and inclination given by God and their wealth in pious works in His service, and thus raise their thoughts and aspirations to things that are concerned with the greater glory of Christ our Lord and the universal good of their country.

For light to know to what pious work and in what manner they ought to employ their means, they should earnestly commend themselves to God our Lord, and make an election worthy of spiritual persons. May Jesus Christ be their guide and enlighten them to know always His holy will and ever fulfill it.

¶ TO JOHN DE MENDOZA
VII, 654-55, Letter 4870

Ignatius says a word in favor of Asconius Colonna, who was imprisoned in Castel Nuovo by order of Charles V. Mendoza was in charge of the castle. He had already made up his mind to enter the Society.

Rome, October 14, 1554

IHS

My Lord in our Lord.

May the sovereign grace and everlasting love of Christ our Lord greet and visit you with His most holy gifts and spiritual graces.

It is many days since I learned of the gifts of God our Lord in the soul of your honor and of the desires He gives you of greatly serving Him, notwithstanding your noble rank and honorable office, which ordinarily provides men with excuses for declining such a call. And although I feel a special affection in His Divine Majesty for the service of your honor and entertain the desire of knowing you and conversing with you personally or by letter, I have not done so up to this. But now it is charity that provides me with an occasion.

I have learned that Don Asconius Colonna is confined in your castle. God has visited him with trials in his old age, as He usually does with those He loves and whom He wishes to dispose all the more to desire their heavenly and eternal country, as they are disappointed in the pilgrimage of this earthly life. I am quite certain of your refinement and nobility of soul, and that as far as you can, without failing in your duty, you have shown and will continue to show his excellency every consideration. And yet I cannot but beg you very earnestly, trusting that you will not object to my doing so, to deal gently with one with whom I have dealt personally on spiritual matters and whom I hold in great affection in our Lord. As I think it is quite proper for me to speak out, I will not omit to tell you that once, when speaking familiarly with Señor Asconius, I heard him say that there were not wanting some who urged him to sympathize with the French, but that he would never do what the prince of Salerno had done; that his family had ever been on the side of the Empire, and that he would be also as long as he lived. I heard this from his own lips.

There is no reason for my going further in this matter, nor, for all that, in any other, except to offer myself to serve you to God's glory. May He in His divine and supreme goodness bring to perfection the gifts of His grace, and bestow it upon us all in abundant measure, so that we may know His most holy will and perfectly fulfill it.

¶ TO HERCULES PURINO
VII, 730-32, Letter 4921

Ignatius consoles him on the death of his only son. Purino was a pious man and a supporter of the College of Mutina.

Rome, November 3, 1554

JHUS

My illustrious Lord in our Lord.

May the supreme grace and everlasting love of Christ our Lord ever be our help and support.

Having yet to answer your lordship's letter of the nineteenth of last month, I received a second which our brother Don Laurence brought me yesterday, and will in this answer both briefly, since in God's goodness the time allowed me by my ailments is so short.

Before your lordship wrote I had learned of the sickness of your little son, and that he had passed from this temporal life to life eternal. Charity lays an obligation upon me because of the spiritual friendship between us, and I have endeavored to help you with the prayers of this community and by repeatedly offering for him to the eternal Father the sacrifice of His Son Jesus Christ our Lord in the holy Mass. Although I could not fail to share the sorrow of your lordship and your spouse because of the separation from this only son, owing to the love in our Lord which I bear you both, I feel myself impelled on the other hand, seeing that this is the will of a most wise God and loving Father, to give Him thanks, and to convince myself beyond the possibility of any doubt that this was best, not only for the son, but for the father and the mother as well. For the son to be free of the toils and perils of this world and of the many snares that could cause him to fall into everlasting misery, to be admitted so early to enjoy, not the private inheritance of his earthly patrimony but that realm of bliss where he shall be forever blessed, is for him a manifest advantage. If your lordships remember that we have not here a lasting city, but seek one that is to come in God's glory, the heavenly Jerusalem, which He shares with His faithful servants and which is our true fatherland, it is not so much a misfortune to be deprived of temporal consolation as a blessing to have the occasion of lifting your hearts and affections to the things of heaven where he is, who, had he remained on earth, might have been able to draw them down to earth. It is certain, as St. Gregory teaches, that, as the weakness of our human nature tends to the things of earth, so it needs to be drawn on high with the hope of things eternal, and impelled from below also by the trials and afflictions of earth, which help it to rid itself of the things of this life and rise to desire and make its way to the other life. Therefore I hope that in the divine mercy and the sweet disposition of His providence your lordships will change this affliction into an occasion for the greatest blessing for the both of you, and likewise of consolation in this world, if you exert yourself, once having understood the will of God, to give yourselves entirely to love Him and serve Him. To this end you could adopt in place of your son some work of charity in which his name could be forever glorified. You will thus have Christ our Lord, in His poor, for heir. . . .

I will say no more here except to beg God's sovereign goodness to deign to take possession of the hearts of both of you, and to inspire you always to greater personal perfection to His greater service and glory. . . .

May the Eternal Wisdom grant us all daily greater light always to know His most holy will and perfectly to fulfill it.

¶ TO FATHER CHRISTOPHER DE MENDOZA

VIII, 58-59, Letter 4959

Ignatius writes concerning some books that Mendoza had asked for. In a postscript Mendoza is seriously taken to task.

Rome, November 17, 1554

IHUS

The peace of Christ.

I see from your letter that your reverence is very anxious about taking some books to the house in Goletta, should it be God's will that you go there.[1] I suppose there is no doubt that they have need of some, but you can set your mind at rest, as I shall have to deal with Cardinal de la Cueva and see that the books which are necessary or useful are provided at his expense or at that of the one who is asking your reverence for them. If they fail you, we shall not fail you here in whatever is necessary. Nor will we wait for this until we are rich, as you say; for in our poverty we will do as much as we would do in abundance. I want your reverence to know, however, that this abundance is not as great as you seem to think. For that money, together with the money that has come to the college from Genoa, is more than five thousand ducats of debt, the house here carries more than six hundred, and added to this are the building operations of the church which have just started. In addition we have over 140 mouths to feed, and just about the sum in question is needed for bread and wine alone. I do not like to wail over these woes, but your reverence has given me the occasion. We should rather look upon them as gifts and visitations of God. As they are the effects of our holy mother poverty, they should not seem to us to be in bad taste.

But enough of this. About everything else, write to Father Master Salmeron. I commend myself especially to your reverence's prayers.

POSTSCRIPT. Dear father, I have been wondering whether I should return your reverence's letter for your further consideration, so that in the future you should take care not to let your pen run on, setting down things which you would regret having written if once you reflected over them.

I must call your reverence's attention to another point, as one really devoted to you in our Lord, as you know I am. In your manner of speaking try not to take such a personal satisfaction for having helped with your property, and so on. It has the appearance of giving one to understand that you are to have greater privileges for having done so. It is all right for us to know that, and let us speak of it to Ours, and keep a proper account of it. But do not let it appear that your reverence, *quasi iure suo,* wishes to be more esteemed on that account. Such conduct would betray petty qualities of soul in one who makes much ado about what he ought to look upon as nothing, compared with what he would like to do, and compared with his debt to God for whom he gives it. This advice is worth more to your reverence than ten *scudi,* a sum which I would look upon as very trifling were I to use it in doing you a service.

That is all for the present.

---

[1] Goletta was a small town and military post in Africa.

¶ TO ASCONIUS COLONNA
VIII, 159-60, Letter 5024

Ignatius sends a letter of sympathy to Asconius Colonna, the duke of Palliani and Tagliacozzi, and constable of the Kingdom of Naples. Although the letter does not state definitely the reasons for Asconius' unhappiness, a letter one month earlier referred to his imprisonment in Castel Nuovo by Charles V. The document referred to in the present letter may be a request for his release. Ignatius consoles Colonna with the hope of future blessings and the favor of Divine Providence.

Rome, December 8, 1554

IHS

Illustrious Sir in our Lord.

May the sovereign grace and everlasting love of Christ our Lord greet and visit your excellency with His most holy gifts and spiritual graces.

Your excellency's letter of October 26 has remained unanswered because of my almost continuous infirmity. But I have often answered it by remembering your excellency in the presence of Christ our Lord. I have begged His divine and supreme Goodness to have your excellency's person and your interests under His protection, and that all these trials (His ordinary way of dealing with those He loves) may cooperate to the great spiritual good and progress of your excellency. I have no doubt that your truly Christian soul will see in them only so many occasions of shaking free of all love and affection for earth and that, united with Him, you will turn all the more fervently to the things of heaven. In adhering to the Creator your love of our supreme and eternal good will grow all the more in purity and selflessness, as experience shows you more clearly how ill placed is that love which is squandered on the weak and fleeting good of things created.

The copy of the document in which the duke of Termoli gives his witness, and which was sent to me by your excellency, had not yet been read by Doimo Nascio. At the moment and since I have had occasion to give warm thanks to God our Lord. May it please His sweet providence to make the truth known in due time, as far as it will be expedient for His glory. I am sure that your excellency holds the glory of God above every other desire.

This will be all for the present, except humbly to commend myself and this community to your excellency. I beg that the supreme and divine mercy will grant us all abundant grace always to know His most holy will and perfectly to fulfill it.

¶ TO VIOLANTE CASALI GOZZADINA
VIII, 183-84, Letter 5041

Ignatius consoles her on the death of her son Camillus.

Rome, December 22, 1554

IHS

Very illustrious Lady in our Lord.

May the grace and love of Christ greet and visit your ladyship.

When we heard of the sickness of your son, Master Camillus, of happy memory, and shortly afterwards of his passing from this temporal life to life eternal, in each instance all the members of this house and college had recourse to Christ our God and Savior in their Masses and prayers to intercede for him. We were moved, not only by the charity which makes us debtors to all but by that special affection which binds us by so many kindnesses to the heart of your ladyship, who have been so kindly disposed to us now for so long a time. I hope in Him who is our true health and everlasting life that, since He has not heard our prayer and granted him this present life, which is subject to so many toils and perils and to death in the end, He will all the more promptly bestow that life which is unending and supremely secure and happy and for which He has created and redeemed us at the price of His blood, and to which all the desires for our own good and the good of our neighbor should be directed. I hope also that the same Father of mercy and God of all consolation, who in such a visitation as this shows how much He loves your ladyship and how confidently He deals with you as a strong daughter and true servant, will have granted you all the light necessary clearly to understand how great a favor His divine and sovereign Goodness does to one whom in faith, hope, and charity, helped by His holy sacraments, He withdraws from the unhappiness of earth and transports to the bliss of heaven; and that likewise He shall have given to your ladyship such conformity of will with the divine will that you will not be so much afflicted by the privation of the human consolation which the presence of your son would have afforded you, but even rejoice that he has anticipated you in that happy state where he is established in our most happy fatherland, where we all hope to arrive and rejoice together forever in the presence of our supreme and infinite good. May He be pleased to make the heart of your ladyship more perfectly His own each day, and keep it united with His, and all the more firmly directly to Himself and His holy kingdom as you have less occasion to be satisfied with anything less than Him.

I will not say more, or make any fresh offering of myself to your ladyship, as you know that for a long time we have been entirely yours in our Lord. May He be pleased to grant us to know His most holy will and perfectly fulfill it.

¶ TO FATHER ANTHONY ARAOZ
VIII, 225, Letter 5061

A few lines full of affection which St. Ignatius wrote to Araoz on the occasion of sending him the report which he had received from certain fathers concerning Araoz. Araoz must recognize the spirit of love with which these fathers wrote and behave with the spirit of meekness and charity. The letter does not describe the behavior for which Araoz is being reprimanded. At about this time, however, he was told he must not be so eager to meddle in worldly affairs.

Rome, January 3, 1555

IHS

May the sovereign grace and everlasting love of Christ our Lord ever be our help and support.

As Master Polanco is writing of other matters in my name, I will merely say here that I have received the reports of several of the members of your province relating to yourself. I am sending you a copy herewith, and charge you very earnestly to take in good part what is here said, for those who have written have done so out of sincere affection and have said what they felt under order from the commissary.[1]

One thing, however, I will say. As it is my practice to consult and confer with some of the house on matters of importance which I have to determine, I should wish that you did likewise. We will thus appear to have one and the same way of dealing, bringing ourselves into agreement with that spirit of meekness and charity which the vicar of Christ our Lord recommends in the bulls of the institution of our Society.

In all other things, He who has given us the will to serve Him will also deign to give us help to bear the burden which for His greater service and praise He has laid upon us.

May He be pleased to give us His most abundant grace always to know His most holy will and entirely to fulfill it.

---

[1] Father Jerome Nadal.

¶ TO CARDINAL REGINALD POLE
VIII, 308-11, Letter 5120

Ignatius rejoices over England's return to the faith and gives news of the college in Rome and of the Germanico. Seventy members of the Society in the Roman College are being taught the sciences. The students of the Germanico are diligently preparing themselves for God's service. Ignatius asks that English youth be sent to Rome to be trained for work in England. He speaks of the mission to Ethiopia.

Rome, January 24, 1555

IHS

From a letter of your most reverend lordship written in Brussels on November 11, at the time of your journey to England, I learned of the good hope which God our Lord had given your most reverend lordship for the desired return of that kingdom to union with the holy Catholic Church. Shortly after the whole city learned of the fulfillment of that hope, and that in so short a time that it well seems to have been the work of Him who beyond the limits of time does everything according to His most perfect and divine will. Your most reverend lordship will have been informed of the widespread joy and consolation over such a rare gift to the Holy See, so intimately communicated from the Father of mercies and God of all consolation. It would be impossible to explain the joy which our least Society has felt and continues to feel. May Jesus Christ our Lord be praised without end by all creatures, who has so plainly revealed to us the treasury of His grace and love and the sweet and potent disposition of His providence in this reconciliation of England. Because His works are perfect, may He be pleased to confirm and extend this singular favor shown His whole Church, so that the knowledge and glory of His holy name may be spread more from day to day, and that the blood and life offered by Him to the eternal Father may be efficaciously applied to the salvation of many souls. I may also tell your most reverend lordship this. The Divine Wisdom has added a very special consolation for us, devoted and beholden as we are to the service of your most reverend lordship, by deigning to make use of your ministry especially in so great a work, and by keeping for that kingdom her most serene majesty the queen and his majesty the king, and over and above this, by retaining your most reverend lordship in authority, thus enabling you to contribute personally to the restoration of the kingdom.

Because of the interest you have always taken, you will be glad to hear what matters of importance have taken place in our college of Rome and in the Germanico, where God's service is always on the increase. We are over sixty in our house, and in the Roman College there are more than seventy of Ours. The sciences, with the exception of law and medicine, are being taught with great success to Ours and to externs, who are actually more than fifty in number. The students of the Germanico are giving a good account of themselves in studies and in virtue, and we hope that the Divine Goodness is preparing them for great service in Germany and the spiritual help of their countrymen. Among them is an Englishman of talent and character, and in our college an Irishman of whom we have great hopes. If your most reverend lordship could find it convenient to send a few good students to either of these colleges, we hope that before long they could be sent back with great profit to their native land and to our holy faith because of their exemplary life and orthodox teaching.

In the consistory which is being held this week the question was being discussed of thirteen of our priests who, I told you, were being sent to the kingdom of Prester John, together with some bishops. The appointments met with the unanimous approval of the Sacred College, the pope remarking that in these bishoprics there would be no chance for avarice to creep in. Indeed, there will be more opportunity for martyrdom in this group than for ambition. In fact, we have this year been notified of nine deaths. May the lives of all be made perfect in our Lord Jesus Christ.

At the urging of the king of Portugal one of them was elected patriarch with two coadjutors having the right of succession. His holiness, *motu proprio,* has approved two of Ours to accompany Cardinal Morone to the diet in Germany, which is surely going to be held. Two others are being sent in another group for a certain task of reform. And because these three missions were created in a few days and almost all together, I did not think it unworthy of your most reverend lordship's notice. You will recognize in what manner Christ's vicar on earth is making use of this least Society.

We hear from England that his majesty the king has written to his holiness and a few of the cardinals, as he did to me, recommending our Roman College. As a result his holiness has shown that he is ready and willing to endow it, and is looking about for means to carry his purpose into effect. The cardinals are behind the pope, and we have hopes that these plans will soon be realized. May Christ our Lord dispose of the whole project to His greater service and glory. I therefore commend myself to the holy prayers of your most reverend lordship, and will say no more except that I beg God our Lord to grant us all His grace always to know His most holy will and perfectly fulfill it.

¶ TO BARTHOLOMEW ROMANO

VIII, 328-29, Letter 5130

In this letter Ignatius reminds his correspondent that his conduct and not his place of residence should be changed. He explains that his disquiet comes from within and not from without. He exhorts Bartholomew to the practice of humility, obedience, devotion, and self-denial. Ignatius invites him to write every month describing the progress he is making in virtue and in his studies.

Rome, January 26, 1555

JESUS

My dear Brother Bartholomew.

The peace of Christ.

From your letters and the letters of others, but especially from yours, we have some understanding of your state of mind. We are all the more disappointed in this as we have such great desires of your spiritual good and eternal salvation. You are mistaken in thinking that the cause of your disquiet, or little progress in the Lord, is due so much to the place, your superiors, or your brethren. This disquiet comes from within and not from without. I mean from your lack of humility, obedience, and prayer, your slight mortification, in a word your little fervor in advancing in the way of perfection. You might change residence, superiors, and brethren, but if you do not change the interior man, you will never do good. And you will everywhere be the same, unless you succeed in being humble, obedient, devout, and mortified in your self-love. This is the only change you should seek. I mean that you should try to change the interior man and lead him back like a servant of God. Stop thinking of any merely external change, because if you are not good there in Ferrara, you will not be good in any college. We are all the more certain of this as we know you can be helped more in Ferrara than elsewhere. I will give you one bit of advice: humble yourself sincerely before your superior, ask his help, open your heart to him in confession or as you like, and accept with devotion the remedy he offers. Busy yourself in beholding and bewailing your imperfections rather than contemplate the imperfections of others. Try to give more edification in the future, and do not, I beg you, try the patience of those who love you in Jesus Christ our Lord and who would like to see you His good and perfect servant. Every month write me a few lines on how you are getting on with your humility, obedience, prayer, and the desire for perfection. Tell me what progress you are making in your studies. May Christ our Lord have you in His keeping.

¶ TO FATHER JOHN OF AVILA
VIII, 362-63, Letter 5154

Ignatius asks John of Avila to excuse his delay in answering because of the poor state of his health. He very delicately thanks Avila for his devotion to the Society and avows his own devotion to him. He gives a report on Guzman and Loarte. Ignatius exhorts him to glorify God in good as in bad health.

Rome, February 7, 1555

IHS

Very reverend Father in Christ.

May the sovereign grace and everlasting love of Christ our Lord ever be our help and support.

I can well believe that, between the great charity of your reverence and the news you have of my poor health, you will excuse my tardiness in answering your letter of July 27, which our brothers Don James de Guzman and Dr. Loarte brought with them. For the prayerful remembrance of me and this Society, which is more yours than ours, and for the special affection from which this remembrance and so many other good deeds and favors proceed, I will not give thanks to your reverence. For one is not accustomed to expect thanks for what he does for his own. And yet there is plentiful occasion to give thanks to God our Lord, the author of all good, and to beg Him to reward the great charity which He has given to your reverence by increasing it and perfecting it day by day, and drawing from it great fruit for many souls and for His own glory, which is all that your reverence ever had in mind. With regard to myself and the rest of the Society here, I can assure you that we shall never permit ourselves to forget the close union of one and the same spirit, the same desires for His service and praise which God our Lord has given us.

As to your spiritual sons, Don James de Guzman and Dr. Loarte, we find that acquaintance only confirms the information which your letter gives us, and we can see that it comes from one who knows them well. Don James gives us all great satisfaction and consolation by his goodness, and the example of his humility and obedience is a source of edification to all. The doctor is also giving a good account of himself, and although he has a much larger task with himself, I hope that God our Lord will cause him to grow daily in all good with the help of your prayers for him and for us all. We beseech Him who is our true health and life to make use of your ailments, so that in sickness and in health He may be glorified in the person of your reverence.

It is only right to be patient in the care and attention which your reverence is compelled to take of your physical strength, since it is done only for His service and not for any personal benefit of your own. In fact, we must all finally conform to what we know to be the will of God our Creator and Lord. May His divine and supreme Goodness give us all His bountiful grace so that we may always know His most holy will and perfectly fulfill it.

¶ TO FATHER PONCE COGORDAN
VIII, 395-97, Letter 5174

Father Cogordan was entrusted by Cardinal Cervini with the reform of the Monastery of Arta Cella in Auvergne, France. St. Ignatius drew up an instruction for the occasion in which he explains with great prudence and tact just how the reform ought to be carried through. The importance of the document consists in the saint's exposition of the broad principles and general norms which were to regulate this new ministry which was to become so frequent in the early Society.

Rome, February 12, 1555

Manner of procedure

1. Master Ponce should deliver the letters to those to whom they are addressed and try to win the confidence of those who govern the province and to whom he carries letters. He should have them write to the rulers of the land and to some men of influence.

2. Deliver the letters to those of the country, and as far as you can cultivate their friendship, especially those who are related to the nuns.

3. Make it understood by everyone, both in public and in private, that you have come for the common good and honor of the monastery and of all the countryside. Deliver the bull of the sacrament and have it solemnly published.

4. You should begin to win their confidence by conversing on spiritual matters with men of birth and others, and by visiting the hospitals and other pious works, if there are any.

5. You should visit the nuns with great kindness and make them understand that the cardinal sent you for their spiritual consolation. Give them his letter, but do not speak of reform to begin with. You should first win their confidence and that of the countryside.

6. During this interval you should give them sermons and exhortations in common, and speak on spiritual topics with individuals, and try to learn who are the most recollected and edifying. Win over some one of them to our Lord, preferably the abbess, and also some others who have influence.

7. When you have made yourself acceptable and come to know the hearts of the nuns, their past life and their mistakes, you should begin the reformation tactfully. Learn who their confessor is. If he is one who cannot be of help, advise him not to visit the nuns for some time (and see to it that he does not), but keep away from them until you yourself have spoken to him. Try to win his friendship.

8. You should know what friar and other persons frequent the monastery and with whom they speak. Advise them to stay away, and see that they do. Do all you can to prevent all visiting, unless you know that some will help in obtaining the desired end. Make use of the help and support you may find in the relatives of the nuns.

9. Persuade the nuns to remain enclosed for some time for their spiritual good, and keep everyone away from the monastery.

10. Get them principally to go to confession and Communion, and be especially careful to get some of them to make a general confession, to gain the plenary indulgences and as an example to the others.

11. Help them with examinations of conscience and with the Spiritual Exercises, especially at the beginning with the exercises of the first week, and leave them some methods of prayer suited to each.

12. Try with tact and charity to inspire them with confidence to open their hearts and make known their defects, and give them to understand in an unmistakable way that you are acting through charity and love and for their own good.

13. If some are hard to deal with and are unwilling to cooperate, do not give up or be annoyed with them. Show them rather a deep charity and a persevering wish to help them.

14. Do not resort to any coercive means with the nuns without fresh advice from us here at Rome.

15. You must not partake of the nun's hospitality or take anything by way of alms or any other way.

16. Show no partiality, but use the same charity toward all.

Matters to be reformed

1. The nuns should observe enclosure, if at all possible, even though their institute does not oblige them to do so. Only rarely should they allow

women, if they are of noble birth and of good name, to enter the monastery. But men, never.

2. They should lead a common life, and no one should have a servant or anything of her own.

3. They should recite the Office in choir, and practice mental prayer and spiritual exercises.

4. They should confess and receive Communion every week, or every month, to a confessor of upright life and teaching, an elderly man in his ways as well as in his years. He should be appointed by the cardinal, or by the bishop with the approval of the cardinal.

5. Those who exercise authority in the land should each year choose two women of influence, elderly and upright, who will undertake to help the nuns in their needs, to see that they are living aright, whether anyone who is open to suspicion visits them, and everything else that has to do with the monastery.

¶ TO CLAUDE, EMPEROR OF ABYSSINIA
VIII, 460-67, Letter 5205

In this letter Ignatius explains to the emperor of Abyssinia the primacy of the Roman pontiff and the unity and authority of the Church. He discusses at some length the error of the Greeks and others in not recognizing the pope as supreme head of the Church. Ignatius praises the king, whom God has inspired with the wish for union with the head of the Catholic Church. Ignatius says that twelve priests besides the patriarch have been chosen to go to the lands of the emperor. He explains that each one of these men is well known and tried. They are ready to give even their lives to save souls.

Rome, February 23, 1555

JESUS

My Lord in our Lord Jesus Christ.

May the sovereign grace and everlasting love of Christ our Lord greet and visit your highness with His most holy gifts and spiritual graces.

His most supreme highness, the king of Portugal, with the great zeal which God our Creator and Lord has bestowed upon him for the glory of His holy name and the salvation of souls redeemed by the precious blood of His only-begotten Son, has written me several letters. In these he tells me how pleased he should be if some twelve religious of our least

Society of Jesus were appointed, among whom his highness would choose one as patriarch and two others as coadjutors with right of succession. The vicar of Christ our Lord would then be asked to give them the proper authority, which would include sending them with the other priests to the kingdom of your highness.

The Society is bound by ties of the greatest respect and devotion to his serene highness the king of Portugal, among all Christian princes, and for this reason I acceded to his wishes and chose twelve priests besides the patriarch, as he had again written to ask me to do. They are all from our ranks, and twelve in number out of devotion to the number which represented Christ our Lord and His twelve apostles. They will offer themselves for every kind of labor and danger which they may have to encounter for the good of souls in the lands subject to your highness. I was all the more willing to do this because of the special desire which God our Lord has given me and all of our Society to be of service to your highness as to one who, following in the footsteps of your predecessors, in the midst of so many infidels who are enemies of our faith, labors to preserve and advance the religion and the glory of Christ our God and Lord. There was all the more reason for wishing that your highness had the help of spiritual fathers with the authority, the true power of the holy Apostolic See, and the pure teaching of the Christian faith. For these are the keys of the kingdom of heaven which Christ our Lord first promised, and later bestowed on St. Peter and his successors. He promised these keys to him alone when He told him, as St. Matthew relates: "And I say to thee that thou art Peter, and upon this rock I will build my church, and the gates of hell shall not prevail against it. And I will give to thee the keys of the kingdom of heaven. And whatsoever thou shalt bind upon earth, it shall be bound also in heaven; and whatsoever thou shalt loose on earth, it shall be loosed also in heaven."[1] He fulfilled His promise by conferring them on the same St. Peter after His Resurrection and before His Ascension, when He said three times, as St. John relates, "Simon, son of John, lovest thou me more than these?" and after Peter's answer, "Feed my sheep," thus giving him charge not over a part, but over all His sheep, bestowing upon him the plenitude of power required to feed the whole body of the faithful in the Christian life and religion, to lead them at last to the pastures of everlasting happiness in the kingdom of heaven.[2]

To the rest of His apostles Christ our Lord gave a delegated authority. But to St. Peter and his successors, it was full and ordinary, to be commu-

---

[1] Matthew 16:18-19.   [2] John 21:15-17.

nicated with all the other pastors as necessity should require. They were to recognize Peter as their chief pastor and receive authority from him. This was prefigured by the words of God our Lord in Isaias, where the prophet, speaking of Eliachim the high priest, says: "And I will lay the key of the house of David upon his shoulder; and he shall open and none shall shut, and he shall shut and none shall open."[3] Here it is St. Peter and his successors who are spoken of in figure, who holds full power, as signified by the keys, which are given in sign of complete and sovereign dominion. For this reason your highness should give thanks to God our Lord for having in your own time done you the favor of sending these true shepherds of souls to your kingdom, who are in union with the supreme shepherd and vicar whom Jesus Christ our Lord left on earth and from whom they have the very ample authority with which they are invested.

It was not without reason that neither your highness' father, nor grandfather, would have a patriarch from Alexandria. A member that has been torn from the body does not receive life from the body or movement or feeling from its head. Thus, the patriarch in Alexandria or Cairo, being schismatic and separated from this Apostolic See and its supreme pontiff who is the head of the whole body of the Church, received for himself neither the life of grace nor authority; nor can he lawfully impart it to any other patriarch. The Catholic Church is but one throughout the whole world, and it is impossible for one to be attached to the Roman pontiff and another to the Alexandrian. As Christ the bridegroom is one, so the Church, His spouse, is only one, of whom Solomon, speaking in the name of Christ our Lord, says in the Canticles, "One is my dove";[4] and the Prophet Osee, "And the children of Juda and the children of Israel shall be gathered together, and they shall appoint themselves one head."[5] In the same sense St. John said later: "And there shall be one fold and one shepherd."[6]

There was one ark of Noah, as we read in Genesis, outside of which there was no possibility of being saved. One was the tabernacle made by Moses. Solomon built one temple in Jerusalem, to which all had to come to sacrifice and adore. There was one synagogue in which all had to unite. All these were figures of the Church which is one, and outside of which there is nothing that is good. For whoever is not united with the body of the Church will not receive from Christ our Lord its head that

---

[3] Isaias 22:22.
[4] Canticle of Canticles 6:8.
[5] Osee 1:11.
[6] John 10:16.

influx of grace which gives life to the soul and prepares it for beatitude. To declare this unity of the Church against certain heretics the Church sings in the Creed: "Credo unam sanctam et catholicam apostolicam ecclesiam." That there are particular churches is an error condemned by the councils—the churches, for example, of Alexandria and Constantinople, independent of the universal head, who is the Roman pontiff, who is in continuous succession from St. Peter, who at the command of Christ our Lord chose this see, as St. Marcellus the martyr tells us, and confirmed his choice with his death. He has been followed by Roman pontiffs who were recognized as the vicars of Christ by so many holy doctors, both Latin and Greek, by all the nations—pontiffs who were reverenced by holy hermits and bishops and other confessors, who confirmed their testimony with so many miracles and the blood of so many martyrs, who died in the faith and in union with this holy Roman Church.

Pope Leo was acclaimed in the Council of Chalcedon[7] by the unanimous voice of the assembled bishops, "sanctissimus, apostolicus, universalis." The Council of Constance[8] condemned the error of those who denied the primacy of the Roman pontiff over all individual churches. And in the Council of Florence,[9] in the time of Pope Eugenius IV, which was attended by the Greeks, Armenians, and Jacobites, this decree was passed in conformity with previous councils: "Definimus sanctam apostolicam sedem, et pontificem romanum, in universum orbem tenere primatum, ac successorem esse Petri, et verum Christi vicarium, totiusque ecclesiae caput; et omnium christianorum patrem et doctorem existentem, et ipsi in beato Petro, pascendi, regendi, gubernandi universalem ecclesiam, a domino Jesu Christo potestatem plenam esse traditam."

His serene highness King David, of happy memory, your highness' father, moved by the Holy Spirit, sent his ambassador to recognize the Holy See and to offer obedience to the supreme pontiff at Rome. Among the many praiseworthy achievements of your father and your highness himself, these will be deserving of everlasting memory and of being perpetually celebrated in all your lands, to give thanks to God our Lord and the author of all good for the great favor He has bestowed on you in return for the diligence and care and the great virtue of your highness; the father, first of all, rendering his obedience to the vicar of Christ our Lord, and the son, bringing to his kingdom the first true and lawful patriarch of this holy Apostolic See. For if it is a singular blessing to be

---

[7] Conc. calced., sess. iii.
[8] Conc. constant., sess. vii and xv.
[9] Conc. florent., sess. 25.

united to the mystical body of the Catholic Church, which lives and is ruled by the Holy Spirit, who according to the Evangelist teaches her all truth; if it is a great gift to be illumined by the light of the teaching of the Church and established in her firmness, concerning which St. Paul says to Timothy that it is "the church of the living God, the pillar and ground of the truth,"[10] and to which Christ promised His assistance when He said, "Behold, I am with you all days, even to the consummation of the world,"[11] there is reason for always giving thanks to God our Creator and Lord in those lands, since His providence has done them so much good by means of your highness and your glorious father. And this all the more as I hope, in His infinite and supreme goodness, that, together with this union and obedience to the holy Catholic and Roman Church, there must come to your realms at the same time spiritual prosperity and an increase of temporal prosperity, together with a great uplifting of your royal estate and confusion to your enemies, to the extent that will promote the greater service and glory of Christ our Lord.

All the priests who are being sent to your highness, especially the patriarch and his coadjutors,[12] are men who are very well known and tried in our Society, and with experience in many works of charity. They have been chosen for this important undertaking because of the great influence of their example and their sound learning. They are very eager to go and happy to be sent, as they hope, to spend their lives in great labors for the service of God and of your highness, and in the help of the souls of your subjects. It is their desire to imitate to some extent the love of Christ our Lord, who laid down His life and shed His blood to redeem them from everlasting misery, as He declared, in the words of St. John: "I am the good shepherd. The good shepherd giveth his life for his sheep."[13] In like manner the patriarch and his companions go to you ready to share, not only their learning and to give advice and spiritual help to souls, but if need be even to give their lives for them. I hope that the more familiarly and intimately your highness deals with them, the more satisfaction and spiritual consolation you will receive in our Lord. In other respects, especially with regard to their teaching and the acceptance of their doctrine, they bear, as your highness knows, and especially the patriarch, the very authority of the supreme pontiff. And believing what they say is believing the Catholic Church, whose teaching it is their duty to interpret.

---

[10] 1 Timothy 3:15.   [11] Matthew 28:20.
[12] Father John Nunez Barreto as patriarch and Fathers Andrew Oviedo and Melchior Carneiro as coadjutors.
[13] John 10:11.

As it is of obligation that all the faithful believe and obey the Church's behests and to have recourse to her in their difficulties, I do not doubt that the great faith and goodness of your highness will command all your subjects to believe and obey and have recourse to the patriarch and those whom he may appoint in his stead, since they hold their office and authority from the supreme pontiff, which is the same authority as that of Christ our Lord and which He has shared with His vicar on earth. In Deuteronomy we have a figure of the Church in those who had difficulties and doubts and were referred to the Synagogue, as Christ our Lord expressly declares: "The scribes and the Pharisees have sitten on the chair of Moses. All things therefore whatsoever they shall say to you, observe and do."[14] And Solomon the wise is thinking of the Church when he says in Proverbs, "Forsake not the law of thy mother,"[15] who is the Church. And in another passage, "Pass not beyond the ancient bounds which thy fathers have set,"[16] who are the prelates of the Church. So great is the trust which Christ our Lord wishes us to give to the Church that He says through the evangelist St. Luke, "He that heareth you heareth me, and he that despiseth you despiseth me";[17] and St. Matthew, "And if he will not hear the church, let him be to thee as the heathen and publican."[18] No trust should be put in anyone who disagrees with the teaching he has heard from the Catholic Church. Let us recall what St. Paul says to the Galatians: "Though . . . an angel from heaven preach a gospel to you besides that which we have preached to you, let him be anathema."[19] This is what the holy doctors have taught us by word and example. This is what the councils have decreed. This is what is approved by the common assent of all the faithful servants of Christ our Lord.

There is no doubt that the patriarch and his companions will always show your highness great respect and reverence. They will try to be of service and give you all possible satisfaction, to the glory of God.

Be assured that we of this least Society who remain at home here, are entirely devoted to your service in the same Lord, and in our prayers and sacrifices we will continue as we have begun to beg and beseech the Divine Majesty to preserve your highness and your royal estate in His holy service, and so to grant you prosperity here below that you attain to the true happiness of heaven.

May He give us all His abundant grace always to know His most holy will and perfectly fulfill it.

---

[14] Matthew 23:2-3.
[15] Proverbs 1:8.
[16] Proverbs 22:28.
[17] Luke 10:16.
[18] Matthew 18:17.
[19] Galatians 1:8.

¶ TO FATHER MELCHIOR NUNEZ BARRETO

VIII, 481-83, Letter 5210

Letters from India are not forthcoming. More information is wanted on the death of Xavier and other members of the order. Nunez is reported to have been elected provincial of India, and this election is ratified and confirmed by Ignatius if the report of Xavier's death is true.

Rome, February 24, 1555

May the sovereign grace and everlasting love of Christ our Lord ever be our help and support.

This year, dear brother, we have had no letters from India, although we have had them from Portugal, where they had word from a single Portuguese ship which came to port, to the effect that our beloved brother Master Francis has departed this life. May he be with God, if the report is true. The fact is that, as we see some contradiction in the report, we are withholding judgment for the time being, as we have had no letter from any of Ours who can speak as eyewitnesses.

Whatever the truth may be, we are convinced that the name of Christ our Lord will be glorified by him both in life and in death, and that his charity will help us on earth, or from heaven, in our works in God's service.

We have also heard that our brothers Master Gaspar, his substitute in India, and Fathers Morales and Urban, and some others have ended their earthly pilgrimage and have passed to the heavenly and lasting city. Whatever truth there may be in this, may God our Lord, the true life and salvation of all, be praised. May it please Him to dispose of us all who are now, or will be, in this least Society to His greater service and glory. Amen.

From reports, apart from letters, we hear that you have been chosen as provincial of India. This can be done, according to our bulls, until the general superior makes other provisions. I have not yet received any certain information, but because of the good report I have of you personally, I will say only that I confirm the choice made by our brothers, and give you all the authority proper to your office, just as your predecessor in office, until other provision be made here. But if our brother Master Francis is still alive among us in this mortal and passing life, it will be his to act, as in our Lord he will judge best, and reason and our Institute demand.

This year you will see a large number of our brothers in India.

¶ TO FATHER MELCHIOR CARNEIRO
VIII, 489-90, Letter 5218

Ignatius bids him not to refuse the burden which the supreme pontiff has laid upon his shoulders for God's service, and gives signs of the tenderest charity. Father Melchior has been chosen as bishop for the Ethiopian mission.

Rome, February 26, 1555

May the sovereign grace and everlasting love of Christ our Lord ever be our help and support.

Although I know that you will take as intended for you also what I write to Fathers John Nunez and Dr. Andrew de Oviedo, I do not wish to omit writing this to you, as I do not know whether I shall soon have another chance of doing so. I want to beg you in our Lord not to make any difficulty about accepting the burden which the vicar of Christ our Lord on earth has placed on your shoulders, because, besides putting an obstacle in the way of the greater service of God, there would be a failure in the obligation which you owe by obedience to the holy and Apostolic See. But I will not pursue this point, since your letters give no reason for fearing that you do not understand this, nor your great virtue that you will not be willing to fulfill your obligations. Those who hold you in such affection in our Lord realize that He is making use of you personally in His holy service. And I know that you have no other desire than personally to glorify His holy name by being of help to many souls.

It only remains for me to commend myself very affectionately to your prayers, and to ask God our Lord to give you His blessing and His grace, so that you may devote all your efforts in His worldwide service and that of His holy Church.

I am quite satisfied that you will maintain the closest possible union with us, and hold it for certain that in whatever state of life you may be, we will always keep you close to our hearts, drawing you all the more closely in an interior union as you are farther removed from our exterior presence.

May Christ our Lord give us all His perfect grace always to know His most holy will and perfectly to fulfill it.

Remember me very especially to all the companions of this journey to Ethiopia, and to all those who are already there whom we have known here by sight, and to those too whom we have never met, for we always hold them in the same charity in our heart and greet them very sincerely in our Lord.

¶ TO GASPAR DE BORGIA
VIII, 535-36, Letter 5248

Gaspar de Borgia, bishop of Segorbe and Albarracin, had always shown "a very paternal spirit toward this least Society," as St. Ignatius wrote.[1] The Jesuits everywhere experienced "the warm affection" of the bishop.[2] On October 15, 1554 he wrote to St. Ignatius offering a revenue of five hundred ducats for the foundation of a college of the Society, and showed himself ready to help in every possible way.[3] St. Ignatius answered by thanking him for the generosity he showed, and pointed out the importance and far-reaching results of helping in works that give so much glory to God.

Rome, March 12, 1555

JHS

My most reverend Lord in our Lord.

May the sovereign grace and everlasting love of Christ our Lord salute and visit your most reverend lordship with His most holy gifts and spiritual graces.

After answering other letters which your lordship did me the favor of writing, I received yours of October 15, from which, as from the letters of Master Estrada, it is clear that from day to day the desire is growing in your lordship of helping and supporting this least Society, which is all yours. God's providence is making use of this desire as the main instrument in the establishment and the prosperity of the Society in the kingdom of Spain. May it please Him to allow your lordship to know, by the increase of charity and the gifts of His grace and spiritual consolation, in how important a work for His divine service and the help of souls and how pleasing in His divine presence your lordship is engaged for His reverence and love. I hope that He will do so, and give your lordship even in this life a clear pledge and proof of the reward He is keeping for you in life everlasting.

As to particular ways of helping, whether by means of pensions or otherwise, your lordship will be able to see what is more to the point. For He who gives the desire will also give understanding to see what is best fitted to obtain our end in God's service.

I will say no more, except to beg your most reverend lordship, not merely to consider as belonging to you the colleges of those three king-

---

[1] *Epistolae et instructiones*, VIII, 8.
[2] *Ibid.*
[3] *Epistolae mixtae*, IV, 394.

doms,[4] together with those who dwell in them, but in the same way all the members of this least Society everywhere, for we are yours with a very special obligation and devotion in our Lord. May it please Him by His infinite and sovereign goodness to give us all His abundant grace always to know His most holy will and perfectly to fulfill it.

¶ TO FATHER ROBERT CLAYSSONE
VIII, 539-40, Letter 5251

Father Robert had written a report the style of which was verbose and bombastic.[1] St. Ignatius points out the qualities he ought to cultivate, recommending that his style be sober and select.

Rome, March 13, 1555

Dear Master Robert in Christ.

Pax Christi.

In this first letter from me you will recognize my affection for you, especially because I want to call your attention, without apology or excuse, to the style of your letter. While your letter is in some respects ornate and learned, we miss a becoming modesty[2] in the ornament used and in the show of learning. It is one thing to be eloquent and charming in profane speech, and another when the one who is speaking is a religious. Just as in a matron that ornament which is modest and chaste is to be commended, so in the style which Ours should use when speaking or writing we do not look for what is wanton or adolescent, but for a style that is dignified and mature. This is especially so in letters, where the writing by its very nature must be more compact and polished and manifest at the same time an abundance of ideas rather than of words.

Your charity will receive this admonition in good part, just as our charity did not permit us to forego it. We do not venture to send your letter anywhere without many a previous correction.

Some selection of topics must also be made, and in the quarterly letter only those items should be submitted which serve for edification. In many passages indeed there is a manful enough declaration of satisfaction in sharing the cross of Christ, but in some others the spirit seems weak and much less vigorous than one would expect in a soldier of Christ.

---

[4] The kingdoms of Aragon, Catalonia, and Valencia.
[1] The letter is to be found in *Litterae quadrimestrales*, III, 194.
[2] The text has the Greek, *to prepon*.

This, beloved brother, is our censure, and from it you will see that it is not only the Sorbonne that is allowed to exercise such a privilege. In return for having written to you, as I think, with such frankness, confidence, and affection, I beg the reward of your prayers, and your admonition in turn, should occasion require it. Yours in our Lord Jesus Christ . . .

¶ TO GERARD HAMMONTANUS
VIII, 583-85, Letter 5280

His family name was Kalckbrenner but he was commonly called Hammontanus, from his birthplace, Hammont. He was prior of the Carthusian monastery at Cologne. Ignatius answers with every manifestation of charity a letter he received from the prior, and gives thanks for timely assistance. He speaks of a college at Cologne, and praises God's wonderful providence for calling young men to Rome who are to be the future defenders and propagators of the faith in Germany. The dependence of Ignatius on God is here made clear, for in spite of the high cost of living and the scarcity of money, he will not refuse suitable candidates.

Rome, March 22, 1555

May the grace and peace of our Lord Jesus Christ be preserved and increased in us unto its consummation in glory. Amen.

I have not yet answered your paternity's letter of September 27, although the kindliness of your charity toward us and its practical effects in the favor bestowed, while they increased our debt of gratitude in our hearts, urge us to give some sign of gratitude to God the author of all good and to your paternity as the special minister of His providence. But when I saw that your paternity (to use your own words) was more desirous of prayers and silence than of a letter of thanks, as one who was moved by the purest intention of charity to send us most opportunely a very special help, I thought that at least for the time being I should refrain from writing, if not from the prayers or from encouraging this mutual bond of charity with your holy order and monastery, by leaving some memorial of this great favor, which would be a reminder, not only for us who are still living but for our successors as well. Blessed be the name of our Lord Jesus Christ, who provides in so many ways for this least Society. And as He grants that it not only grows daily in numbers and in spiritual fruit, so He gives in addition all these other things to those who are seeking the kingdom of God.

As to the opening of a college of our Society in Cologne, we well understand your paternity's interest and support, and we pray that God will reward you abundantly. I have no doubt that your active devotion and that of others who wish to provide the youth of Germany with teachers to train the minds of the best of them in letters and virtue will find the opportunity when it will be pleasing in the sight of His Divine Majesty. But while God's providence is disposing the souls of men to open a college in Germany itself, He has given us an eager desire to train in Rome the youth of Germany whom He has called to the ministry of the orthodox Catholic faith. He is also moving many young men of excellent character who are flocking here to Rome with the intention either of entering the Society or of enrolling in the German College, of which I am sure your paternity has heard. Many come, not only from lower but also from upper Germany, and amongst them some come from association with heretic parents or friends, like roses growing among thorns. We have between seventy and eighty German students here.

Young men of excellent character are coming from other nations as well, and even men with years of learning and an authority that is far from common. Here at Rome there are 180, more or less, who belong to the Society, although some are repeatedly being sent off to various posts in different parts of the world. But about fifty live in the German College, so that our Lord Jesus Christ would seem to be preparing soldiers for some exceptional campaign, and out of this training camp wishes to produce some rich fruits in His Church. Although those who are worldly-wise, wonder, and perhaps consider it rash for us to permit our numbers to grow when we are without resources, and without regard of the high cost of living together with the scarcity of money, we who have cast the anchor of our hope in the goodness of God, who feeds many as easily as few, in times of both want and abundance, think we neither can nor should exclude those called by His holy inspirations to our Society.

And although, as your paternity writes, it seems that the gospel is being transferred to the infidel and taking leave of the western nations because of their tepidity, nevertheless we ought to hope and strive with all our might to do everything we can by prayer, word, and example, and in every possible way, as worthless instruments of the Divine Wisdom, to bring what help we can. But enough of this.

It remains for your paternity to be good enough to commend this whole Society of ours to God, in your own holy prayers and those of your order. May His boundless charity bestow His grace and Holy Spirit upon us all, so that we may always know and fulfill His divine will.

¶ To JOHN PEREZ DE CALATAYUD

VIII, 631-33, Letter 5313

An answer to letters received. Ignatius consoles him on the death of his beloved wife, treats of a business matter, and refers him to the Jesuits of Saragossa.

Rome, April 4, 1555

Very honorable Sir in Christ Jesus.

May the grace and peace of Christ our Lord be ever present and grow in our souls.

I have received two letters from you, and in the second I see that you did not receive my answer to the first. This, then, will be an answer to both. It was a comfort indeed to know that you remember me. Although I should not possess the very special charity that will properly equal yours, I must ask it of God our Lord. He knows that I have kept you, and do still keep you, very close to my heart, and that I entertain the desire of finding some occasion to prove myself useful in your service, to God's glory, as far as my slight ability and my profession will allow me.

The fact of God's having deprived you of so good a companion can be considered only as one of those visitations which Divine Providence uses with its chosen ones to detach them all the more from the things of earth and make them see that there is nothing stable or lasting here below. Indeed, the more gifted a soul, the more God is wont to raise it aloft with the hope and the desire of heaven, where each one will rejoice forever in the divine worship with those he loves.

If we had our fatherland and true peace in our sojourn in this world, it would be a great loss to us when persons or things which gave us so much happiness are taken away. But being as we are pilgrims on this earth, with our lasting city in the kingdom of heaven, we should not consider it a great loss when those whom we love in our Lord depart a little before us, for we shall follow them before long to the place where Christ our Lord and Redeemer has prepared for us a most happy dwelling in His bliss. May He be pleased to comfort your soul, and direct all your affairs, as He so well knows how, to bring you and all your family to the last end for which we are created and redeemed by His blood and death.

Señor Gomez has spoken to me of your affairs, and I have given him my opinion. I refer you to what he will write you. I regret the embarrassment in which you have become involved from your having done me a kindness. May God our Lord direct all to His greater pleasure and to your greater good.

I can well believe that you will have some association with the members of our Society who are resident in Saragossa, and that you will try to profit spiritually from it. I will not enlarge on this point now.

Should you wish to know anything of me personally, they will be able to satisfy you.

God does me a great favor in employing me in the service of this holy Society, although I carry out my part with great negligence and imperfection. May He increase His grace in all of us, so that by our ministry He may add to the glory of His name. Amen.

¶ TO FATHER SIMON RODRIGUES
VIII, 657-58, Letter 5329

After his case had been examined and settled at Rome, Rodrigues retired to Bassano, near Venice, where he lived in some independence, spending the alms which were sent him from Rome without giving anyone an account of his expenditures. He thought it was enough "to mention it . . . without giving a detailed account." Despite the Society's shortness of funds, Ignatius would not hear of Rodrigues wanting what was necessary, and supplied his needs even generously. But, mindful of his profession of poverty, he wanted to know how the money was spent, and of what Rodrigues had need. He gave orders to the rector at Venice that Rodrigues was to get double the allowance he himself got. If this could not be done at Venice, Ignatius would see that it be done elsewhere.

Rome, April 6, 1555

Pax Christi.

I received your letter, and as it was an answer to mine, I shall make no reply to it here. In what you say about supplying you with money after Easter, I suppose you will be mindful of our profession, and yours, holy poverty being the mother of us all. Here we have about two hundred mouths to fill, prices are high, our debts amount to many thousands of *scudi,* the Holy See is vacant, our food and clothing are bought with money borrowed at a high rate of interest; and yet the truth is we would rather be lacking in what is necessary than have you go without your comfort. But in order that our father may have more light on the whole matter, it would be good if you wrote to the rector, Master Cesar [Helmi], or had a letter written to him, to tell him how you are making out in having your personal needs supplied by that college, how these things help you, and how any expenses incurred for your personal needs may be paid for with money solicited elsewhere. It is not a year since you belonged to that college, and having placed 130 *scudi* on deposit for you at Venice, besides the traveling money you took from Rome, we should not know how to give an account of the money you have spent, should any one ask for it. He would like to be able to do this, and as he does not know how you are going to be provided with what you need, it would be good for you to write us, or make the matter known to your rector there, to whom we shall write to see to it that you lack nothing that is necessary. If provision cannot be made either at Venice or at Padua for what is necessary to your comfort, our father says that he will see to it that you are taken care of in another college that is better supplied than where you are. However, no matter where you are, everything possible will be done from here, and even more than is reasonably possible, to see that you lack nothing of what is necessary.

No more, except that we all commend ourselves to your prayers.

Our father tells me again that the rector is to give you a double portion of everything, and if he is not prepared to do this, he himself will see to it that it is done in some other college.

¶ TO FATHER JOHN NUNEZ BARRETO
VIII, 680-90, *Appendix de rebus Ethiopicis*, Letter 2

St. Ignatius sent the following instruction to the recently appointed patriarch of Ethiopia, Father John Nunez Barreto, which the Franciscan, Father Charles Santis, does not hesitate to qualify as "a document which is fundamental, not only because of its exact knowledge of oriental psychology, but because it manifests the supreme prudence and discretion of the saint."[1]

Without a doubt this is indeed one of the most important missionary documents of St. Ignatius. In it we see the tactics which he wishes employed, the delicacy of his care that the missionary adapt himself to the customs and way of life of the natives, the prudent norms he gives for eradicating as mildly as possible the prevailing superstitions. He directs him to begin with persons of wider influence by trying to make himself agreeable and to gain the hearts of the Abyssinians. The missionaries should introduce those Christian practices which are more in conformity

[1] *Enciclopedia cattolica*, Vol. V, p. 691.

with native mentality and tastes, and be careful not to wound susceptibilities. The people should proceed gently in uprooting their own prejudices by means of an excessive austerity, and substitute acts of charity in place of acts of penance. The missionaries should give much emphasis to the sacramental and liturgical life, open centers of instructions, provide the required books, and give the Ethiopian clergy canonical appointments when circumstances make such appointments opportune.

Probable date February 20, 1555

IHUS

Some suggestions which may help to bring the kingdoms of Prester John into union with the Catholic faith and Church.

Since, humanly speaking, the principal factor in this undertaking will be found primarily in Prester John, king of Ethiopia, and secondarily in the people, a few suggestions will be offered which may be of help in winning over Prester John. They will be followed by others which may help in dealing with the people and Prester John conjointly.

For the king

Besides the bulls which the pope addresses to him, the letters which are written him from here will afford some help in winning over the heart of Prester John. They recall to mind the submission which his father David sent to the Holy See, and contain certain recommendations of those who are sent and accredited to him. They also make other friendly advances. But the principal and final help, after that of God our Lord, for winning the heart of Prester John must come from the king.[2] Not merely letters from his highness, but, if he will agree to it, a special ambassador will be required, who on the part of the king will call on Prester John and present the patriarch, the coadjutor bishops, and the other priests, and explain the order that will be followed, so that it will be no longer necessary to take patriarchs from Moorish lands or from schismatic Christians. The more solemnly this presentation is made on the part of his highness, the more authority it seems the patriarch will have for God's service.

It might be good to see whether his highness thinks that some presents should be sent, especially of things that are held in esteem in Ethiopia; and in offering them he could indicate that a true union of friendship will exist among Christian princes when they all hold the one religion. When this is recognized, he could send him every kind of official he de-

---

[2] John III of Portugal, who had asked that the patriarch be sent with the missionaries and who had begun the negotiations with the negus.

sired, and God will give him the grace to overcome the Moors, so far as this will be for God's greater service.

Some letters from the king to individuals will also be of help, especially to those who are closer to Prester John and with whom he consults and whom he holds in esteem, notably the Portuguese. Other letters, if the king agrees, could be brought unaddressed, the proper addresses being supplied in Ethiopia. But whether by letter or otherwise an effort should be made to make such men friendly.

The viceroy of India likewise could do much to add to the authority of the patriarch with Prester John, by letter or a personal representative, if the king does not send one.

The patriarch and those with him should try to be on familiar terms with Prester John and gain his good will by every honorable means. Should he be receptive and the opportunity present itself, give him to understand that there is no hope of salvation outside the Roman Catholic Church, and whatever she determines about faith or morals must be believed if one is to be saved. If you succeed in convincing Prester John of this general truth, you have already gained many particular points which depend on this fundamental truth and which can little by little be deduced from it.

If you can win over men of influence who have great weight with Prester John, or, on the other hand, if you can get him to make the Exercises and give him a taste for prayer and meditation and spiritual things, this will be the most efficacious means of all to get them to think less of and even to abandon the extreme views which they entertain concerning material things.

Remember that they have a prophecy to the effect that in these times a king from this part of the West (apparently they have no other in mind than the king of Portugal) is destined to destroy the Moors. This is an additional reason for a closer friendship with him, and this in turn will be recommended by a closer uniformity. For if there is no opposition in the matter of religion, there will be a closer union of love between them.

You should also remember that up to this Prester John holds both ecclesiastical and civil jurisdiction. Consider whether it would be good to let him know that kings and great princes of the Catholic Church usually have the right of presentation to important positions, but that the actual conferring of the dignity is done by the supreme pontiff and by bishops, archbishops, and patriarchs in their respective spheres of authority. Conforming himself in this matter with the Roman Church and her princes could be of much help to him.

For the people and king conjointly

Take along with you the amplest faculties and see that you are able to explain them. The exterior appearance of the bulls or briefs should be as beautiful to the eye as possible. It will be all the better if they are translated into Abyssinian.

To the best of your ability you should have ready the proofs for the dogmas against which they err, with the definition of the Apostolic See or the councils when there is any. For if they can be brought to admit this one truth, that the Holy See cannot err when it speaks *ex cathedra* on matters of faith and morals, it will be easy to convince them of the others. You should be well prepared, therefore, to prove this thesis and you should approach this matter in a way that is accommodated to those people, or the understanding of anyone.

Concerning the abuses which exist, first try to bring over Prester John and a few individuals of wider influence, and then, without making a fuss over it once these are disposed of, see what can be done about calling a meeting of those in the kingdom who are held in high esteem for their learning. Without taking away from them anything in which they are particularly interested or which they especially value, try to get them to accept the truths of Catholicism and all that must be held in the Church, and encourage them to try to help the people to come to some agreement with the Roman Catholic Church.

After having removed the more substantial abuses—those which are in conflict with a sincere belief, such as the obligatory observance of the Old Law—it would be better to begin, with the support of Prester John, to remove or lessen other abuses if it can be done. If this cannot be done, try at least to make it as plain as possible that there can be no obligation to observe such practices and that, even though they are tolerated, it would be better not to observe them. In this way they will lapse, especially if some of the leading men can be induced to give the example.

The austerities which they practice in their feasts and other corporal penances might be gently moderated, it seems, and brought within a measure of discretion. This could be done in four ways. The first would be to quote the testimony of Holy Scripture, to praise spiritual exercises over those that are corporal, since these latter are but of little avail.[3] But you should not withdraw your approval from external exercises, which are necessary up to a certain point. Thus if they lose that esteem for things which they now hold in honor, these things will fall of their own weight,

---

[3] 1 Timothy 4:8.

since they are rather repugnant to the flesh anyway. The second is rather to praise and prefer a golden mean to its extremes.[4] The third means is taken from reason, which will convince them that it is against charity and the common good so to weaken themselves for good works by their fasting that their enemies invade their lands and put them to the sword, with so many offenses against God our Lord. This is an argument which will readily appeal to Prester John, and others too who have more than ordinary intelligence. The fourth means is that of example, which could be given by some of those whom they regard as holy, once you convince them that they should so act for God's greater service. It is quite likely that they will do so. Observe too that God calls some individuals to a life of penance and austerity; and when He does, praise what they do in this matter. But in general a measure of discretion is necessary if such austerities are to be praised.

Perhaps some exterior feasts would be a great help in getting rid of certain abuses. I am thinking of Corpus Christi processions and others which are in use in the Catholic Church. These would replace their baptisms, and so forth. Our own people, who are not so coarse, are helped by these feasts.

Be very careful that public services such as Mass and Vespers are conducted in a way that will be edifying to the people. The recitation should be slow and distinct, since they do the opposite, and think that our way is more perfect. If the king approves having a choir with organ, this might be a help in the beginning. But let them be in charge of some externs, as it is foreign to our Institute.

Vestments of priest, deacon, and subdeacon, altar ornaments, chalices, altar stones, and equipment for making hosts ought to be of the best. Try to get them into the habit of making hosts for the Blessed Sacrament as they are made here. In bringing them to Communion let them know that confession should precede, and that Communion is not distributed any day one comes to the church. In the case of the sick who cannot come to the church, see that the Blessed Sacrament is brought to their homes.

It would be good to instruct them in the ceremonies of baptism. It must be conferred but once and not many times, accustomed as they are to baptize every year.

As they have never made use of confirmation, it ought to be administered to all the people after they have been prepared for the sacrament.

---

[4] *Constitutiones*, Pars X, n. 10. St. Ignatius had used the word *mediocridad*, which is here described.

You should also introduce the practice of extreme unction, as they know nothing about it there.

At first you could hear the confessions of those who can understand you. For the others, it would be good for you to bend your efforts to learn the Abyssinian language. The confessors they have among them could be instructed in the proper procedure by means of interpreters. They should be told of reserved cases, which are restricted to bishops and patriarchs; and very severe penalties should be meted out to confessors who reveal matter of confession, something which they say is done there. Lastly, see that the abuses regarding these sacraments are diligently corrected.

With regard to holy orders, some reform is necessary with respect to age, integrity, competence, and other aspects in the candidate for orders, as far as circumstances which prevail there permit.

As to matrimony, and generally speaking the same must be said of all the sacraments, give heed to the form which must be observed. Ceremonies can be introduced gradually, in the measure in which they contribute to greater edification. These exterior rites should not be few in number, considering that the people are much given to ceremonies.

It would be a great help for the complete conversion of those lands, both at the beginning and throughout the rest of the time, to open a large number of elementary schools there, and secondary schools and colleges, for the education of young men, and even of others who may need it, in Latin and in Christian faith and morals. This would be the salvation of that nation. For when these youngsters grow up, they would be attached to what they have learned in the beginning and to that in which they seem to excel their elders. Before long the errors and abuses of the aged would lapse and be forgotten. If it appears hard to the people of that kingdom, habituated as they are to their old ways, to see their children properly trained, think about the advisability of Prester John's sending abroad a large number of those who have talent. A college could be opened in Goa and, if circumstances called for it, another in Coimbra, another in Rome, another in Cyprus, on the opposite side of the sea. Then, armed with sound Catholic teaching, they could return to their lands and help their fellow countrymen. If they came to love the practices of the Latin Church, they would be all the more firmly grounded in her ways.

The patriarch could, by himself or through an interpreter or someone else, begin to give discourses and exhortations to the people within the limits of their capacity. The bishops and others could do likewise. Teaching the catechism in many different places by good teachers would also be of great importance.

Those among the native population who excel in talent and exercise some influence by reason of their good lives should be won over by making much of them. They could be given some ecclesiastical revenues and dignities, but only under the probability that they would turn out to be faithful ministers. You could even have some of these preach.

Some Portuguese who are acquainted with the Abyssinian language would be good as interpreters, should any of Ours preach, and for conferences, after the manner of the Abyssinian preachers. Some could even be brought from Goa or other parts of India; and if there were children's catechism classes in India, they could serve as a beginning for a children's school in the kingdom of Prester John. This would seem to be very much to the point.

Take thought of beginning in the course of time some universities or liberal-arts courses.

Consider the abuses or disorders which can be corrected gently and in a way that will give the people of the country a chance to see that a reform was necessary, and that it begins with them. This will furnish you with authority for the reform of other abuses.

Since Ours have to lessen the esteem for corporal penance which the Abyssinians have, in the use of which they go to extremes, set before them charity in word and example. To this end it would be good to establish hospitals where pilgrims and the sick, curable and incurable, could be gathered, to give and cause others to give public and private alms to the poor, to arrange for the marriage of young girls, and to establish confraternities for the redemption of captives and the care of exposed children of both sexes. They would thus see that there are better works than their fasts. It seems that Prester John, who is generous with his alms, should if possible have a finger in all these pious works.

In works of spiritual mercy also the people of the country should behold in you a tender solicitude for souls. This would be shown in teaching them virtue and their letters, all of which should be done gratis and for the love of Christ. These works should be praised in sermons and conversations and supported with texts from Holy Scripture and the example and sayings of the saints, as we indicated above.

Although you are ever intent on bringing them to conformity with the Catholic Church, do everything gently, without any violence to souls long accustomed to another way of life. Try to win their love and their respect for your authority, preserving their esteem of learning and virtue, without harm to your humility, so that they will be helped in proportion as they esteem those by whom they are to be helped.

Take along some good books, especially pontificals, and others which explain the external rites of the Church, such as decrees of the Apostolic See and the councils with which they have to be made acquainted. They should know the number of bishops attending the councils (in Ethiopia much importance is attached to this point), and all this will be a very efficient help. You should also take along some lives of the saints, and be well acquainted with them, especially the life of Christ our Lord and His miracles, for the reason given. You should have some calendars of the feasts. And lastly, it would be good for you to be well versed in matters ecclesiastical, even the smallest items, because it is a branch of learning which they best understand there, and they have for this reason a higher esteem for it than for other branches that are more subtle, of which they understand nothing.

It will also be a help for you to go well supplied with church ornaments for the altars, and vestments for priests, deacons, subdeacons, and acolytes; chalices, crosses, vessels for holy water, and other items which are used in external worship.

You might think over and suggest to his highness in Portugal whether it would be a good idea to send along with you some men of practical genius to give the natives instructions on the making of bridges, when they have to cross rivers, on building, cultivating the land, and fishing. And other officials too, even a physician or surgeon, so that it may appear to the Abyssinians that their total good, even bodily good, is coming to them with their religion.

You should think also of the propriety of taking along with you a few well-chosen books on law and civil relations, so that they may have a sounder policy in their government and in the administration of justice.

Think also of the advisability of taking along some relics of the saints for the devotion of the people.

Recall that, according to their prophecies or traditions, their patriarchs were expected to come from Rome after a hundred had come from Alexandria. The Alexandrian line ended in Abimamarco,[5] and so they received a pseudopatriarch who went to them in the name of the Apostolic See. It would appear therefore that they are ready to give a good reception to the patriarch, and consequently to his teaching. Be sure that you are informed

---

[5] It stands thus very clearly in the manuscript. Nevertheless this patriarch, the last before the time of St. Ignatius, received his authority from Alexandria. His name was Marcos, or more accurately, Marqos. He died in 1530. At his death a Portuguese adventurer named John Bermudes, whom St. Ignatius calls in the next line *pseudopatriarcha*, wished to be taken for metropolitan, as well as by the negus as by Pope Clement VII.

in every respect of all that is known of the history of those kingdoms. It will be good to know this, for it will protect you from dangers and enable you to give greater help to the people.

Consider whether it would be well if the patriarch were able to dispose of abbeys and other revenues which become vacant, as a reward for the good ministers among them.

The bishops should set aside all pomp and circumstance and, as far as possible personally discharge the office of pastors. They and their assistants should avoid all appearance of avarice.

The patriarch should have his council, which he should consult on matters of importance. After hearing their opinions he should come to a decision. The council should consist of four, and for the present among them shall be the two coadjutors. As a rule they should live together, except for temporary separations which may be required by some affair of importance, especially in the beginning. If one happens to be absent for a short time, the three, together with the patriarch, ought to choose another in his place.

If one of the four chosen in Portugal should die or be necessarily absent, the patriarch and the others of the Society who were sent with him ought to choose as a substitute him who receives the largest number of votes.

Once the dioceses are set up, consider who of the natives would be suitable as bishops and archbishops. If there are any such, they could be consecrated. But if there is none, write to the king of Portugal and to Rome for others to be sent from here.

It also seems good to set up beneficed curacies, and give them to persons of good lives and sound learning, as far as possible. Revenues should be assigned and conferred by the election of the bishops with the approval of the patriarch.

You will have to be very expert if you are going to neutralize the authority of the *Book of Abtilis*,[6] which, so they say, contains the canons of the apostles. It is the source of their abuses and excesses, and because they look upon it as part of the canonical Scriptures, from which there can be no dispensation, their errors, up to the present, have been as it were irremediable.

---

[6] This is the name which St. Ignatius gives to the book called by the Abyssinians *Fides patrum*. It is an Arabic anthology, called in its original tongue *I'tiraf al-aba (Confessio patrum)*, containing passages from the fathers from St. Irenaeus to the Alexandrian patriarch Cristodulus (1047-1077). Translated from Arabic to Ethiopic, it received the title *Hajmanota Abau (Fides patrum)*.

Consider whether it would not be better to eat apart by yourselves. The people, being much given to fasting, do not ordinarily eat before night. This will avoid giving them bad example, or making them suffer.

The churches of canons should be visited and also the monasteries of religious of both sexes. Find out what is in need of reform and make what provisions are possible.

Everything set down here will serve as directive, the patriarch should not feel obliged to act in conformity with it; rather with what a discreet charity, considering existing circumstances, and the unction of the Holy Spirit, who must direct him in everything, will dictate. Thus with your own prayers, with those of the whole Society and the faithful everywhere, we must urge our petitions before the throne of God's kindness and goodness, so that, having compassion on these nations, He will deign to lead them back to the unity of His holy Church and the true religion and the way of salvation for their souls, to His honor and glory.

¶ ON THE METHOD OF DEALING WITH SUPERIORS
IX, 90-92, Letter 5400a

It appears from other documents that these instructions were drawn up by St. Ignatius December 1, 1554 and sent to the colleges and houses of Spain and Sicily.

IHS

1. He who has business with a superior should have the matter well in hand, arranged in order and thought out by himself or others, in keeping with the greater or lesser importance of the matter. In smaller matters, however, or when there is need of hurry and no time is available for study or conferring, it is left to his own judgment as to whether he should represent the matter to the superior or not, if he has not been able to confer with others or study the matter himself.

2. After he has examined and studied his proposals, he should place them before the superior, and tell him that this point has been examined by himself or with others, as the case may be. He should give the superior the results of his examination and study, but he should never say to a superior in discussing a point with him, "This or that is right, or this or that will be," but he should speak conditionally and with a certain amount of reserve.

3. Once he has proposed the matter to the superior, it will be the superior's duty to make a decision, or wait for further study, or refer the proposals back to those who submitted them, or name others to examine them, or make the decision then and there, according to the nature of the difficulty involved.

4. If I point out some drawback in the decision of the superior, and the superior reaffirms his decision, there should be no answer or discussion for the time being.

5. But if, after the decision of the superior, he who is dealing with him sees that something else would be better, let him call the superior's attention to it, adding his reason. And even if the superior had withheld judgment, this may be done after three or four hours, or a day. He could then represent to the superior what he thinks would be good, preserving, however, a manner of speaking and using such words that there would neither be nor appear to be any dissension or altercation. He should then accept in silence what is then and there decided.

6. But even supposing that a decisive answer was given the first time, or even the second, he might, a month or more later, re-present his view in the manner already indicated. For time and experience uncover many things, and the superior himself may change his mind.

7. He who deals with a superior should accommodate himself to the character and abilities of the superior. He should speak distinctly and so that he can be heard, clearly, and whenever possible at an hour that is suited to the superior's convenience.

8. As far as possible, they should not wait until the day or the evening before to write what is supposed to be written by Saturday, nor at other ordinary or extraordinary times should they wait until the post is ready to leave for places beyond Italy, and then write in a hurry. But they should try to arrange that what should be written by Saturday be begun the Sunday previous, and continue until the end of Wednesday, leaving as little as possible unwritten of the answers to letters received before that date. In this way Thursday, Friday, and Saturday will be free to deal with and answer matters of importance which may turn up and need an immediate answer.

9. Ordinarily do not write to different parts of Italy oftener than every month, informing the rectors of this order which is given, unless there be cases which do not admit of greater delay.

10. Write every three months to places that are more distant, unless there is an occurrence of some importance or the posts are more convenient than usual.

11. With regard to the reception of candidates for the Society in Italy, the following points[1] are sent to the colleges, which deal with the qualities required of those who are to be admitted to the Society. And they should not receive anyone, or send anyone here, until we have been informed about them, point by point.

12. However, if there are some who very strikingly and beyond the possibility of any doubt fulfill the conditions set forth in the points, they may be received, or even sent to Rome, if they are of such high standing or if there be danger in delay, in which case superiors will have to use their own judgment. But it would be much better to advise the general in Rome and wait for an answer. There might be no difficulty about the candidates, but there might well be difficulty for the house in Rome.

13. We are sending the same points and directions everywhere, which have been made out for Italy and Sicily (which is always to be understood when we speak of Italy). It will be of advantage to know in other places what goes on in Italy, as this will be of the greatest possible help to them. True it is that in places far distant from Rome, such as in other kingdoms, there is no need of consulting with the general about admissions, or of sending men to Rome. But the charity and discretion of the commissary or provincial with whom lower superiors such as rectors will consult, will take the place of the general's consultation. There could well be cases which would not admit of the delay in consulting the general.

14. Provision has been made that a copy of this notice be sent to all places where there are any of the Society, and in the book in which this is entered in Rome a note has been made at the foot of the page that it has been sent everywhere, and that it has been received. Let a reminder be made of this notice each time that a letter is written until such time that a notice comes of its receipt.

15. The same instructions will be sent to India, and the provincial should send the same to the remote parts of his jurisdiction. The same dispatch can be sent from Portugal to Brazil and the Congo, although in such remote places, especially among infidels and recently converted Christians, even though they should be helped by what is written, it is left to the discretion of superiors, who, taking into consideration the condition of the region and other circumstances, will act according to their judgment of what is best for the greater glory of God and the greater spiritual progress of souls.

---

[1] Nothing more is said in the letter of these "following points." He may have been referring to the "enclosed points" *(capitulos siguientes)*, somewhat like the questionnaire, now called *informationes*, that accompanies every application for admission to the novitiate.

¶ TO FATHER MANUEL LOPEZ
IX, 180-83, Letter 5446

A newsletter announcing the happy death of Marcellus II and the election of Paul IV. The condition of the Society in Rome, and Nadal's successful work in Germany.

Rome, June 17, 1555

IHS

The peace of Christ.

Long before the arrival of this letter you shall have heard that God has taken to an eternal pontificate our holy father Marcellus II, of happy memory, having allowed him only twenty-three days of labor in his temporal pontificate. A happy exchange for him, and for us a great help to place in God alone our trust for the fulfillment of our desires for the Church universal and for our Society. If we had to found this hope on human means, it must have seemed that our mainstay would be the pontiff who from the very first days of his elevation by word and example worked only for the reform of the Church. He was so devoted to the Society that the very first time our father went to the Vatican to kiss his foot, he asked for two of Ours to remain with him in his palace to confer with him and advise him. Master Lainez and Master Nadal were appointed. He wished to endow not only our colleges in Rome, but his desires went even farther, with all the affection that one of the Society could have had. But God our Lord called him away. May He be blessed who is able "of these stones" to make as many others as He wishes, as good and even better than He.[1]

Four of us had asked our father permission to make a pilgrimage to Our Lady of Loretto to petition for the pope's restoration to health, Fathers Louis Gonzalez, Dr. Loarte, Don James de Guzman, and myself. He granted the permission; but before we arrived there we heard of the pope's death. In a sense God gave us more than we asked for. Instead of bodily health He gave that of heaven, and taught us, as I said above, to place our trust in Him alone.

A few days after our return to Rome the present pope was elected. May it please Christ Jesus, our Lord and God, to make him a successful minister and agent of His providence for the universal good of His Church. Your reverence, together with the members of your community, should earnestly ask this of the divine and supreme Goodness.

[1] Matthew 3:9; Luke 3:8.

There has been no little consolation in the obedience which three ambassadors of the king and queen of England have given these days to the Holy See and the vicar of Christ our Lord. His holiness has made high festival over it, as well he might.[2]

The pope has spoken warmly about the reform of the Church, saying that he wants to make deeds an answer to so much talk, or die in the attempt. May God our Lord grant that we may see something soon.

Here in Rome we have become very numerous, for although some have been sent away these days to various places, the number in the college is higher than 112, and in this house we are between 60 and 70.

Services are held in our church as usual, especially sermons and confessions. The Spiritual Exercises are given outside, enemies are reconciled, old and obstinate sinners recalled, catechism taught, and other works of mercy, corporal and spiritual, practiced. It would take too long to go into particulars.

There is a little letup in studies because of the heat, but care is taken to see that there is steady application. The attendance is good for this country. Before long some young men, good prospects all, will be sent from the house to the college. They come from various nations, and were sent to us these last few months by God. They have a strong desire of entering the Society.

The German College is also doing very well, and this September, in accordance with an agreement between the king of the Romans and Father Nadal, forty-eight students will be sent to the college, with all their expenses paid. He himself is thinking of bringing others with him. In this large number from the northern nations coming to the Society, and the large number to the German College, God our Lord gives us the hope that He intends to have pity on the poor people who are living in such great darkness of error. It is difficult to help them otherwise than by training laborers who speak their own language. And while it is true that Father Nadal does not speak it, he is not idle in that country. For since the legate Morone's return for the election of the pope, he remained behind at the earnest request of the cardinal of Augsburg,[3] to visit the college at Dillingen and Ours in Vienna, as can be seen from copies of his letters, which we will send if we can. In Vienna something has been accomplished by him which has greatly consoled us, although we have not had

---

[2] The English legation had been decreed while Julius III was still alive, and consisted of Anthony de Montague; Thomas Goldwell, bishop of St. Asaph; and Sir Edward Cherne. They arrived in Rome on the very day of Paul IV's coronation.

[3] Otto Truchsess.

any letter from him. But the cardinal of Augsburg has heard from two sources that King Maximilian had a preacher whom he much favored who was a Lutheran and who preached that doctrine publicly with great scandal because of the actual harm done and sorrow caused by the suspicion that the king sympathized with such teaching.[4] We now understand that Master Nadal so deported himself that the preacher took flight and escaped only with his life for having deceived the king. And not only did he rid the city of this pest, but he even left souls consoled and edified when they understood that, if the king had favored that evil man, it was not because he believed his false doctrine but because he insisted that he had the true doctrine. Praised be God our Lord, who does not abandon His own in the end, and may He be pleased everywhere to increase the knowledge and glory of His holy name. Amen.

¶ TO FATHER ALBERT FERRARESE
IX, 266-67, Letter 5500

St. Ignatius gives some norms for use in the confessional regarding women whose dress is not altogether modest and who spend too much money on it, especially if they frequent the sacraments.

Rome, June 29, 1555
JESUS

My dear Father Master Albert.
Pax Christi.

From father rector's letter we learn that your reverence is uneasy about the dress and personal adornment of the women of Venice. You are quite right, for in this matter they frequently offend both God our Lord and are the cause of others offending Him. Where the practice is common, however, and there neither is nor appears to be any excess other than the said practice and no intention of sinning or of causing others to sin, it is not considered mortally sinful. Moreover, if any woman should do it to please her husband, there would not be even venial sin. On other occasions

---

[4] Sebastian Pfauser, of whom Polanco has much to say (*Chronicon*, V, 230 and 235). Polanco corrects himself (*Chronicon*, V, 273) later, and discloses the cause of his mistake. "On the very day of Father Nadal's arrival in Vienna, the heretic preacher departed, which gave rise to the rumor that the preacher had been driven from Vienna by Father Nadal. But Nadal writes that he left Vienna as a result of the sermons of Canisius against him and the letters written by Canisius to the king of the Romans, and the letters of Lanoy to the bishop of Laybach." See Braunsberger, *Beati Canisii epistulae et acta*, I, 53-55.

we have written on this matter as follows. Where there is no notable curiosity—nothing beyond what is common—and no bad intention, although there might be some vanity in a woman so presenting herself as to display her charms, and so forth, they could be absolved the first time with an admonition and a bit of advice. But if they confess this again, especially if they are frequent communicants, you must make them give up this vanity and restrain this bad habit as much as possible. Should they be unwilling to comply, you could tell them that for this time you will absolve them but not in the future, and that they should go elsewhere to confession if they do not wish to give up their vanity. Even though you do not condemn them as guilty of mortal sin, there is great imperfection, and if one does not wish to give up such an imperfection the Society will have nothing to do with her. And yet your reverence may be allowing your zeal to mislead you, and so, in such cases, you should be guided by the judgment of the rector, since it is possible for him to know outside of confession what everyone knows and sees. Do not be timid or scrupulous whenever he thinks you should not be.

I will say no more, except that charity and the desire to help souls is wont to make the members of the Society brave, and in this way God helps them. I beg of Him to bestow upon your reverence the abundance of His grace.

¶ TO FRANCIS JIMENEZ DE MIRANDA
IX, 308-11, Letter 5525

Francis Jimenez de Miranda, abbot of Salas in the province of Burgos, was living in sacrilegious wedlock in Rome from 1554 to 1556, and was also making illicit use of the ecclesiastical revenues he held. He wished to found a college in Burgos and entrust it to the Society in atonement for his faults. But he kept putting off the carrying out of his purpose because of the difficulties his own sins put in his way and the covetousness of a brother, who claimed the abbot's income for himself and for his children. St. Ignatius, with the disinterestedness which will appear, had the conversion of this unfortunate man much at heart. To obtain this grace the fathers in Rome said two Masses daily. Besides having recourse to God, the saint endeavored by means of visits, letters, and so forth, to have this old man make a radical change in his life, and he succeeded to the extent of removing the occasion of his sins from his house. The unhappy man, nevertheless, clung to his evil ways and refused to receive the visits or answer the letters of the saint. Ignatius finally sent him the following letter. It is an excellent example of his unselfish, courageous, and untiring apostolic zeal.

Rome, July 11, 1555

IHS

My very reverend and honorable Lord in Jesus Christ.

As I have not been able to gain admittance to your presence, either by messenger, note, or personal call, I might easily give up from weariness if I were looking for something for myself. But as I am sincerely seeking something that has to do with God's service and your salvation, I should not yield to weariness, or give up trying to accomplish by letter what I could not do by word of mouth, if the least vestige of charity remained in me.

My lord, what urges me most is not to get the college in Burgos started. God will bring that about in His own time by some one or other, since it is a work of such great service to God. I do indeed desire that your worship be the founder; and seeing that we have done everything possible to satisfy your conditions, even to our father's offering to turn over to your lordship's disposal the houses we now have there, I have nothing further to ask in this matter. What hurts me most is the continual delay you resort to in what concerns the welfare of your soul, as I see that in this negligence there is a very great and imminent danger. As I love you in Christ our Lord and daily beg God for your salvation in my Masses and prayers, I cannot help feeling a great sorrow until I behold you once more traveling on the road to salvation. I recognize your advanced years, I recognize the condition of your health, your disposition, your physical ailments, to be such that, when we least expect it, death may overtake you. What would cause me extreme anguish is that death should find you unprovided with the penance which your sins demand, and with the good works that are necessary if you are to attain to eternal happiness.

My lord, this is no time for pretenses with those who love you. Do not look upon him as a friend or servant, but as a mortal enemy of your soul, who attends you with flattery, especially those who reassure you and hold you in your sins. What you need is penance, and much of it.

This means that you must not only withdraw from your sin and be sorry for it, but that you must make satisfaction for past sins and unburden your conscience of so much church property that has been misappropriated. I am not talking about injustice *in foro externo,* but of church property which is not necessary for the support of your state and which belongs to the poor and to pious works. According to the holy doctors, it is a great injustice to deprive them of these goods. It will not be enough that the Rota or the papal tribunals give you the possession and enjoyment of these revenues when you come to stand before the tribunal of Christ our Lord, who will have to demand of you a strict accounting of all that you have taken from the Church. Very soon it will be necessary for you to appear in person before His infinite justice to await a peremptory sentence, from which there shall be no appeal. It will be either to a happy and most blessed life full of joy and consolation and inestimable honor, or to a most unhappy death and eternal damnation, full of all the miseries and torments which the rigor and severity of divine justice has prepared for those who die impenitent and without having made satisfaction for their sins.

You do not know whether you will be summoned to this judgment this coming September, or this month, or this very night. Many a man in better health than you enjoy, more conservative in his personal habits, has gone to bed without a care, and was not alive when morning came. Do not put your soul in such peril. By the love of Jesus Christ, by the blood He shed to redeem your soul, make ready to give a good account of yourself and of all that God our Lord has given you to dispense. As He has awaited you this long with so much mercy, do not allow the short time of life that remains to slip by fruitlessly, so that you find yourself at the last moment, when you would give everything you have and all that the world is worth for an hour in which to repent and do good. And it will not be given you if now in the time granted you by the wisdom of God you refuse to help yourself.

You will pardon my straightforward speech. But my love constrains me, and I should not want my conscience to accuse me of having omitted this service expected of one who is devoted to you and who desires your eternal salvation. Every day, most unworthy though I am, I beg God's supreme clemency, and I feel that you lack those who should remind you of your duty. I know that there are some who speak in a contrary sense, let alone the fact that the flesh and the devil add their contribution.

I am so anxious to see you dispose yourself for the grace of God our Lord by good and pious works that, if you thought that our college ought to be deferred in favor of any other work which you had in mind, for the relief of your conscience and your own greater merit in the eyes of our Lord, I would readily agree. But it would not be a good work to bestow wealth on one's relatives who already have enough according to their state; nor to set up monuments of little spiritual advantage and little help for the common good. But to give to the poor and to pious works is what raises everlasting monuments in heaven for those to enjoy who make them, while for those which are worldly and vain, they merit torment and the severest pain. You should remember that you are not absolute master of your possessions but their steward, and that you will be held accountable for them. This will suffice for one of your understanding.

Here we do not, and will not, cease to ask God's goodness in behalf of your lordship, whether you thank us or not. God is our end, and these many years now I have been a kind of chaplain of yours, although you do not look upon me as such or give me credit for my good intention. It is enough, however, to have God and my conscience for witness. May the Holy Spirit be with your lordship.

¶ TO PETER CAMPS
IX, 507, Letter 5653

A letter of courtesy. Ignatius is glad that the affairs of the Society are prospering in Barcelona. He hopes that the opposition that has arisen, once the truth is known, will turn to greater good. He gives thanks for the support given to Ours, and promises to remember the living and the dead whom Peter recommends to his prayers.

Rome, August 29, 1555

My dear Sir in our Lord.

May the sovereign grace and everlasting love of Christ our Lord ever be our help and support.

From your letter of May 13 last, I see that you rejoice that the members of the Society have established themselves in Barcelona by taking a house and opening a church. It is easy to see that the source of your rejoicing is the great charity that God has given you in our regard especially. He too will be your reward. Even I find no little consolation in the same Lord because what we are trying to do for His service in your city is a source of satisfaction to those for whom we ought earnestly to desire it together with every service for God's glory. The opposition which was, and continues to be, manifested is nothing new for us. Rather, from the experience we have had in other places, we hope that Christ our Lord will be all the better served in Barcelona the more obstacles he raises who is always trying to hinder His service, and to this end urges this one and that one to think, with every good intention, but under the influence of misinformation, that they oppose, because they do not understand it, what they think should be opposed. I am persuaded in our Lord that our college will not be disappointed in the help and support they look for from yourself and the archdeacon,[1] seeing that you have offered to help in words that betray only love and affection.

In our prayers we will be mindful of our duty toward the living and the dead whom you recommend. May the divine and supreme Goodness hear them, and may it please Him to give us His bountiful grace always to know His most holy will and perfectly to fulfill it.

¶ TO DONA JOAN DE VALENCIA
IX, 552-53, Letter 5683

The young nobleman Don Frederick Manrique de Lara, having heard the sermons of Father Lainez in Genoa, made up his mind to enter the Society of Jesus. After he had spent a year in the religious life, St. Ignatius answered his mother, Doña Joan, with the following letter, in which he praises the mother's conformity with God's will in the vocation of her son. He assures her of the great satisfaction he feels in the novice's progress in virtue and learning.

Rome, September 5, 1555

JESUS

My dear Madam in our Lord.

Your letter was the occasion of great consolation to me in our Lord, as I learned from it that the same spirit that moved Don Frederick, your son, to adopt the Society's way of life, moved you likewise to find satisfaction in his decision. This is a proof that the great love you bear him is not so much merely the tenderness of flesh and blood as the spirit of charity with which we desire true and eternal blessings for him we love rather than the temporal and passing goods of this life. This I can tell you with complete assurance, that, as far as we have observed up to the present, there is good reason for one who loves Don Frederick to be consoled at seeing him in his present state of life. Besides his great peace of mind, it seems that God our Lord is daily giving him an increase of His grace and virtue. In this way He gives us all great edification and offers the hope

---

[1] Dimas Camps, Peter's brother.

that His Divine Majesty will be greatly served and glorified in him. He is also doing very well at his studies and is making more than ordinary progress. We are therefore very well satisfied with him, God be praised.

I have written what we think of him because I know it will give you consolation. If in any way our Society can be of service to you, we would be only too glad to have you command us with every confidence.

No more for the present, except to beg the divine and supreme Goodness to deign to give us all His plentiful grace, so that we may always know His most holy will and perfectly fulfill it.

¶ TO FATHER FRANCIS BORGIA
ix, 626-27, Letter 5736

Although Ignatius was wont to look to God for everything in all he did, yet he never thought that human plans and helps were to be neglected. He lays down two directives, one that Borgia undertake to help the Roman College to the extent of his powers, and the other that he take the means which most recommend themselves to him. He approves in advance whatever decision Borgia makes in the matter.

Rome, September 17, 1555

IHS

May the sovereign grace and everlasting love of Christ our Lord ever be our help and support.

As I look for God in all things and try to please Him in everything I do, I hold it a mistake to put my trust in any means or plans, and in them alone. I do not think it a safe practice either so to trust in God our Lord as not to wish to help myself with what He has already given me, because it seems to me, in our Lord, that I must make complete use of both, seeking only His greater praise and glory and nothing else. I have therefore given orders that the principal members of the community meet together in order that they may be able to see better in our Lord what ought to be done concerning the college and its students after they have read what has been written you on the subject. For two reasons I am persuaded with complete peace of mind that it will be to God's greater glory. The first is that you devote yourself with all care to this work; and the second, that whatever means you shall judge to be better in our Lord, I fully approve; so that whatever you judge in His Divine Majesty, I fully approve as better and more certain of success. In this matter we have but one will, but you are in closer touch with affairs where you are and with the princes, concerning whom information is asked by those who write. Full information of developments will be given from here.

I close, asking God our Lord through His infinite and sovereign goodness to give us His perfect grace always to know His holy will and perfectly to fulfill it.

¶ TO FATHER SIMON RODRIGUES
IX, 707-08, Letter 5799

Ignatius answers a letter with every mark of affection. He forgets the past and asks Rodrigues that, mindful of his profession, he continue in every way to help the souls for whom Christ shed His blood.

Rome, October 12, 1555

I received your letter of September 4, and learned likewise from Master Nadal by word of mouth what had best be done in your regard. As one who loves you very much in our Lord, I am greatly consoled by anything I hear concerning your well-being. As to your submission and the prompt willingness to obey which you show, I give thanks to God our Lord. May it please Him to grant you the plenary indulgence with remission of fault and penalty which you ask of me, because on my part I have always been, and still am, very faithful in forgetting the past, and especially with one whom I have always loved to God's glory. Indeed, instead of lagging behind, I am ready to go much further in what you ask of me. If you are well in the hermitage where you are, stay there in that part of the country, or go to Padua or Venice, just as you think best and will be more consoling to you. Superiors of our colleges and houses will receive word to take all the care of you that you need, and we will help you from this end even more than our slender resources would seem to warrant. But we must believe that the divine and sovereign wisdom will direct all things for the good of all, to serve and glorify Him and attain in Him our ultimate and supreme good.

But wherever you are, I would not have you forget to help the souls that have cost Christ our Lord so dear, in keeping with our profession, even though you do no more than converse with individuals and exhort them, or in any way that you will find convenient.

This will be all, except to beg God our Lord to keep you in His holy grace, and give us the grace to know and fulfill His holy will.

¶ TO ISABEL DE VEGA
x, 5-7, Letter 5825

A letter of sympathy. Ignatius consoles Isabel on the early death of Ferdinand de Silva, and promises many prayers for him, her father, and her uncle. He will look after the College of Bibona, which owes its foundation to Isabel's charity, and hopes that it will turn out to God's glory. He entrusts further messages to Domenech, who is on the point of setting out.

Rome, October 20, 1555

JHS

My Lady in our Lord.

May the sovereign grace and everlasting love of Christ our Lord greet and visit your ladyship with His most holy gifts and spiritual graces.

I received your letter of August 10 a little late. Because of weak health I have delayed even longer in giving you an answer, although I have not delayed in the prayers and Masses for the soul of Señor Ferdinand de Silva[1] which you ask of me. God rest his soul. Even if there was no chance of his receiving the last sacraments before he died, there is every reason to hope that Divine Providence from the depths of His infinite mercy will have supplied that lack—that mercy from which the sacraments and all the other means of salvation derive their efficacy. I know that when he passed through Genoa he made a general confession to Master Lainez, and this earnest wish to confess is a proof of that interior contrition which God our Lord gives to those to whom He wishes to show mercy.

Likewise, the remembrance which your ladyship bids me have of his lordship the duke[2] and his affairs is so much a duty that it would be a great fault on my part to be unmindful of it. May it please the author of all good to pour His abundant grace on your ladyship and your illustrious family, which is my desire and earnest prayer in His divine presence.

Our Society should have much at heart the health of Señor John de Vega, not only because of his fatherly interest in us, but very especially because this interest has so important a bearing on God's glory and the general good of souls, in whose service he has so truly and so successfully employed these many years. If the rumor in Rome about a change proves

---
[1] Isabel's young and worldly cousin. He died suddenly before a priest could reach him.
[2] Peter de Luna, duke of Bibona, Isabel's husband.

true, we have all the more reason to pray earnestly for his health to Him who is the true health of all. May it please His infinite wisdom to direct Señor Ferdinand de Vega[3] in the important decision of which your ladyship writes. In this house we will so beseech Him.

As to the College of Bibona, the information which Master Jerome Domenech gives us shows the devotion and charity which assisted at its foundation. Because of this I hope in God our Lord that He will be well served in it. As to the staff needed to make a beginning, at least in one of our colleges, Master Jerome knows that we have done what we could, although not all that we could have wished to do if our resources were greater. God will add to them for His service, and the event will show that we all have the proper regard for a work begun with such charity and carried on for God's service.

Referring you to Master Jerome for other matters, I will restrict myself to asking God constantly to increase in your ladyship, along with an increase of purity and a greater share of His light and love, contempt of self and a great esteem of the blessings of His goodness and liberality. May it please Him to give us all His grace always to know His most holy will and perfectly to fulfill it.

¶ TO JEROME VINES
x, 154-56, Letter 5919

Some practical direction on prayer.

Rome, November 17, 1555

Most honorable Lord in Christ Jesus.

The peace of Christ.

Concerning the method of prayer which your lordship asks about, it necessarily consists of various ways, not only in general but in particular. I should think that your lordship should come to a decision, and do what you can calmly and gently. Do not be disturbed about the rest, but leave to God's providence what you cannot manage yourself. God is well pleased with the earnestness and moderate anxiety with which we attend to our obligations, but He is not pleased with that anxiety which afflicts the soul, because He wishes our limitations and weakness to seek the support of His strength and omnipotence, with the trust that in His goodness

---

[3] The brother of John de Vega.

He will supply what is lacking to our weakness and shortcomings. If one is involved in much business, even though his intention be good and holy, he must make up his mind to do what he can, without afflicting himself if he cannot do all that he wishes; let him do all that a man ought to do who follows the dictate of a good conscience. If other things permit, you must have patience and not think that God our Lord requires what man cannot accomplish, nor that He wishes you to be cast down. And if one satisfies God, what difference does it make whether he satisfies men? There is no need to wear yourself out, but make a competent and sufficient effort, and leave the rest to Him who can do all He pleases. May it please His divine goodness always to communicate the light of His wisdom so that we may see and fulfill His will in us and in everyone else. Amen.

¶ TO JEROME VINES
x, 206-08, Letter 5945

Ignatius consoles Jerome in the sickness of Michael and Fabricius Vines, his brothers, and begs him to moderate his anxiety about money affairs. God will not abandon him.

Rome, November 24, 1555

IHS

Very honorable Sir in Jesus Christ.

The peace of Christ.

. . . With regard to the illness of our dear brother Michael Vines, I pray that Christ be his spiritual health. We are rightly envious of him, because he has the double merit of patience in his trials and of charity, with which he accepts and recognizes the favor as coming from God's hands, in the certainty that our most wise and loving Father will send him only that which is good for his ultimate and supreme end. Considering how He also visits our other brother Fabricius (although without threat of death), and your lordship too with no slight trials, and your parents (whom I must judge to be of similar virtue with their children), I am convinced that God loves all of your blessed family because He treats them as true sons whom He wishes to console in His eternal kingdom rather than in their exile. And yet I hope that He will give them great consolation in this present life also, seeing that they are sons who are given to every virtue as good servants of Christ, and consequently heirs of supreme and everlasting happiness. . . .

The anxiety which your lordship shows at the approaching time for the payment of a large sum of money should, I think, be moderated. It ought to beget diligence rather than worry. Remember that God our Lord, whose service is our sole aim, is very rich in power and mercy, and no matter what difficulty may be experienced in the management of temporal affairs, which is a natural consequence of poverty, He does not and will not abandon us. He is more interested in our not forgetting our profession, and would have us exercise confidence in Him and not rely too much on the things of earth. Nevertheless, we shall not fail to cooperate with His grace, and will seek those means which, according to the course of His providence, we ought to seek.... May the Holy Spirit be your consolation and continual spiritual progress.

¶ TO HENRY DE LA CUEVA
x, 222-24, Letter 5953

Ignatius is surprised that his letters have not reached Henry, and tells him that he is no longer to doubt or deliberate about his vocation to the Society, since he was moved by God's grace to take a vow to enter religion. He recommends that he follow Borgia's direction as to where he should finish his studies and that he allow himself to be guided by obedience to him. He bids him go to Borgia, to whom he also writes, and earnestly exhorts him to humility. Ignatius tells him to consider no one in the Society of less importance than he.

Rome, November 28, 1555

JHUS

The peace of Christ.

May the sovereign grace and everlasting love of Christ our Lord ever be our aid and support.

From your letter of September 29 to the most reverend cardinal,[1] our common lord and father in our Lord, I gather, not without some surprise, that you have not received the decision we reached here concerning your state of life and the place where you could spend a few years in recollection and study. You must have known this from the letters of Father Francis and Dr. Araoz,[2] of September 10, supposing them to

---
[1] Bartholomew de la Cueva.
[2] Fathers Francis Borgia and Anthony Araoz.

have sent you my letter. This was the second I sent you to let you know of the decision arrived at here and which I had sent on to you in different letters. By this time you should not only be acquainted with this decision, but already in the course of carrying it out. And yet I will repeat here the first part of that decision. After conferring, reflecting, and praying over the matter, we came to the conclusion that you should accept the call to the Institute to which God has inspired and moved you and to which you have dedicated yourself by special vow, having made a total offering of yourself to His Divine Majesty. As I have no doubt on this score, I write you as though you were already one of my brothers, whom God has entrusted especially to my care.

As to the second part which concerns a place to which you can retire, you can be sure that I very much desire in our Lord that you manage to get to a place that is best suited to contribute to your greater spiritual consolation and advancement, where you can lay the foundation for the strong course in letters that will be needed in your vocation. There is no such place at present in Italy. Such is the opinion of the most reverend lord cardinal, and it will have to be elsewhere, some place that will be judged most appropriate. It seems to me in our Lord that it would be much more perfect on your part to leave this choice to the free judgment of Father Francis as our commissary, who in the Society in those kingdoms has all the authority of Christ our Lord. Because, over and above your thinking that the Divine Wisdom will have greater communications with him because of the office He has entrusted to him, it is fitting that you and every true religious, having made the sacrifice of yourself by offering yourself whole and entire as a holocaust to the divine and supreme Goodness, keep nothing for yourself, as they do who hold their own wills in reserve and seek to follow their own opinions. Thus they take back for themselves the principal part of what they had surrendered to God our Lord through the hands of their superiors. And because I have a very special reason and obligation for desiring in you all the perfection that I wish in the best of my brethren, I would be much pleased if in this matter you put yourself with all confidence into the hands of Father Francis, whom I have again reminded to take the greatest care of you personally. It seems to me that, if you are to deal with him, it would be better if you go to him, for you can come to a better understanding in this way than you could by letter. I am sending with this a letter for him which I should like to have you deliver personally.[3]

---

[3] See the following letter.

I cannot help opening my heart to you, my dearest brother, as to one whom I dearly love in our Lord. Be assured that I would not want anyone to enter this Society who was not willing to humble and abase himself more than you have given signs of being willing to do. Take into account also that in all those kingdoms there is no one in the Society of less importance than yourself, or anyone of whom you should think less than of yourself. In this way, before God our Lord and those who think as God does, you will enjoy a greater reputation, while if you acted otherwise, you would neither help your own soul nor would you give satisfaction either in heaven or on earth by your procedure. But I hope in Him who by word and example recommended this virtue of humility so earnestly to us, inviting us especially to imitate Him in it, that He will bestow it upon you, and that upon it as a foundation He will raise up in your soul many very great spiritual gifts, by means of which you will serve and glorify His divine and supreme Goodness. May He be pleased to give us all the fullness of His grace, so that we may always know His most holy will and perfectly fulfill it.

I commend myself very especially to your prayers.

¶ TO FATHER FRANCIS BORGIA
x, 225, Letter 5954

Ignatius mentions previous letters, and desires that Henry de la Cueva be sent by Borgia to Portugal to finish his studies. He earnestly recommends the young man and his interests to Borgia.

Rome, November 28, 1555

JHUS

May the sovereign grace and everlasting love of Christ our Lord ever be our protection and support.

I am sending herewith the copy of a letter I am writing to Don Henry de la Cueva. You will learn from it that he had not received my letter by September 29, although I think he must have got it later, and of the decision reached here concerning his case. Anyhow, if the other was lost, I am sending this. Although I exhort him to the indifference becoming a religious in the matter of where he is to go, and even if he puts himself freely in your hands, I think nevertheless in our Lord that for good reasons he ought to be sent to Portugal, and because he himself desires it. As far as his spiritual interests are concerned, I would not have him go just because he wanted to go, but I would be glad to have him go because you did.

I commend him personally and his affairs to you as earnestly as I can in our Lord, as you know the obligations we are under to the most reverend lord cardinal, to say nothing of what charity asks of us in his regard.

Master Polanco is writing about other matters.

I commend myself to your prayers, and I beg of God our Lord to give us all His bountiful grace always to know His most holy will and perfectly fulfill it.

¶ TO JOHN PEREZ
x, 307-09, Letter 5998

Ignatius affectionately answers a letter brought to him. He rejoices that such happy fruits have been reaped from the opposition raised against Ours in Saragossa. He thanks Perez for the kindness which he and other friends showed, and hopes that God will reward them for the efforts they made. He cautiously explains to Perez the opinion he asked about his affairs and especially his desire to enter the Society, and promises that he will pray for him. He has a word about the members to be sent to Calatayud. In a postscript he speaks of his health and gives the number of Jesuits in Rome.

Rome, December 12, 1555

JHUS

Very honorable Sir in Christ Jesus.

May the grace and peace of Christ our Lord be ever present in increasing measure in our souls. Amen.

I received your letter of September 12 from those friends of yours who very charitably have promised to carry this answer back. I was greatly consoled in Christ our Lord to see that His Holy Spirit, and the desires and holy aims that come from Him, shine through your letter. As one who loves you dearly in our Lord, I cannot but greatly rejoice and give Him many thanks for His gifts which I behold in you. I beg Him to add to them and to carry you from virtue to virtue until you reach the perfection which He is wont to bestow on His chosen servants both in this world and in the next.

As to the trials which Ours have met in Saragossa and the reparation which has been made to them, there is occasion in both to recognize a great favor of our most kind Father and Lord, since in the first He gave them so great an opportunity to serve Him in patience; and in the second, He gives them an opportunity to help others in His service and gather no little fruit for their own progress and merit and in the spiritual edification and consolation of their neighbors, to God's glory.

For the kindly service which you and your friends have rendered us, and for the share in our trials which their charity has caused them, they will have Christ our Lord to reward them, for whose love and reverence they have acted. May it please His divine and sovereign Goodness to answer for us as only He can do. Amen.

We are convinced that the Evil One has caused all this turmoil in Saragossa because he fears the losses our work there will inflict upon him. We hope therefore that the help given to the souls He loves will be all the greater in the service of God our Lord, which after all is only what we are trying to do everywhere.

I was delighted that you went to Valladolid and Simancas to console Father Francis and to counsel him. I hope that so much good will is not going to be in vain, since He who gives it and moves you so will surely provide some good fruit for the spiritual progress with which you will have returned home after having made the Exercises, and in the desire you indicate of entering the Society if you can reconcile that step with the obligation of caring for five children. I am very eager to have some word of what God our Lord has given you to understand.

You ask me to give you my opinion, but I can hardly comply except in general terms, as I have no knowledge of many particulars on which a sound opinion should be based if it is to have any value. I can say in general that your desires are good and holy, since they partain to a state in which God our Lord is served with greater security and perfection. But the prudence and reflection which you must use to satisfy the obligation which God has laid upon you of educating your family for His service is very holy and necessary. You will have some one nearer at hand to advise you. This I would say with confidence and without fear of error, that you should have a very upright intention, keeping in view only God's will and seeking perfect conformity with it. Thus if you remain in your present state, try to perfect yourself in it, and perhaps it will happen that your sons, or one or other of them, may take the place which is not open to you. Train them in the fear and love of God, and give them as good a religious education as you can. Should you ever change your state, you will not do so without leaving everything provided for, and thus you will be able to give a good account of all that God has entrusted to you. You could not do so if you shirked what is of precept for what is of counsel. The most I can say is that I will promise to ask God to deign to direct all your affairs and to increase daily your soul's knowledge and love of Him.

You will receive news of the Society from Ours in Saragossa. And I should like to have news of what has been done about having some of Ours come to Calatayud for your spiritual consolation and that of the city.

May Christ our Lord give us all His grace ever to know and to fulfill His most holy will.

POSTSCRIPT. Our father master Ignatius is in good health, God be praised—as good as usual—as are all of us in this house. As a rule we are some sixty here, with about a hundred of our college students. We should have many more if since last September we had not sent more than a hundred from Rome to various colleges. But we have received many others to replace them. May Christ our Lord be pleased with them all.

¶ TO JEROME VINES
x, 322-23, Letter 6007

A letter of consolation on the death of Michael, on whom he heaps praises.

Rome, December 15, 1555

JHUS

My very honorable Lord in Jesus Christ.

The peace of Christ.

From your lordship's letter of the eighth of this month we learned that our beloved brother Michael was on the point of taking flight for heaven. Thanks be to Christ Jesus, our life and everlasting happiness, whose wisdom and goodness has thought it best not to leave so good a servant any longer among us, but to free him from the trials and perils of this pilgrimage and give him in exchange the repose, the peace, and the happiness that have no end. Yesterday we received word of another of our young brothers, Gerard Cools, a Fleming, a very learned youth and a great servant of God, whom we were sending from Rome to his native land on the advice of his doctors. Having passed some distance beyond Cologne, he was approaching his own country when he rendered his soul to His Creator. We cannot say anything else than that we envy rather than compassionate them, for both of them have lived in our Society with great purity, obedience, and self-abnegation, together with a desire of serving and glorifying God. We have no doubt that He has gathered them like ripe fruit, not wishing to withhold any longer the inexpressible and inestimable reward which He has prepared for His true and faithful servants. If we find ourselves deprived of the consolation which their physical presence gave us, we should not so much grieve over that as congratulate ourselves on the supreme blessing and happiness of our brothers who will help us better from heaven than they could have done on earth in all that pertains to God's service. This I can assert of Master Michael, that in all the places and for all the time he has lived in our Society, he has left the sweet odor of his rare virtue, and we have heard nothing that would gainsay this. We look upon him as a holy child of God, possessed of the spirit of Christ our Creator and Lord. And although we believe there is but little need, yet as an exercise of charity we have recommended him, and shall continue to do so, to God's sovereign goodness. May it please Him to console his parents and your lordship, with the complete conformity of your own will to His. Amen.

¶ TO THE RECTORS OF THE SOCIETY
x, 451-52, Letter 6068

In the name of St. Ignatius Father Polanco communicates to superiors the order that all shall learn the language of the country where they are living, thus promoting greater union among themselves.

Rome, January 1, 1556

Pax Christi.

It seems to be required for the benefit and edification of the peoples among whom our Society is living and for the increase of union and charity and kindliness among Ours, that in places where we have a college or a house all who do not know the language which is in common use should learn it and as a rule speak it. If each one spoke his mother tongue, there would be much confusion and lack of union, seeing that we are of different nations.

For this reason our father has given orders that in all places where the Society exists, all of Ours should speak the language of that country. In Spain, Spanish; in France, French; in Germany, German; in Italy, Italian; and so on. He has given orders that here in Rome all should speak Italian, so that every day there are lessons in Italian grammar to help those learn it who are unable to use it. No one is allowed to speak to another except in Italian, unless it be to make clear the meaning of some words and thus be better understood. Once a week in the refectory, either at dinner or supper, there is an Italian sermon in addition to the *toni* which are ordinarily held. Care is taken that some of those who are skilled in Italian help the others, so that they can compose their sermons with greater ease. A good penance is given to those who fail in their observance of this regulation.

Likewise our father has given orders that this same rule be written out and kept everywhere in the Society as carefully as possible, due consideration being had for differences of places and persons. For this reason we are writing to your reverence to see that the regulation is kept. Let us know when you receive this.

May Jesus Christ be with us all.

¶ TO JEROME VINES
x, 528-30, Letter 6110

Ignatius consoles him and bids him be at peace, to put all his hope in God, to cast off his melancholy, and to take some kind of recreation. He says that Salmeron is in Vienna and that Ribadeneira is preaching in Louvain, much to the edification of his audience. Jerome's prayers are requested for Ignatius, whose health is poor.

Rome, January 18, 1556

JHUS

The peace of Christ.

... I am not surprised that your lordship is so indisposed, as we have heard that you are considerably worn out, and seemingly allow things that can annoy you to make too great an impression on you. We should desire moderation on both points, because in work, even when it is of a religious nature, there should be moderation, to the end that one will be able to bear up under fatigue, which is impossible when work becomes excessive. In all these events it would be good for the soul to be ready to accept either alternative—that is, success or failure—with a good will, as though coming from God's hand. Let it be enough for us to do what we can according to our weakness, and be willing to leave the rest to Divine Providence, whose business it is. Men do not understand the course of divine providence, and as a result sometimes afflict themselves when they really should be glad.

I am persuaded that God our Lord now wishes to make use of your lordship here below for a while before bringing you to eternal happiness, for the help of many souls, and in many kinds of service, thus laying up for you a greater reward in heaven. Consequently, away with that troublesome imagination! Be ready for any hour when God will be pleased to call you, but leave it to His Divine Wisdom, without giving too much thought to your own fancies. I would even add this, that you ought to take more recreation than you do, and not yield to any of these melancholy thoughts, which are usually encouraged by the devil in order to interfere at least with a greater good.

We had a letter from Master Salmeron from Vilna, dated November 3. Vilna is a city of Lithuania, not far from Moscow and Lesser Tartary. We heard later that he arrived at Vienna in Austria, which is rather close to Italy, but we have had no word from him. When we hear again we will let your lordship know.

Master Peter Ribadeneira reached Louvain and the imperial court, and has begun to preach to the great edification and admiration of all, as your lordship will see from a copy of a letter which I enclose from our master Bernard Olivier, who is himself a good preacher.

Nothing more, except that we recommend ourselves to the prayers of your lordship. About the ninth our father's health took a bad turn, but he is now improving. Please show to Ours what is said about Ribadeneira and Salmeron.

¶ TO JOHN DE MENDOZA
x, 650-51, Letter 6177

While praising his eager desire to come to Rome to enter the Society, Ignatius urges Mendoza to wait until he can get the king's permission, at least until the receipt of letters from the Jesuits of Flanders.

Rome, February 7, 1556

JHUS

My Lord in our Lord.

We have been informed by a special letter from the rector of our college in Naples of the eager desire you have of coming to Rome, as you seem to think that permission from the court is too long delayed, and there is apparently no other way of obtaining your desire. While your eagerness to get into the state of perfection and the impatience consequent on the delay in carrying out these good and holy desires is a source of great edification to all of us, I think in our Lord that it would be better both for your own interests and those of the Society to wait a little longer. It is quite possible that any moment now the king's permission will be granted. You will then very shortly accomplish with the kind grace of his majesty what you would do now without it. I ask this favor of you for the love of Christ our Lord, and your love of me, to wait at least until we get an answer from Ours, and that you remember that you are really there where your heart is, and that this waiting is one of the greatest trials you could undergo.

I will close, asking God our Lord to guide you with a very special providence in the way of His greater service, and for us all the grace of always knowing His most holy will and perfectly fulfilling it.

¶ TO ALEXIS FONTANA
xi, 5-6, Letter 6216

The saint admires the good example of detachment from this world which was given by the abdication of Charles V.[1] He hopes that Philip II will make use of his royal office for the good of the people and the salvation of his soul. All the others should pray for him with this intention. As to Fontana, he is quite right in accepting his personal disgrace as a gift from the hand of God. The peace that he experiences proves that God has placed a sincere desire for His service in his heart. Ignatius hopes God's grace will help Fontana in the task of reorganizing his life.

Rome, February 16, 1556

My most excellent Sir in Jesus Christ.

After the enclosed notes were written, but which we were not able to send by means of Melan, we received yours of the eighteenth of January

---

[1] The abdication of Charles V, which took place October 25, 1555, was a cause of great surprise to the statesmen of his time. It left Prince Philip, who was already governing the Low Countries, master of the whole realm. Concerning both of these events Ignatius has an exchange of thought with one of the secretaries of the emperor. This same secretary, Alexis Fontana, lost his place when Philip II ascended the throne. He accepted this change without any attempt to regain favor. From the correspondence of Ribadeneira and the chronicle of Polanco (*Chronicon*, VI, 445, 454, 464, 474), we learn that he remained some time at the court of Brussels, supporting, as he had always done, the affairs of the Society. He finally retired to Sardinia, his native land, where he later built a college of the Society. Ignatius, informed of his disgrace, helped him with his virile advice to bear his lot like a Christian—this especially in the second of the two letters which follow.

with others from Señor Peter de Zarate. But the letters from Master Peter Ribadeneira which you said were coming by the same post with yours have not arrived. The news which the letters of your excellency contained brought us great comfort and consolation, and our father gives you his personal thanks for the news of the renunciation of his estates and the departure for Spain of his imperial majesty. To be sure, the world has good reason to give thanks to God our Lord for such an example. One would have to see it to believe it, as men are usually attached to the things of earth, things that are sometimes such trifles in themselves. The infinite and sovereign goodness of God is filling the heart of the father with the blessings of heaven. May He increase His gifts in the son, so that He may not allow him to be crushed under the weight of the government of these vast and important kingdoms; and may the son administer them to the greater glory of Him who bestowed them, to the good of all men, so as to merit for himself the crown of eternal glory. It is only right that all good men be instant in their prayers to the divine and sovereign Goodness, and ask very special graces for his majesty to enable him to bear this burden upon his shoulders, be it ever so great.

You will do us a great favor by letting us know the address of Señor Vargar, and consequently your own.

What you say of Master Peter Ribadeneira's method of doing business and preaching carried great weight, as one might expect, with our father and all of us, and has given us no little satisfaction in our Lord. When the letters that are due arrive, we hope to learn something in detail.

¶ TO ALPHONSE RAMIREZ DE VERGARA
xi, 184-86, Letter 6327

Ignatius answers that he is very much interested in the affairs of Vergara, and tells him that reason is the best guide in attaining perfection. There is no need of having recourse to fresh and interior movements of the will. In a postscript he bids Borgia try to accommodate Vergara.

Rome, March 30, 1556

IHS

My dear Sir in our Lord.

May the sovereign grace and everlasting love of Christ our Lord ever be our help and unfailing support.

From your letter of February 4 and another from Father Francis Villanueva I understand your situation and the decision you have come to. As to praying for you and having others do so, that I will undertake very willingly because I desire for you, as I ought, not only every perfection but every consolation as well.

The Holy Spirit will teach you better than anyone else the means to take to relish with affection and to put into execution with sweetness that which reason points out to be for the greater service and glory of God. It is true that reason gives us sufficient motives for seeking what is better and more perfect. And yet the will, even when this determination and execution do not precede, can easily attain it, since God our Lord rewards the confidence we place in His providence and the complete surrender of self and giving up of one's consolation, with a deep contentment and relish and all the greater abundance of spiritual consolation, especially when one does not seek it, but seeks rather His glory and good pleasure alone. May it please His infinite and sovereign Goodness to direct all your efforts as may best conspire to this end. . . .

May Christ our Lord give us all His grace always to know His most holy will and perfectly to fulfill it.

I am writing to Father Francis that I would be glad to satisfy you in having Father Villanueva come to Alcala if it can be done without prejudice to God's greater service. I hope that he can do so, although getting the work started at Plasencia may detain him somewhat. This project at Plasencia will be as much yours as is that at Alcala. Entirely yours in our Lord . . .

¶ TO ALEXIS FONTANA
xi, 189-90, Letter 6330

In this letter of consolation and advice Ignatius is dealing with a man who showed that he knew how to accept disappointments as from God's hand.

Rome, March 31, 1556

My Lord in our Lord.

. . . In the new distribution of secretarial offices, it seems to me that you are making no mistake in accepting this blow as from the hand of God, whose greater service and glory we should seek in all conditions and states of life. When a man with that end in view tries one means and then another, he should be convinced that the one that does not succeed is not suited for the end he has in view. He should therefore give thanks to the Sovereign Goodness no less sincerely for having failed in what he was seeking than he would if he had succeeded. The peace and satisfaction which you experience in this regard is a sure sign of your sincerity of purpose and the desire which God gives you for His greater service. God grant that in the decision to be made you will have the benefit of His light and His Spirit, which will insure your choosing that which will be for His greater glory and praise and your own perfection. As is only right, we are remembering this intention in our prayers. I will merely add that I think it quite reasonable for you to have some regard for your health. Do not take upon yourself more work than you can conveniently carry, but husband your strength for God's greater service. . . .

May Christ our Lord grant us the grace to know His most holy will and fully to accomplish it.

¶ TO FATHER ANTHONY SOLDEVILA
XI, 275-77, Letter 6386

Soldevila was a restless and hardheaded man, and something of a health crank, who had given much trouble by his disobedience. He is here threatened with dismissal unless he mends his ways.

Rome, April 19, 1556

JHUS

The peace of Christ.

I could wish that this my first letter to you were concerned with matters of greater spiritual comfort than this is going to be, for him who is writing it as well as for him who is going to read it. However, it is not advisable to shirk this annoyance, to wait to see whether you will improve more than seems likely, especially if we are to judge the future by the past. And yet God our Lord is almighty, great is His grace, and it is His to set our hearts aright. The desire I have for the good of your reverence gives me some hope where there is little ground for it if we take a purely human view of the situation.

We have been informed that you have not kept the promise you made to Father Madrid (not to mention others) of obeying like a dead body and signalizing yourself in this respect, after all the failures of the past, of which your memory together with your conscience, if you take the trouble to recall, will bear you frequent witness. For one who has found himself so often mistaken in his own judgment, it would be reasonable to accept and put into practice that saying of Solomon, "Lean not upon thy own prudence."[1] For beyond the fact that we are to believe the Scriptures and the dictate of reason, that no one is a good judge in his own cause, experience has taught you this to your own great cost. It seems to me that because you have studied what the logicians have to say of obedience, you have profited so much that both yourself and those who associate with you are apparently making yourselves out to be great interpreters and circumscribers of obedience, going about protesting that you have no wish to kill yourselves, and so on. Nothing could be worse than such teaching, or have a more pernicious effect on the union we aim at in the Society and the perfection of obedience which ought to be governed by charity. Like a pestilence, it will not take long to infect a whole college. This is properly the spirit of pride and makes shipwreck of the simplicity and magnanamity of obedience, and its end is voluntary apostasy or dismissal to prevent others from being infected. Nevertheless, in this matter the Society will have regard for the charity it can exercise toward individuals, without prejudice however to the general good.

We are writing to the rector to see that obedience is observed, and that he make out a list of those with whom each of those who need to be curbed may speak. You will have yours. And be careful not to give those to whom you do speak the doctrine mentioned above, which shall not be at all tolerated in the Society. And look to a general repentance and amendment, taking care not to fall into the old difficulties you had at Rome and at Genoa. If you cannot acquire the spirit and way of the Society, it would be better for you to go. For the rest, you may see the rector, to whom we are writing.

May it please Christ our Lord to grant us true humility and abnegation of will and judgment, so that we may deserve to begin to be His disciples. Amen.

¶ TO OCTAVIUS CESARI
XI, 351, Letter 6443

In this letter Ignatius expresses his concern for Octavius' health. He asks him to observe the rules for the sick, and promises to pray for his

---

[1] Proverbs 3:5.

restoration to health. Octavius was the son of Nicholas and the only previous letters concerning him dealt with his mother's desire to have him visit her in Naples. This request Ignatius refused because he felt it might jeopardize her son's vocation.

Rome, May 10, 1556

JHUS

The peace of Christ.

Although you do not write to us, my dear brother Octavius, we have weekly news of your condition according to directions we have given to father rector, as we want to know whether you are better in health of body and of soul. If God is pleased with the former, we have no doubt He is also pleased with the latter. You should especially give proof in this illness that you are more observant than ever of our rules, those which in your situation can and should be observed, such as that which tells us that the sick should try to edify those who are about them by their patience and that they should be obedient to the doctor and the infirmarian. We strongly urge, dear brother, that in this trial you show your good spirit to all. You will then recover your health more rapidly, if, with it, you are to give our Lord greater service. We also recommend that respect and reverence due to your relatives in those matters which do not interfere with your spiritual progress.

You will have other news from the letter which we are writing to Ours today. Here we are merely recommending ourselves to your prayers, even though they be short, and exhort you to maintain your good will and receive your illness cheerfully from God's hand, and give more diligent attention to recovering your health.

May Christ our Lord give you life and perfect health. Amen.

¶ TO FATHER ADRIAN ADRIENSSENS
XI, 374-75, Letter 6454

Ignatius gives some prudent advice on eating and drinking and the preserving of health.

Rome, May 12, 1556

JHUS

The peace of Christ.

We received your reverence's letter dated the last of March, and to answer all your points briefly, I praise your thriftiness and economy and your doing your best to give a good example in all that concerns food. I do not think it is good, however, to withhold what the doctor thinks is necessary for the recovery or the preservation of health, although he too ought to be mindful in this of our poverty. This much in general. It is good, moreover, to get accustomed to what is common and more easily obtained in the matter of food and drink, especially if one enjoys good health, and it is quite in keeping with reason and our Institute, which directs that Ours make use of a menu that is common and ordinary. Therefore if health permits, one should get accustomed to beer, or even water, or cider, where this drink is in common use, and not make use of imported wines, at greater expense and with less edification. Some, however, may be in ill health, such as Master Adrian White, and Master Bernard Olivier and Master Peter Ribadeneira. If they treat their poor bodies well, they will have strength enough for works of zeal and charity for the help and edification of their neighbor. If they don't, they grow weak and feeble, and are of little advantage to the neighbor. They are rather a burden, as happened to Master Bernard and Master Adrian when they were in Italy. I would by no means make these men get used to a coarser diet unless it could be done without injury to their health. Rather, I would prefer God's servants and all those who are ready for heavy labors for Christ to have these comforts than to see others enjoy them who are less useful for the common good. Care should be taken, however, lest what is merely superfluous should be allowed to slip in under the guise of necessity, and things that merely flatter the senses as conducive to health, thus turning a praiseworthy practice into an abuse. Should it be against edification to take some of these extras in public, such things as have been ordered by the doctors as necessary, see that they are taken in private. In a word, all that is needed for health should be provided, but without scandal. This is what may be said in general, and prudence will make the application to particular cases. Decide what is to be done in each case after weighing all the circumstances.

May our Lord give us the light of holy discretion to make use of creatures in the light of the Creator.

Spiritual men will not think it strange or reprehensible to have different food and drink on the same table to answer the requirements of good or ill health. But to avoid scandalizing weaker brethren, should any be present, these special foods can be taken apart. We must not forget Paul's warning against scandalizing the weak.[1]

---

[1] 1 Corinthians 8:13; Romans 14:21.

¶ TO ELEANOR MASCARENHAS[1]
xi, 415-16, Letter 6487

Ignatius faithfully retains sentiments of gratitude which he felt toward Eleanor. The uncertainty she feels because of her ailments ought to be directed to God's service. But since she asks his advice, he suggests that she write to Philip II and explain her position, her desires, and so forth, with perfect frankness. That done, she should abide by the prince's decision. Ignatius prays daily for the new king of Spain, and will continue to do so as long as he lives. He sends Eleanor Mascarenhas ten Agnus Deis.

Rome, May 19, 1556

IHS

May the sovereign grace and everlasting love of Christ our Lord be always in our continued favor and help.

Your two letters, of November and December, reached me on the same day toward the end of April, and I behold in them what is written in my own heart from the first time that we met in our Lord—I mean the intense love and affection which you have for me in His Divine Majesty. I trust that in His divine goodness these sentiments will remain both in your soul and in mine, and go on increasing forever and ever.

With regard to your position and the ailments you suffer, I have done what you so earnestly recommended in your letters; that is, I have had recourse to God to ask Him to show you how you may best serve Him. You ask moreover that I write you what I think and advise you as to what you should do. Speaking as it were in the presence of God, this is my thought in His Divine Majesty, that if I were in your place, I would remain firm and constant in that condition and state decided upon by his highness until I should be ordered to do otherwise. To this end, and that everything be arranged for God's greater glory, I would lay the whole matter before the prince in writing—that is, my desires, my ailments, and any other point which might have connection with the subject. Having done this, I would not have the slightest possible doubt that what his high-

---

[1] Eleanor Mascarenhas was at the time a lady in waiting of the Empress Isabella, and had known Ignatius at Alcala. When he was taken into custody by the vicar of the Inquisition Figueroa, she offered to use her influence to have him freed. But the prisoner refused this help, and from that moment began the profound veneration of Doña Eleanor for Ignatius (Ribadeneira, *Vida*, I, c. xiv). She took a deep interest in the first works of the Society in Spain (*Chronicon*, I, 163). She was governess to Philip II and later to Don Charles, Philip's son. When he outgrew feminine hands, Eleanor entertained the thought of retiring to a convent. She disclosed her perplexities to Ignatius and asked his advice.

ness decided, having a complete view of the situation, would be for God's greater glory. And with this your grace should be consoled and at peace in our Lord.

Your grace urges me to remember Prince Philip in my prayers, who by God's grace is now ruler of such vast states. Indeed, I do so daily, and I hope in His Divine Majesty to continue my prayers for him and to increase them throughout the few days that still remain to me, because he is our prince and we are under great obligations to him, to say nothing of the lively desire and devotion with which your grace reminds me of a duty that is so close to me and to all of this least Society.

Some twelve or fifteen days before the arrival of your letters a devoted friend of mine in the Lord sent me a spiritual present, from which I chose two ornamental Agnus Deis to send to your grace with a word to remind you, as I have said above, that I have held you and still hold you in my heart of hearts, and will do so in the future, even more, if that were possible. Since the receipt of your letters others were sent from the pope's palace, and I have decided to add eight more to the two. Your grace can have them decorated according to your own devotion, or use them as you may think more to God's greater glory.

May it please His infinite and sovereign Goodness to give us His plentiful grace, so that we may know His most holy will and perfectly fulfill it.

¶ TO JOHN BAPTIST[1]
xi, 437-38, Letter 6502

Ignatius tries to strengthen him against the devil's temptation, and urges him to be content with his lot. He asks John to allow himself to be ruled by obedience.

Rome, May 23, 1556

JHUS

My dear Brother John Baptist.

The peace of Christ.

We are not surprised at your temptation regarding studies, for we know that it is the devil's work to annoy and disturb the servants of God. But you should be surprised at yourself for having admitted it, forgetting

---

[1] Although John Baptist gets frequent mention, his family name never occurs.

that the religious should have no will of his own, and in order to do God's will should do the will of his superiors. And you have all the less reason for admitting the suggestion of the devil in this matter, as from the very beginning you were expressly told not to think of studies, but to exercise yourself in the offices of charity and humility. It was thought, taking into account your age and your aptitudes, that you would lose your time at study, and could make better use of it in other employments in God's service.

In the body all the members are not eyes, nor ears, nor hands, nor feet. And as each member has its function, and is satisfied with it, so likewise in the body of the Society all cannot be learned, nor all priests, but each one must be content with the employment given him according to the will and judgment of the superior, who will have to give an account to God of all his subjects.

Finally, John Baptist, if you have given all to God, allow yourself to be guided by God, and act not in your own way, but in God's way. And this you will have to learn by obedience to your superior.

If someone tells you anything else, even though he is transformed into an angel of light, be sure that he is the devil who is trying to draw you out of the Society. The Society will not put up with this self-will of yours if you do not really amend. You may have the name of religious, but if you fail in obedience, you are not a religious at all. Now, for the good we desire for you, we want you to examine yourself and get over the way of acting you have had in this matter for some time now.

May God our Lord give you His grace.

¶ TO EMERIUS

XI, 439-40, Letter 6503

Ignatius allows an excellent man to make a change for his peace of mind and offers him some timely advice on avoiding the snares of the enemy and for correctly dealing with the neighbor.

Rome, May 23, 1556

JHUS

My dear Master Emerius in Christ.

The peace of Christ.

Our father has understood what you wrote. Although you show great courage in overcoming the enemy who up to the present has annoyed, but by God's grace not overcome, you, judging that it would be to your greater consolation, he leaves it to you to decide about coming to Rome next September, or to remain in Padua, or to make a change to some other college in which you could take charge of the first class, as you did here.

In this way you will with God's help defend yourself. Besides your prayer, make it a point not to look at anybody fixedly in the face, which might cause you any uneasiness of heart. In general, when you deal with the neighbor, let your eyes be averted, and try not to think of this one or that one as handsome or ugly, but rather as the image of the most holy Trinity, as a member of Christ and bathed in His blood. Moreover, do not become familiar with anyone. It will be enough in the colleges if you fulfill the task of master through pure charity and obedience. Always deal with your students in the open, and not apart, and extern students should not be allowed the run of the house, unless in some particular case the rector has given permission. By attending to your progress in God's service and the way of perfection, God will continue to help you.

Be on your guard also against those times and occasions when you are usually attacked. Make a slight elevation of the mind to God. And above all, make a real effort to abide in His presence, recalling frequently that His Infinite Wisdom is present both to the inner and exterior man.

There is no call to multiply remedies if these are faithfully made use of. And do not forget the first, which concerns the eyes. You will, then, never complain with him who says: "My eye hath wasted my soul."[1]

Our father and all of us commend ourselves to your prayers.

¶ TO CHARLES CARDINAL OF LORRAINE
xi, 448-51, Letter 6512

A short but accurate refutation of the decree issued by the theological faculty of the University of Paris against the Society of Jesus.

Rome, May 23, 1556

IHS

For the information of the illustrious and most reverend monsignor the cardinal of Lorraine on the decree or censure of the faculty of theology of the University of Paris.

---

[1] Lamentations 3:51.

It would be good to show your most reverend lordship the decree or censure of the said faculty. But we have been unwilling to produce it here in Rome, either to the pope or to any of the ministers of the Apostolic See or to the cardinals, because of the respect and love we bear so celebrated a university, of which our first members are alumni.

In the points which the censure touches upon condemning our Institute, it would not be proper for us to undertake the formal defense of what the apostolic authority itself defends. It was only after several examinations and against the opposition of some that it approved our Institute in the year 1540, confirmed it in 1543, and again in the year 1550. Consequently the censure is rather against the Apostolic See than against the Society.

We have refrained from producing the decree out of respect for the authority and the good reputation of the said faculty of theology, for it would be a blot on their reputation to wish to pass a censure in a matter of such importance and in which, as has been said, the Apostolic See is involved, without having reliable information or a true understanding of the Society and its affairs. That this is true is evident when they say that the Society accepts without distinction all persons, no matter how wicked or infamous they are. The very opposite of this is true of the Society, such men being absolutely excluded by its Constitutions. It receives neither homicides nor those guilty of heresy or schism, or other serious sin of any kind, even when such persons have been restored to good standing.

They are clearly lacking reliable information when they say that the Society gives occasion for apostasies from other orders by offering an asylum to those who abandon them. The fact is that their Constitutions do not allow them to accept one who is actually a member of another order, or has left after having worn the habit for a single day. The Society has a very good opinion of every approved order, and has led many an apostate back to his order. This is especially true of the order of St. Francis, of St. Dominic, the Carmelites, and even others, as can be seen. In these orders there are many who have returned from their apostasy or who have entered for the first time with our help.

It is also a matter of wonder that they say we have no rules, because if they had wished to be informed in the matter, they could have found in the apostolic letters themselves mention made of the Constitutions.

They claim that the Society works to the prejudice of the bishops, parish priests, secular rulers, the people, and the university. The truth is quite the contrary. Our purpose is to help them and serve them in spiritual matters with all the forces at our command, and even in the works of corporal mercy. If our most illustrious and reverend protector wishes, he can see the public testimony of princes and Christian lords, nations, the universities, and the peoples, and even bishops throughout all Christendom, wherever Ours are living, and even among the infidel, which we can collect and send on, from which all who so wish can see that God our Lord makes use of this young plant for the help of souls in every walk of life, and by His grace it will be seen that this is true, for our Society makes its way in the light and before the eyes of men, not only in this Apostolic See, but also in other important lands which it has been able to reach, and from which it will not be difficult to have similar testimony.

We understand that there are only a few, and they perhaps not of the faculty, who by means of this misinformation have procured the said censure, and that they are trying by themselves, or through other means, to misinform your most reverend lordship, and even his most Christian majesty. But truth is mighty, and we hope will overcome falsehood, as it usually does, which is spread either by error or deliberate ill will, insofar as it will be to the greater service and glory of God.

What we wish to do by the present letter, therefore, is to inform our most illustrious and reverend protector, who could, if he judged it proper, also inform his majesty the king. He might also be good enough to deal with the theological faculty, and get it to recall their decree, rather than wait for the Apostolic See to do so, which would redound little enough to their honor. When his most Christian majesty is informed, he can hardly help condemning the decree and showing his dissatisfaction. But this is a move which belongs to the most reverend and illustrious monsignor of Lorraine, our protector, to make.

¶ TO JOHN DE VEGA
XI, 496-98, Letter 6545

Ignatius consoles the viceroy of Sicily on the death of his brother.

Rome, June 5, 1556

My Lord in our Lord.

May the sovereign grace and everlasting love of Christ our Lord greet and visit your most illustrious lordship with His most holy gifts and spiritual graces.

From several letters written by Master Peter Ribadeneira, a priest of our Society, we have learned of the course of Señor Ferdinand de Vega's[1] illness and its conclusion. He is now in glory. But the sorrow we feel at his departure from this life could never have been so great in spite of all the love and affection we felt for him in our Lord, as not to be eclipsed by the consoling assurance we must have of his greater good, when we see that he departed from this mortal and miserable life in such a way as to leave no doubt that it was to make an early entry into life eternal, through the mercy of God, who gave such clear signs of holding him both in life and in death among the number of His chosen servants, and treated him as such. In the same way I hope that the divine and supreme Goodness, who has enriched your lordship with so great a soul and imprinted on it such a lively faith and hope in His changeless and eternal blessings, will not allow you to mourn the brief absence of so good a brother, to such an extent that you fail to recognize and delight in the rare favor shown him, and thus bear with patience the lack of consolation which your lordship would have drawn here below from his presence. And all this because of the bliss and felicity to which our Lord has raised him, bestowing upon him in the very midst of his years what he would have devoted all his years to gain—the last and blessed end for which he was created and redeemed by the life and blood of God's only-begotten Son.

We have taken great care here to commend him to God our Lord throughout all his illness, and later to pray for the eternal salvation and happiness of his soul, although we hope that there will be little need of our prayers, as we may judge from a letter which I am herewith sending you open, in which Master Peter writes to Master Jerome Domenech. I think it will give your illustrious lordship much satisfaction to see it. It will cause you to give thanks to Him who is our life and all our good. May it please Him in this and in all His visitations to give the abundant unction of His grace to your lordship and thus enable you to accept these visitations with complete conformity to His grace, growing through them in merit and love of our most kind and wise Father who with exceeding charity sends them for our greater good.

I close here, begging the same God our Lord by His infinite and supreme goodness to grant us His perfect grace so that we may know His most holy will and perfectly fulfill it. Your illustrious lordship's most humble servant in our Lord . . .

---

[1] John de Vega also had a son, Ferdinand, who died in 1550.

¶ TO FATHER JOHN BAPTIST DE FERMO
XI, 501-02, Letter 6547

Father de Fermo was at work in Siena. He felt himself extremely weighed down by the labor of preaching. In this letter Ignatius tells him his burden will seem heavy only if he keeps his eyes on himself. He tells him instead to put his trust in God and reminds him that God ordinarily helps those who undertake a duty through obedience. Ignatius says he had thought the church was in the center of the city, but whatever its location, it may be suitable for a college.

Rome, June 6, 1556

JHUS

Pax Christi.

From several letters of your reverence we perceive that you lament the weight of the burden which preaching is laying upon you. You have good reason and to spare, as I see it, to consider it heavy if you keep your eyes only on yourself. But consider how powerful is God our Lord to achieve great results even with instruments that are of themselves pure weakness. Such instruments when moved by holy obedience are dismayed at nothing; rather, the lower they are in their own eyes which look upon their own littleness, the more they are encouraged when they consider the power of God, who in His usual mercy avails Himself of the weakest instruments in His Society. Therefore, as long as your reverence is engaged in this office, carry on with courage and confidence in the power of obedience; that is to say, in the power of Christ our Lord, in whose place you obey the superior.

That the church is in an out-of-the-way place does not agree with the information we first had; namely, that it was in the center of the city.[1] Even if what you say is true, and the neighborhood is not thickly populated, it might be suitable for a college. As time goes on, something can be done about it, if it is judged proper.

Cosmas and John Baptist are doing well in their noviceship. May God make them His servants, and give us all the grace always to know and do His most holy will.

All of us here commend ourselves to your reverence's holy sacrifices and prayers.

---

[1] Polanco has something to say about this in *Chronicon*, VI, 125. He has much praise for the site and the church.

¶ TO FATHER MARIN VALENTINE
XII, 30-31, Letter 6615

Ignatius offers a remedy for the scruples of Father Marin.

Rome, June 24, 1556

JHUS

From the letters of Father Jerome,[1] and also of Father Eleutherius[2] our father has learned what God is pleased to accomplish through the ministry of Ours in your city. I am sure that He would make more use of them if the excessive scrupulosity, reinforced by the lack of humble resignation on the part of your reverence, had not proved an obstacle. Up to a certain point scruples will not harm one who is suffering from them, when such a person becomes, because of them, more vigilant and careful about not offending God, without forming a judgment that this or that is sinful, even though he has some doubt or fear that it is, and when he places his confidence in another whom he should trust, setting aside his own judgment and accepting that of his adviser. If these two points do not help the scrupulous person, he is in the gravest danger, not only of offending God by failing to avoid what he erroneously thinks is sin but also of losing the opportunity and the ability to serve Him, and even his own good natural judgment.

So there, Master Marin, make up your mind to keep these two points fixed in your memory: (1) not to make any judgment, or determine by yourself that something is sinful when it is not clearly evident that it is and others do not think so; (2) when you fear that there is sin, you should refer the matter to the judgment of the superior, Father Eleutherius, and believe what he says, not because he is Master Eleutherius (even though he is a man of fine spirit and entirely trustworthy), but as superior, who holds the place of Christ our Lord. You should do the same with any other superior you may have: humble yourself and trust that Divine Providence will rule and guide you by means of your superior. And believe me, if you have true humility and submissiveness, your scruples will not cause you so much trouble. A kind of pride is the fuel they feed on, and it is pride which places more reliance on one's own judgment and less on the judgment of others whom we trust. Do you also beseech God in your prayers and Masses to free you from this suffering or infirmity, as far as is needful to avoid offending Him, or being an

---

[1] Father Jerome Domenech, provincial.
[2] Father Eleutherius Pontano, rector of the College of Bibona.

obstacle to His greater service, and ask the prayers of others for the same intention. Offering you mine, I commend myself to yours.

May Christ our Lord give us all His grace always to know and fulfill His most holy will.

¶ TO BROTHER JOSEPH
XII, 71-72, Letter 6647

Brother Joseph had misled his superiors in Rome by pretending to want to be a Jesuit when in reality he had no purpose whatever of remaining in the Society. This letter is addressed to him in Loretto. St. Ignatius reminds him of his unworthy conduct, but at the same time offers to forgive him. He will be ready to receive him if he truly wishes to serve God in the Society.

Rome, July 4, 1556

YHS

My dear Brother Joseph.

We have put up for some time with this levity of spirit, not to give it a harsher name, because of the kindliness and love and charity we profess to have for you and all your traveling companions in Christ Jesus and for all your nation. It is this lightness of mind that has caused you to fail in your holy purpose of following our Institute, or to pretend to be doing so when all the time you were quite alien in heart from the sentiments you expressed in words and deed. We have left no stone unturned to help you spiritually. But seeing at last that all our efforts are useless, we feel that we ought to take some thought for the common good of the Society. We are writing, therefore, to father rector, Master Oliver,[1] to allow you to go in peace wherever you like, if you continue in this frame of mind and have no further wish to follow our Institute. We are ready to forgive you sincerely for any offenses or any loss arising from the expenses you have occasioned the Society. But it is your responsibility to repent in the divine presence and to make up for what you have done so ill by other good works that are worthy of a religious man. You should not think it a slight thing or of little moment that we have received you into our Society at your own repeated request and with so much affection have dealt with you as with others of our most beloved brothers, only

---

[1] Father Oliver Manare.

to be so unjustly deceived by you. Not only in our house, where you went through the customary probations, but also in the College of Loretto you have occupied the place and used up the revenues of the servants of God, who have consecrated themselves to God's service and the good of their neighbor. I do not say this to cause you any shame, but rather to move you to repentance.

I commend you to God. If you are quite determined to follow some other way of life, go wherever you like. But if you remain with us, you may stay on at Loretto, or come to Rome after the heat of the summer. But if you are still doubting, make up your mind any way you like, but do not remain in one of our colleges. Wherever you go we will commend you to God and hope and pray for your eternal salvation. Farewell in our Lord Jesus Christ.

¶ TO FATHER ALPHONSE ROMAN
XII, 119, Letter 6677

Ignatius hopes that the opposition in Saragossa will cause the spiritual edifice to rise all the higher.

Rome, July 14, 1556

It is an ordinary experience that, where there is much contradiction, much fruit will follow; and although the Society is accustomed to better foundations, one would judge that we can expect a great and outstanding spiritual edifice here, seeing that you have laid such deep foundations of contradictions. We hope in God our Lord that this will be so.

¶ TO LOUIS DE CALATAYUD
XII, 120-22, Letter 6678

An affectionate answer. Ignatius consoles Louis who was annoyed because he desired to start a college of the Society at Ocana.

Rome, July 14, 1556

JHS

My dear Sir in our Lord.

May the sovereign grace and everlasting love of Christ our Lord ever be our protection and support.

I have received several letters from you, dated in December and January, which were very late in arriving, although by another post I had already learned from other sources (official letters and news reports from Ours), of the holy desires with which God has inspired you to undertake a lasting work in His service and for the help of many souls in Ocana.

Later, from the letters I mentioned above, I saw what annoyance and discouragement, even to a stay in prison, this work is costing you. I should think that God's divine and supreme goodness wishes to give you the fullest and most abundant reward in His kingdom for the service you are doing Him. For where others are accustomed to find consolation and support in their good works even from men, you have found annoyance and such extraordinary opposition. The love of God our Lord and of your neighbor which moves you must be especially pure and courageous, for only such a love could make you persevere where forces so opposed are found to embarrass you. And yet I hope in God our Lord that with the example of others this attempt will have a better ending than is augured by its beginnings....

Whether the project succeeds or not, we all feel under the deepest obligation to you for your devoted interest, and we hope that you will always hold us to be entirely yours in our Lord. May He by His infinite and sovereign goodness deign to give us His bountiful grace so that we may know His most holy will and always fulfill it. Your servant in our Lord ...

¶ TO FATHER FULVIUS ANDROZZI
XII, 141-43, Letter 6692

A kindly answer to a letter received. Ignatius congratulates him on his success and gives him some very sound advice. He recommends the Spiritual Exercises. Many others bear witness to the good influence exercised by Fulvius and his companions. A word about Fulvius himself and some news of the brethren.

Rome, July 18, 1556

JESUS

The peace of Christ.

We have two letters from your reverence, one dated the twentieth of last month and the other the fourth of this. We rejoice in our Lord on the occasions which His goodness allows you to serve Him by helping and consoling souls, not only of our benefactors but of their families and the people of their lands, and because of the health and peace of mind He vouchsafes you. However, if little time is left you to prepare your sermon, Christ our Lord will supply that defect. But throughout the day things might be so arranged as to give you more time, if more time is necessary for one thing than for another. The good disposition and devotion of your patrons will be a great help to you in setting to order what should be better arranged.

Your reverence knows that there is one outstanding means among those which of their nature are wont to be a help to men. I mean the Exercises. I remind you therefore that you should make use of this weapon, which is so much a familiar part of our Society. The first week could be given to many so as to include some method of prayer. But to give them exactly as they are, one should have retreatants capable and suitable for helping others after they themselves have been helped. Where this is not the case, they should not go beyond the first week. Your reverence should look about to see whether you can find some good prospects for the Lord's service, for whom there is no better way than the one I have indicated. The frequent reception of the sacraments is usually of much help to this end.

If you are very busy, you should make a choice and employ yourself in the more important occupations where there is greater service of God, greater spiritual advantage for the neighbor, and the more general or perfect good. Keeping a little time to put order in yourself and your activities will be of considerable help to you in this respect....

With regard to the personal experiences of your reverence, which you say are the cause of some pain and sadness, I hope that you will daily be freer of them by God's grace, since all of these things and even greater pains of our human nature can be cured by greater enlightenment and an increase of charity. I hope that your reverence will find such a master in the Holy Spirit, who will make it less necessary on our part to multiply advice.

I am enclosing a letter from Hortensius, and if you wish I will send you other letters which were sent us from Loretto. I understand that Curtius is advancing with great strides along the way of virtue and edification. Master John Philip will write you about other matters.[1]

May God grant us all His grace always to know and do His will.

---

[1] Hortensius and Curtius Androzzi were brothers of Fulvius. John Philip Vito was an assistant to Polanco.

¶ TO STEPHEN CASANOVA
XII, 151-52, Letter 6699

Ignatius does not think that his resistance to sinful suggestions is the whole cause of his decreasing physical strength, but much of it will be due to immoderate and untimely mental activity. He should, therefore, observe the order laid down for him. He explains two possible ways of resisting sinful suggestions and cautions Stephen to use only the first, even though he is most eager to please God.

Rome, July 20, 1556

JESUS

Dear Master Stephen.

The peace of Christ.

I received your letter, in which you put it down as a certainty that it is the repression of your sensuality which is robbing you of your strength and that you are determined to attend to the principal business of your soul. First, although it could easily be that this weakness of yours comes partly from such repression, I do not believe it to be the sole cause. There are also mental exercises, especially those undertaken immoderately and out of time, which also play a part. Go on observing what I have previously told you, until you write again and permission is given you to bring about a change in that order.

This repression, however, can be done in two ways. One, when the reason enlightened by God becomes aware of a movement of sensuality or of the sensitive part of nature against God's will, yielding to which would be a sin, you repress it through the fear and love of God. This is well done, even though some weakness should ensue or some bodily ill, since sin should not be committed for this or any other reason. There is another way of repressing this sensuality. You may be looking for some recreation, or anything else that is perfectly lawful, in which there is no sin, but out of a desire for mortification or love of the cross you deny yourself what is sought. This second way of repression is neither good for all, nor should it be used at all times. Rather, at times there will be more merit in taking some honest bodily recreation in order to be able to remain active for a long period in God's service than in repressing oneself. From this you will understand that the first kind of repression is good for you and that the second is not, even when you are eager to travel by the more perfect way and one that is more pleasing to God.

In every other detail I refer you to your confessor, to whom you will show this letter. I commend myself to your prayers.

¶ TO PETER, A PRIEST OF BOLOGNA
XII, 173-74, Letter 6718

In this letter Polanco encourages a priest who has been considering becoming a member of the Society. He tells him that he should not be concerned about his bodily weaknesses and should resign himself into the hands of God. It may be a human affection which is making him so timid in his spiritual progress.

Rome, July 23, 1556

JESUS

My dear Peter in Christ Jesus.

The peace of Christ.

As our father is indisposed at the moment, I will take his place and answer your letter of the fifteenth of this month, in which you make known your bodily indisposition, although you still have the determination to serve God in the Institute of our Society. The truth is, we desire nothing else than that one wait upon the Divine Majesty in the way that will best please Him. If you find some other way better adapted to your attaining the same end, that would please us even more. And yet there is certainly room for reasonable doubt that this spirit that makes you so timid about making progress is the spirit of God. Instead, it would seem to be some weak human affection toward relatives and country, or a desire to live at greater liberty. For the fatigues which we understand you underwent at the beginning of your pastorate were no less than what awaits you in our Society, although they were less meritorious, and the style of living as to meals and so on was no better. As far, therefore, as health is concerned, you will enjoy as much or more in the Society than out of it. To throw a clearer light on this spirit, therefore, it would be good for you to try to resign yourself once more into God's hands, and to give your case the consideration that a man of judgment and a servant of God would give it. If you find that God gives you enough confidence to serve Him in the state of religious perfection, let us know. But if you think that you ought to return to the world, we will be your friends as before, because we are interested in nothing else than your good and the greater service of God. May His grace remain and ever grow in your heart.

Your friend Don Pantaleone sends his greetings, and thinks perhaps that he might have you near him in Messina, obedience so arranging it. But before his desire can be realized, your constancy would require a longer trial.

We commend ourselves to your prayers.

¶ TO N. N.
XII, 290-93, Appendix I, Letter 41

This document is without date. There is no name attached to it, and the editors of the Monumenta *decline to make any attempt to assign a recipient. They even surmise that it might be something of an experimental exercise, and leave to others the task of identifying the recipient. Certain details point to the probability that the writer had an individual in mind. The college referred to is likely the Roman College.*

Rome, date uncertain

JESUS

Motives which might prove convincing to N— for founding the College N—.

1. If he is aware of what he owes to God, who without any effort or merit of his has bestowed so many favors on him and blessings both interior and exterior, he will find a great occasion of showing his gratitude to the Divine Liberality by interesting himself in a work like this college, which will give such great service and so much glory to God. Of all the colleges which the Society has anywhere in the broad expanse of Christendom, there is none, we believe, which will render so great and so widespread a service as this, as experience has already begun to prove.

2. If he is zealous for the common good and the help of souls and the spread and increase of the Catholic faith, this is a work which is especially destined to such an end. For not only will the youth of Rome be taught and trained in learning and good morals, but in time students can come from all parts of Italy and beyond for the same purpose. As its reputation spreads, it is very probable that they will come. More than this, many from Germany and those northern regions that have been so damaged by heresy will be instructed here, and they can then be sent back as faithful workers, who by teaching and example will try to bring back those nations to the bosom of our holy mother the Church. Likewise, a large number of apostolic workers of our own Society will be educated there, with their studies directed solely to the same end of the common good. From here they will be sent to every part of Christendom, wherever there is need, among heretics and schismatics, Moors and pagans. And although this is a part of our Institute everywhere, those who are educated here under the eyes of the supreme pontiff and the Apostolic See can be expected to be better prepared in this matter than others. Thus this college will be a never-failing nursery of ministers of this Apostolic See for the service of holy Church and the good of souls.

3. If zeal for God's glory and the universal good must move him, so will the desire for personal advantage. For that is advantageous in everything which helps toward its end. And of all human advantages the greatest is that which helps to the last and most happy end of man. This being true, according to Catholic teaching, of good works and those which are meritorious of everlasting life, one can see how advantageous it would be to have a share, or rather to make all good and meritorious works one's own which will have their origin in this college, to God's glory and the good of many souls.

4. There are other great advantages in life and in death from the suffrages of the Masses and prayers of the whole Society, to which the founders of houses and colleges are entitled according to our Constitutions, as may be seen from the enclosed paper concerning the remembrance to be kept of founders.

5. It is also to be considered an advantage for N— and all his household and his successors to have these good people bound to his love and service by special ties. Because in many things that are spiritual and temporal in which they will have part they will be glad to cooperate, and they will do so not only freely out of their own charity but even from a sense of obligation.

6. He will have many an occasion of being helped in education and spiritual matters, because, as the college is his, where there will be professors of all faculties and many men of virtue who are servants of God, association with them and the facility with which he will be able to avail himself of their labors cannot but be very useful to him. Should he wish to retire with them for some days, he will be retiring as it were in his own house.

7. After all is said, the main advantage is that, if N— undertakes so good a work, God, who is the most generous rewarder of what is done for love of Him, will repay him with the abundance of His spiritual gifts both in this life and in the next.

8. Such a work would be very important for the easing of his conscience. N— has a large ecclesiastical revenue and is under the obligation of making a proper disposition of such income. According to the learned doctors he is entitled to keep for himself what is necessary to maintain his state properly and becomingly, while the remainder should be spent on the poor and good works. In this good work, by which so many of Christ's poor will be helped, he has a very good way of unburdening himself, and even of helping the soul of him who left him such a fortune in church possessions.

9. These are the motives which ought to have the greatest weight with him. But for one who is likely to be moved by other considerations, such as respect for his authority and reputation, or honor and fame, this work would be of prime importance. It would be outstanding among all the colleges of the Society, and might even be called their head, just as this house is the head of the other houses of this order, which God has raised up in our time to render Him such great service. It would be under the eyes of the pope and all the court, who would be constantly informed concerning its interests, and from Rome alone would spread the good odor of such a work throughout the world. One who is eager of making himself a name would, as the author of such a work, have a greater opportunity of distinguishing himself in this work than in any other I know of.

10. If he were thinking of leaving a monument to himself after finishing his days, it is evident that this work is quite to his purpose. It would be a great and lasting ornament for his whole family, being an enterprise of so public a nature, and such extended possibilities for good, that it would bring distinction on its author in many ways.

11. This work would bring him great and immediate contentment and satisfaction, if such a motive has any weight with him, because he could begin to enjoy it at once. And yet, as the work would grow with time, so also would the reason for his gratification as he saw the excellent results of his work.

12. The ease with which it could be accomplished might be some enticement to him. For payment could be made in installments as the building advanced, and the college could be maintained in great measure from the contributions which would come in from other places. As he is still young, he could space his contributions according to his devotion and as God would inspire him.

May it please His Eternal Wisdom to grant him understanding to know, and firmness of will to carry into effect, that which will give greater pleasure to His Majesty. We have no other purpose in view.

¶ TO THE COMMUNITY AT ALCALA
XII, 674-76, Appendix VI, Letter 11

The editors of the Monumenta *reason that these rules were given about the year 1541, before the Constitutions were written and immedi-*

ately after Ignatius was elected general. Ribadeneira says that they were written for the members of the Society living in Alcala and that they were read frequently and kept with the greatest care. These rules are concerned with dealing with others.

1. We should be careful to preserve great purity of heart in the love of God, loving nothing but Him, and desiring to converse with Him alone, and with the neighbor for love of Him and not for our own entertainment and delight.

2. We should speak only with necessity, and for the edification of ourselves or others, and avoid those things which offer no profit to the soul, such as the desire for news and worldly affairs. We should try always to treat of matters connected with humility and mortification of the will, and not of things that give occasion for laughter or criticism.

3. Let no one seek to be considered a wit, or to affect elegance or prudence[1] or eloquence, but look upon Christ, who made nothing at all of these things and chose to be humbled and despised by men for our sake rather than to be honored and respected.

4. We should not wish to see or do anything which could not be done in the presence of God and His creatures, and we shall thus imagine that we are always in His presence.

5. We should not dispute stubbornly with anyone. Rather we should patiently give our reasons with the purpose of declaring the truth lest our neighbor remain in error, and not that we should have the upper hand.

6. One of the things which we must be very firm about, if we are to please our Lord, is to cast far from us everything that could remove us from the love of our brethren. We should make every effort to love them with a tender charity, for Supreme Truth has said, "By this shall all men know that you are my disciples, etc."[2]

7. Should anyone do anything that is disedifying, and it seems that as a result he should be held in less esteem than he was held before, let him not be so discouraged as to wish to give up, but let him humble himself and ask forgiveness of those who might have been scandalized by his bad example and a penance from his superior. He should give thanks to God, who has permitted him to be humbled, so that he can be known by all for what he is. He should not wish to appear better in the eyes of men than he is in the eyes of God. The brethren who behold him should think

---

[1] The prudence of which Ignatius speaks is of course the prudence of the world, as is evident from the context, a prudence which our Lord did indeed condemn. The Spanish word *discreto* could also mean cleverness, shrewdness.

[2] John 13:35.

that they could fall into even greater weakness, and should ask God to strengthen them.

8. In our superiors we should always behold the person of Christ, whom they represent, and have recourse to them in our doubts and hold it as certain that our Lord will direct us through them.

9. We should not conceal our temptations, nor even our good thoughts, but make them known to our confessor or superior, because "Satan himself transformeth himself into an angel of light."[3] We should always act according to the judgment and counsel of our spiritual father rather than our own, which we should always regard rather with suspicion.

10. In dealing with others we should bear ourselves modestly, and try not to appear glum or too serious, nor, on the other hand, overcheerful and gay, but as the Apostle says, "Let your modesty be known to all men."[4]

11. We should never postpone a good work, no matter how small it may be, with the thought of later doing something greater. It is a very common temptation of the enemy to be always placing before us the perfection of things to come and bring us to make little of the present.

12. Let us all persevere in the vocation to which God calls us, and not make our first loyalty an empty word. For the enemy is wont to tempt those in the desert with thoughts of dealing with the neighbor and improving him, and to those who are helping the neighbor he will propose the great perfection of the desert and solitary life. Thus he lays hold of what is far off to prevent us from taking advantage of what is at hand.

¶ TO THE MEMBERS OF THE SOCIETY IN PORTUGAL

XII, 676-78, Appendix VI, Letter 12

In his letter Ignatius aids the members of the Society in Portugal in directing their activities where they will be most effective.

Undated

To Ours in Portugal, for their protection and progress in our Lord.

With perfect frankness I will set down a number of points by way of direction. I do this with that trust with which you inspire me, in the full confidence that my words will be taken and understood with the same

---

[3] 2 Corinthians 11:14.   [4] Philippians 4:5.

intention and good will with which I write them. I am giving these directions as though I were admonishing my own soul.

If I were with you in Portugal, I should try to write out my sermons first before giving them. I should not touch on topics that were dubious or that presented any difficulty, but simply correct faults and sins in a modest and orderly way.

If I were giving the Exercises in their entirety, I should give them to very few, and they educated, or persons who are very desirous of perfection, or very prominent, or who might be thinking of entering the Society. As a rule, I would give only the exercises of the first week together with the general confession, and some of the examens, but not go further.

I would rarely give the elections, and only with persons who are educated and very desirous of making them, or to persons who are not likely to cause us any embarrassment. It sometimes happens that, when they come out of the Exercises without having made all the progress hoped for, they are tempted, and say out publicly that Ours wanted to reduce them to poverty by urging them to religious poverty.

I would not have any dealing with young women of the common people, except in church or in an open place. On the one hand, they are lightheaded, and whether there be foundation for it or not, it frequently happens that such dealings give rise to evil talk. Such females are in general more inclined to be giddy and inconstant in God's service. After their devotions are over, they not infrequently turn, sometimes to the flesh, sometimes to fatigue. For this reason many allowances have to be made as to their corporal needs.

If I had to deal with women in matters spiritual, it would be with women of birth against whom no breath of evil rumor could arise. Above all, I would not talk with any woman behind closed doors or in remote places. In this way I would avoid all criticism and suspicion.

In all spiritual associations I should try to make one step of progress safely, and prefer this to making a hundred by putting myself in danger, or to advance another at the cost of a serious difference of opinion with him, although I might have been right. A scandal, whether it has foundation or not, does us more harm and neutralizes more than half the progress which God our Lord accomplishes through us, especially in times and places such as these.

I should make it a point to satisfy all, of both sexes, with whom I dealt or talked, so that they would get the idea that I was a lowly and humble person and not one full of obstinate conceit, especially in matters that are of little or no importance.

¶ INDEX OF NAMES

Abimamarco (Marqos), 388 *note*
Abtilis, Book of, 389 *note*
Acevedo, James, 185 *note,* 191
Adam, 36
Adrian, Master, 310, 311
Adrienssens, Adrian, 420
Alcala, 88, 440
Alcuin, 45 *note*
Alvarez, Andrew, 194 *note*
Alvarez, John, 190
Amadeu (John de Menezes da Silva), 198 *note*
Amador, Sebastian, 26 *note*
Amaroni, Thaddeus, 328, 330
Ambrose, St., 193
Ambrose, 199
Androzzi, Curtius, 434 *note*
Androzzi, Fulvius, 433, 434 *note*
Androzzi, Hortensius, 434 *note*
Anthony, John, 328, 330
Aragon y Gurrea, Martin de, 305, 339 *note*
Araldo, John Francis, 352 *note*
Araoz, Anthony, 38 *note,* 39, 40, 42, 44 *note,* 49, 50, 52, 53 *note,* 54, 68, 72, 84, 93, 101, 121, 139, 150, 153, 165, 166, 172, 200, 201, 209, 220, 229, 243, 349 *note,* 350, 360, 406 *note*
Araoz, Magdalene, 39 *note,* 44 *note*
Archinto, Philip, 111
Ardevoll, Jerome, 3
Arta Cella, Monastery of, 365
Astrain, Anthony, 59 *note,* 107 *note*
Athanasius, St., 193
Attino, Francis de, 336
Augustine, St., 45 *note,* 72 *note,* 148, 183, 184, 193
Azpeitia, 39
  Ignatius in, 39 *note*
  letter of Ignatius to people of, 42

Badia, Thomas, 117 *note*
Barbaran, 110, 111
Barcelona, 399
  Ignatius' sentiments toward, 16
  residence of Ignatius in, 3
Baroello, Stephen, 157
Barreto, John Nunez, 342, 343 *note,* 371 *note,* 374, 381
Barreto, Melchior Nunez, 373
Bartolome, 36
Basil, St., 193
Benedict, St., 294
Benet, Dr., 9, 12
Benoist, John, 27 *note,* 36
Bermudes, John, 388 *note*
Bernard, St., 126, 127, 143, 147, 160, 161, 170, 289, 290, 292, 293
Berse, Gaspar, 298, 315, 324, 325 *note,* 373
Bibona, College of, 403
Black, John, 320 *note*
Blessed Sacrament of the Minerva, Confraternity of the, 43, 44 *note*
Bobadilla, Nicholas, 57, 72, 73, 105, 118 *note,* 120, 162, 229
Bonaventure, St., 183
Book of Abtilis, 389 *note*
Boquet, John, 347, 348 *note,* 349
Borgia, Charles, 218, 226 *note*
Borgia, Francis, 58, 86 *note,* 91, 106, 107 *note,* 108, 137, 138, 153, 179, 184, 194, 195, 196, 219 *note,* 229, 244 *note,* 257, 287, 305, 306, 307, 315, 338 *note,* 339 *note,* 349 *note,* 401, 406 *note,* 407, 408, 410, 416
Borgia, Gaspar de, 375
Borgia, John, 227 *note,* 244 *note,* 266
Borgia, Louise, 305, 339 *note*
Borrell, John Paul, 108 *note,* 109
Bosch, John, 109

443

Botello, Francis, 65 *note*
Braganza, Theotonius, 317 *note*
Brandao, Anthony, 234 *note*, 237, 238
Brandina, Lucretia, 100
Broet, Paschase, 51, 67 *note*, 118 *note*
Burgos, John, 57 *note*, 105, 139, 184, 190

Caceres, James, 19, 35, 36 *note*
Cajetan, Thomas de Vio, 184
Calatayud, John Perez de, 379
Calatayud, Louis de, 432
Camara, Louis Gonzales de la, 282
Camps, Dimas, 349 *note*, 400 *note*
Camps, Peter, 399
Canal, Peter, 320
Canisius, Peter, 96, 212, 260, 300, 301, 344, 395 *note*
Cano, Melchior, 182, 191
Caraffa, John Peter (Pope Paul IV), 28, 393
Cardoli, Fulvius, 132 *note*
Cardona, Alduncia de, 13
Cardona, Joan de, 100, 101
Carneiro, Melchior, 371 *note*, 374
Carpi, Countess of, 70
Carpi, Faenza, 57, 105
Carpi, Pius Rodulphus de, 350
Carvajal, D. Gutierre, 59
Casanova, Stephen, 435
Cassarubios, Blase de, 338
Cassian, John, 169, 211, 289, 291
Castillo, Francis de, 349 *note*
Castro, Christopher, 16, 23, 26 *note*
Castro, Eleanor de, 86 *note*, 92 *note*
Catalonia, 91, 92, 153, 257
Catherine of Aragon, 304
Catherine of Austria, 328 *note*
Cazador, James, 13 *note*, 14, 52, 53, 153
Cervini, Marcellus (Cardinal Santa Croce, Pope Marcellus II), 77, 81, 83 *note*, 106, 121, 152, 153, 365, 393

Cesari, Nicholas Peter, 308, 313, 420
Cesari, Octavius, 308, 313, 419, 420
Chalcedon, Council of, 370 *note*
Charles V, of Holy Roman Empire, 26, 64, 89, 104, 257, 260, 261, 262, 327 *note*, 338 *note*, 339, 354, 358, 415 *note*
Charles, cardinal of Lorraine, 425
Cherne, Edward, 394 *note*
Chrysostom, St., 183, 193
Church
  Our Lady of Aranzazu, 349
  Our Lady of the Wayside, 99
  St. Mary Major, 38, 39
Claret, John, 14, 15 *note*
Claude, emperor of Abyssinia, 367
Clayssone, Robert, 376
Clement VII, Pope, 388 *note*
Codacio, Peter, 69, 70, 110, 119
Codure, John, 67, 99
Cogordan, Ponce, 365
Coimbra, College of, 56 *note*, 120, 233, 254, 326
College
  German, 259, 301 *note*, 378, 394
  of Bibona, 403
  of Coimbra, 56 *note*, 120, 233, 254, 326
  of Ferrara, 331 *note*
  of Gandia, 138, 140
  of Goa, 315
  of Mutina, 355
  of St. James of the Compostella, 57 *note*
  Roman, 57 *note*, 226, 227 *note*, 362, 401, 437
Colonna, Asconius, 68, 274, 275, 276, 277, 323, 354, 358
Colonna, Fabricius, 68
Colonna, Mark Anthony, 68, 276 *note*
Compeggio, Alexander, 114 *note*
Confraternity of the Blessed Sacrament of the Minerva, 43, 44 *note*
Constance, Council of, 370 *note*

Constitutions of the Society of
   Jesus, 233, 261, 344 *note*
Contarini, Gaspar, 31 *note*, 36, 37
Contarini, Lawrence, 31 *note*
Contarini, Peter, 31 *note*, 36
Conversini, Benedict, 37, 38
Cools, Gerard, 411
Cordova, Anthony de, 338 *note*
Cordova, Catherine Fernandez
   de, 337, 338 *note*
Cordova, John de, 339
Cordova, Peter Fernandez de,
   339 *note*
Cornet, Peter de, 36
Cosmas, 429
Cottaneo, Francis, 310
Coudret, Louis, 320 *note*, 324 *note*
Council of
   Chalcedon, 370 *note*
   Constance, 370 *note*
   Florence, 370 *note*
   Trent, 82, 91, 93
Coutinho, Anna, 100
Crescenzi, James, 77
Crescenzi, Marcellus, 110, 111
Cruyllas, Frances, 100
Cueva, Henry de la, 306, 307, 339, 357, 406, 408
Cueva y Toledo, Bartholomew
   de la, 339, 340 *note*, 406 *note*
Cuvillon, John, 321

David, king of Abyssinia, 370
Desiderius, 320 *note*
De Soto, Peter, 89
Diaz de Luco, John Bernal, 219
Dilligen, 86
Doctis, Gaspar de, 32
Domenech, Jerome, 27, 54, 108, 158, 228, 296, 319, 403, 404, 428, 430 *note*
Domenech, Magdalene Angelica, 318
Dudon, Paul, 35 *note*

Edward VI, of England, 304
Eguia, James de, 53 *note*

Eleanor of Austria, 26
Eleanor of Toledo, 114, 253 *note*
Emerius, 424
England, 304
Enriquez, Anthony, 331, 332
Ercole d'Este, Duke, 322 *note*
Estrada, Francis, 192 *note*, 194, 229, 375
Eugenius IV, Pope, 370
Exarch, Sebastiana, 101

Faber, Peter, 26, 31 *note*, 35 *note*, 57, 62, 73, 82, 93, 97, 98, 99, 104, 121, 150, 219
Faria, Balthasar de, 104
Farnese, Octavius, 119 *note*
Farnese, Ottavio, 57 *note*, 200
Ferdinand I, of Holy Roman
   Empire, 111, 115, 232, 249, 253 *note*, 324 *note*, 328 *note*
Fermo, John Baptist de, 429
Fernandes, Urban, 233
Ferrao, Bartholomew, 98, 99 *note*, 115
Ferrara, 244, 321
Ferrara, College of, 331 *note*
Ferrarese, Albert, 320 *note*, 395
Ferrer, Francis, 101
Flanders, 327
Florence, Council of, 370 *note*
Florence, Master (Florentius
   Pauletus), 158 *note*
Fontana, Alexis, 415 *note*, 417
Francis, John, 329
Francis of Assisi, St., 31, 208
Frassona del Gesso, Mary, 321, 330
Frusius, Andrew, 114, 189 *note*, 229, 269, 271, 352 *note*

Gaddi, Nicholas, 119
Galatino, Cardinal, 199
Gallaiztegui, Bertram Lopez de
   (Lord of Ozaeta), 41 *note*, 49, 267 *note*
Gandia, 86, 101
   College of, 138, 140

Garate, Peter, 310
Garcia, Lawrence de, 53 *note*
Gaudano, Nicholas, 311
German College, 259, 301 *note*, 378, 394
Goa, College of, 315
Godinho, Manuel, 254
Goldwell, Thomas, 394 *note*
Gomez, N., 379
Gonzales, Louis, 283, 284, 297
Gonzalez, Louis, 341, 393
Gonzalez de Villasimplex, John Louis, 309
Gouvea, James de, 35 *note*
Gozzadina, Violante Casali, 359
Gralla, Doña, 13
Gralla, Mosén, 12
Gregory, St., 142, 183, 193, 288
Guevara, John de, 266 *note*
Guia, Stephen de, 49
Guijeno, John Martinez (Siliceo), 256
Guzman, Gabriel, 26 *note*
Guzman, James de, 364, 393

Hammontanus, Gerard, 377
Harmeville, Louis, 320 *note*
Helmi, Cesar, 320 *note*, 380
Henry VIII, of England, 304
Hernandez, Bartholomew, 341
Herp, Henry, 209, 210 *note*
Hospital, St. Anthony of the Portuguese, 92

Ignatius, St.
  accusations against in Rome (1538), 36
  accusations renewed (1545), 79-81
  departure of from Paris, 25
  letter of resignation, 230
  persecutions, 79-80
  residence of in Barcelona, 3
  residence of in San Pietro, 32
  threats to lives of companions of, 100
  visit of to Azpeitia, 39 *note*
  visit of to Rouen, 26 *note*
  visit of to Venice, 31 *note*

Japan, 255
Jeremias, the prophet, 124
Jerome, St., 183, 193
Joan of Aragon, 68, 274
Joan of Austria, 64, 327 *note*, 336 *note*, 350
John, St., the evangelist, 196, 348, 368, 369, 371 *note*
John III, of Portugal, 35 *note*, 55, 64, 79, 82 *note*, 282 *note*, 334, 335, 382 *note*
John, prince of Portugal, 283, 335 *note*, 336 *note*
John, Fray (John de la Pena), 26 *note*
John Baptist, 423 *note*, 424
John of Avila, 182, 341, 364
John of Guise, 223, 224 *note*
Josa, Isabel de, 13
Joseph, Brother, 431
Juarez, John, 341
Julius III, Pope, 221, 304, 349, 394 *note*

Kalckbrenner, Gerard, 377
Kessel, Leonard, 280 *note*

Lainez, James, 31 *note*, 67 *note*, 78, 87, 93, 104, 113, 114, 115, 132, 147, 227, 229, 232, 269, 272, 323, 324 *note*, 393, 400, 403
Landivar, Michael, 27 *note*
Lara, Anthony Manrique de, 265
Lara, Frederick Manrique de, 400
Lara, John Stephen Manrique de, 265
La Sepilla (Eleanor Zapila Rocaberti), 10 *note*, 12
Lasso, Francis de, 89
Lasso, James, 116, 120
Lawrence, Thomas, 36
Leerno, Philip, 316, 320 *note*, 353

Le Jay, Claude, 57, 67 *note*, 82,
    83 *note*, 86, 93, 94, 105, 111,
    115, 116, 117, 118 *note*, 119,
    132 *note*, 212, 233, 249, 259
Leo I, Pope, St., 293
Leo X, Pope, 71
Leon, Anna Ponce de, 339 *note*
Lhoost, James, 154, 156, 157
Lippomani, Andrew, 90 *note*,
    110 *note*, 146, 188, 253 *note*,
    270 *note*
Loarte, Gaspar, 364, 393
Lopez, Manuel, 393
Lorenzo, John, 316
Louis, prince of Portugal, 314
Louis, Master, 132
Loyola, Bertram de Onaz y, 38,
    39, 41 *note*, 42, 49, 53
Loyola, Magdalene, 41 *note*, 50, 267
Loyola, Martin Garcia, 5, 38,
    39 *note*, 44 *note*, 267
Loyola, Millan, 39, 40 *note*, 49,
    53, 54
Luke, St., 148, 372 *note*
Luna, Peter de, 403 *note*

Madrid, Christopher, 191 *note*,
    418
Maffei, Bernard, 105, 106, 116,
    117, 163 *note*
Manare, Oliver, 431 *note*
Marcellus II, Pope. *See* Cervini,
    Marcellus
Margaret of Austria (Duchess
    of Parma), 69, 119 *note*,
    310 *note*
Marqos (Abimamarco), 388 *note*
Martha, St., 108, 110, 111
Martin, St., 98
Mary I (Mary Tudor), of England, 304, 327 *note*
Mary, princess of Portugal, 64,
    82 *note*
Mascarenhas, Eleanor, 100,
    422 *note*
Mascarenhas, Peter, 35, 42
Matthew, St., 368, 372 *note*

Matthias de Sancto Cassiano,
    105 *note*, 106, 108, 110, 114
Maximilian, king of Bavaria, 395
Medici, Cosmo de, 114 *note*
Mediterranean Sea, 261, 263
Mendoza, Christopher de,
    111 *note*, 356
Mendoza, Francis, 191 *note*
Mendoza, John de, 354, 414
Meneses, Joan de, 86 *note*, 100,
    102 *note*, 140, 257
Mercurian, Everard, 320 *note*
Miona, Manuel, 27, 229
Miranda, Francis Jimenez de, 396
Miron, James, 93 *note*, 229, 278,
    279, 282, 296, 302, 303, 334
Monastery of
    Arta Cella, 365
    St. Peter, 31
    San Pietro in Riccasolo, 32
    Santa Clara, 18
Montague, Anthony de, 394 *note*
Monte, John Mary, 106
Morales, Emmanuel, 373
Morone, Cardinal, 77, 106,
    301 *note*, 362
Morrano, Matthew Sebastian de,
    186
Muniz, Anthony de, 86 *note*, 91,
    92, 93 *note*
Mutina, College of, 355

Nadal, Jerome, 260, 261, 267, 303,
    315, 317 *note*, 340, 341,
    360 *note*, 393, 394, 395 *note*
Napi, Aloysius, 320 *note*
Nascio, Doimo, 99, 322, 358
Nazianzus, Gregory, 193
Nobrega, Michael de, 350

Ochino, Bernard, 86 *note*, 87
Olave, Martinus, 271, 321
Olivier, Bernard, 414, 421
Oluja, Jeronyma, 187
Onaz, Laurentia de, 266, 267 *note*
Onaz, Martin Garcia de, 5, 38,
    39 *note*, 44 *note*, 267

Onaz y Loyola, Bertram de, 38, 39, 41 *note*, 42, 49, 53
Onfroy, Francis, 194, 196, 198, 201, 202, 203, 206, 207 *note*, 211
Ori, Matthew, 26 *note*
Orlandini, Nicholas, 107 *note*
Ortiz, Peter, 87
Osorio, Alvaro de, 229
Osorio, Eleanor de, 105, 109, 214, 215, 216, 222, 229 *note*
Osorio, Suero de, 229
Otello, Jerome, 270
Our Lady of Aranzazu Church, 349
Our Lady of Loretto Shrine, 393
Our Lady of the Wayside Church, 99
Oviedo, Andrew, 101, 139 *note*, 164, 194, 202, 207 *note*, 209, 229, 371 *note*, 374
Ozaeta, Lord of, 41 *note*, 49, 267 *note*

Padua, 146
Paeybroeck, Daniel, 154
Palmio, Benedict, 108, 109 *note*
Palmio, Francis, 320, 329
Palou, Berengarius, 17 *note*
Paris
  departure of Ignatius and companions from, 25
  University of, 425
Parma, Duchess of, 69, 119 *note*, 310 *note*
Pascual, Agnes, 3, 4, 12
Pascual, John, 4, 5, 12, 13
Pascual, Peter, 3
Patarinis, John Laurence de, 320 *note*
Paul, St., the apostle, 43, 85, 124, 126, 141, 161, 170, 193, 196, 201, 208, 267, 284, 288, 292, 293, 301, 325, 371 *note*, 372 *note*
Paul III, Pope, 39, 44 *note*, 70, 81, 90 *note*, 101, 102 *note*, 112 *note*, 200, 339, 341

Paul IV, Pope, 28, 393
Pauletus, Florentius (Master Florence), 158 *note*
Pelletier, John, 244, 321, 322, 330, 331 *note*
Pena, John de la (Fray John), 26 *note*
Peralta, Peter de, 26 *note*
Perez, John, 409
Peter of Toledo, 253 *note*
Pezzano, Baptist, 109
Pfauser, Sebastian, 395 *note*
Philip II, of Spain, 64, 82 *note*, 153, 175, 184, 185 *note*, 256, 257, 304, 327 *note*, 415 *note*, 422 *note*, 423
Picard, Francis, 36, 52
Pignatelli, Hector, 313
Polanco, John de, 35 *note*, 72, 99 *note*, 113, 132, 137 *note*, 146, 188, 190, 209, 212, 226 *note*, 229, 233, 237, 255, 256 *note*, 258, 260, 270, 274, 284, 300, 301, 316, 335 *note*, 360, 395 *note*, 409, 412, 415 *note*, 429 *note*, 434 *note*, 436
Pole, Reginald, 57, 106, 301, 304, 361
Pompilius, 337
Pontano, Eleutherius, 430 *note*
Portugal, 441, 442
Postel, William, 199
Prester John, 104, 362, 382, 383, 384, 385
Pujol, Agnes. *See* Pascual, Agnes
Purino, Hercules, 355

Recalde, Joan de, 41 *note*
Recalde, John Lopez de, 41
Rejadell, Louise, 71
Rejadell, Teresa, 17 *note*, 18, 24, 71, 153, 187
Ribadeneira, Peter, 28, 105 *note*, 132 *note*, 136, 146 *note*, 287, 413, 414, 415 *note*, 416, 421, 428, 440

Ribagorza, Countess of, 306, 307
Riva, Augustine de la, 320 note
Rocaberti, Eleanor Zapila (Anna de), 10 note, 12
Rocca, Francis John de la, 92, 110, 138, 139
Rodrigues, Simon, 55, 59, 61, 80, 82, 112 note, 118 note, 121, 130, 132, 159, 237, 254, 282, 287, 296, 297, 300, 302 note, 303, 326 note, 380, 402
Rojas, Francis, 38, 49, 59 note, 229
Roman, Alphonse, 432
Roman College, 57 note, 226, 227 note, 362, 401, 437
Romano, Bartholomew, 363
Rome
  German College in, 259
  opposition to Ignatius in, 36
Romei, Francis, 194 note
Roser, Isabel, 9, 12, 14, 16, 52, 54, 100, 101, 102 note, 108, 109
Roser, John, 9, 11
Rouen, visited by Ignatius, 26 note

Sa, Callistus de, 4
Sa, Manuel de, 229
Sagrista, Peter, 3
St. Anthony of the Portuguese Hospital, 92
St. James of the Compostella, College of, 57 note
St. Mary Major Church, 38, 39
St. Peter, Monastery of, 31
Salamanca, University of, 339
Salazar, 88
Salmeron, Alphonse, 51, 67, 87, 93, 212, 271, 352, 357, 413, 414
Salviatti, John, 119
San Antonio, 56 note
Sancto Cassiano, Matthias de, 105 note, 106, 108, 110, 114
San Pietro in Riccasolo, Monastery of, 32
Santa Clara Convent, 186, 187

Santa Clara, Monastery of, 18
Santa Croce, Cardinal. See Cervini, Marcellus
Santa Croce, Prospero de, 163 note
Santa Cruz, Cardinal. See Cervini, Marcellus
Santini, Peter, 147
Santis, Charles, 381
Santos, Manuel, 131
Saragossa, 306, 379, 409, 411, 432
Savonarola, Jerome, 198
Sea, Mediterranean, 261, 263
Sebastian, prince of Portugal, 335, 336 note
Sendo, Magdalene de, 38
Sfondrato, Francis, 106
Shrine, Our Lady of Loretto, 393
Siliceo (John Martinez Guijeno), 256
Silva, Ferdinand de, 403
Silva, Michael de, 55, 57 note, 65 note
Society of Jesus, Constitutions of the, 233, 261, 344 note
Soldevila, Anthony, 418
Solomon (Prince of Peace), 372 note, 419
Sonorza, Martin, 31
Sousa, Christopher de, 55
Spes, Michael, 309, 310 note
Spinola, Thomas, 310
Stella, Thomas, 44 note

Tablares, Peter, 229
Talpino, 173, 174
Tavono, John Baptist, 320 note
Tejeda, John, 138, 139, 195, 207 note, 208
Tellez, Balthasar, 93 note
Thaddeus, 328, 330
Theatines, 28
Thomas Aquinas, St., 183
Thomas of Villanova, 296
Toledo, John Alvarez de (Cardinal Burgos), 57 note, 105, 139, 184, 190

Torres, Michael de, 99 *note,*
    100 *note,* 101, 103, 108, 115,
    152, 153, 192, 194 *note,*
    279 *note,* 287, 303
Trent, Council of, 82, 91, 93
Truchsess, Otto, 83 *note,* 94,
    394 *note*
Tudor, Mary (Mary I), 304,
    327 *note*

Ugoletti, Elpidius, 78, 252, 253
University of
    Paris, 425
    Salamanca, 339
    Vienna, 249
Urban, 373

Valencia, Francis de, 341
Valencia, Joan de, 400
Valentine, Marin, 430
Vasconcelhos, Ferdinand, 131, 343
Vega, Alvaro de, 214, 226
Vega, Ferdinand de, 214, 227, 228,
    229, 231, 404
Vega, Isabel de, 214, 215, 222, 228,
    231, 403 *note*
Vega, John de, 89, 104, 105, 109,
    119, 214, 217, 221, 223, 225, 227,
    231, 253, 403, 404 *note,* 427,
    428 *note*

Vega, Suero de, 214
Vela, Andrew, 338
Venice
    studies of Ignatius in, 13 *note*
    visit of Ignatius to, 31 *note*
Vergara, Alphonse Ramirez de,
    416
Vicuna, Mary de, 41 *note,* 49, 54
Vienna, University of, 249
Villanueva, Francis, 59 *note,* 121,
    417
Vines, Fabricius, 405
Vines, Jerome, 404, 405, 411, 413
Vines, Michael, 405
Viola, John Baptist, 60, 223, 328
Viseo, diocese of, 57
Vito, John Philip, 434 *note*

Wancob (Robert Wauchop), 36
Weber, Urban, 115, 252 *note*
White, Adrian, 421
Wied, Hermann von, 97
William IV, of Bavaria, 212

Xavier, Francis, 35 *note,* 42, 255,
    298, 315
Ximenez, Peter, 104 *note*

Zapico, D. Fernandez, 38
Zarate, Peter de, 416

www.ingramcontent.com/pod-product-compliance
Lightning Source LLC
Chambersburg PA
CBHW032013230426
43671CB00005B/67